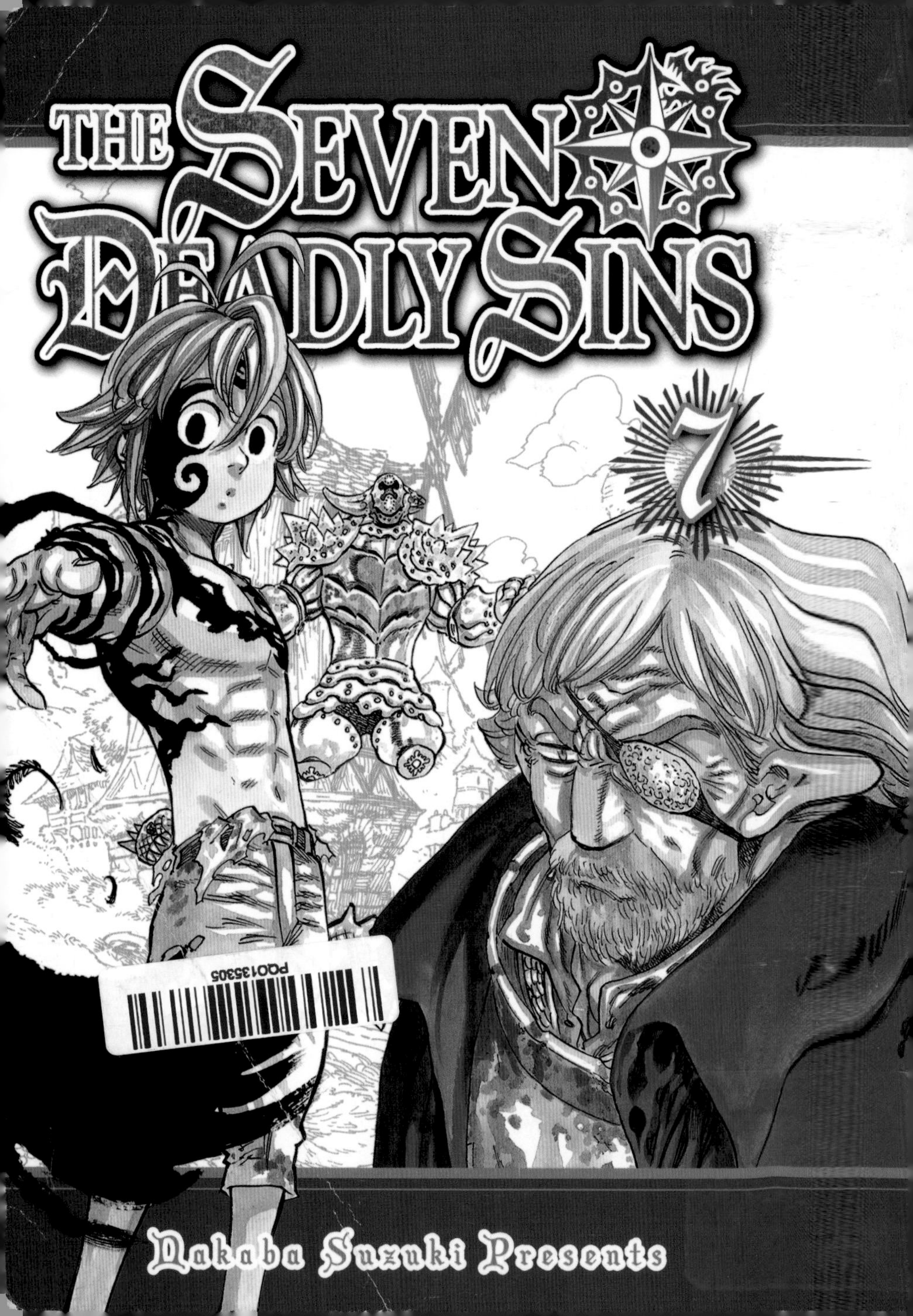
THE SEVEN DEADLY SINS
7
Nakaba Suzuki Presents

THE SEVEN DEADLY SINS 7

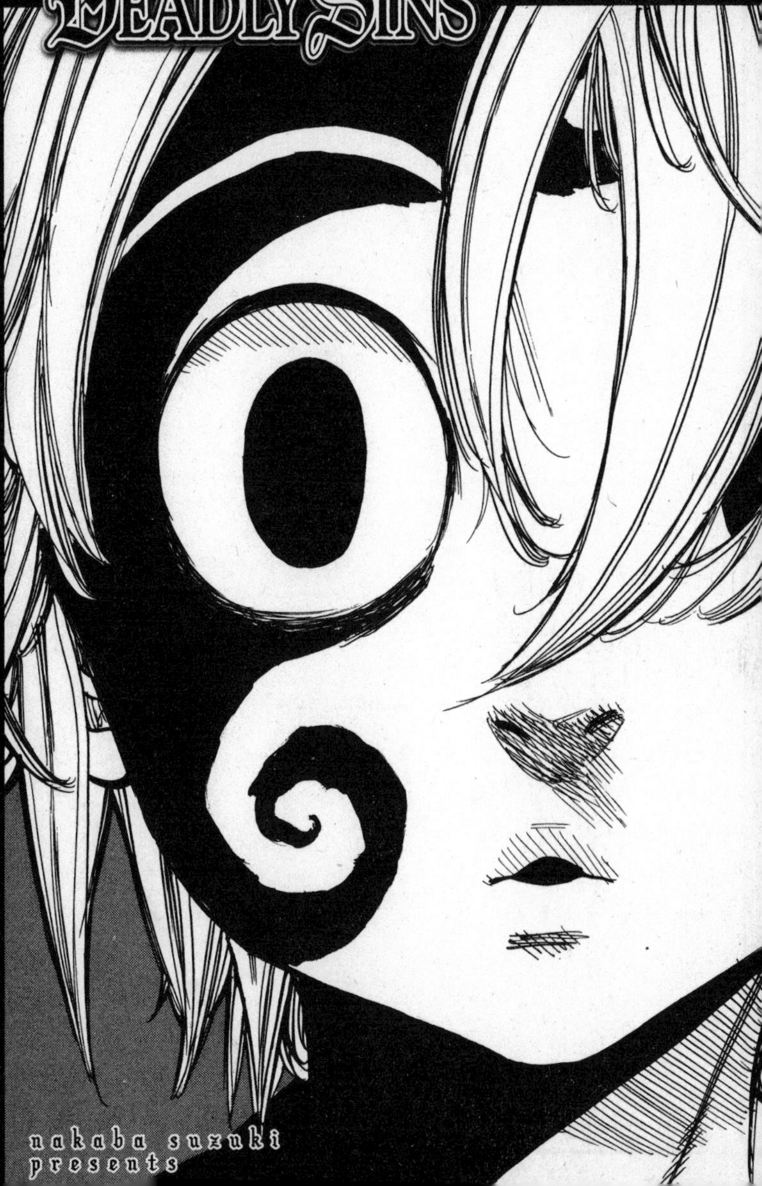
nakaba suzuki
presents

CONTENTS

BOAR HAT

The Seven Deadly Sins

THE SEVEN DEADLY SINS

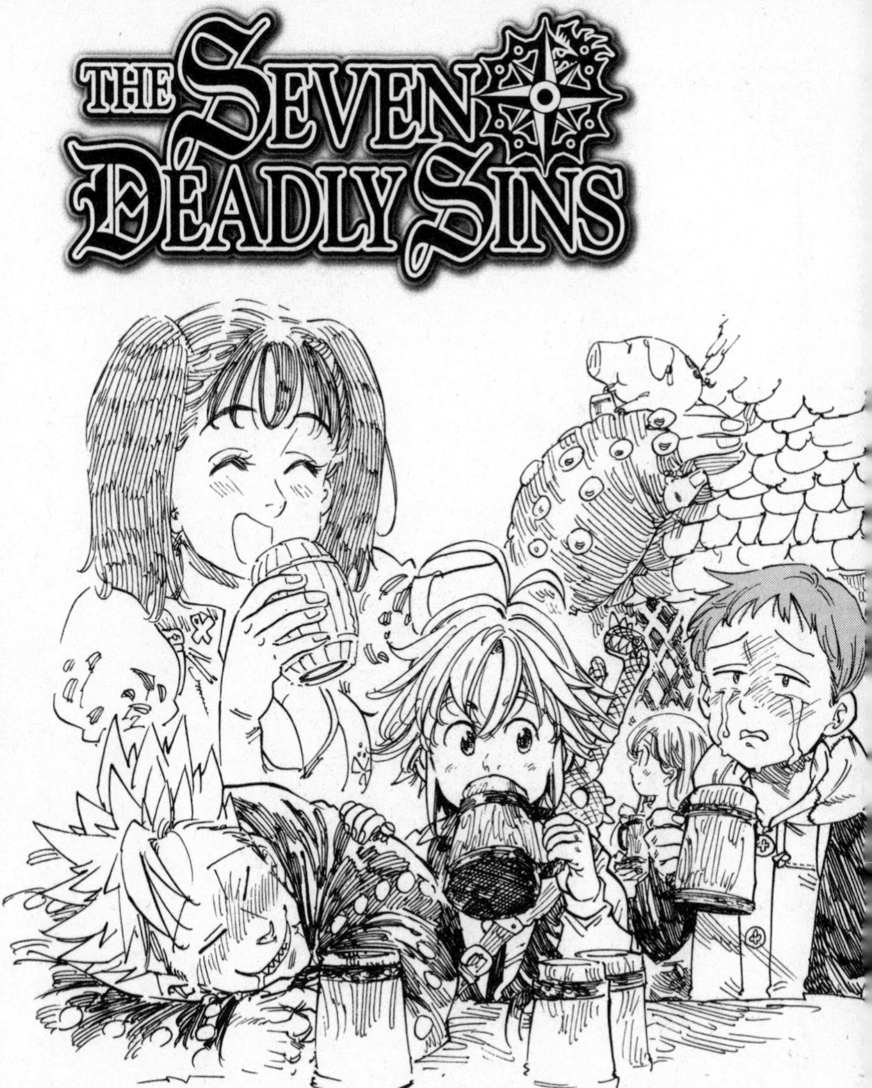

Chapter 47 - Apostle of Destruction

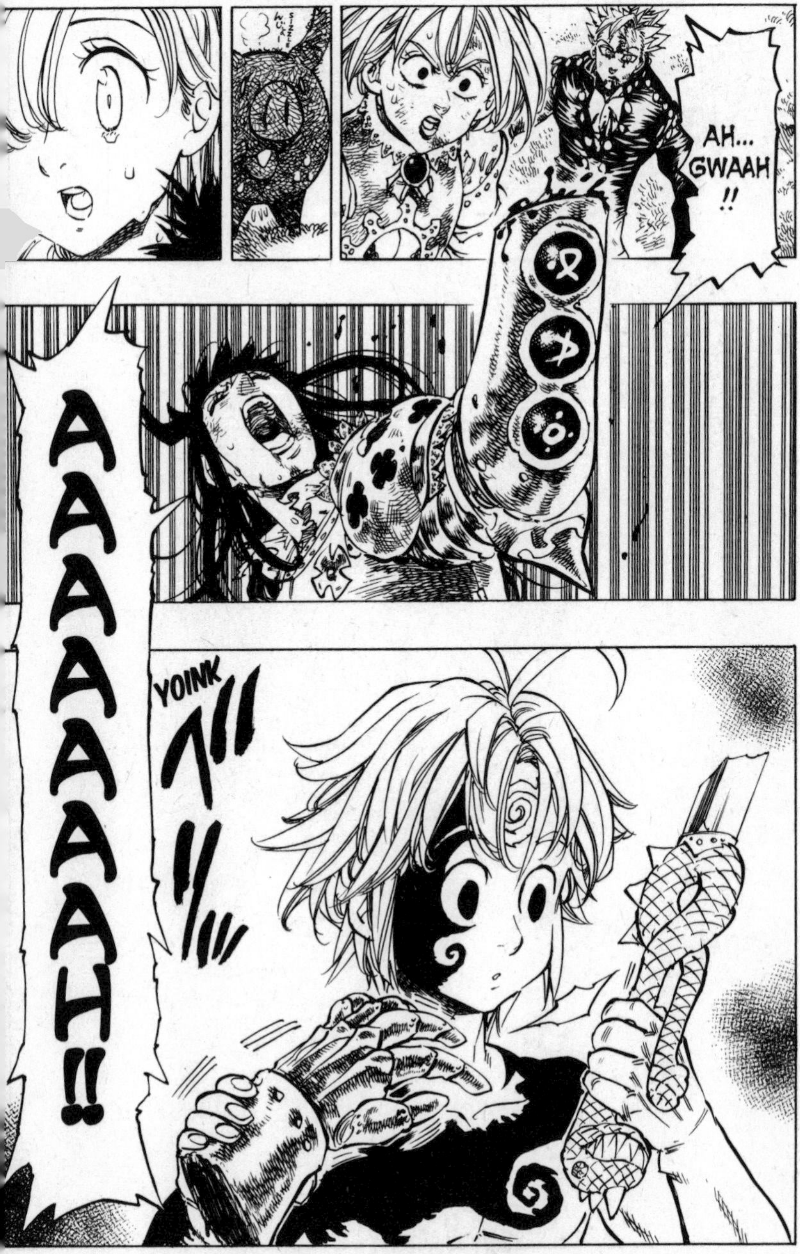
AH... GWAAH !!
SIZZLE
んじょー
AAAAAAAH!!
YOINK

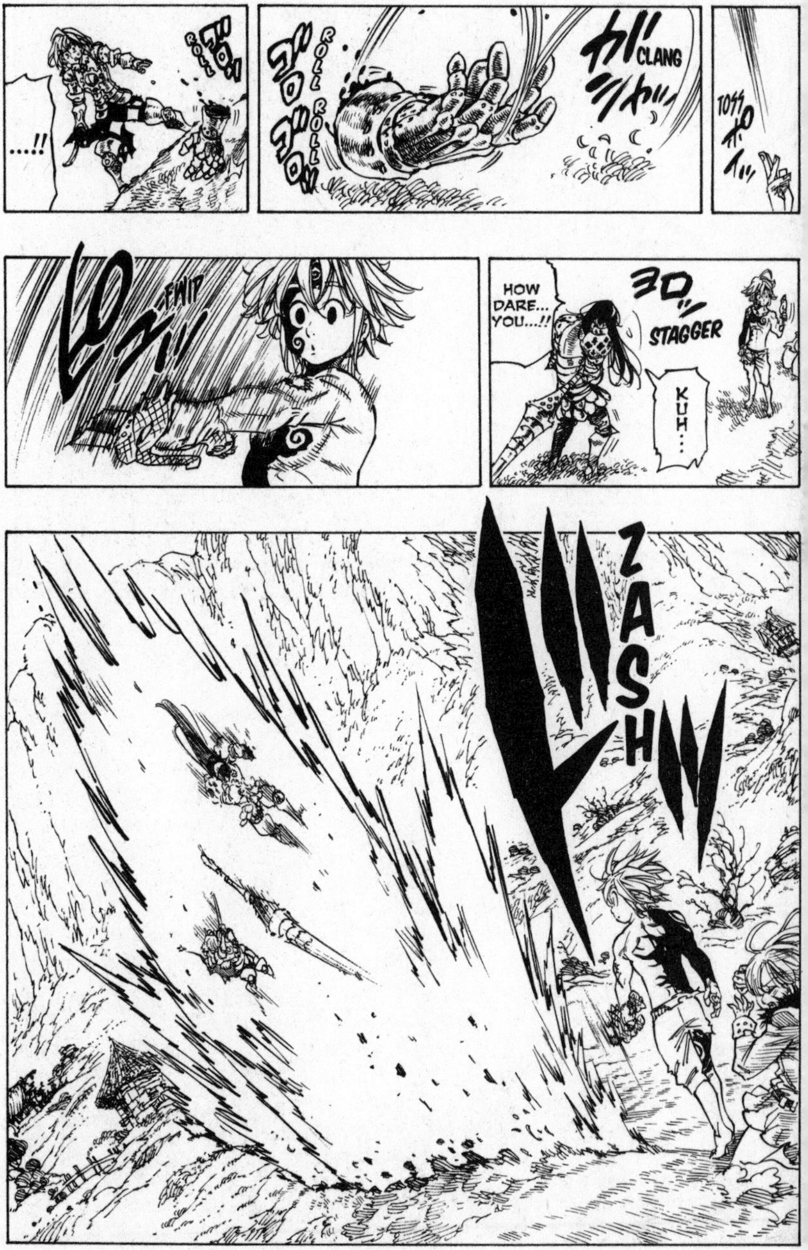
TOSS
CLANG
ROLL ROLL
ROLL
...!!
STAGGER
HOW DARE... YOU...!!
KUH...
FWIP
ZASH

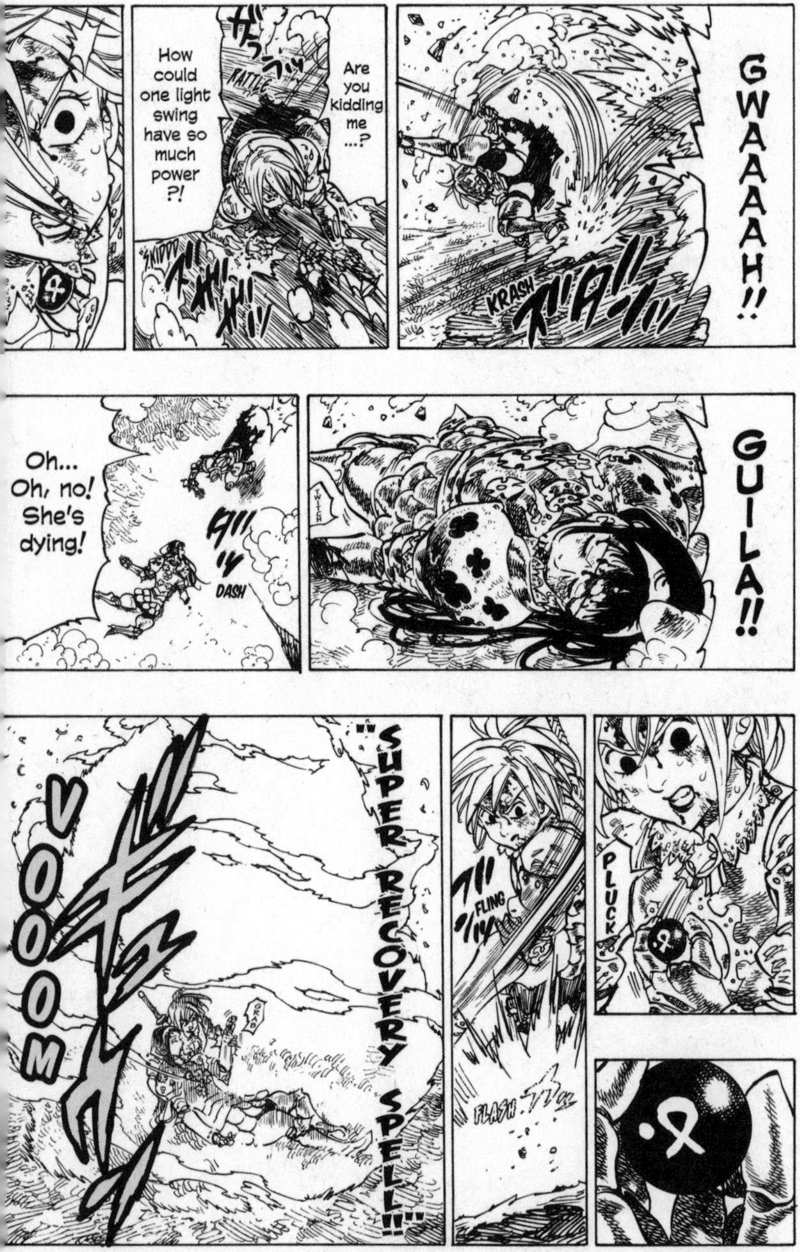
GWAAAAH!!
KRASH
Are you kidding me ...?
How could one light swing have so much power ?!
RATTLE
SKIDDD
GUILA!!
TWITCH
Oh... Oh, no! She's dying!
DASH
PLUCK
FLING
FLASH
"SUPER RECOVERY SPELL!!"
GRAB
VOOOOM

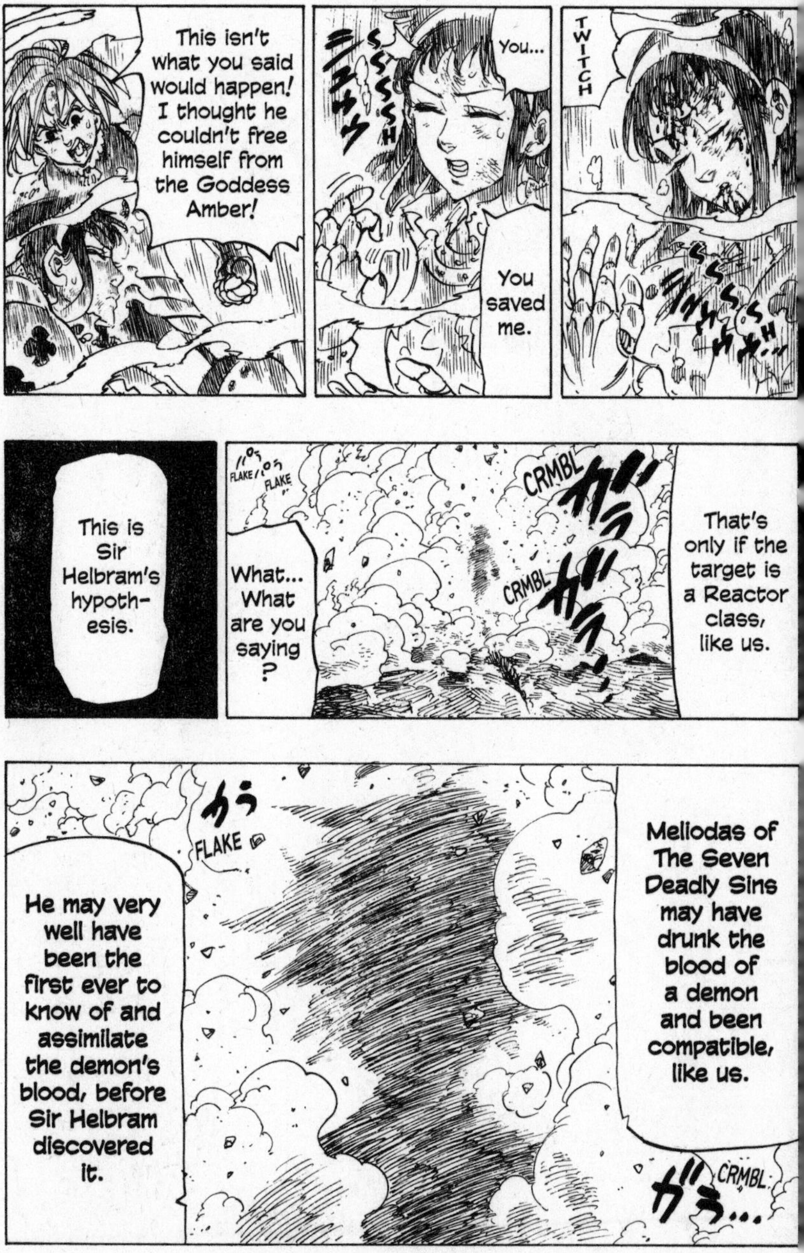
TWITCH
SSSH...
SSSSH
You...
You saved me.
This isn't what you said would happen! I thought he couldn't free himself from the Goddess Amber!
That's only if the target is a Reactor class, like us.
CRMBL
CRMBL
FLAKE FLAKE
What... What are you saying?
This is Sir Helbram's hypothesis.
Meliodas of The Seven Deadly Sins may have drunk the blood of a demon and been compatible, like us.
CRMBL...
FLAKE
He may very well have been the first ever to know of and assimilate the demon's blood, before Sir Helbram discovered it.

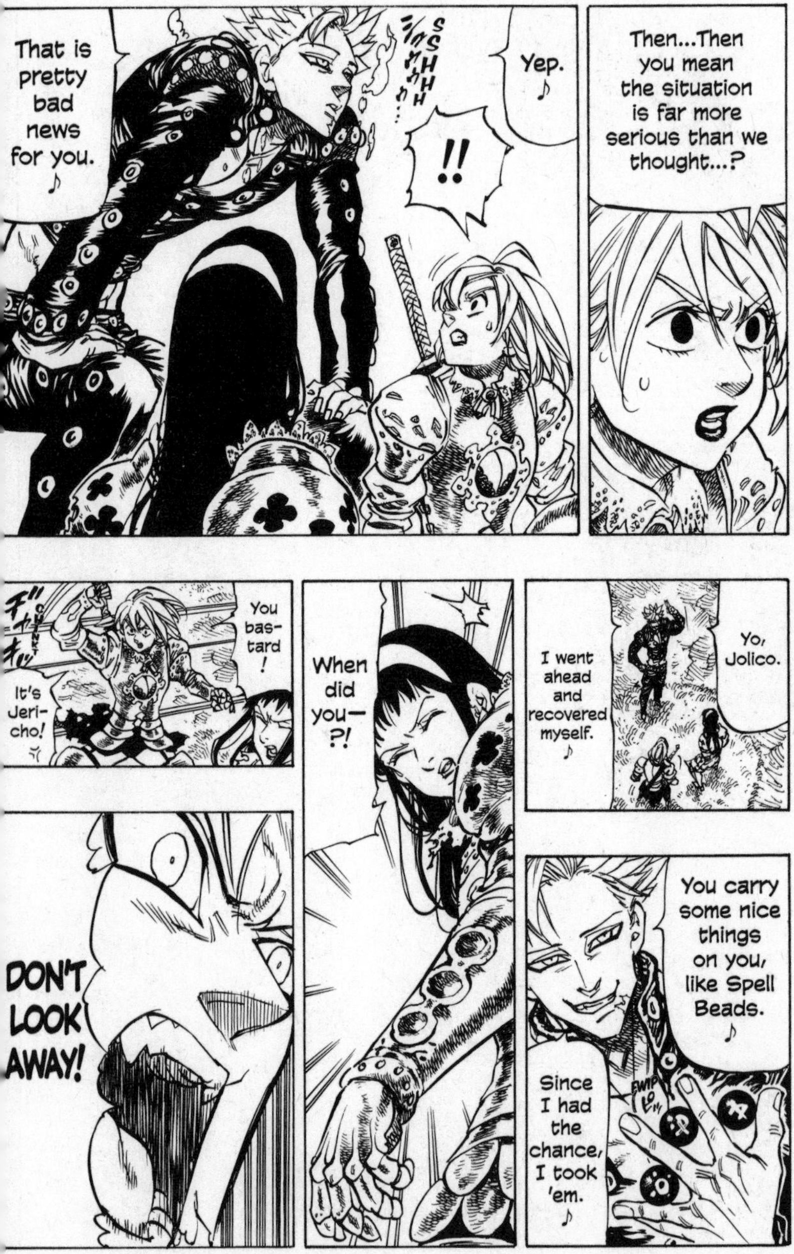
Then...Then you mean the situation is far more serious than we thought...?
Yep. ♪
!!
SHHH
That is pretty bad news for you. ♪
Yo, Jolico.
I went ahead and recovered myself. ♪
You carry some nice things on you, like Spell Beads. ♪
FWIP
Since I had the chance, I took 'em. ♪
When did you—?!
You bastard!
CHINK
It's Jericho!
DON'T LOOK AWAY!

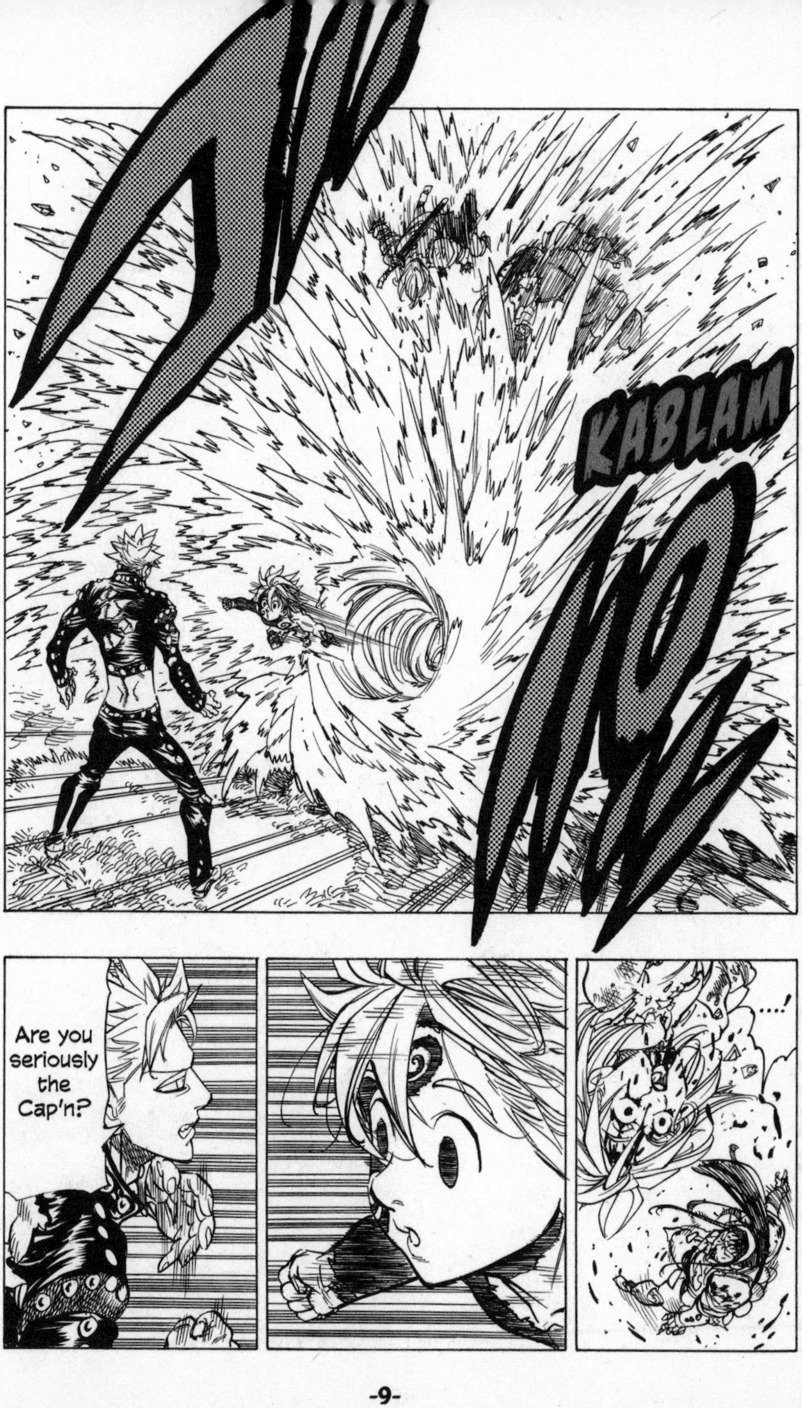
KABLAM
....!
Are you seriously the Cap'n?

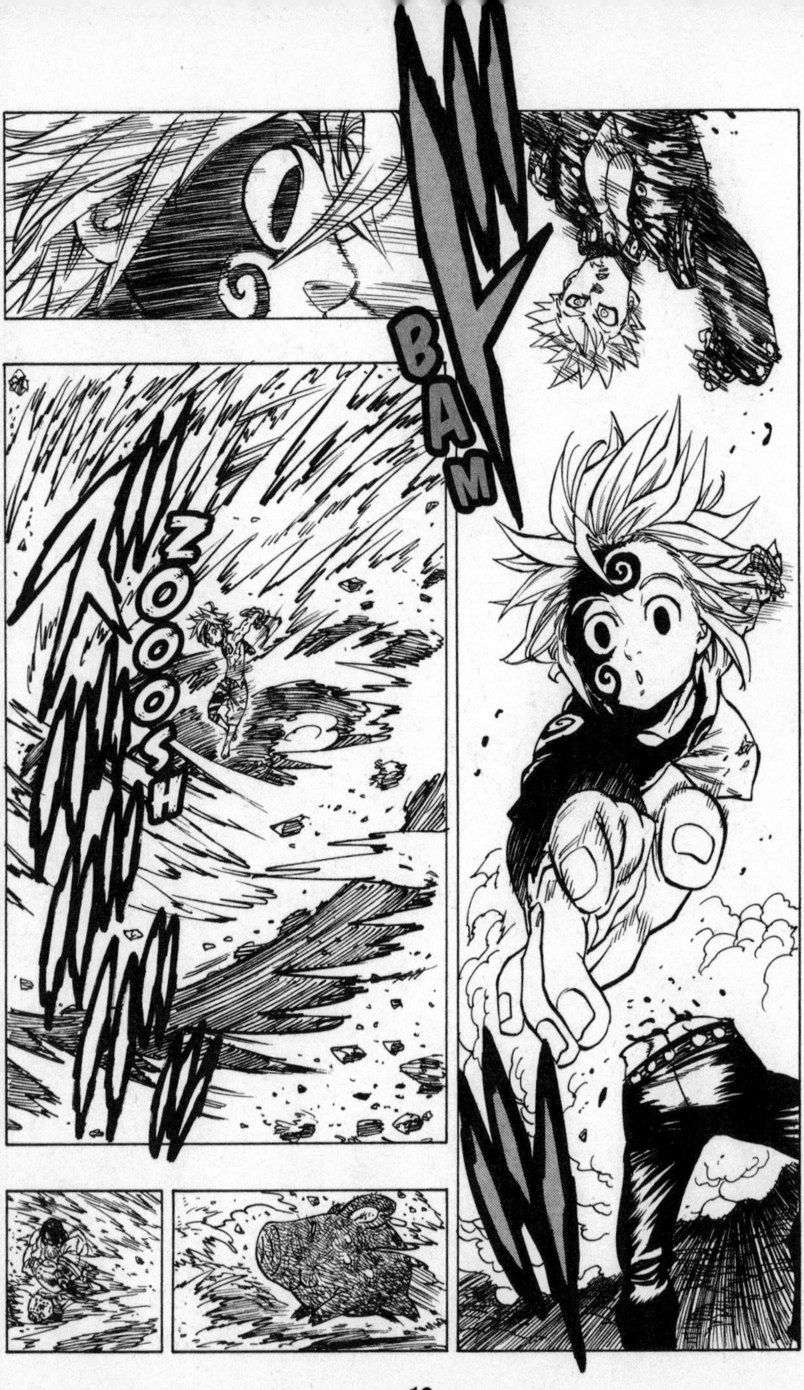
BAM
ZOOOSH

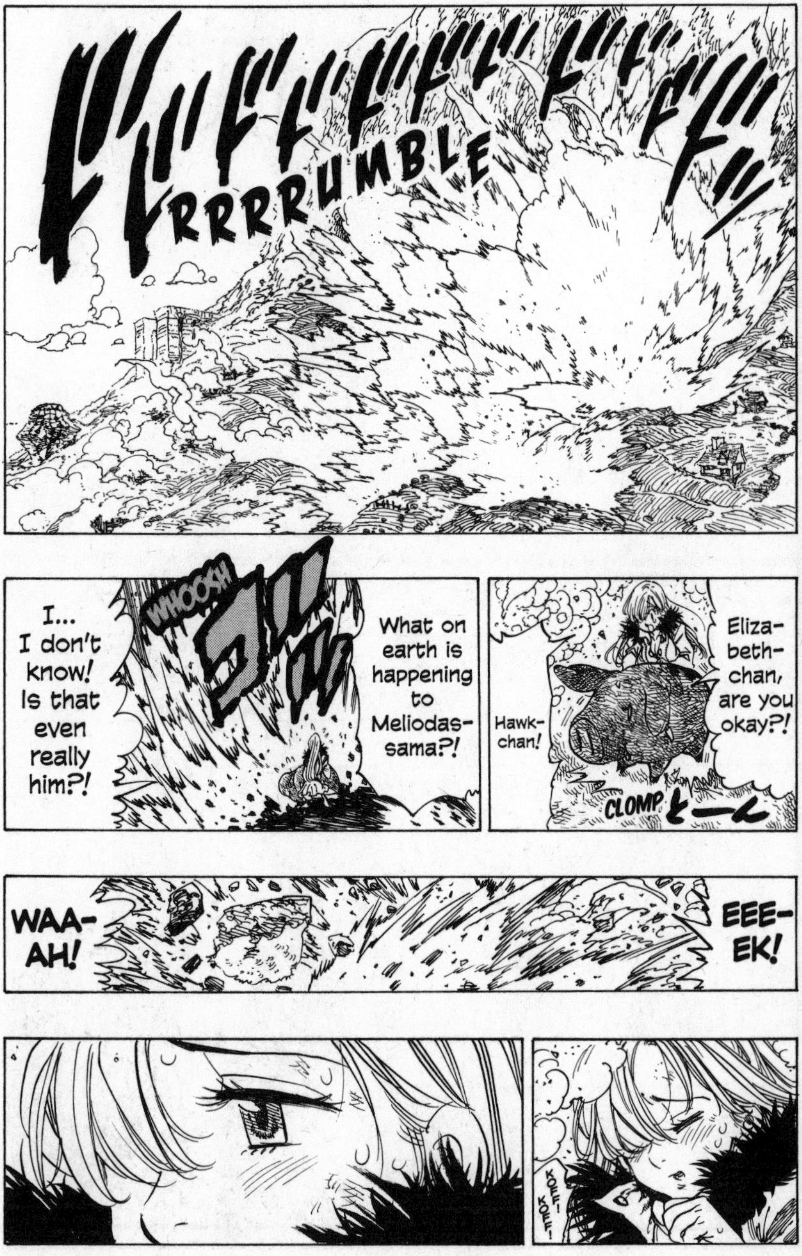
RRRRUMBLE
Eliza-beth-chan, are you okay?!
Hawk-chan!
CLOMP
What on earth is happening to Meliodas-sama?!
I... I don't know! Is that even really him?!
WHOOSH
EEE-EK!
WAA-AH!
KOFF! KOFF!

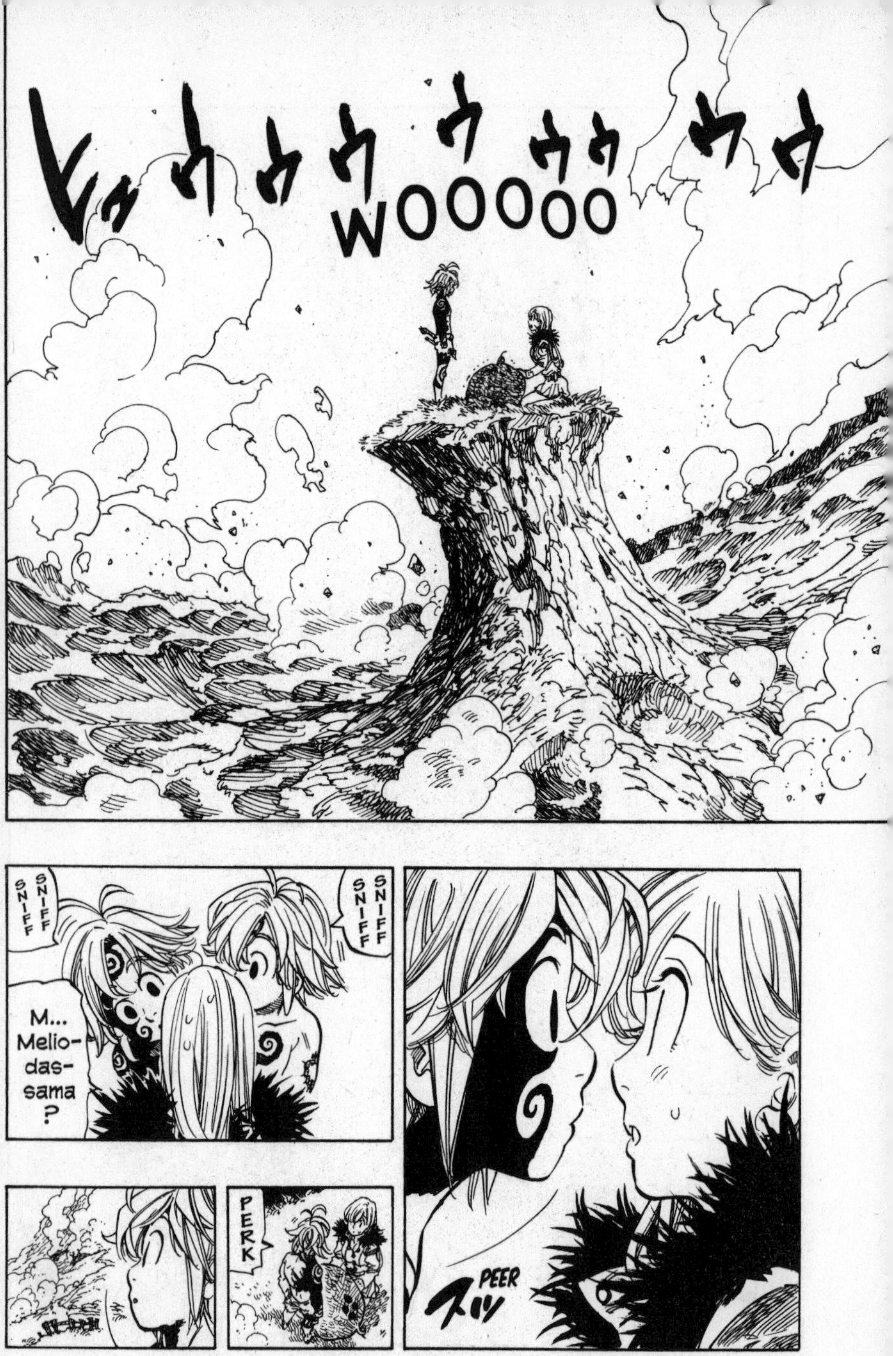
WOOOOO
PEER
SNIFF SNIFF
SNIFF SNIFF
M... Melio-das-sama?
PERK

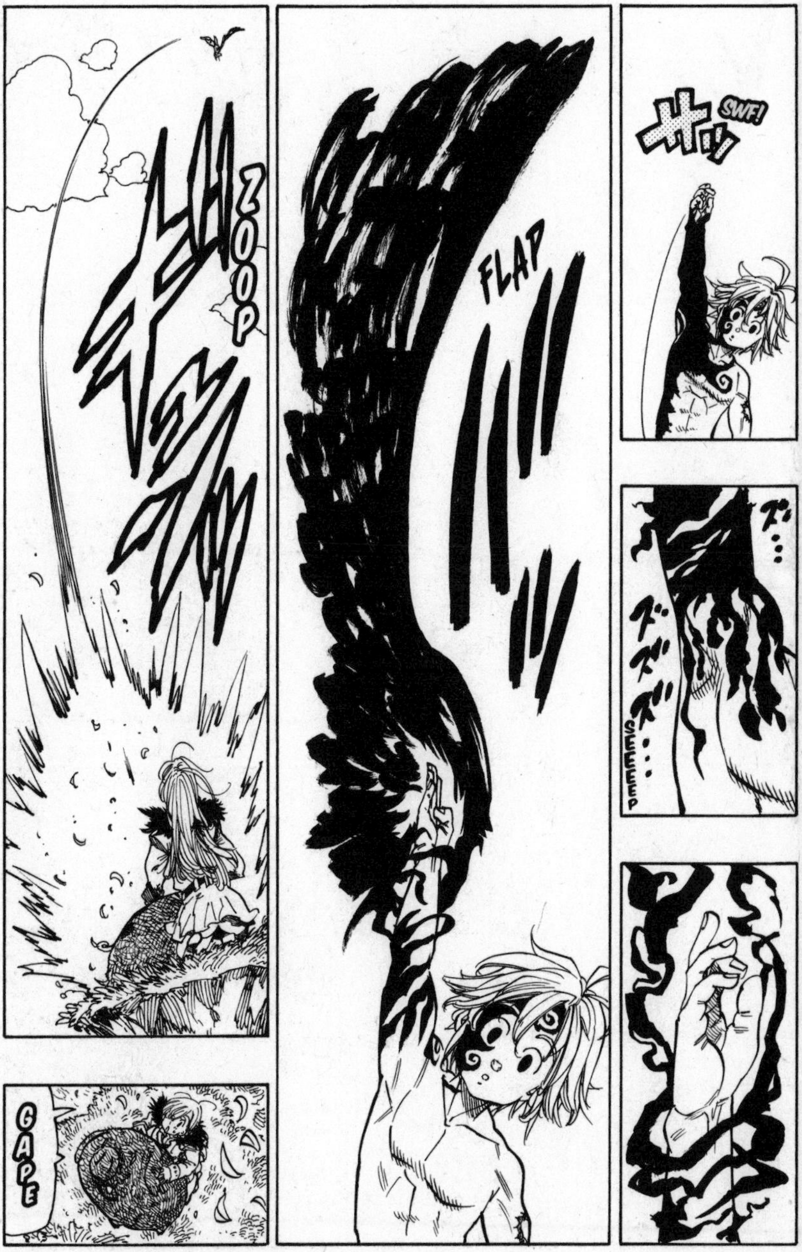
SWF!
SEEEEP...
FLAP
ZOOOP
GAPE

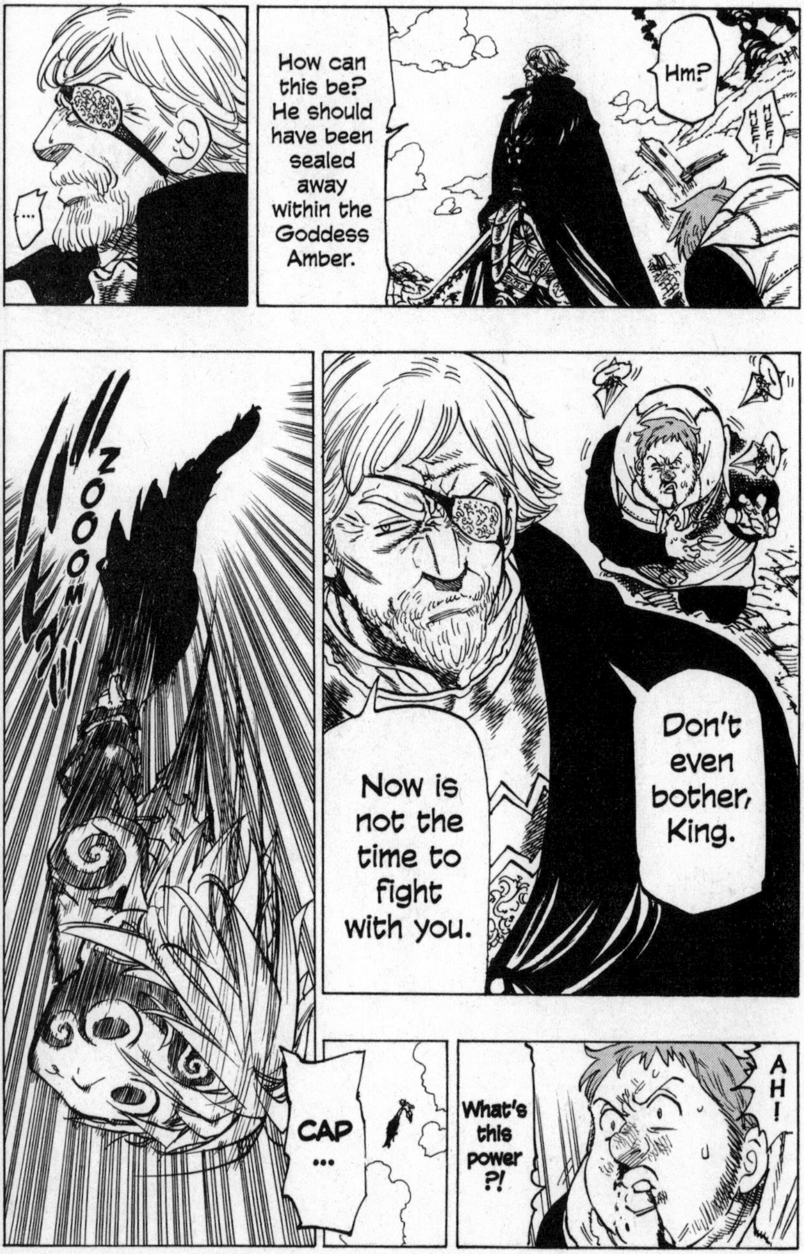
Hm?
HUFF! HUFF!
How can this be? He should have been sealed away within the Goddess Amber.
....
Don't even bother, King.
Now is not the time to fight with you.
AH!
What's this power ?!
CAP ...
ZOOOOM

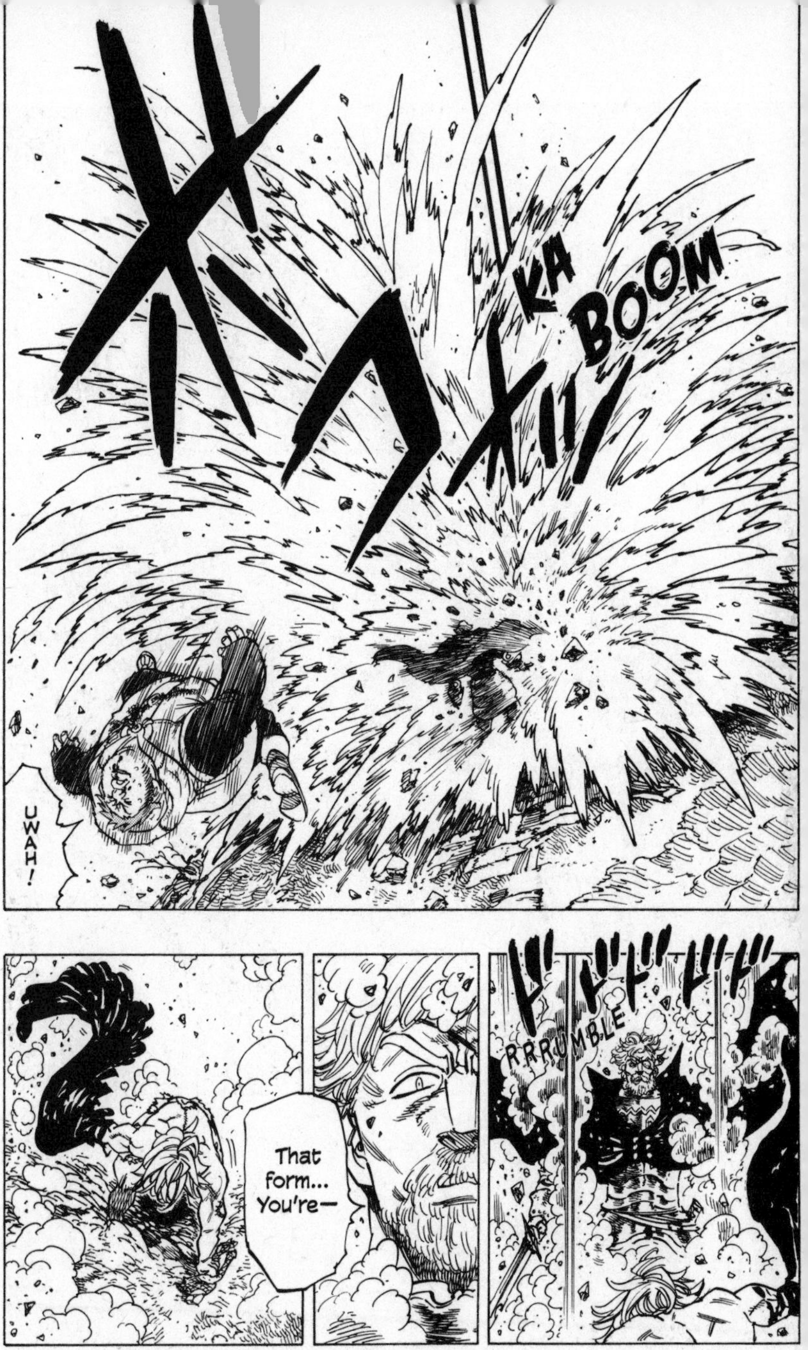
KA BOOM
UWAH!
RRRUMBLE
That form... You're—

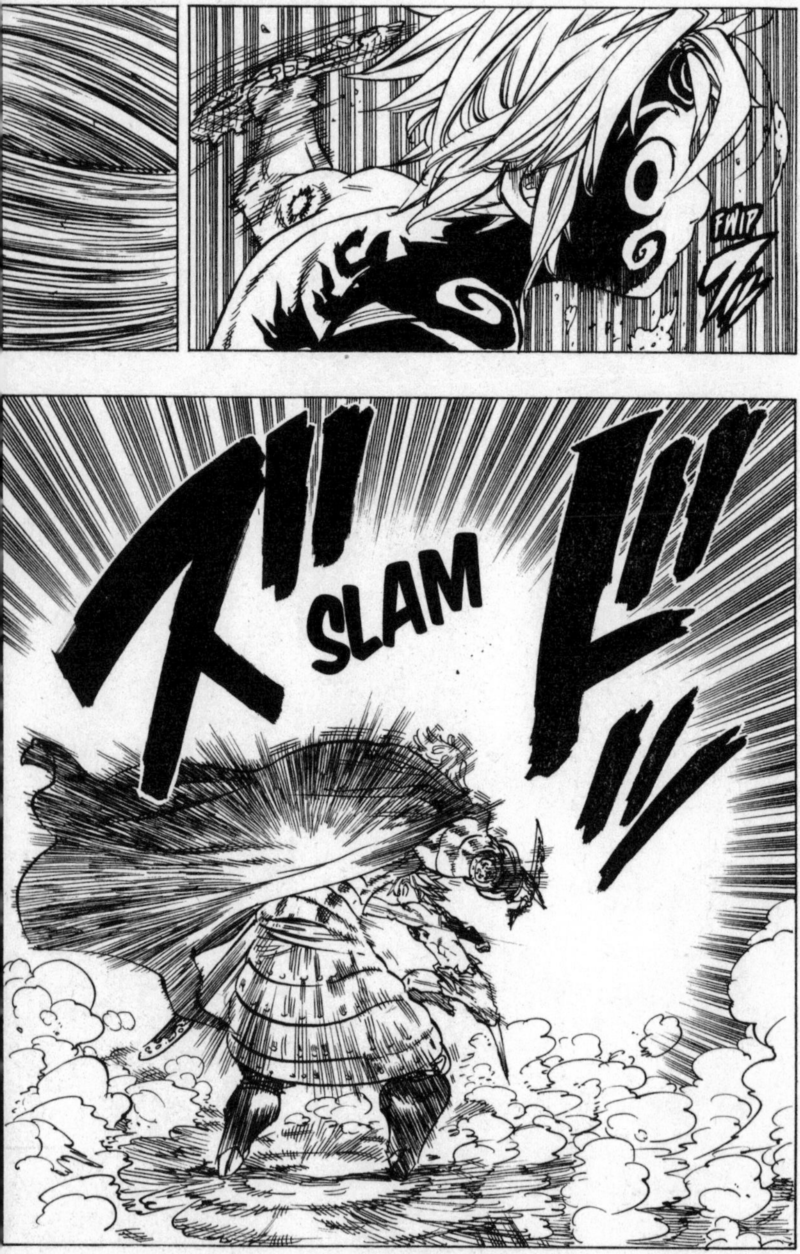
FWIP
SLAM

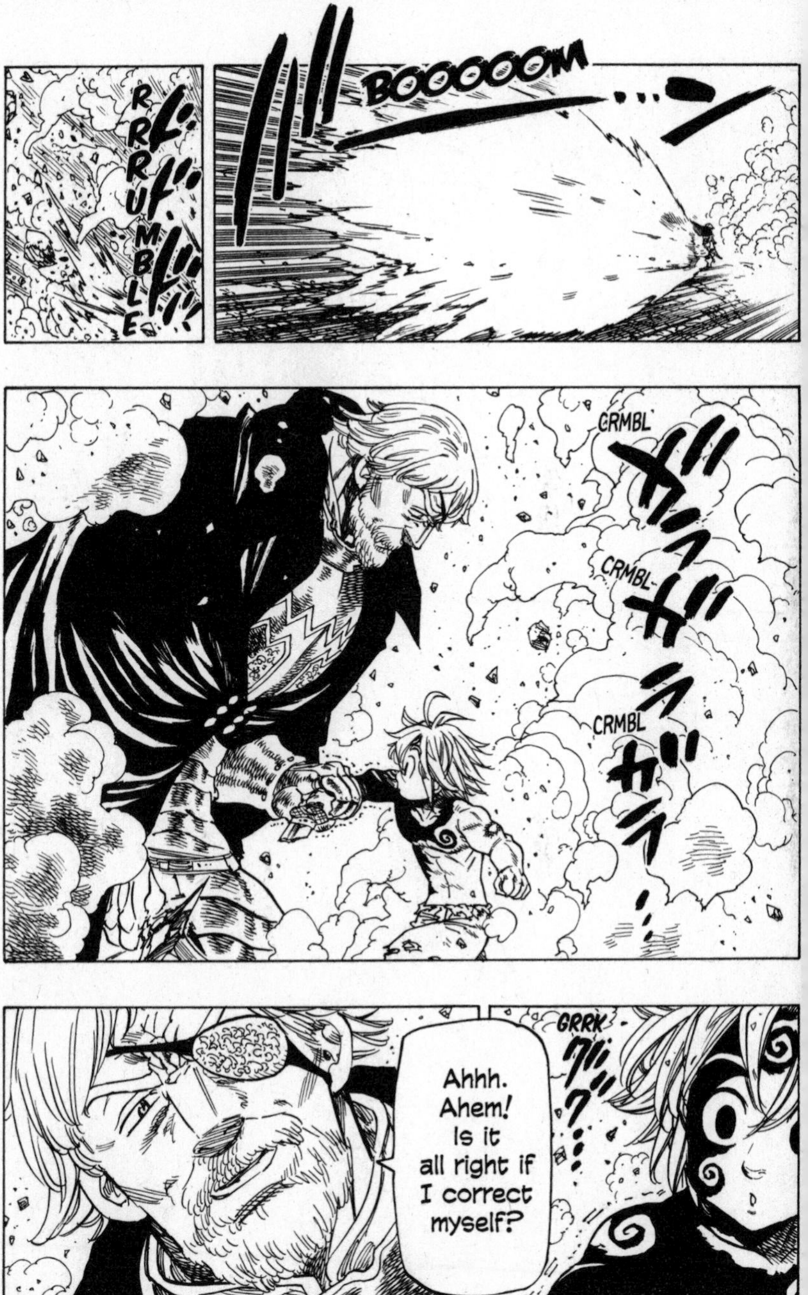
BOOOOOM
RRRUMBLE
CRMBL
CRMBL
CRMBL
GRRK
Ahhh. Ahem! Is it all right if I correct myself?

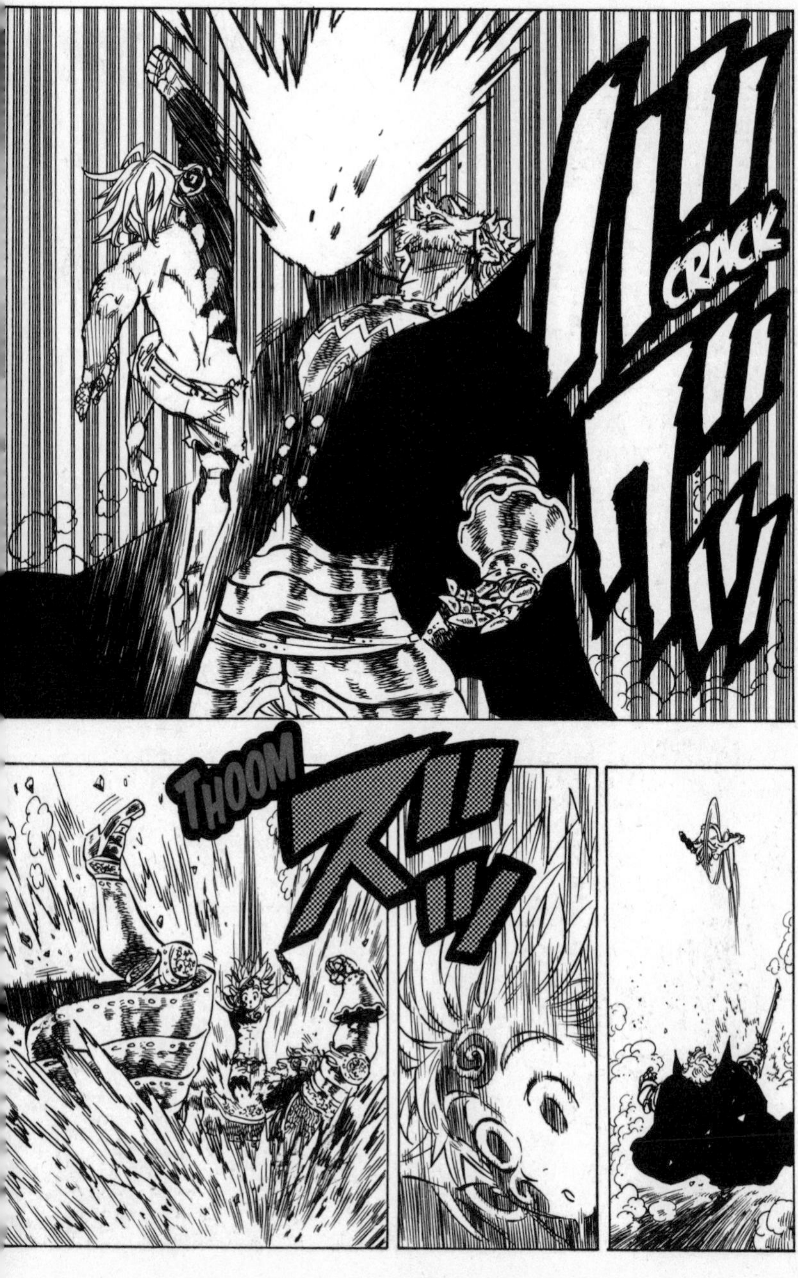
CRACK
THOOM

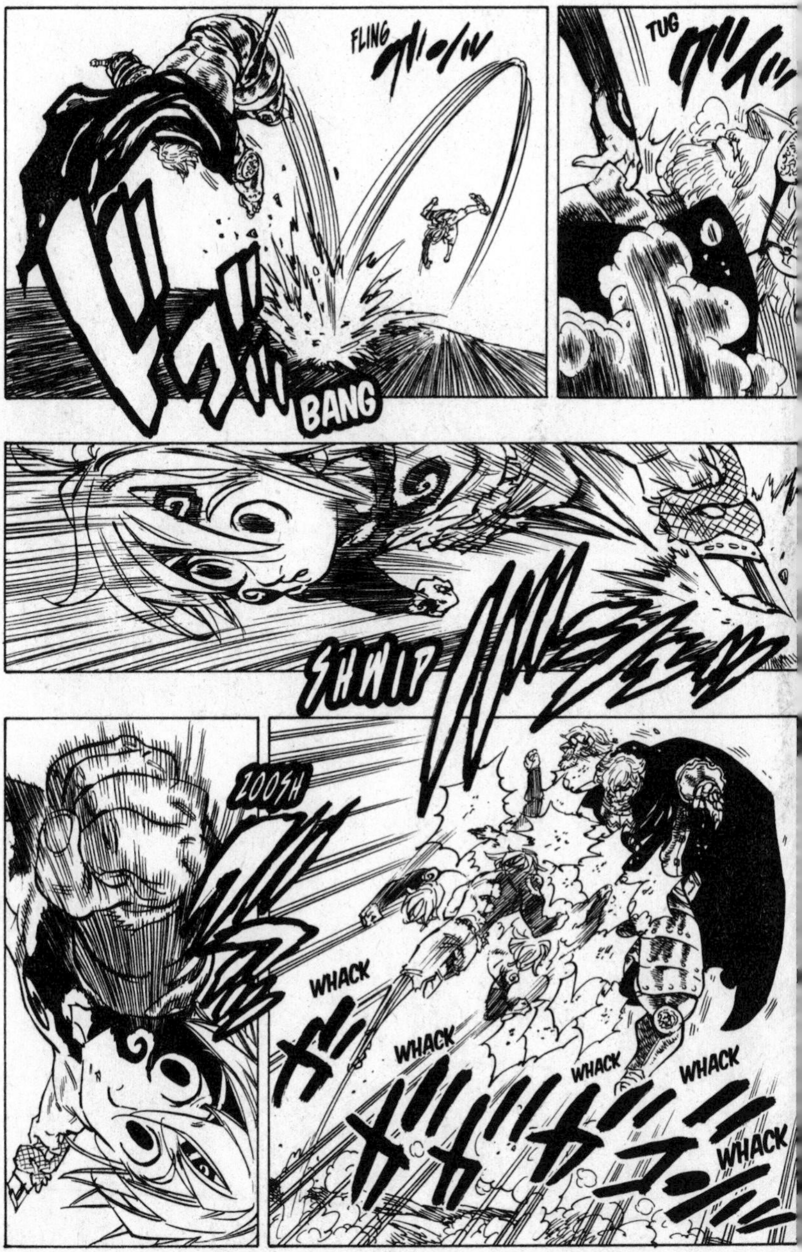
TUG
FLING
BANG
SHWIP
WHACK
WHACK
WHACK
WHACK
WHACK
ZOOSH

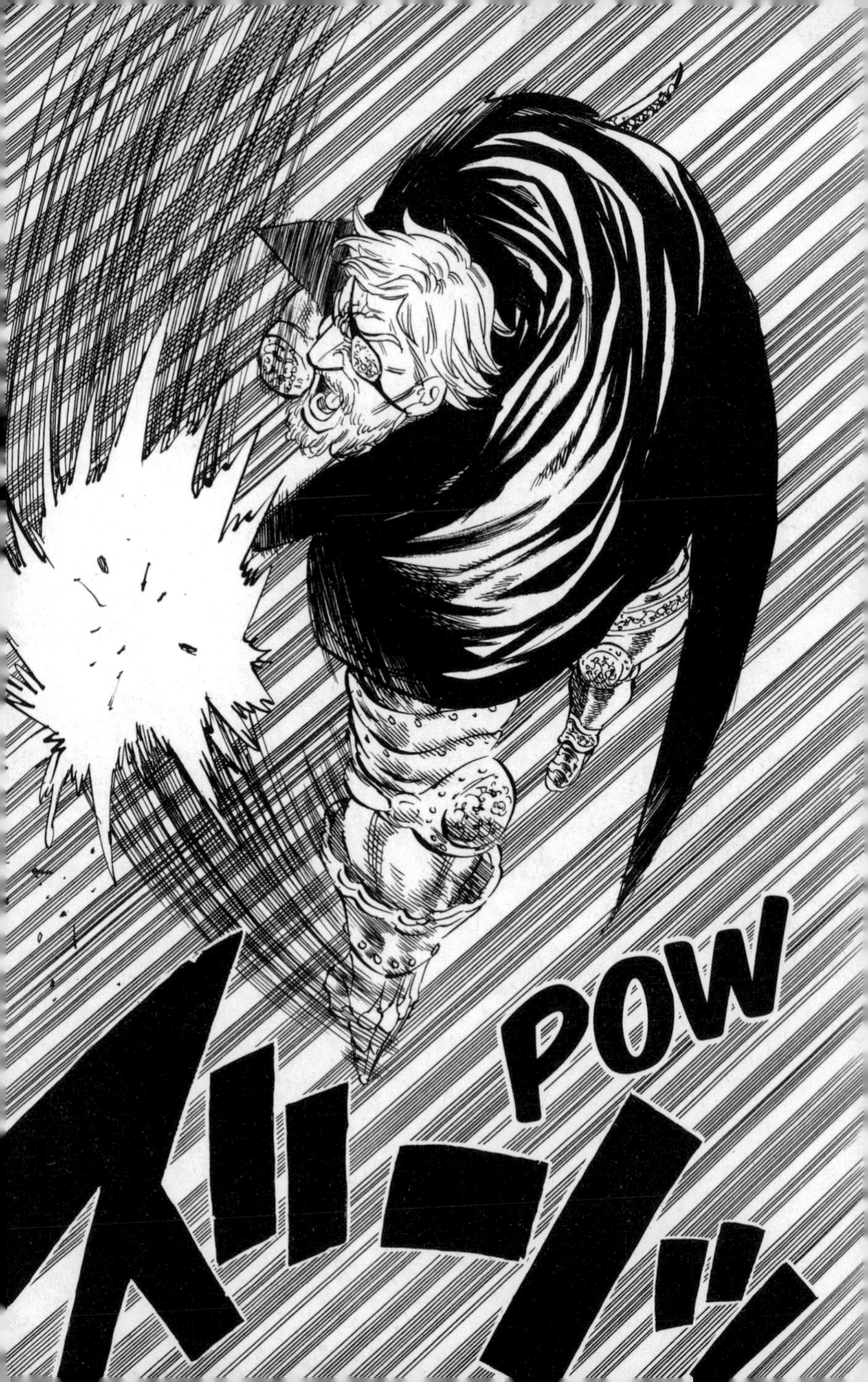
POW

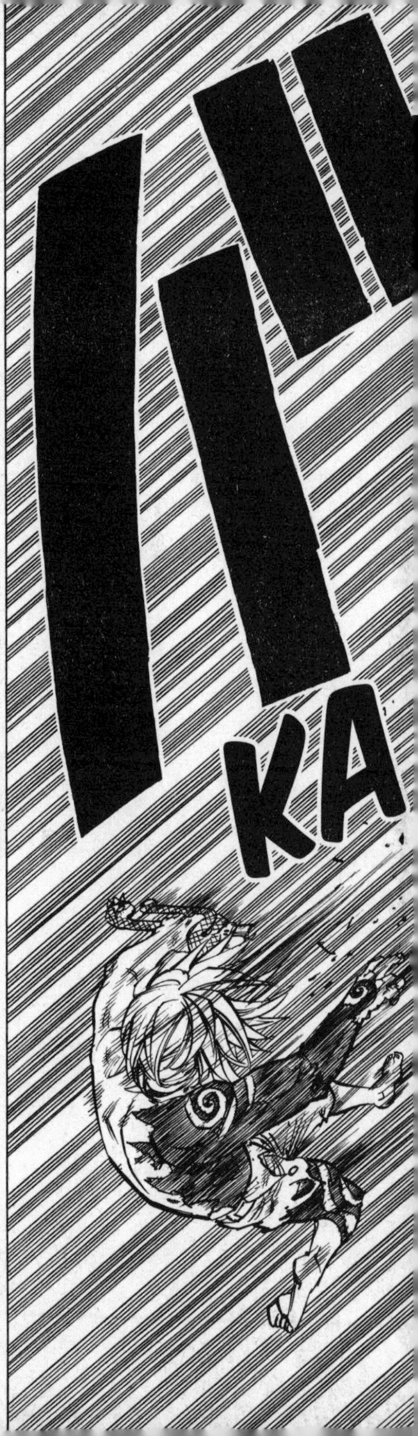
KA
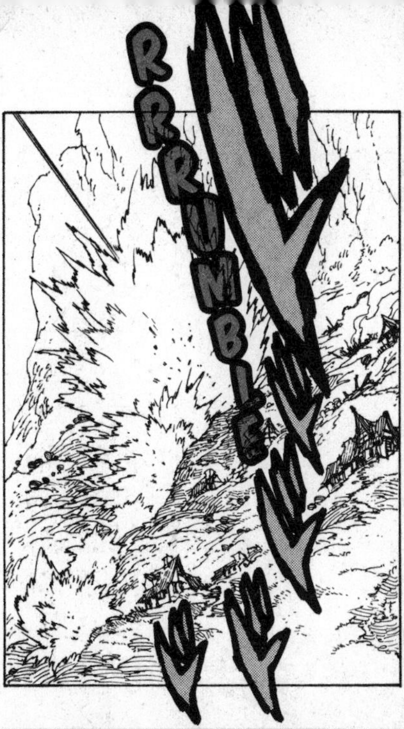
RRRUMBLE
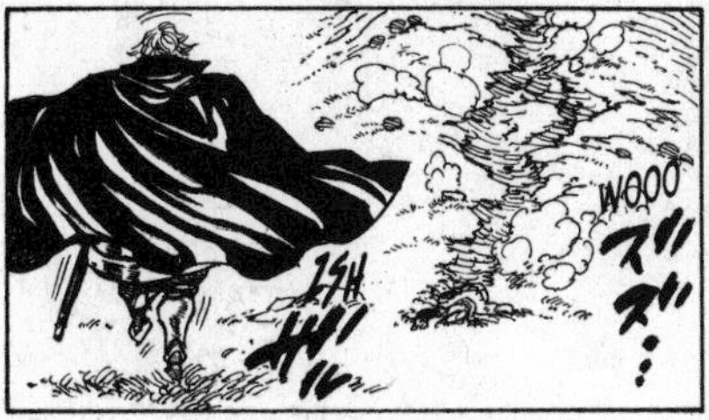
WOOO
ズズ…
ZSH
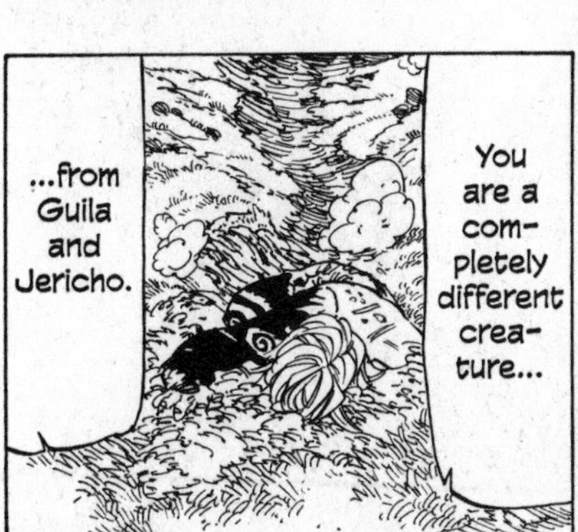
You are a completely different creature...
...from Guila and Jericho.

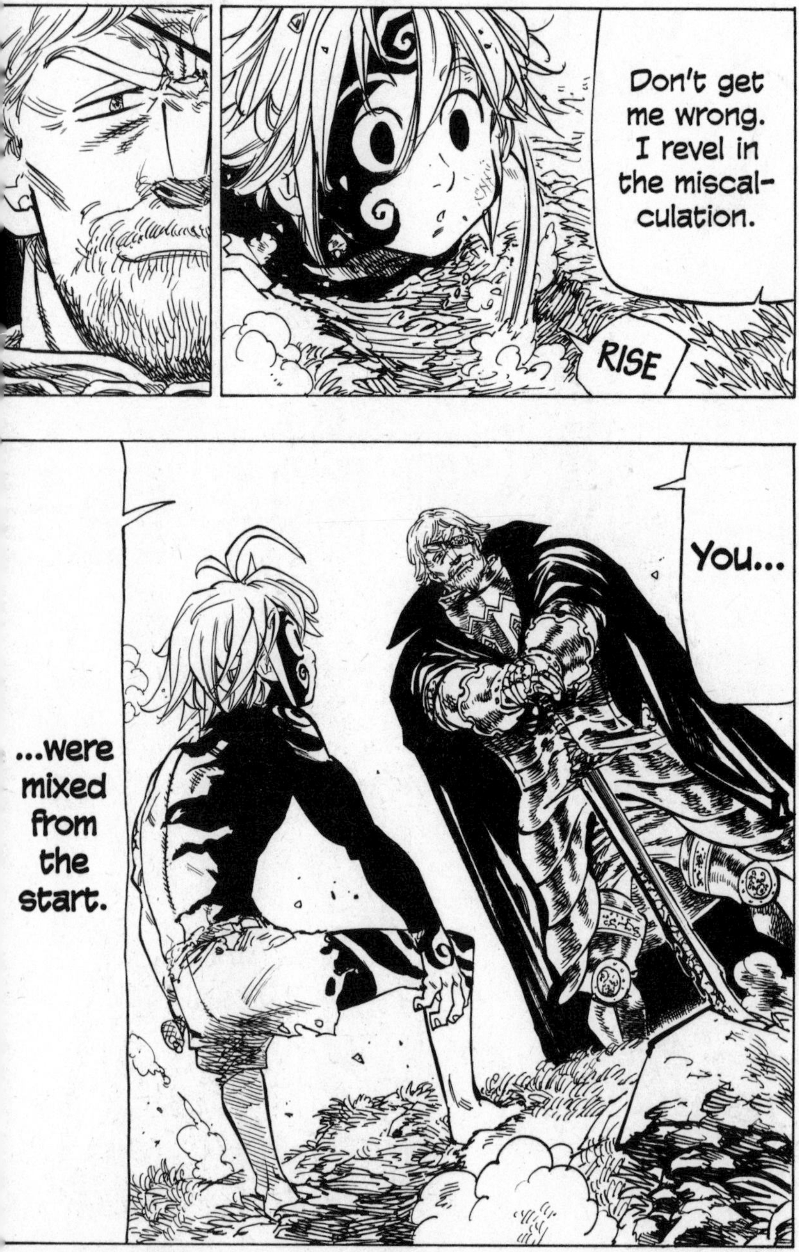
Don't get me wrong. I revel in the miscal-culation.
RISE
You...
...were mixed from the start.

Chapter 48 - Happy Annihilation

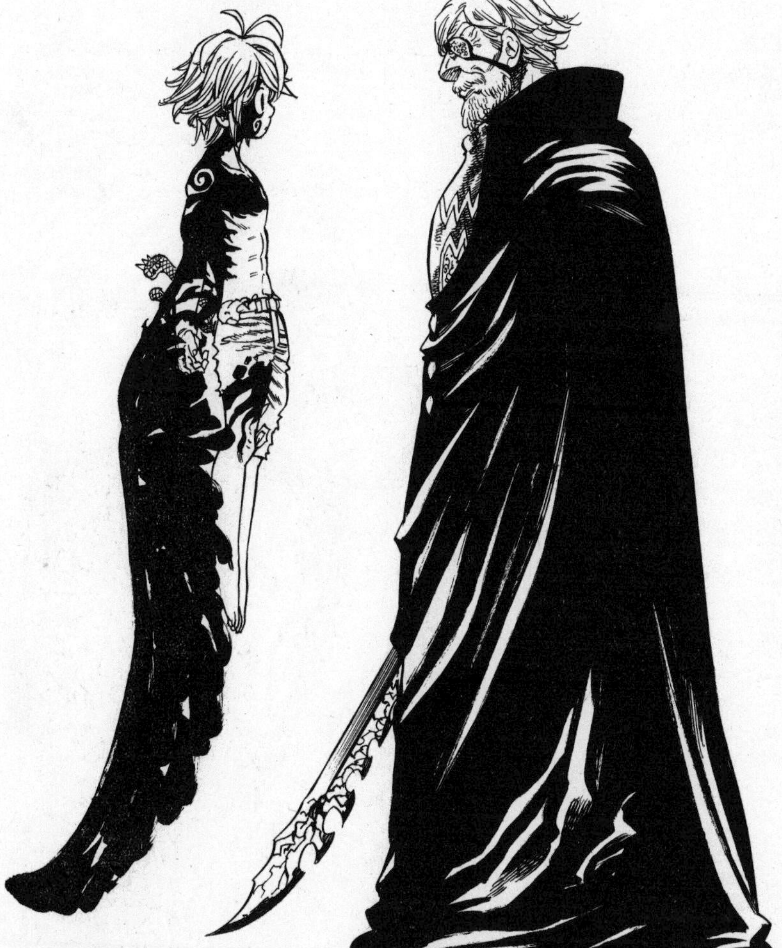

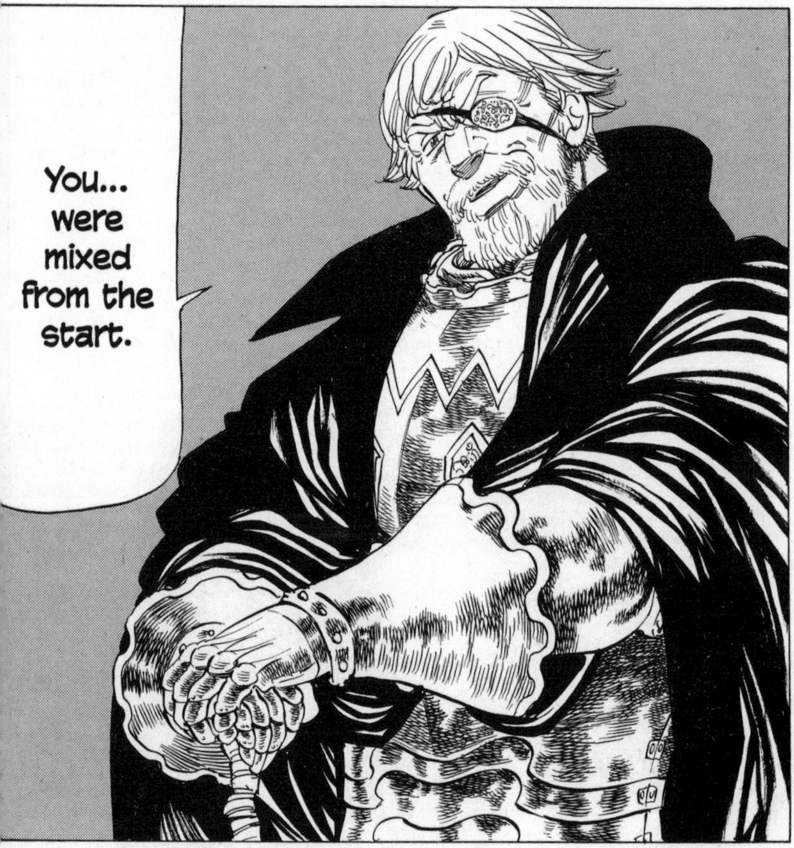
You... were mixed from the start.
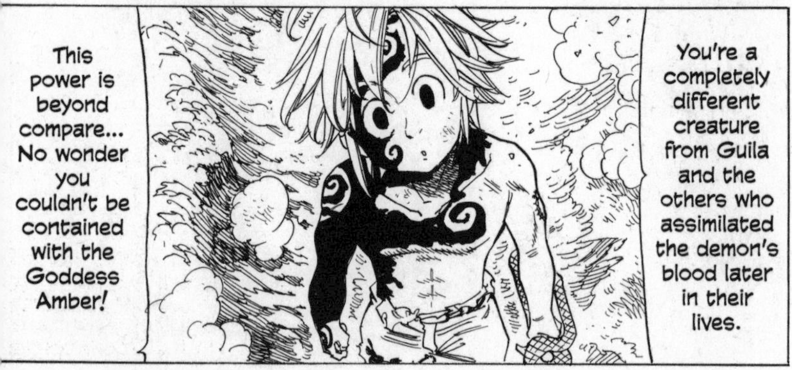
You're a completely different creature from Guila and the others who assimilated the demon's blood later in their lives.
This power is beyond compare... No wonder you couldn't be contained with the Goddess Amber!

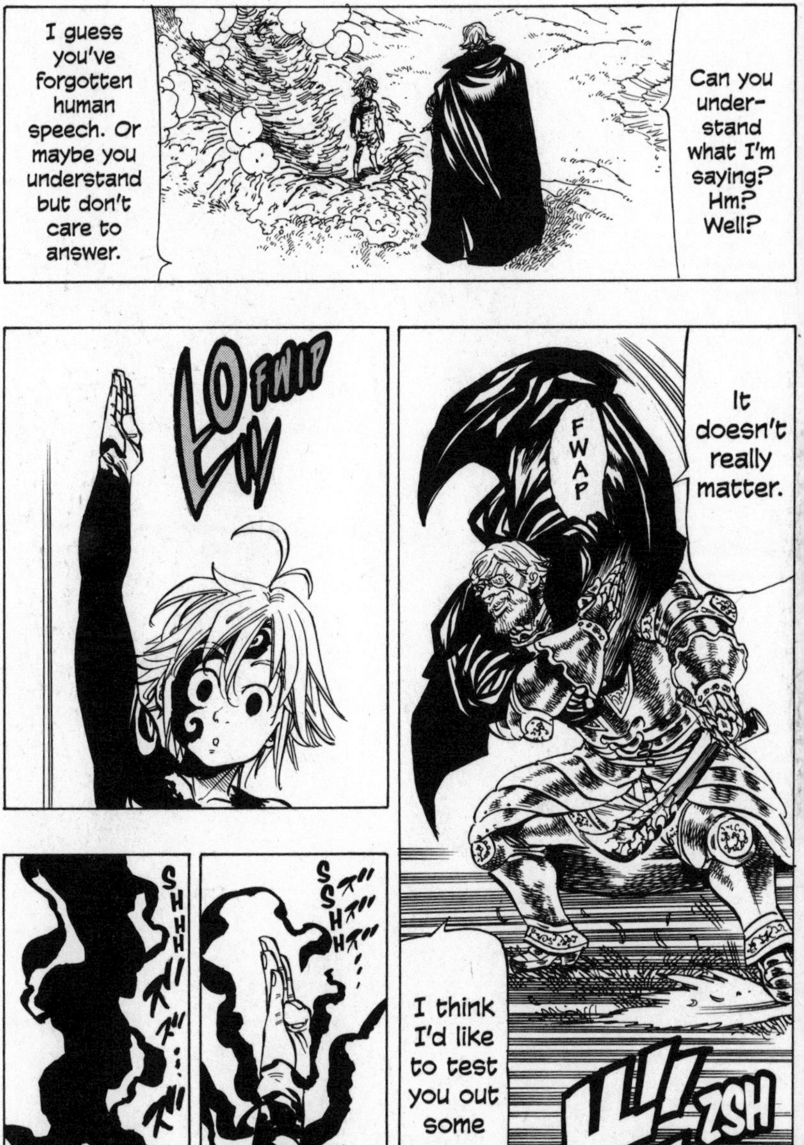

Can you understand what I'm saying? Hm? Well?
I guess you've forgotten human speech. Or maybe you understand but don't care to answer.
It doesn't really matter.
FWAP
I think I'd like to test you out some more. ♡
ZSH
FWIP
SSHH
SHHH

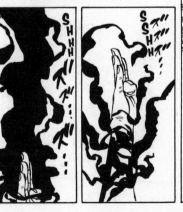

ZOOSH

WHOA!

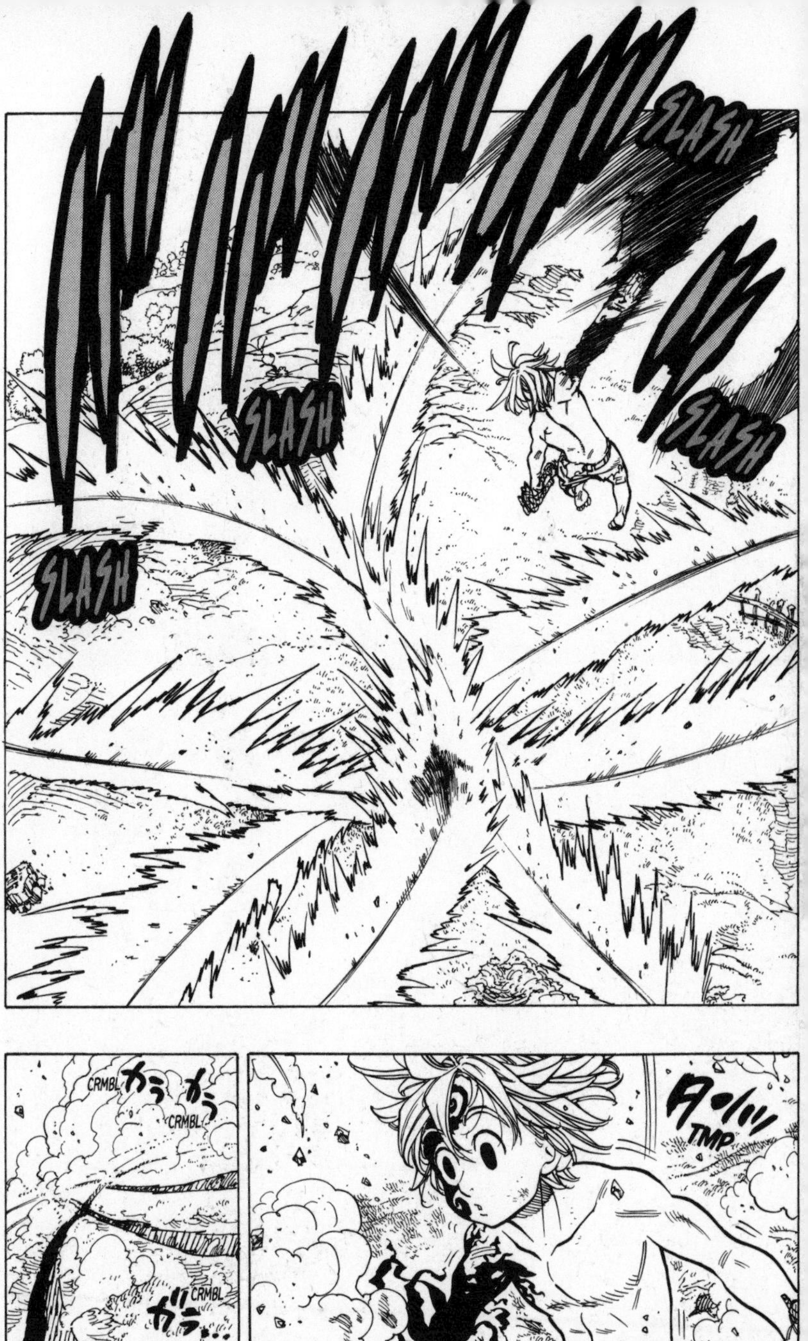
SLASH
SLASH
SLASH
SLASH
TMP
CRMBL
CRMBL
CRMBL

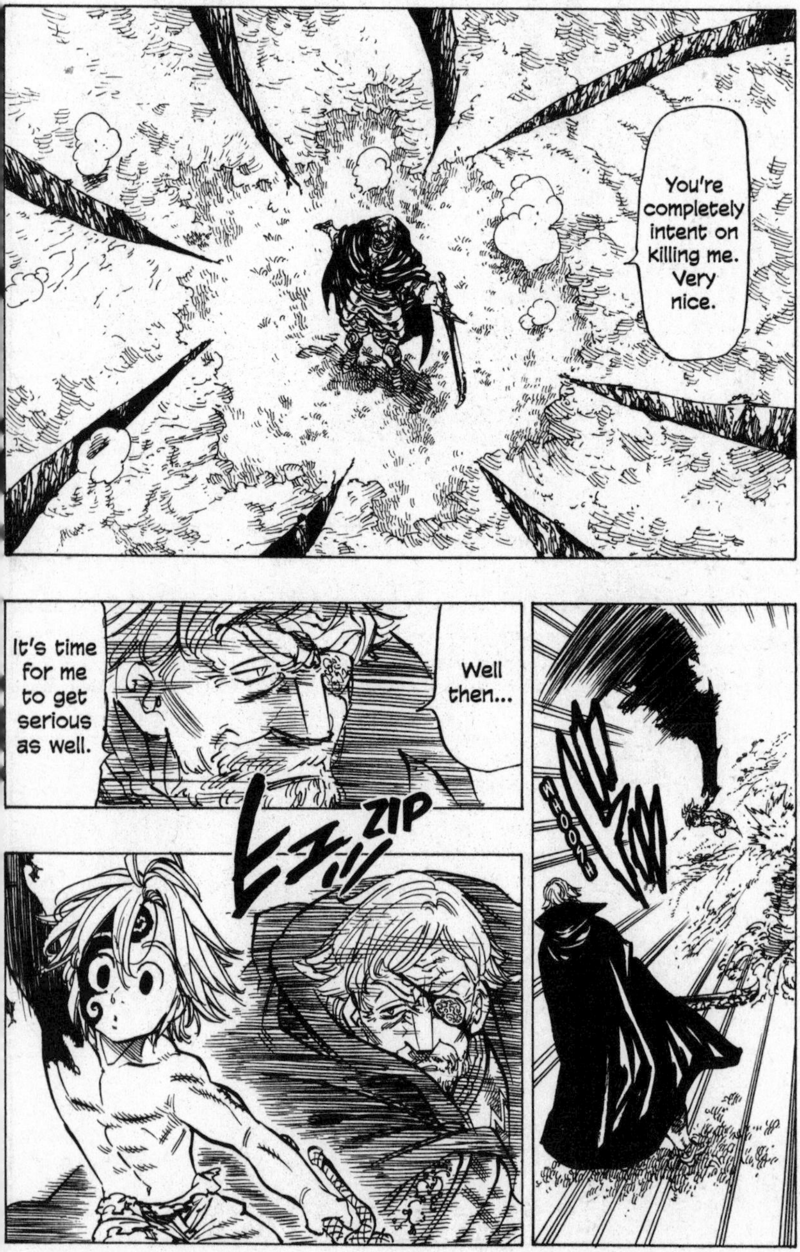
You're completely intent on killing me. Very nice.
WHOOSH
Well then...
It's time for me to get serious as well.
ZIP

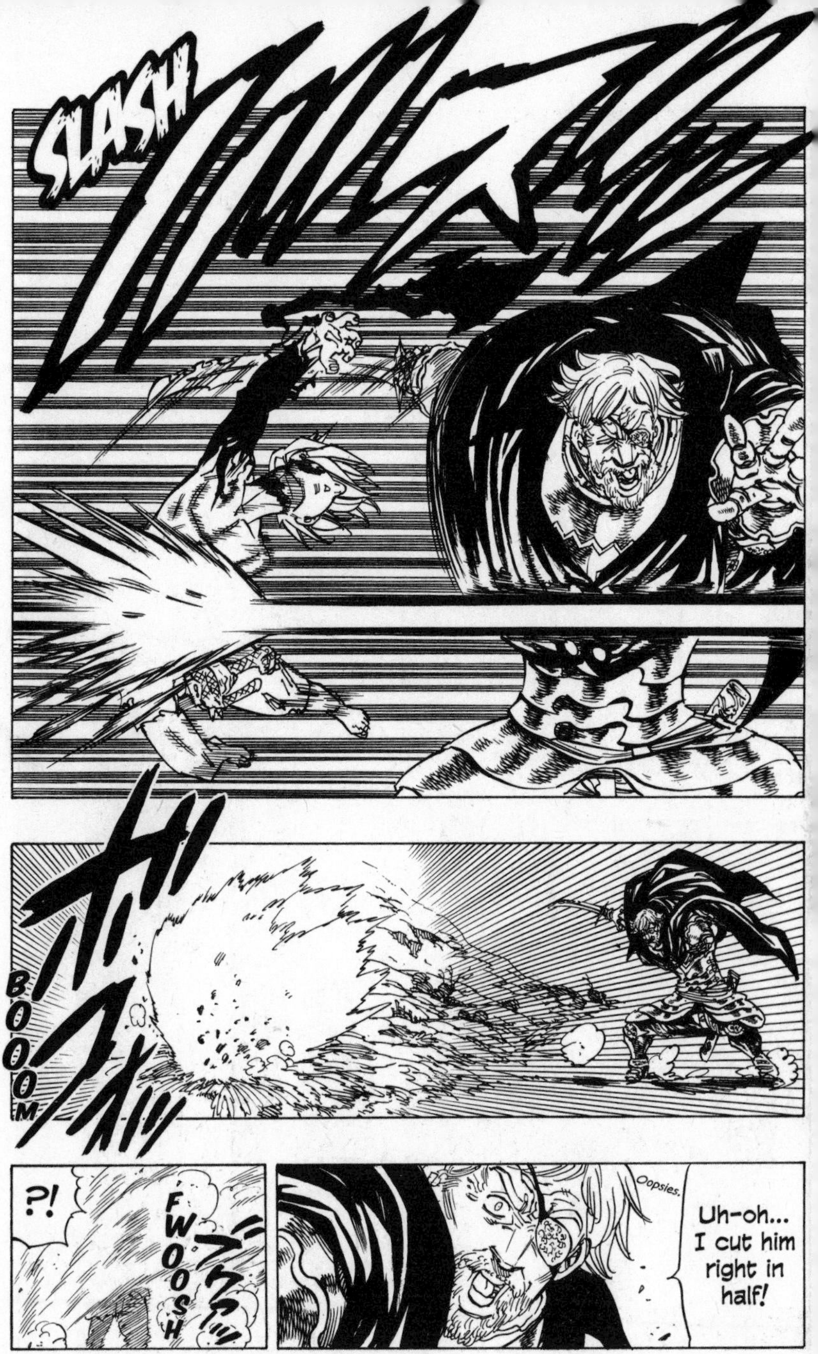
SLASH
BOOOOOM
Oopsies.
Uh-oh... I cut him right in half!
?!
FWOOSH

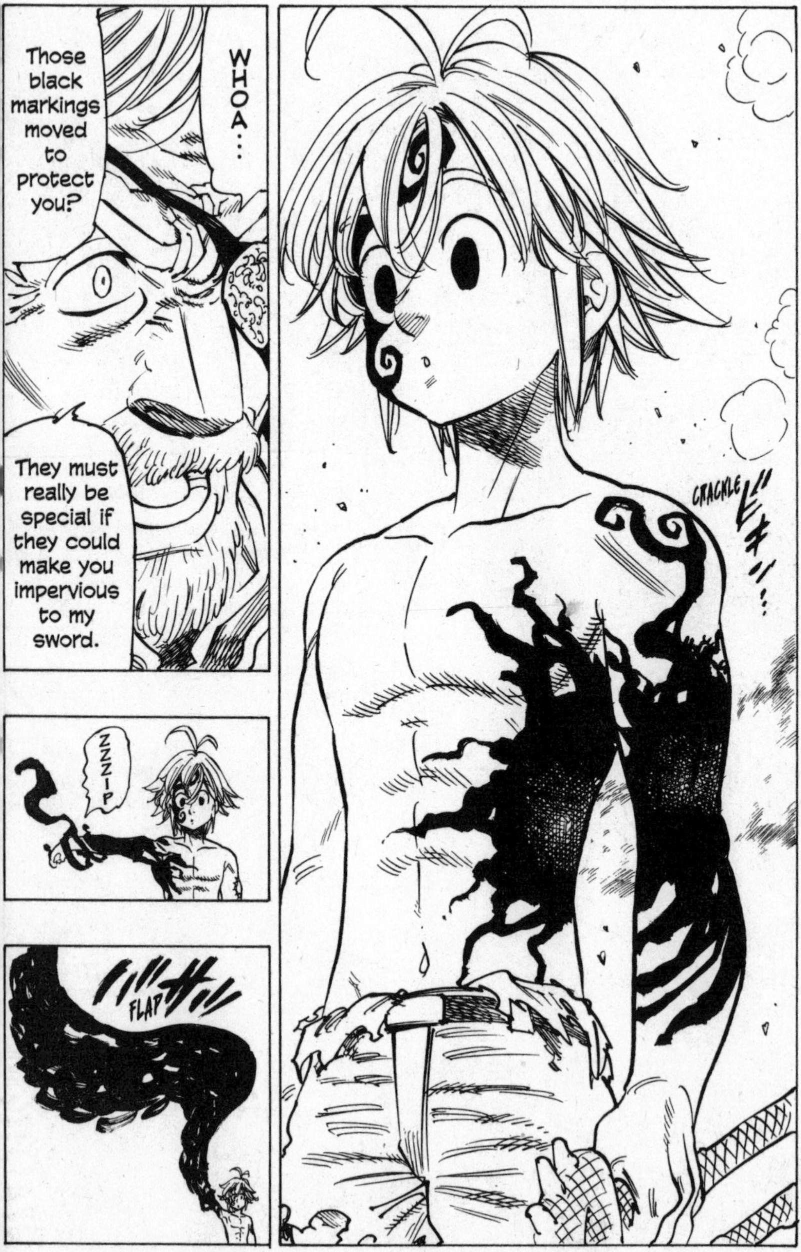
CRACKLE
WHOA...
Those black markings moved to protect you?
They must really be special if they could make you impervious to my sword.
ZZZIP
FLAP

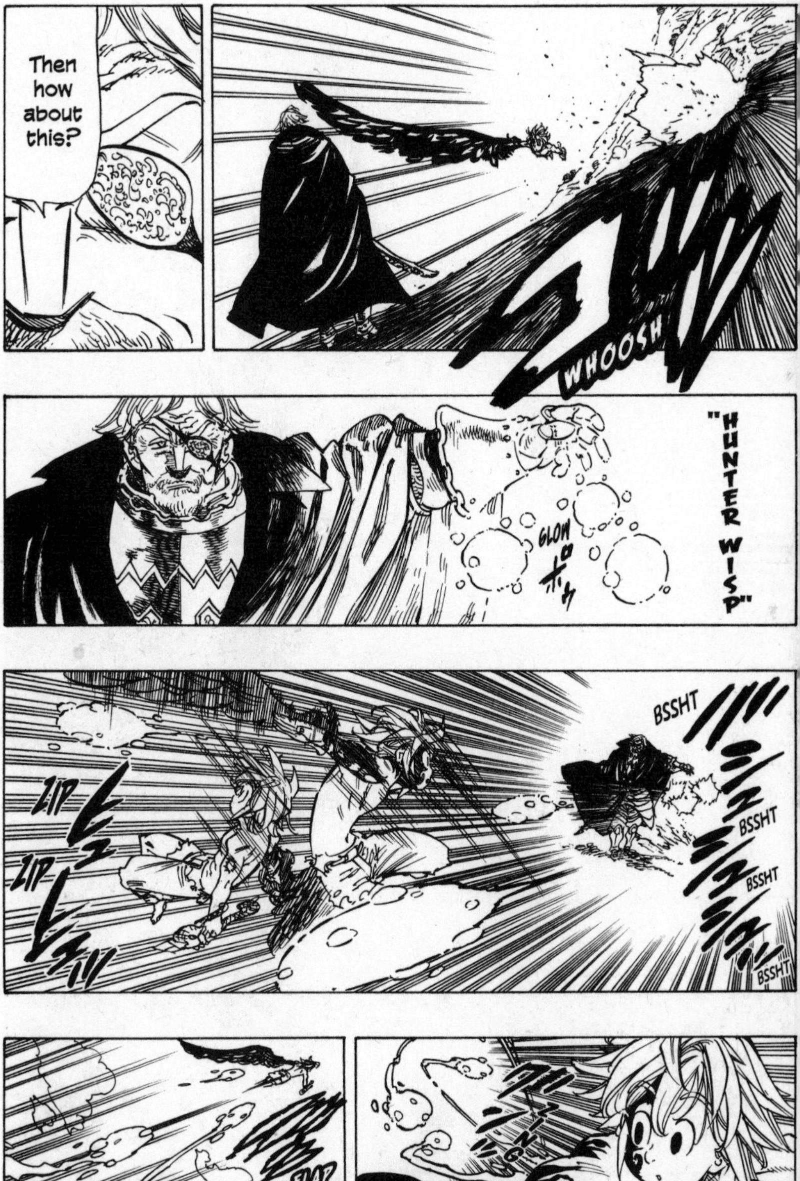
WHOOSH
Then how about this?
"HUNTER WISP"
GLOW
BSSHT
BSSHT
BSSHT
BSSHT
ZIP
ZIP
ZING
FLAP

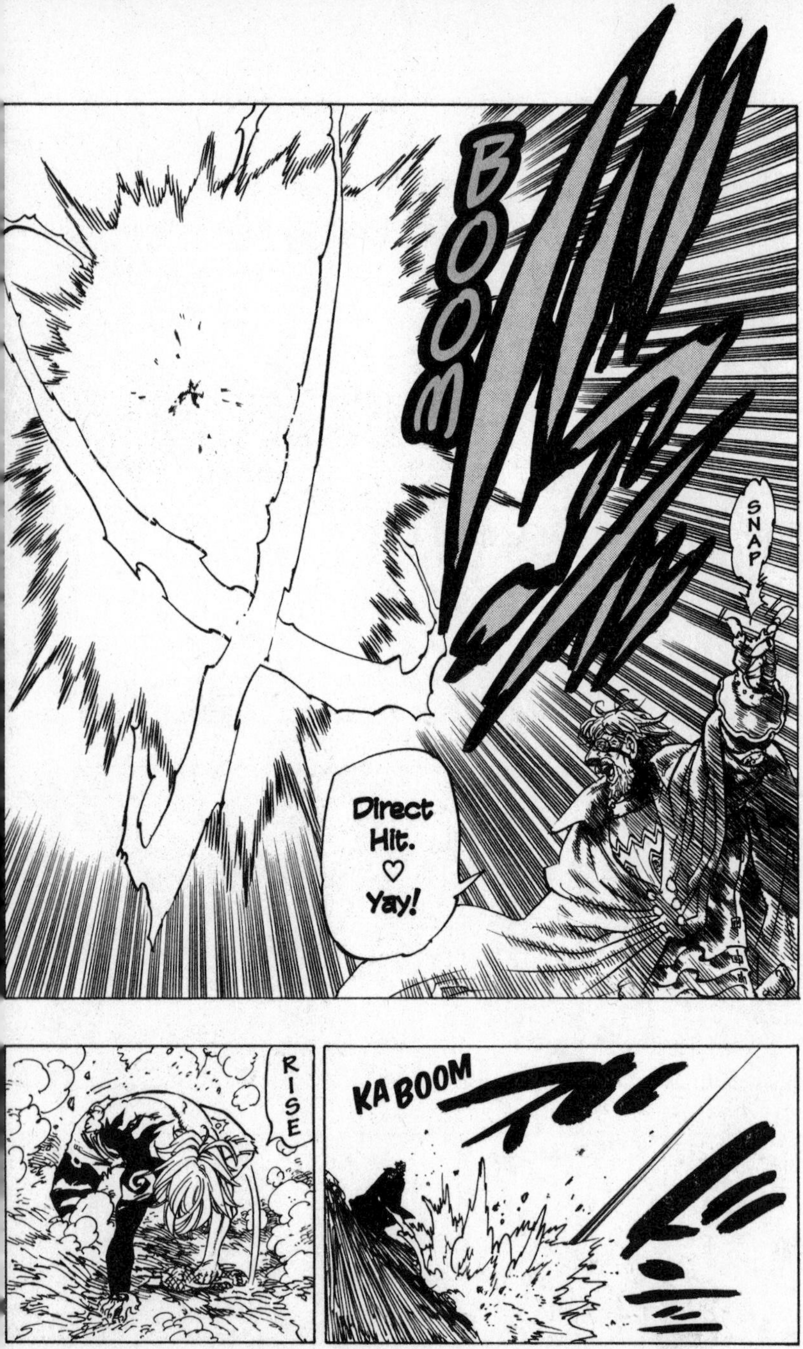
BOOM
SNAP
Direct Hit. ♡ Yay!
KABOOM
RISE

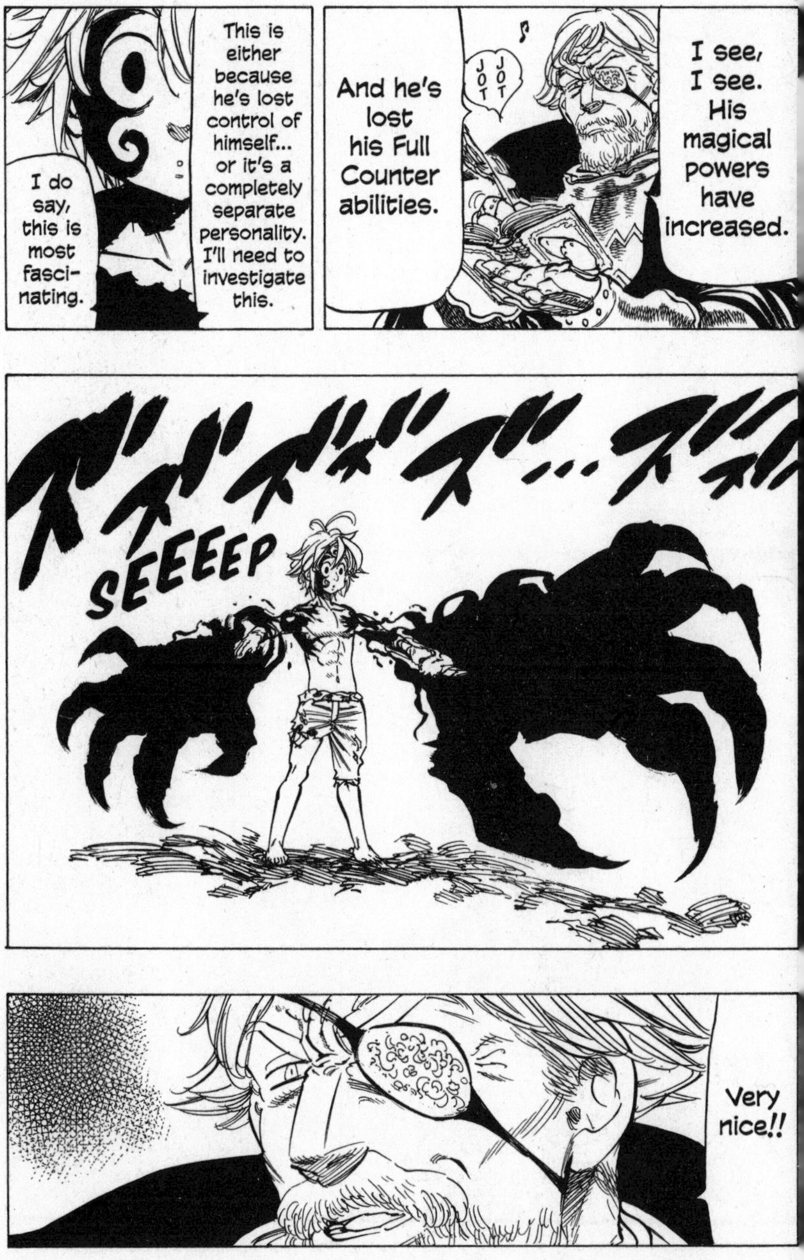
I see, I see. His magical powers have increased.
JOT JOT
And he's lost his Full Counter abilities.
This is either because he's lost control of himself... or it's a completely separate personality. I'll need to investigate this.
I do say, this is most fasci-nating.
SEEEEP
Very nice!!

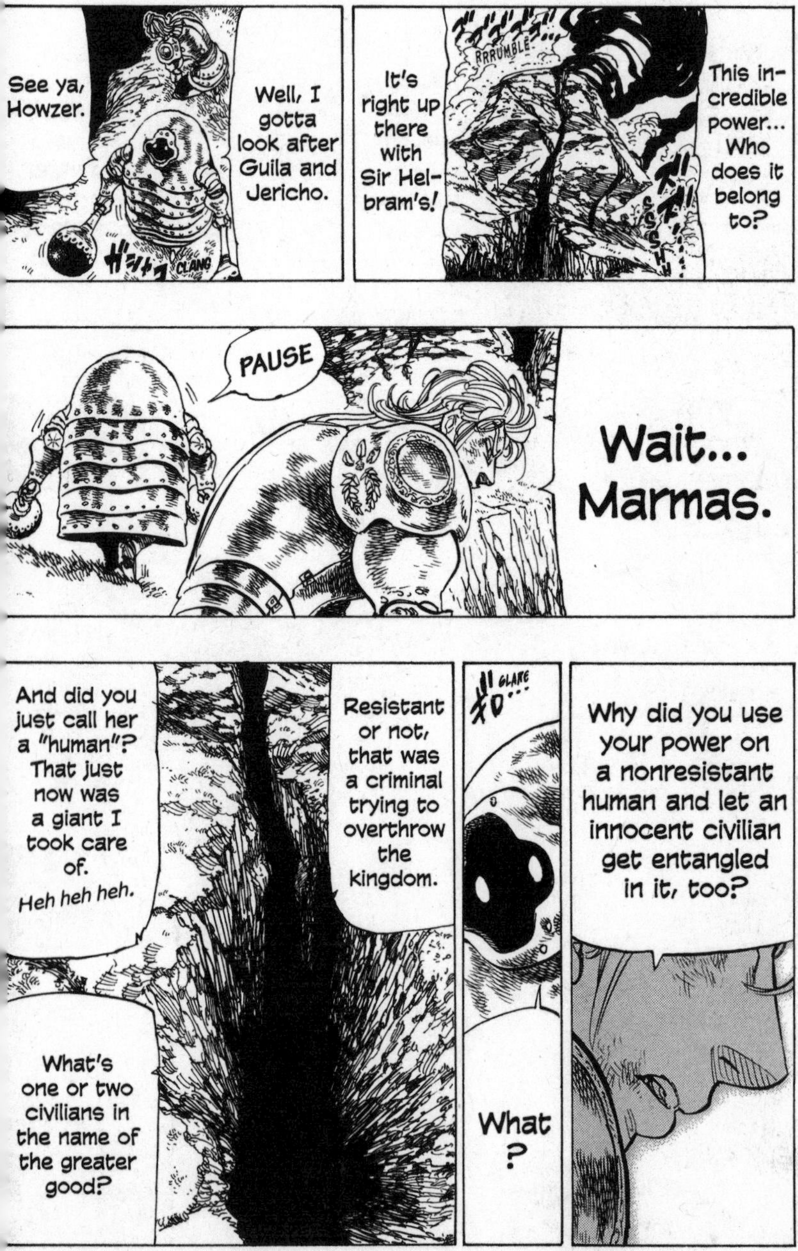
RRRUMBLE
This in-credible power... Who does it belong to?
It's right up there with Sir Hel-bram's!
Well, I gotta look after Guila and Jericho.
See ya, Howzer.
CLANG
Wait... Marmas.
PAUSE
Why did you use your power on a nonresistant human and let an innocent civilian get entangled in it, too?
GLARE
What?
Resistant or not, that was a criminal trying to overthrow the kingdom.
And did you just call her a "human"? That just now was a giant I took care of.
Heh heh heh.
What's one or two civilians in the name of the greater good?

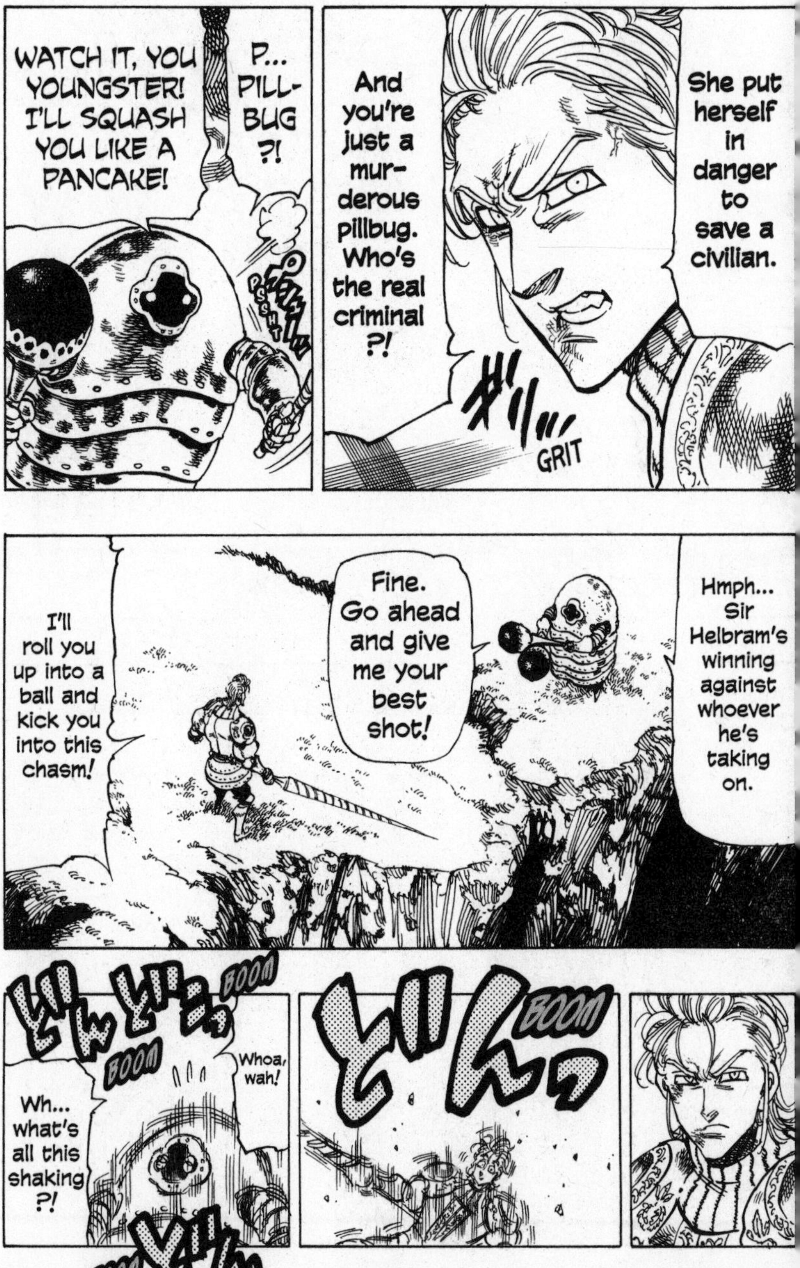
She put herself in danger to save a civilian.
And you're just a murderous pillbug. Who's the real criminal?!
GRIT
P... PILLBUG?!
WATCH IT, YOU YOUNGSTER! I'LL SQUASH YOU LIKE A PANCAKE!
PSSHT
Hmph... Sir Helbram's winning against whoever he's taking on.
Fine. Go ahead and give me your best shot!
I'll roll you up into a ball and kick you into this chasm!
BOOM
BOOM
BOOM
Whoa, wah!
Wh... what's all this shaking?!
BOOM

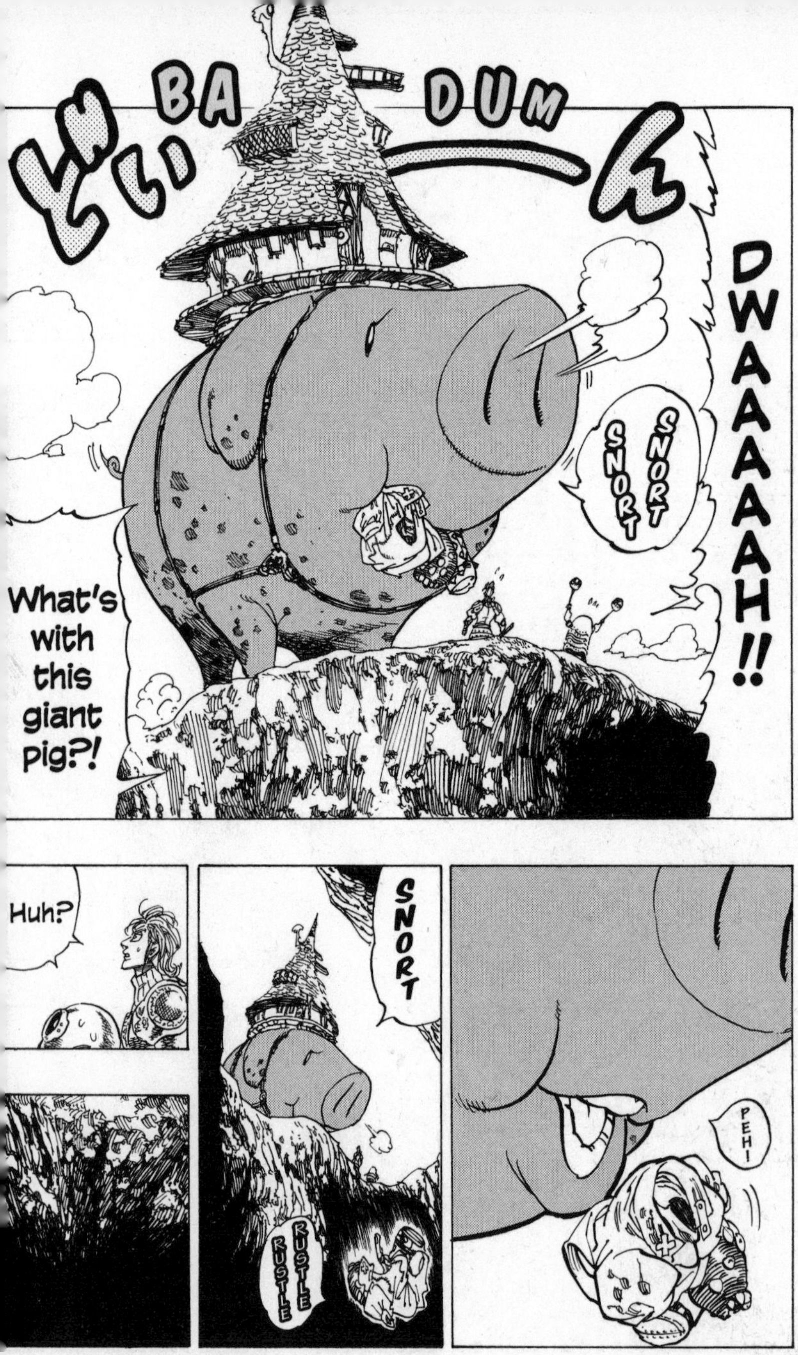

BA DUM
DWAAAAAH!!
SNORT SNORT
What's with this giant pig?!
PEH!
SNORT
RUSTLE RUSTLE
Huh?

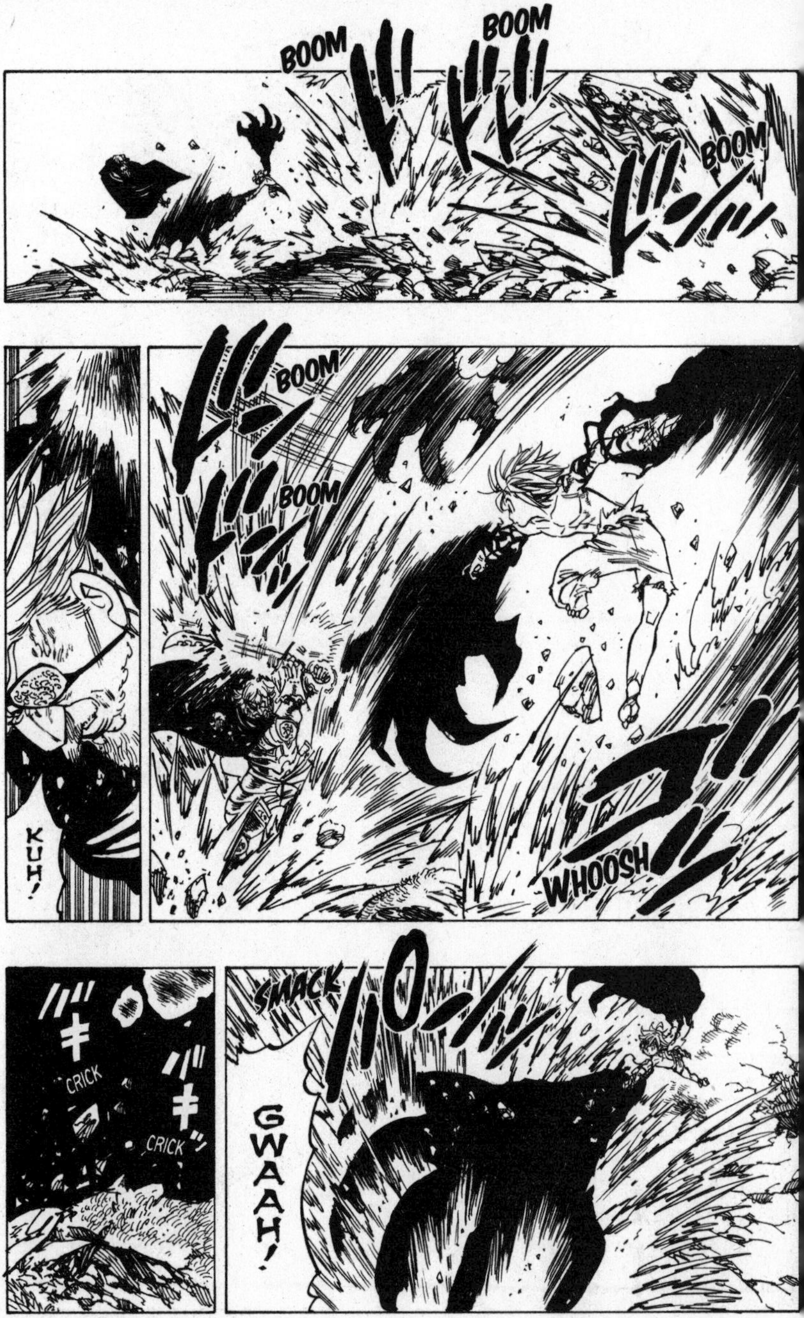
BOOM
BOOM
BOOM
BOOM
BOOM
WHOOSH
KUH!
SMACK
GWAAH!
バキ
CRICK
バキッ
CRICK

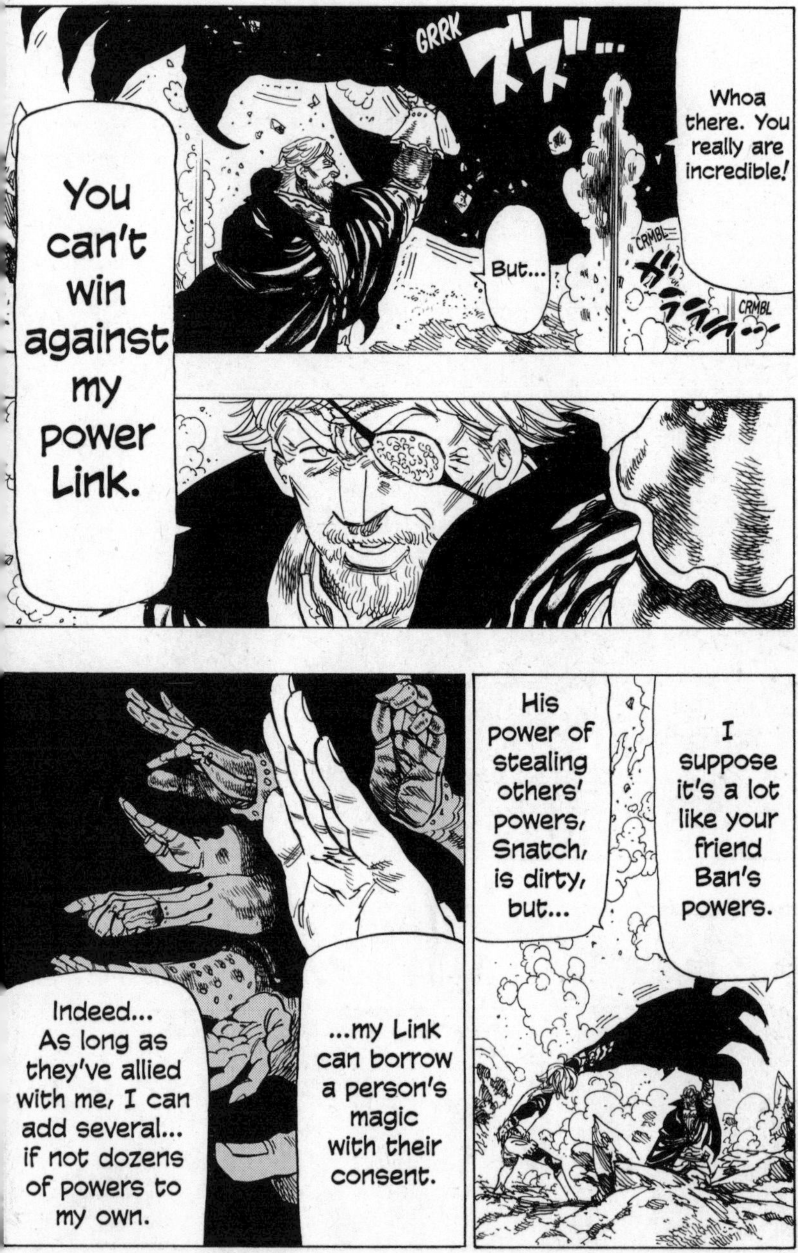
Whoa there. You really are incredible!
ズズ…
GRRK
But...
CRMBL
CRMBL
You can't win against my power Link.
I suppose it's a lot like your friend Ban's powers.
His power of stealing others' powers, Snatch, is dirty, but...
...my Link can borrow a person's magic with their consent.
Indeed... As long as they've allied with me, I can add several... if not dozens of powers to my own.

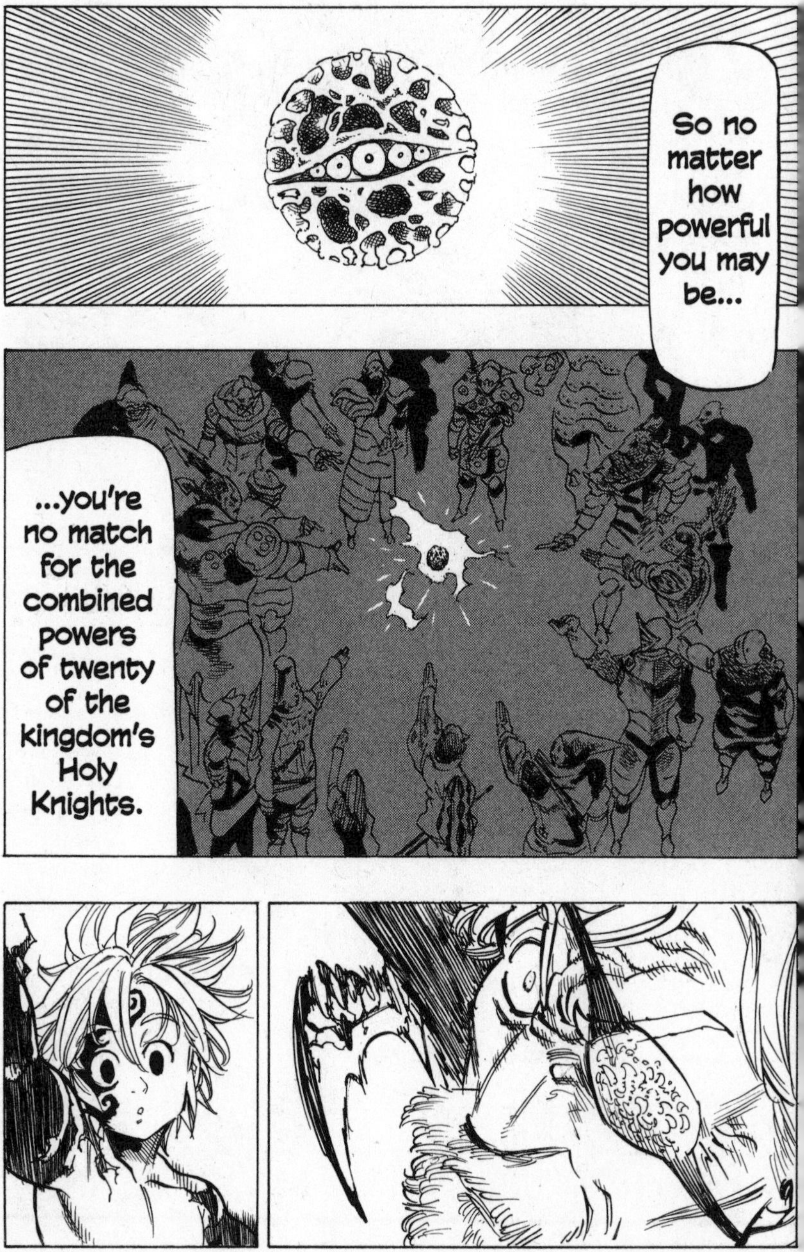
So no matter how powerful you may be...
...you're no match for the combined powers of twenty of the kingdom's Holy Knights.

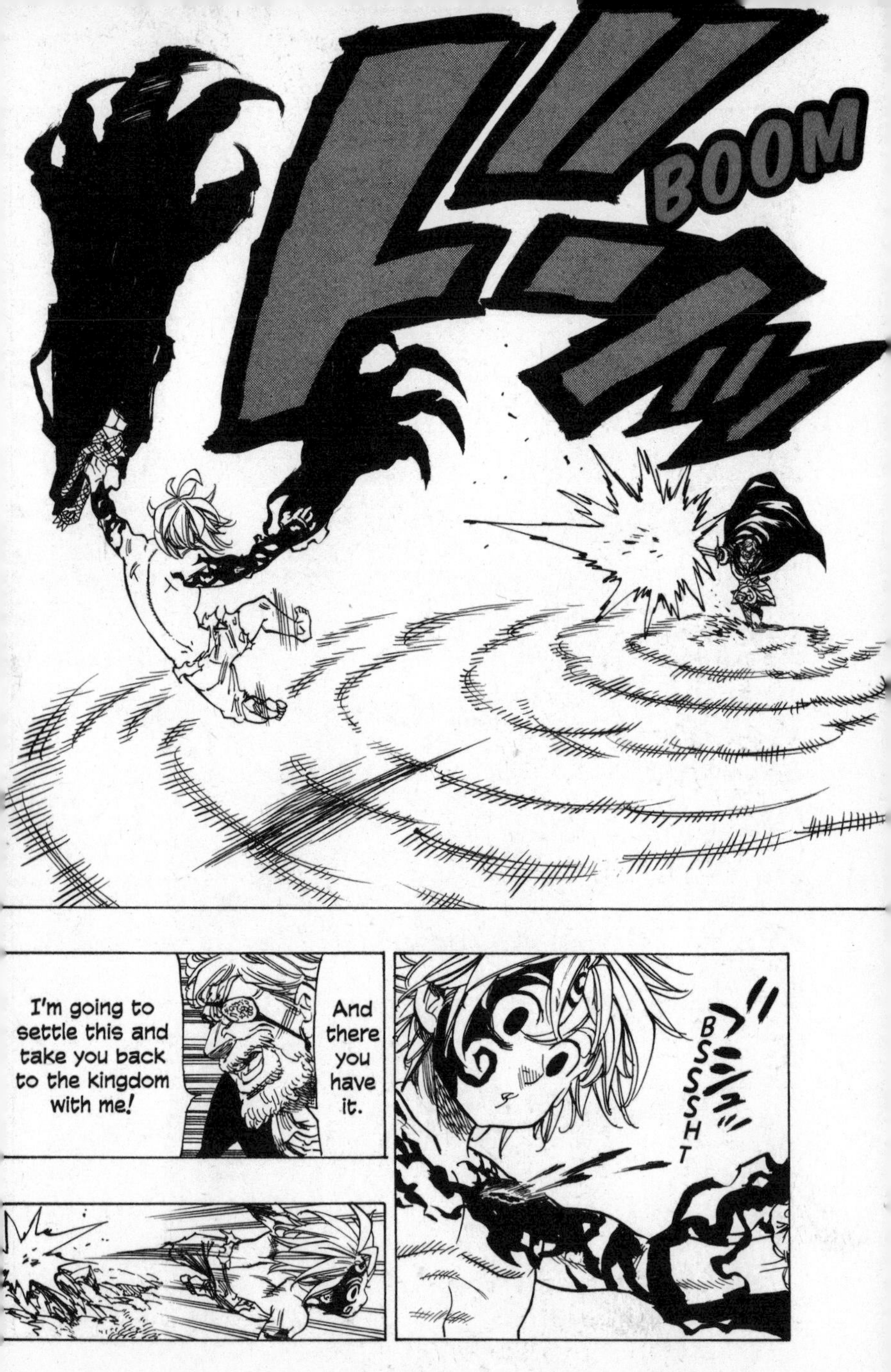
BOOM
BSSSHT
And there you have it.
I'm going to settle this and take you back to the kingdom with me!

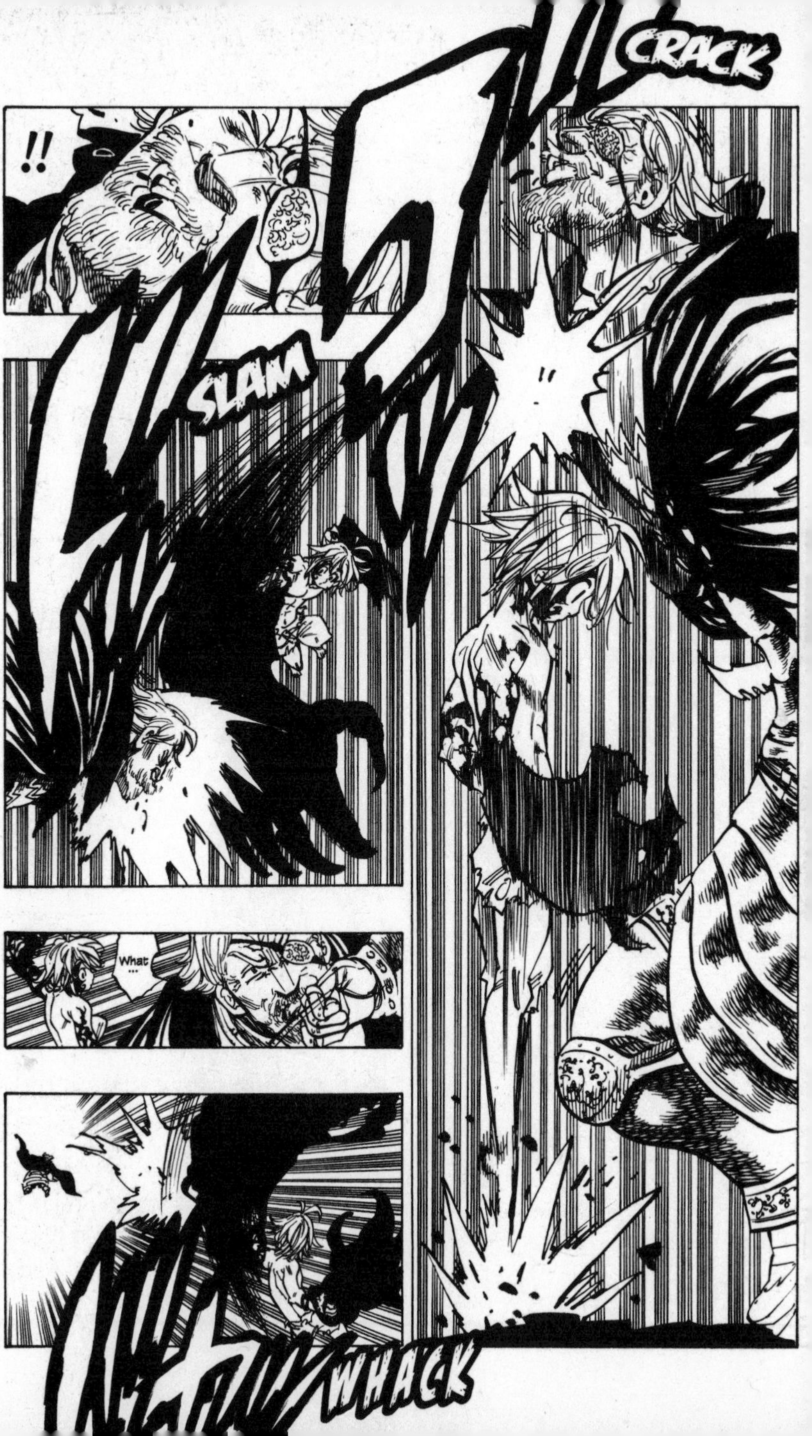
CRACK
!!
!!
SLAM
What ...
WHACK

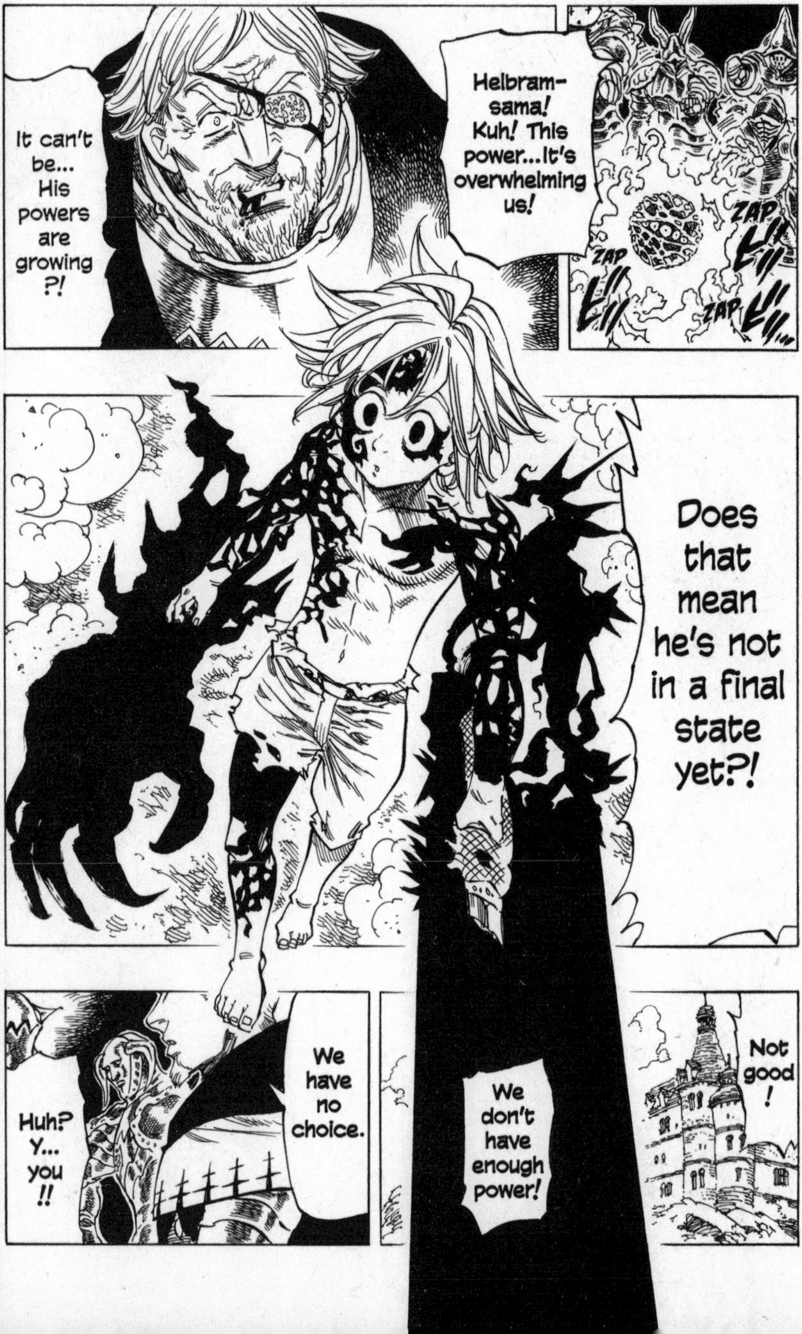
Helbram-sama! Kuh! This power...It's overwhelming us!
ZAP
ZAP
ZAP
It can't be... His powers are growing?!
Does that mean he's not in a final state yet?!
Not good!
We don't have enough power!
We have no choice.
Huh? Y... you!!

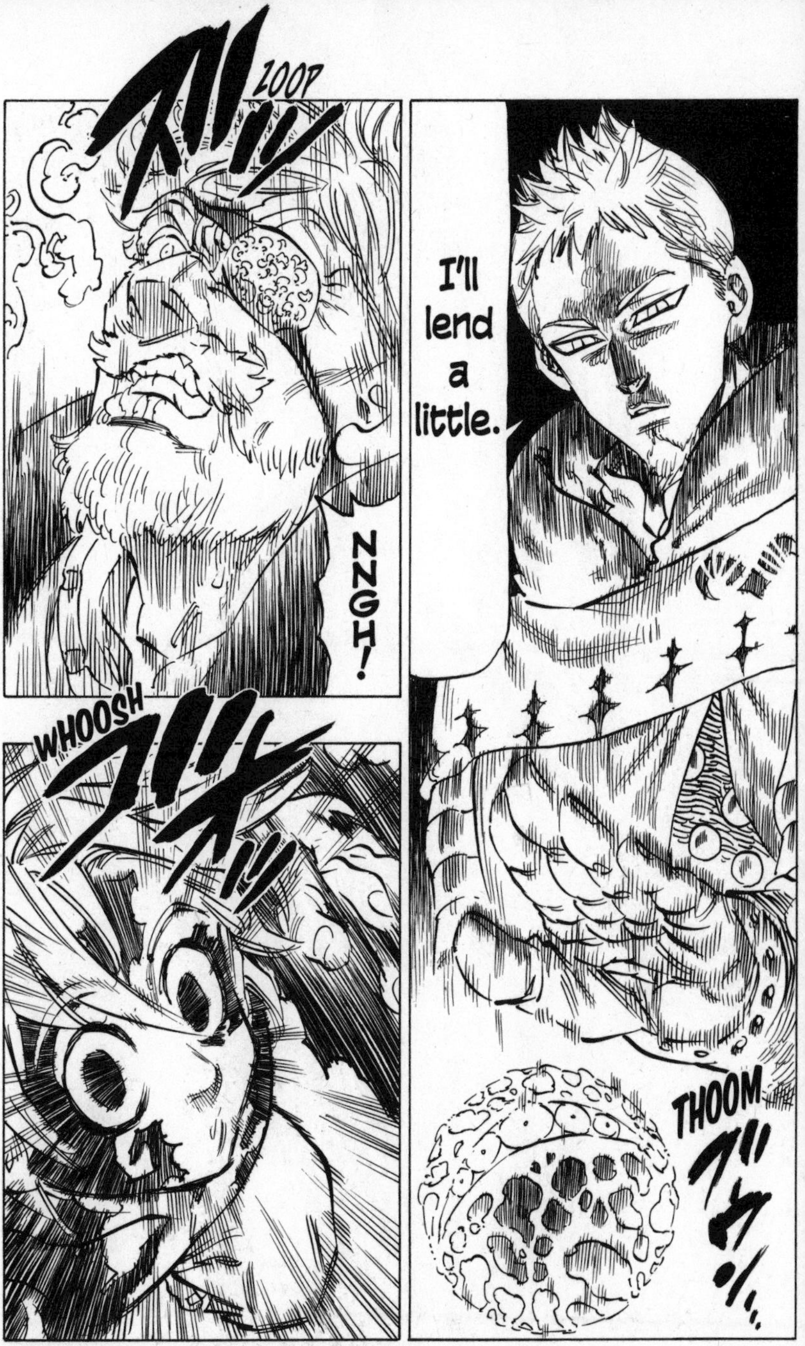
I'll lend a little.
THOOM
ZOOP
NNGH!
WHOOSH

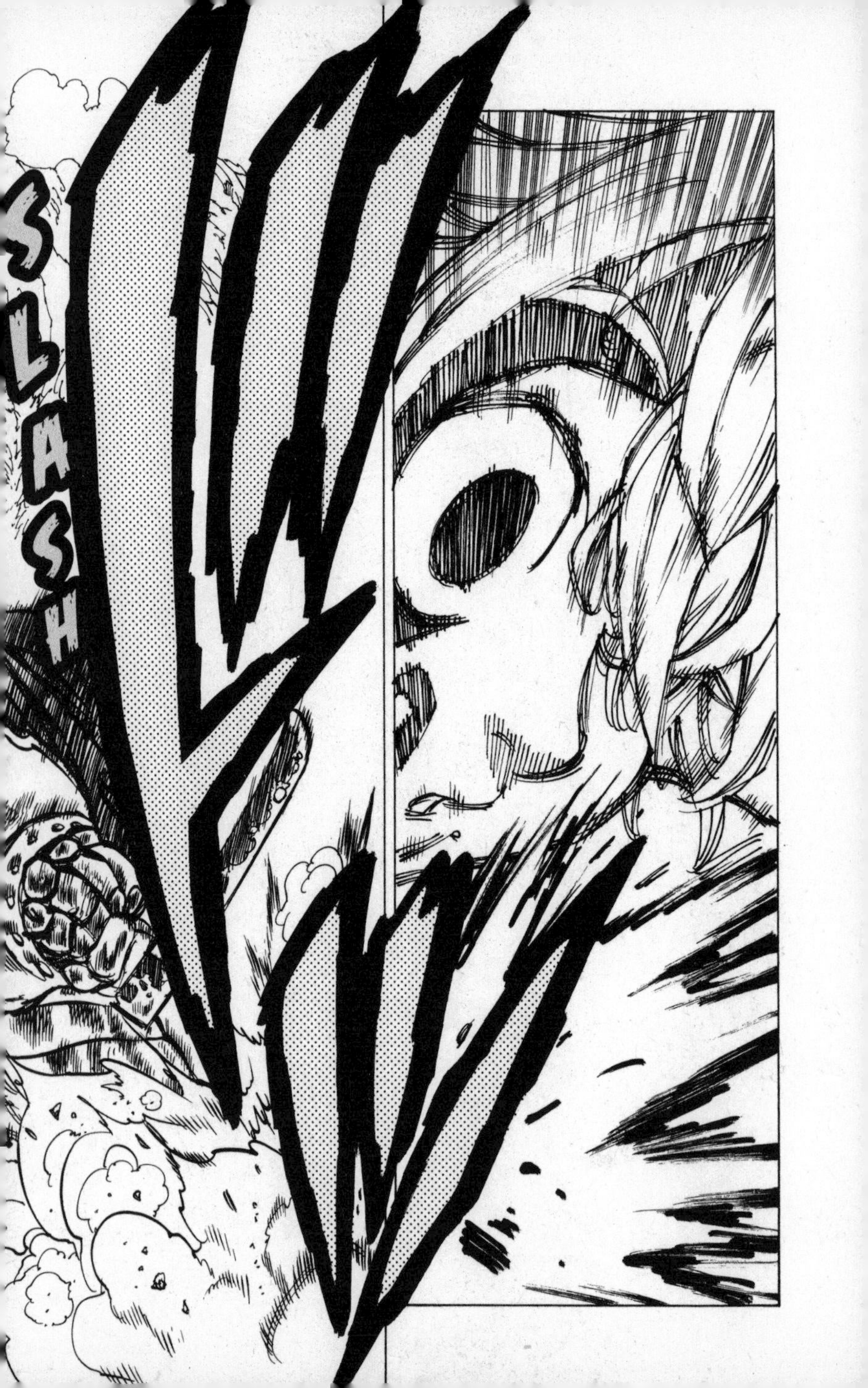
SLASH

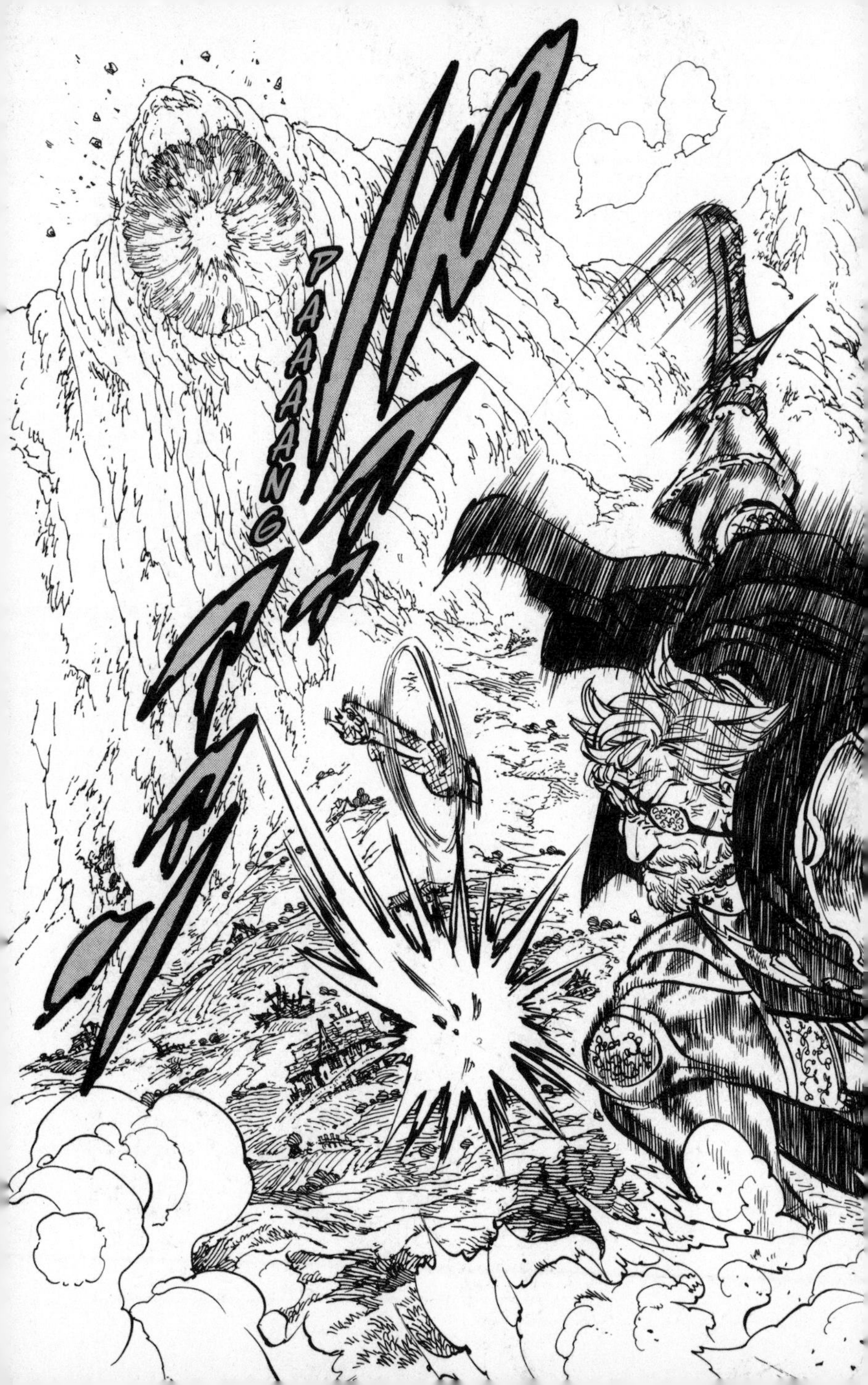
PAAAAANG

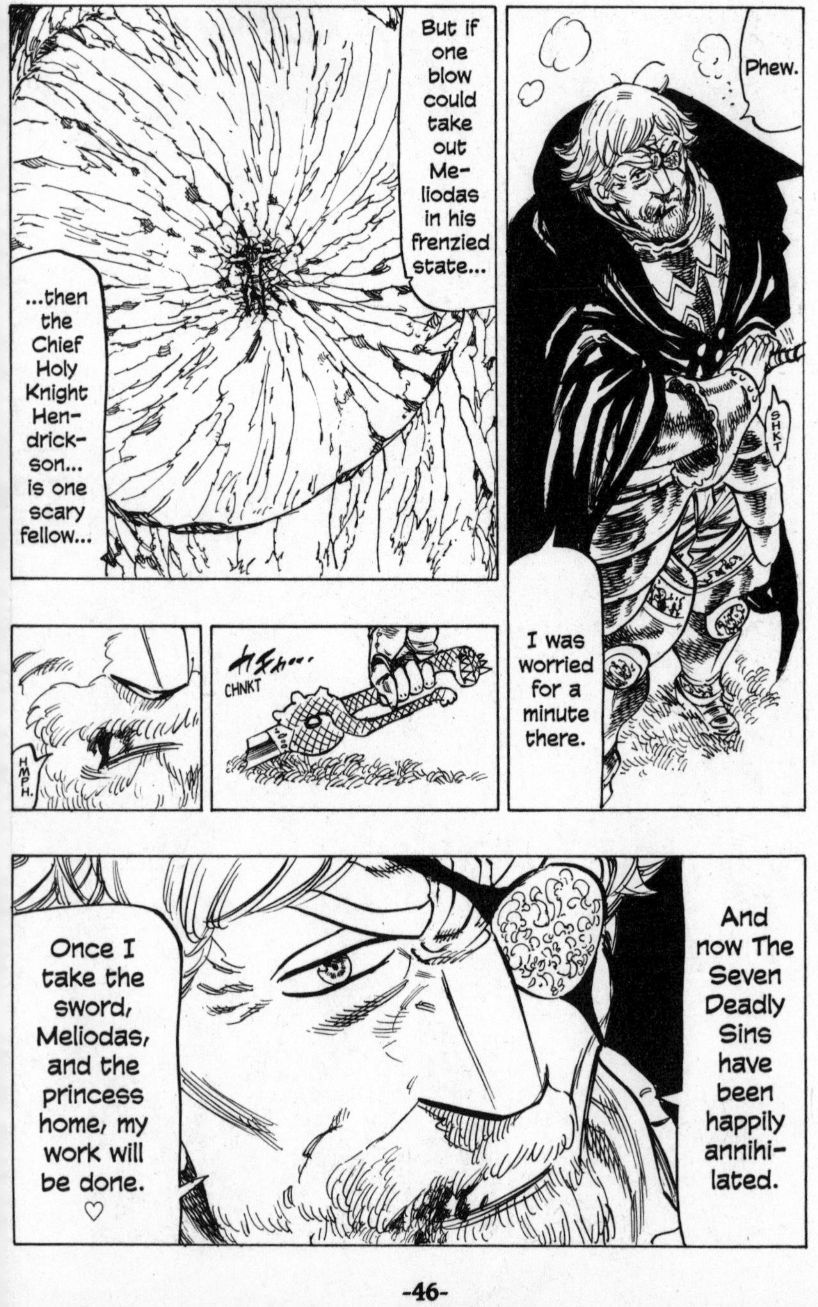
Phew.
SHKT
I was worried for a minute there.
But if one blow could take out Meliodas in his frenzied state...
...then the Chief Holy Knight Hendrickson... is one scary fellow...
CHNKT
HMPH.
And now The Seven Deadly Sins have been happily annihilated.
Once I take the sword, Meliodas, and the princess home, my work will be done. ♡

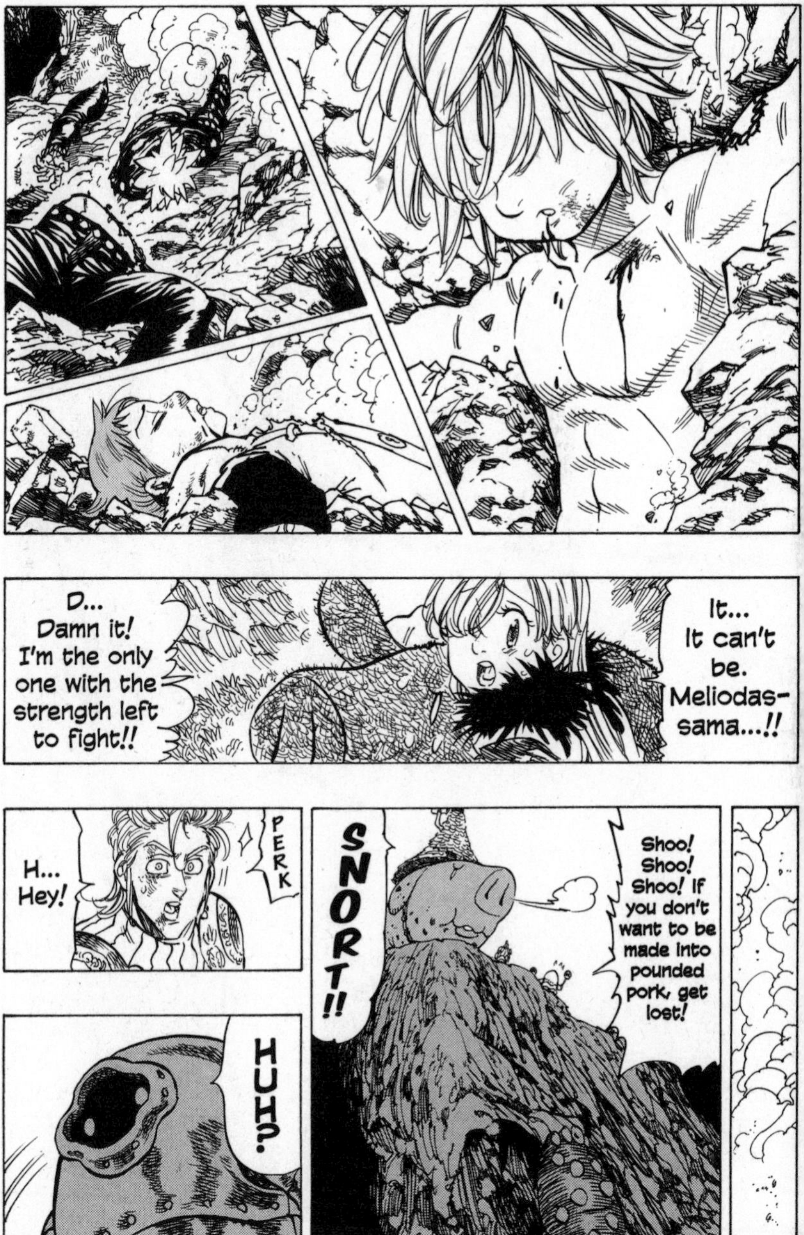
It... It can't be. Meliodas-sama...!!
D... Damn it! I'm the only one with the strength left to fight!!
Shoo! Shoo! Shoo! If you don't want to be made into pounded pork, get lost!
SNORT!!
PERK
H... Hey!
HUH?

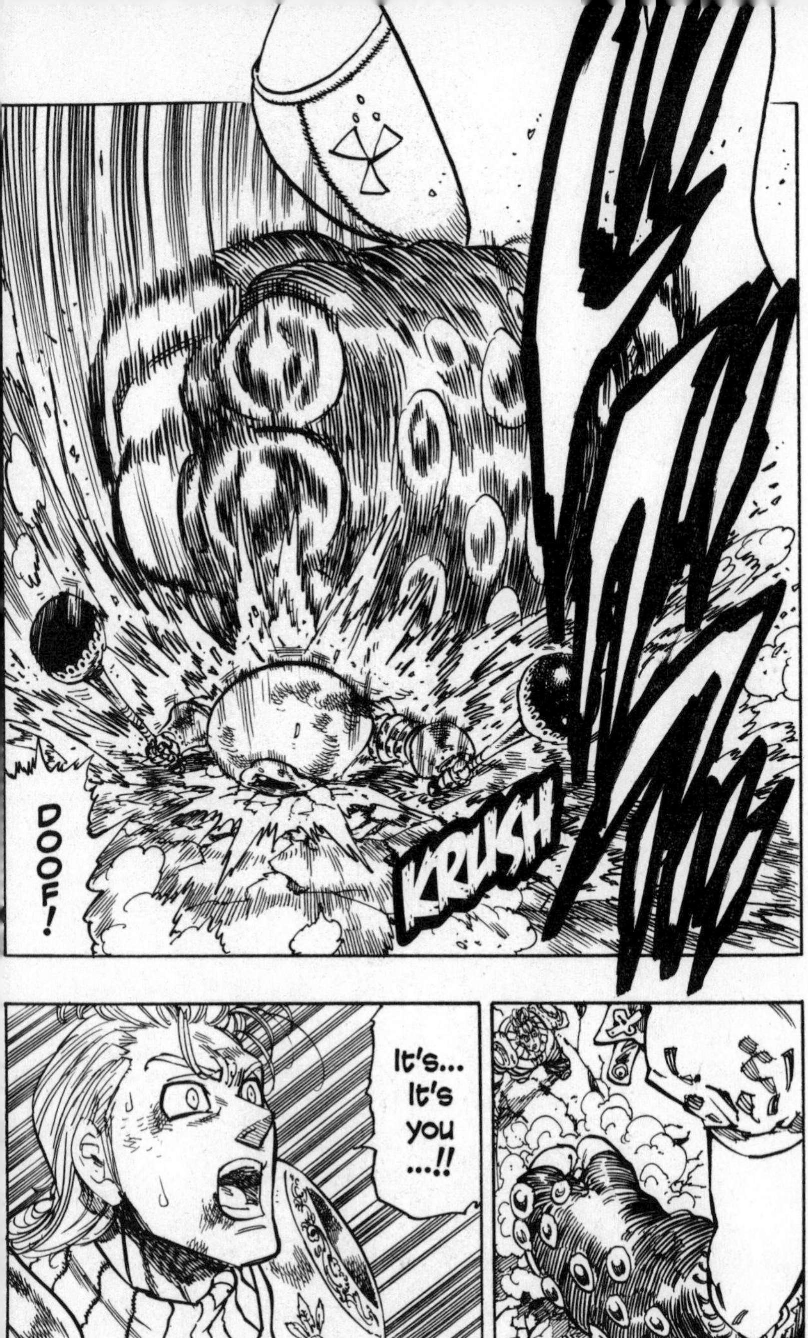
KRUSH
DOOF!
It's... It's you ...!!

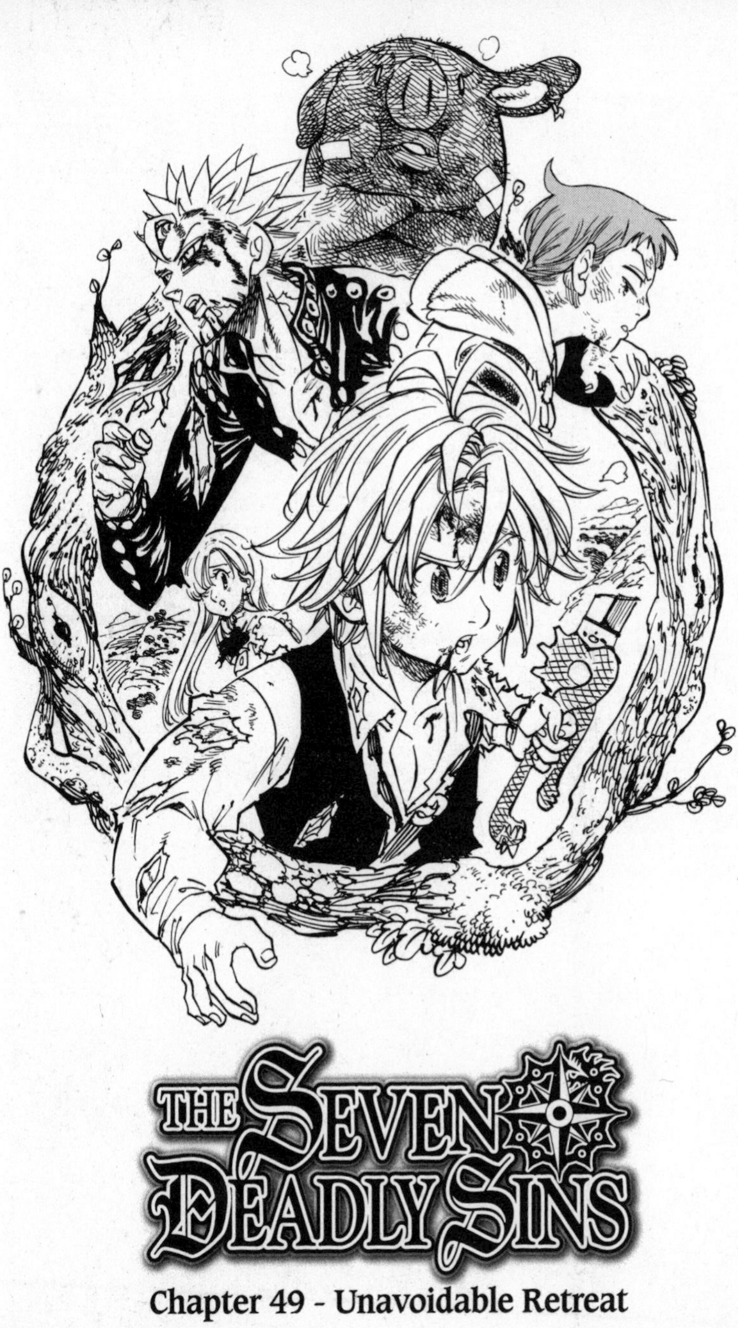

THE SEVEN DEADLY SINS

Chapter 49 - Unavoidable Retreat

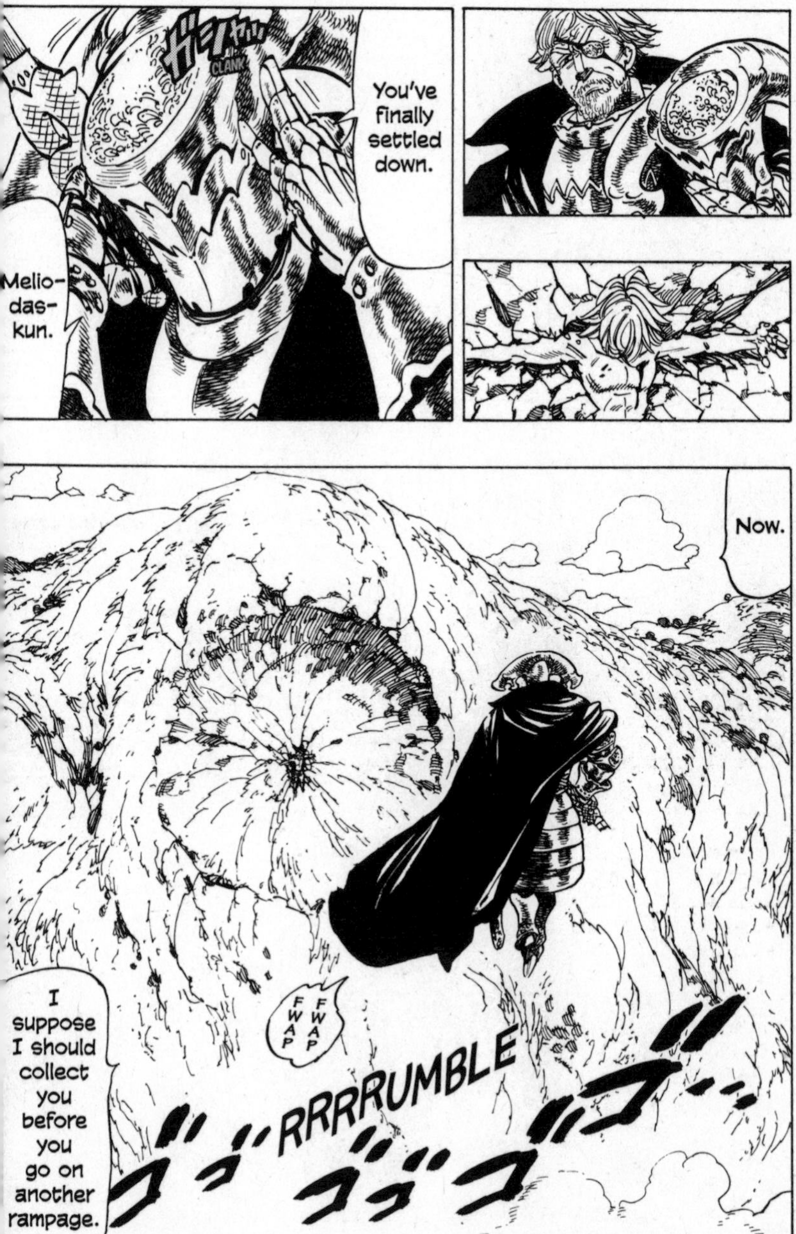
CLANK
You've finally settled down.
Melio-das-kun.
Now.
FWAP FWAP
RRRRUMBLE
I suppose I should collect you before you go on another rampage.

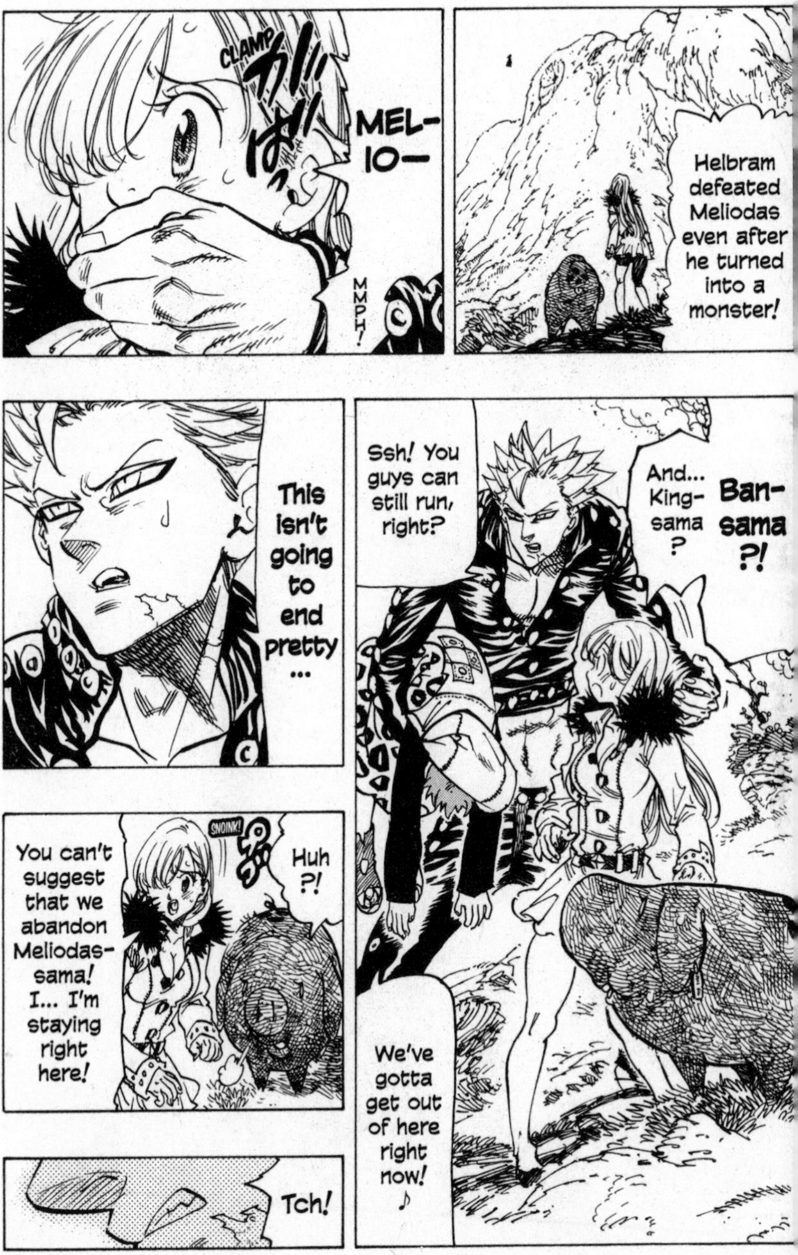
Helbram defeated Meliodas even after he turned into a monster!
CLAMP
MEL-IO—
MMPH!
Ban-sama?!
And... King-sama?
Ssh! You guys can still run, right?
We've gotta get out of here right now! ♪
This isn't going to end pretty...
Huh?!
SNOINK!
You can't suggest that we abandon Meliodas-sama! I... I'm staying right here!
Tch!

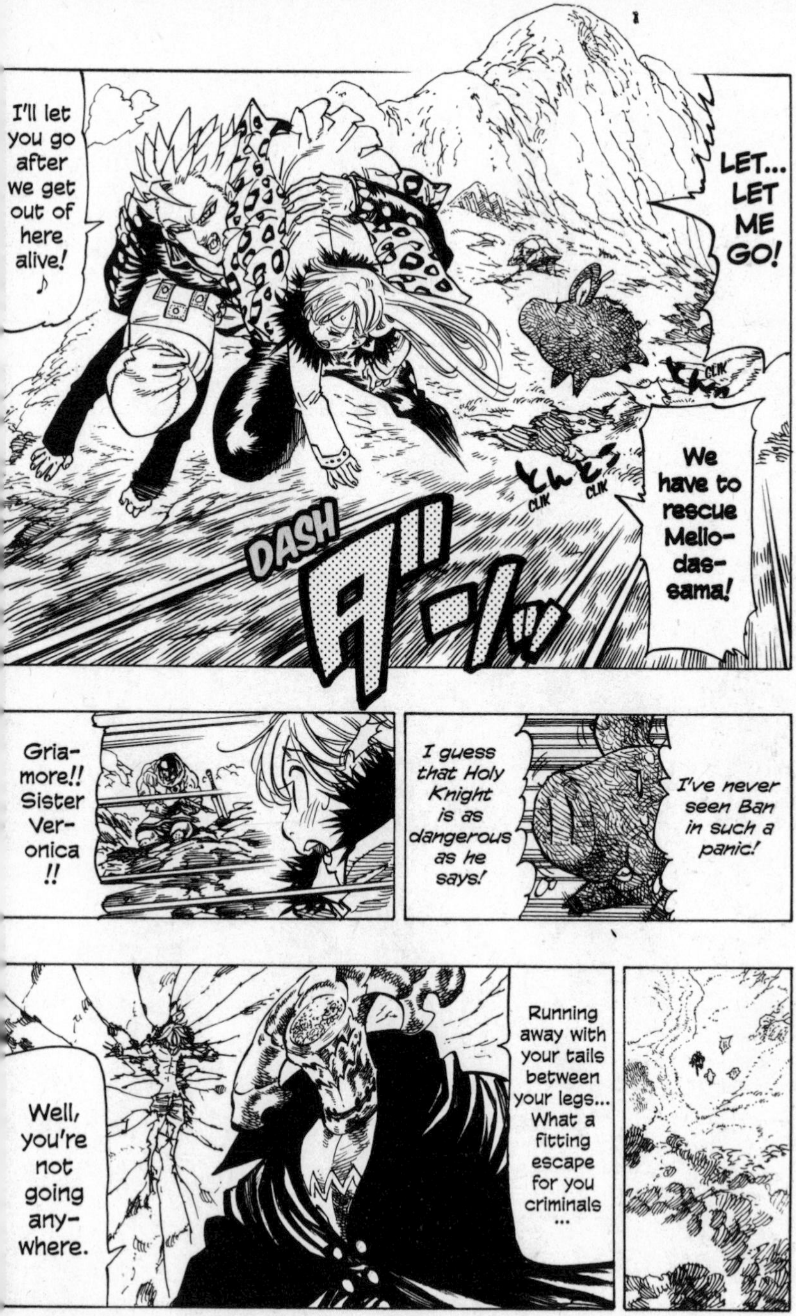
LET... LET ME GO!
I'll let you go after we get out of here alive! ♪
CLIK
CLIK CLIK
We have to rescue Mellodas-sama!
DASH
I've never seen Ban in such a panic!
I guess that Holy Knight is as dangerous as he says!
Griamore!! Sister Veronica !!
Running away with your tails between your legs... What a fitting escape for you criminals ...
Well, you're not going anywhere.

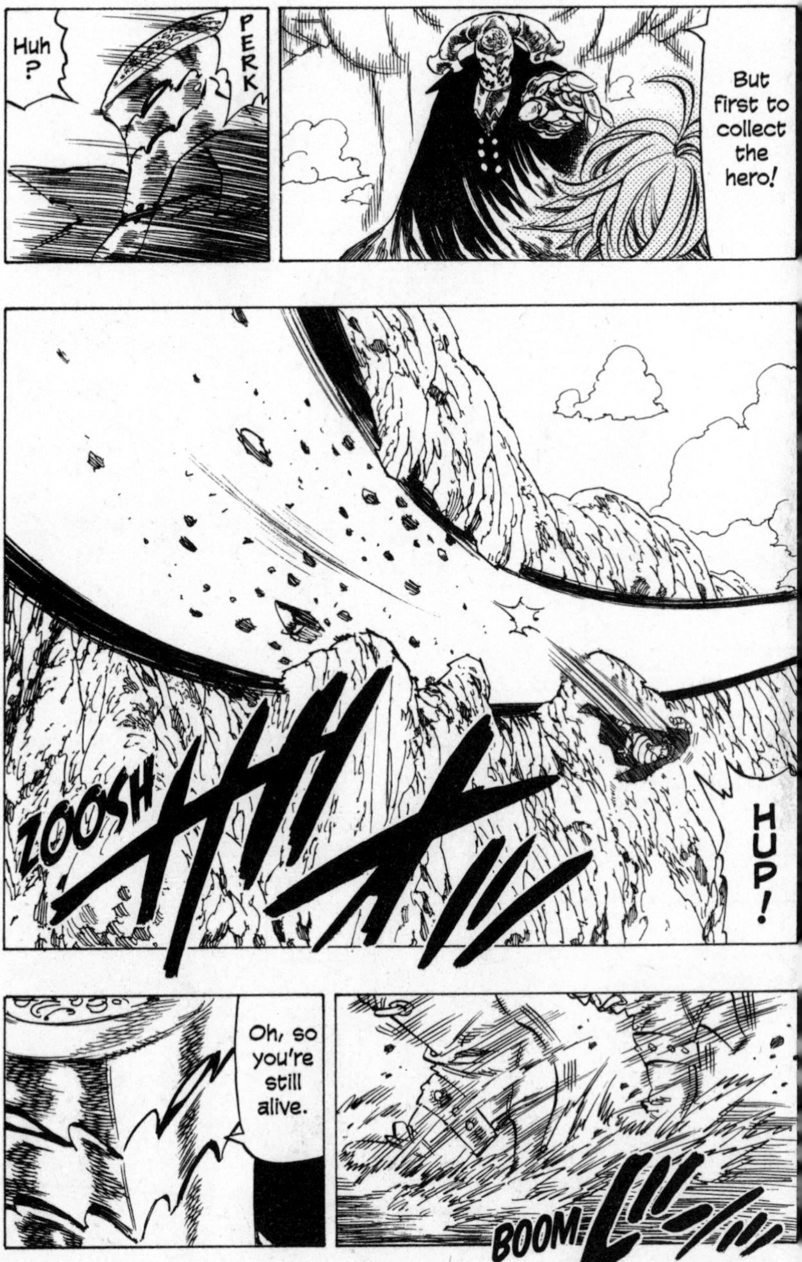
But first to collect the hero!
PERK
Huh?
HUP!
ZOOSH
BOOM
Oh, so you're still alive.

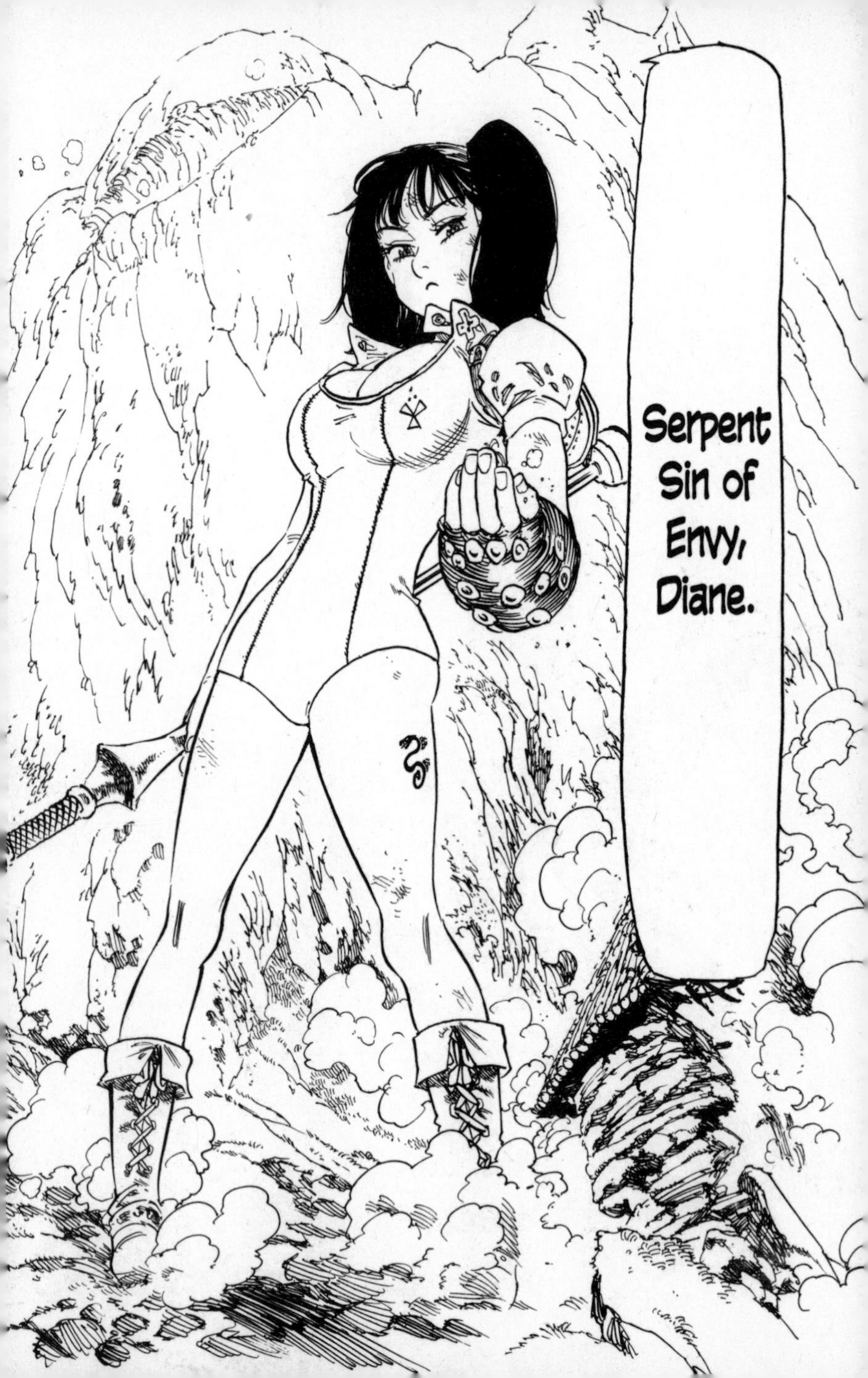
Serpent Sin of Envy, Diane.

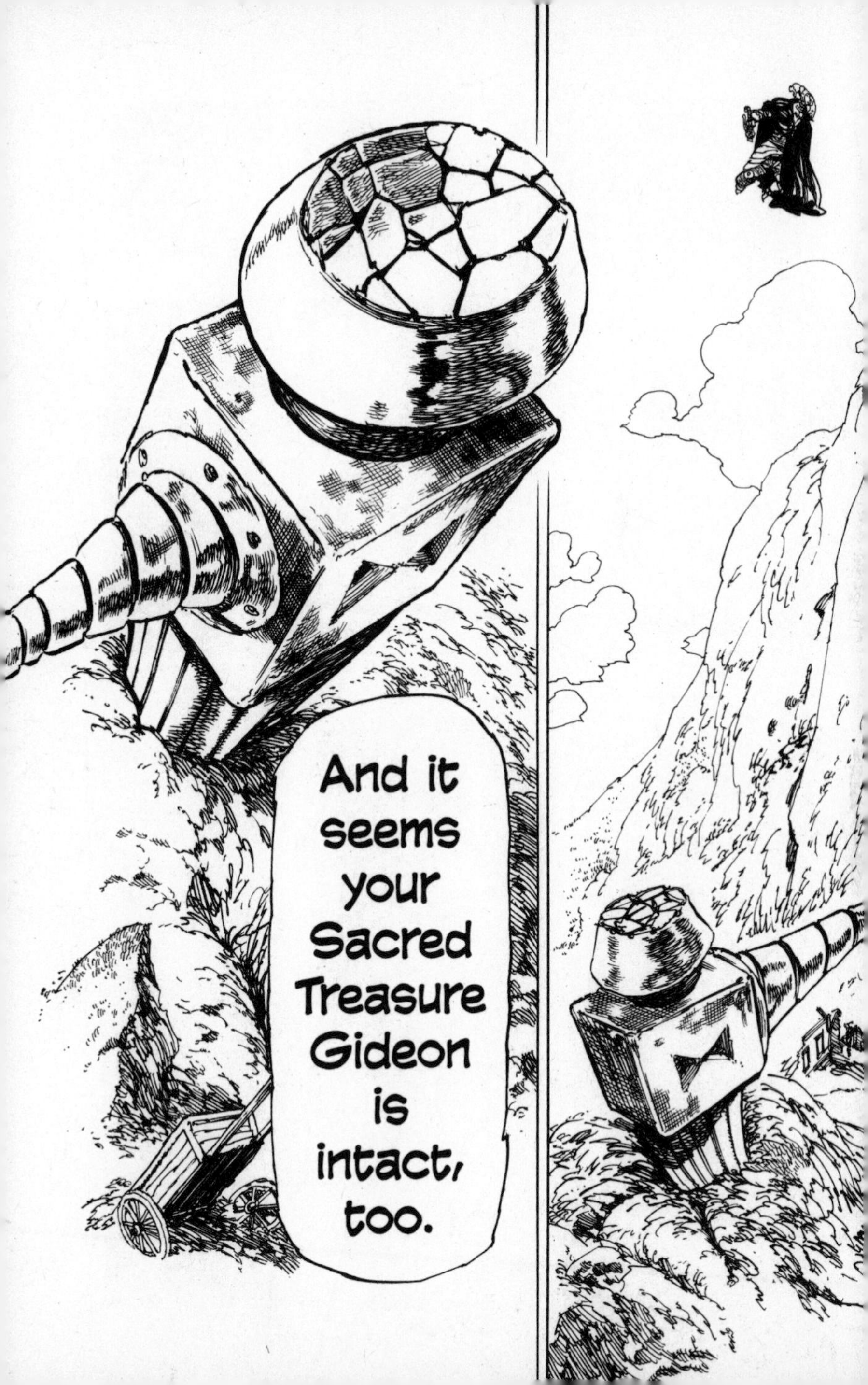
And it seems your Sacred Treasure Gideon is intact, too.

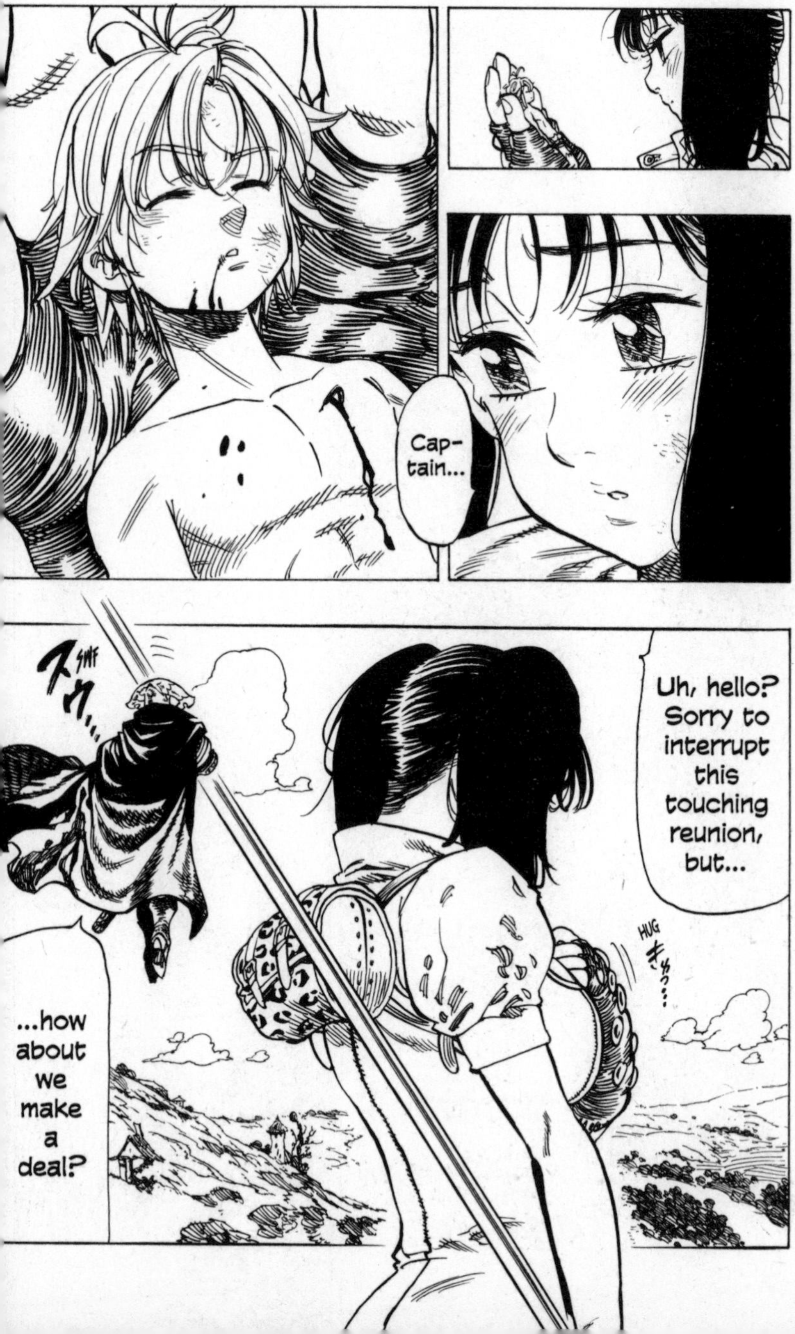
Cap-tain...
Uh, hello? Sorry to interrupt this touching reunion, but...
HUG
SWF
...how about we make a deal?

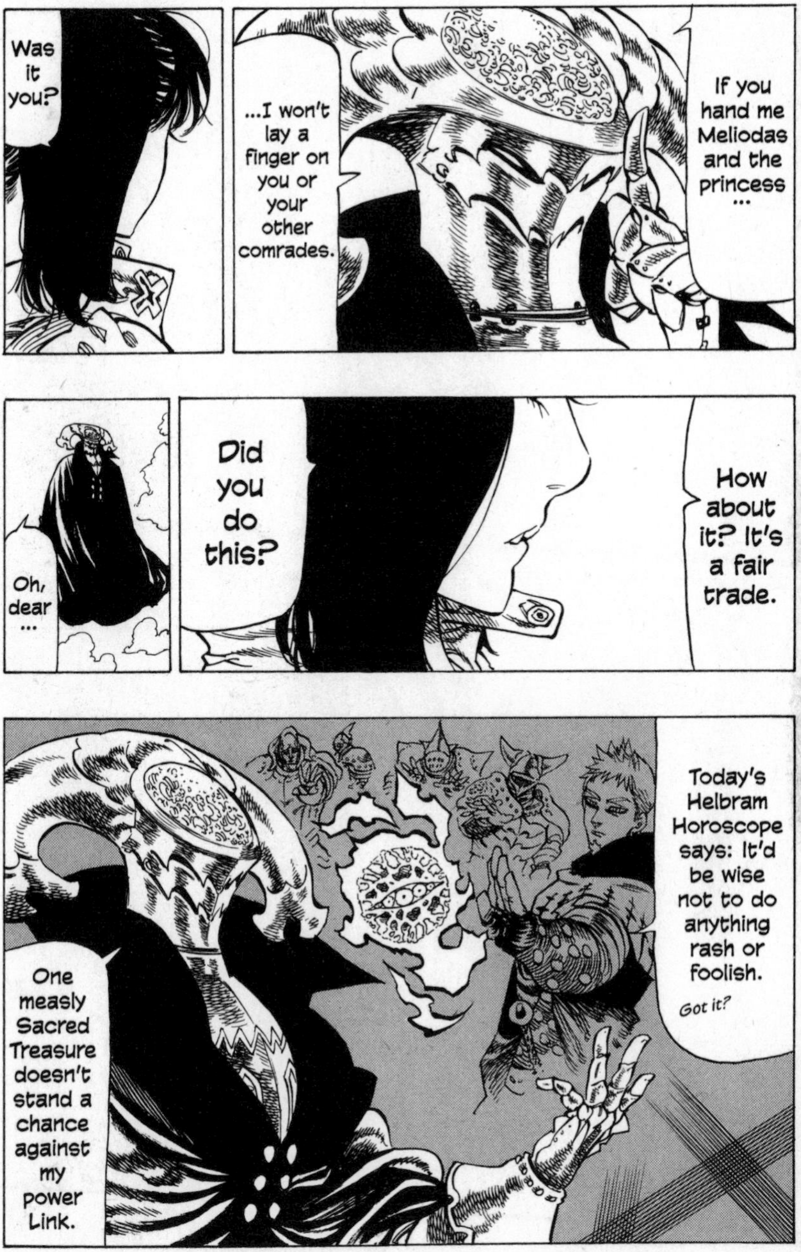
If you hand me Meliodas and the princess ...
...I won't lay a finger on you or your other comrades.
Was it you?
How about it? It's a fair trade.
Did you do this?
Oh, dear ...
Today's Helbram Horoscope says: It'd be wise not to do anything rash or foolish.
Got it?
One measly Sacred Treasure doesn't stand a chance against my power Link.

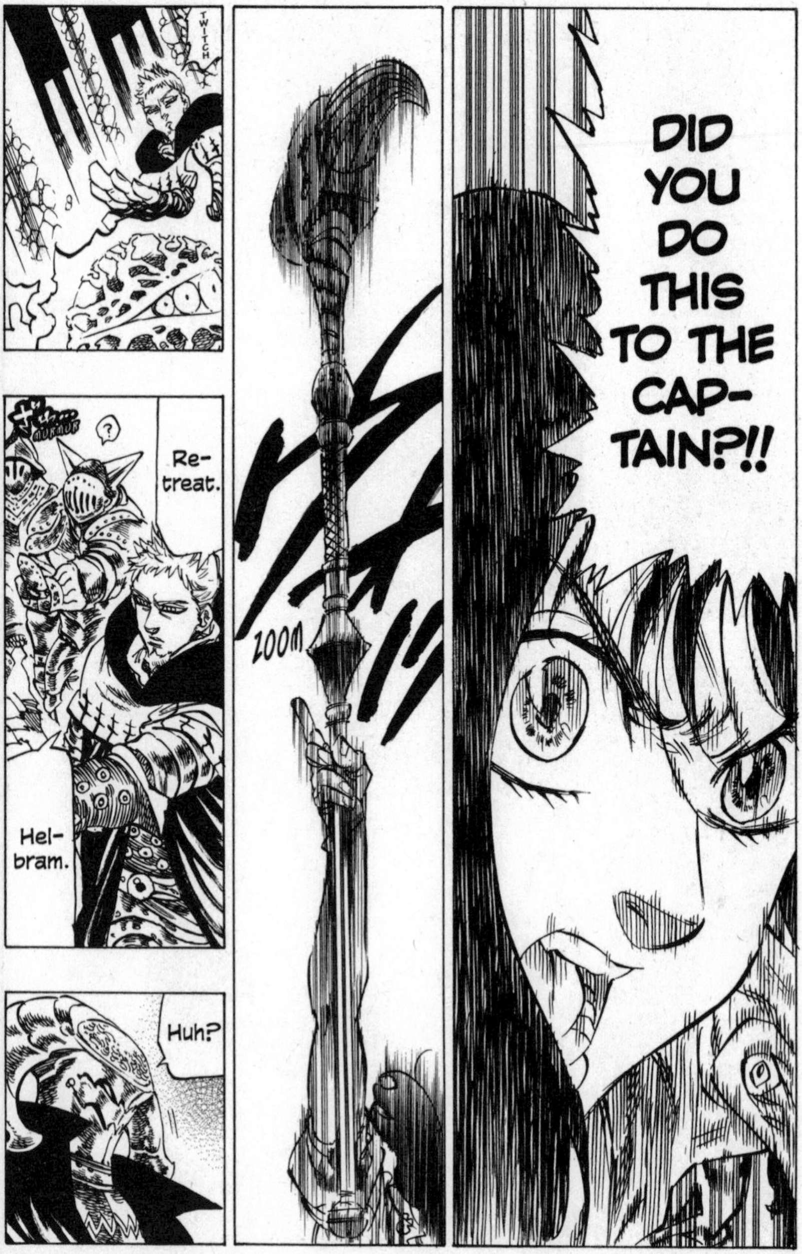
DID YOU DO THIS TO THE CAP-TAIN?!!
ZOOM
TWITCH
ザワ…
MURMUR
?
Re-treat.
Hel-bram.
Huh?

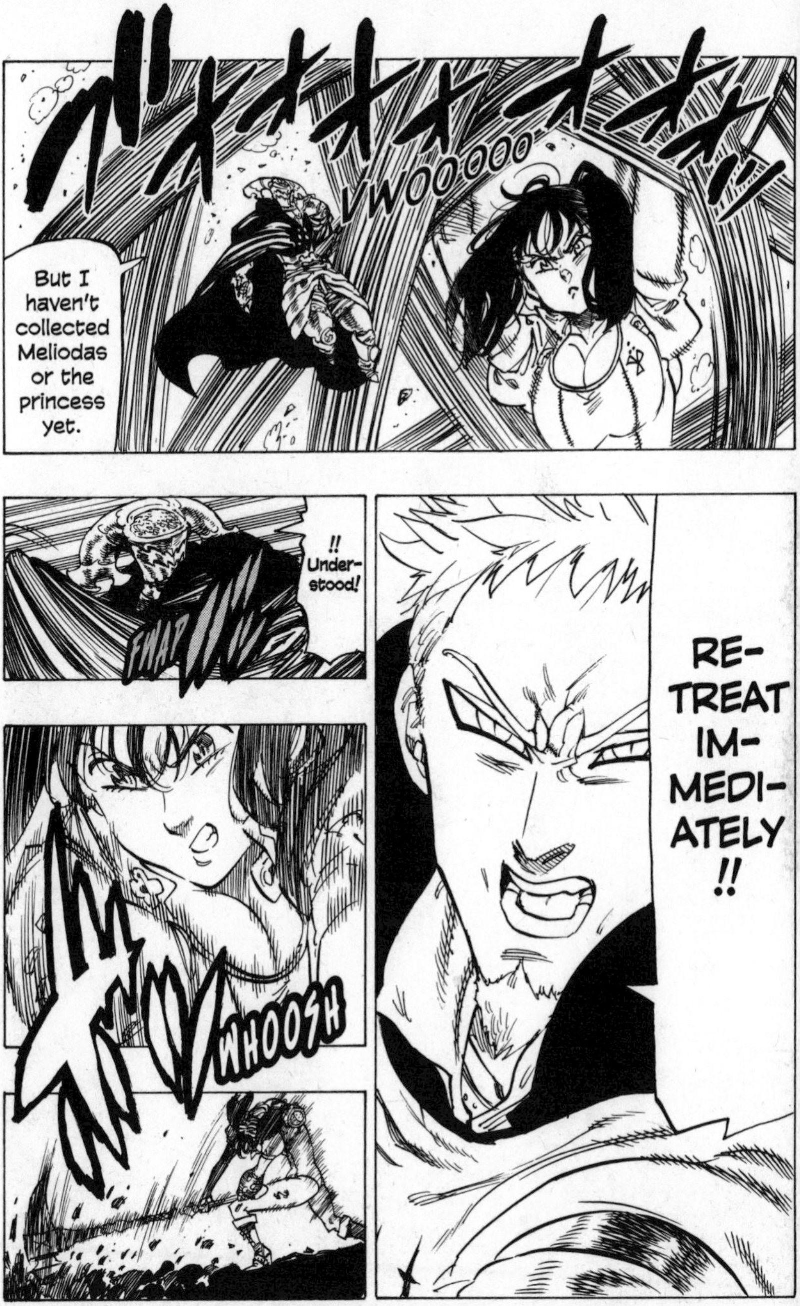
VWOOOOOO
But I haven't collected Meliodas or the princess yet.
RE-TREAT IM-MEDI-ATELY!!
!! Under-stood!
FWAP
WHOOSH

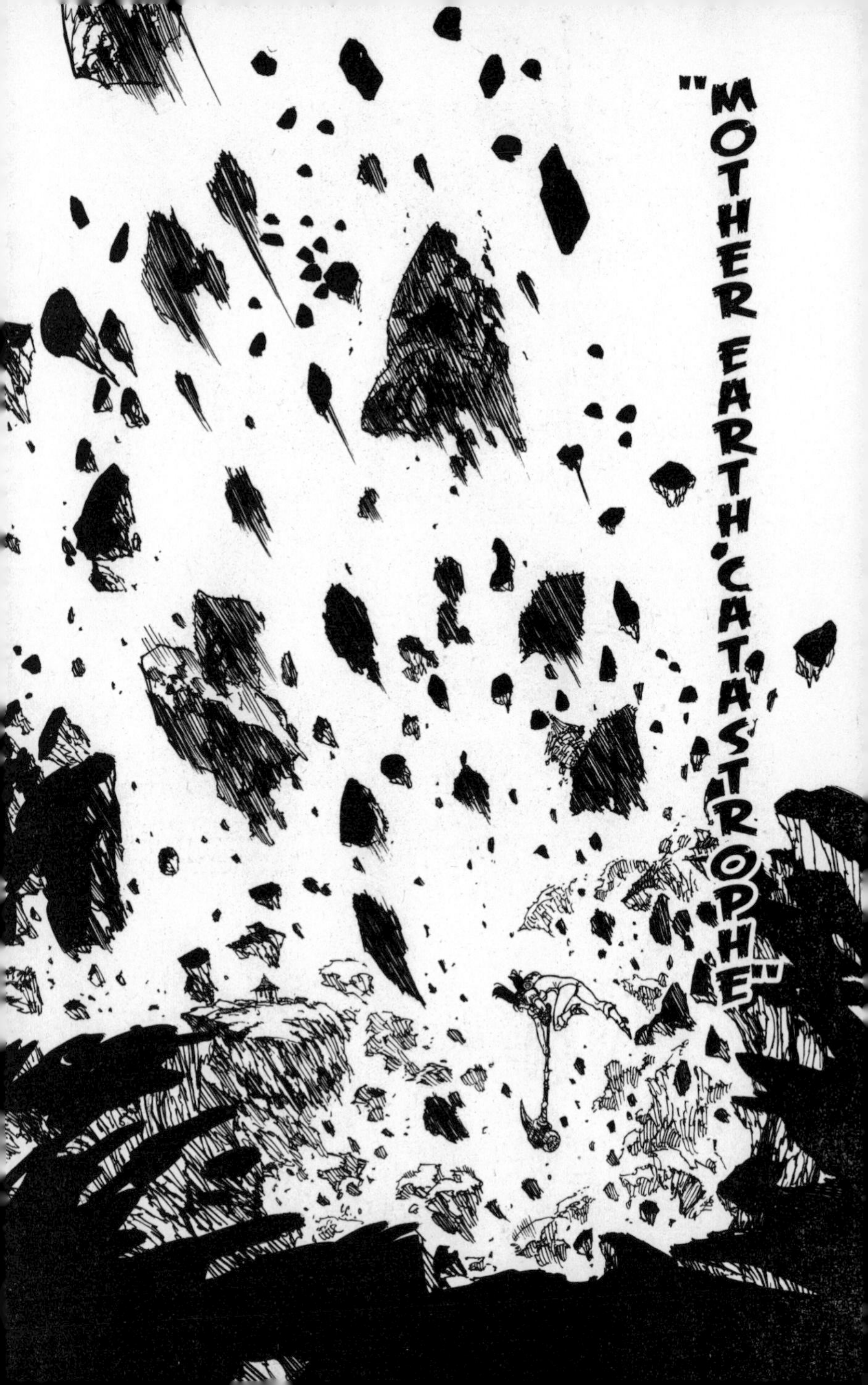
"MOTHER EARTH CATASTROPHE"

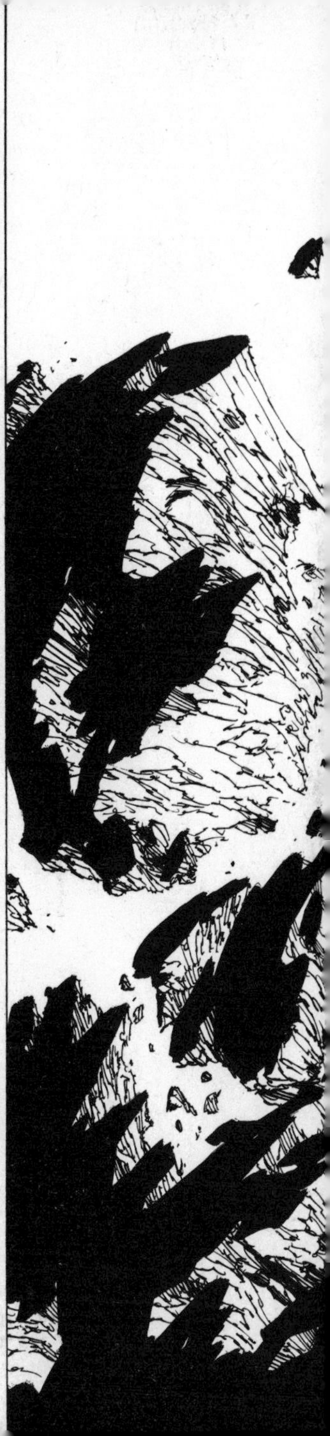

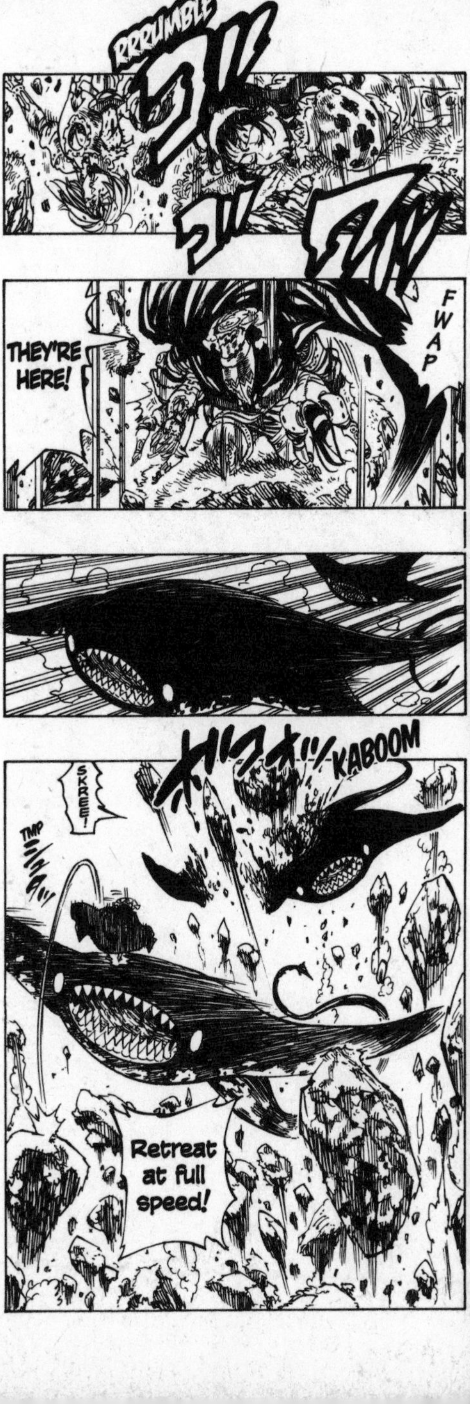
RRRUMBLE
FWAP
THEY'RE HERE!
KABOOM
SKREE!
TMP
Retreat at full speed!

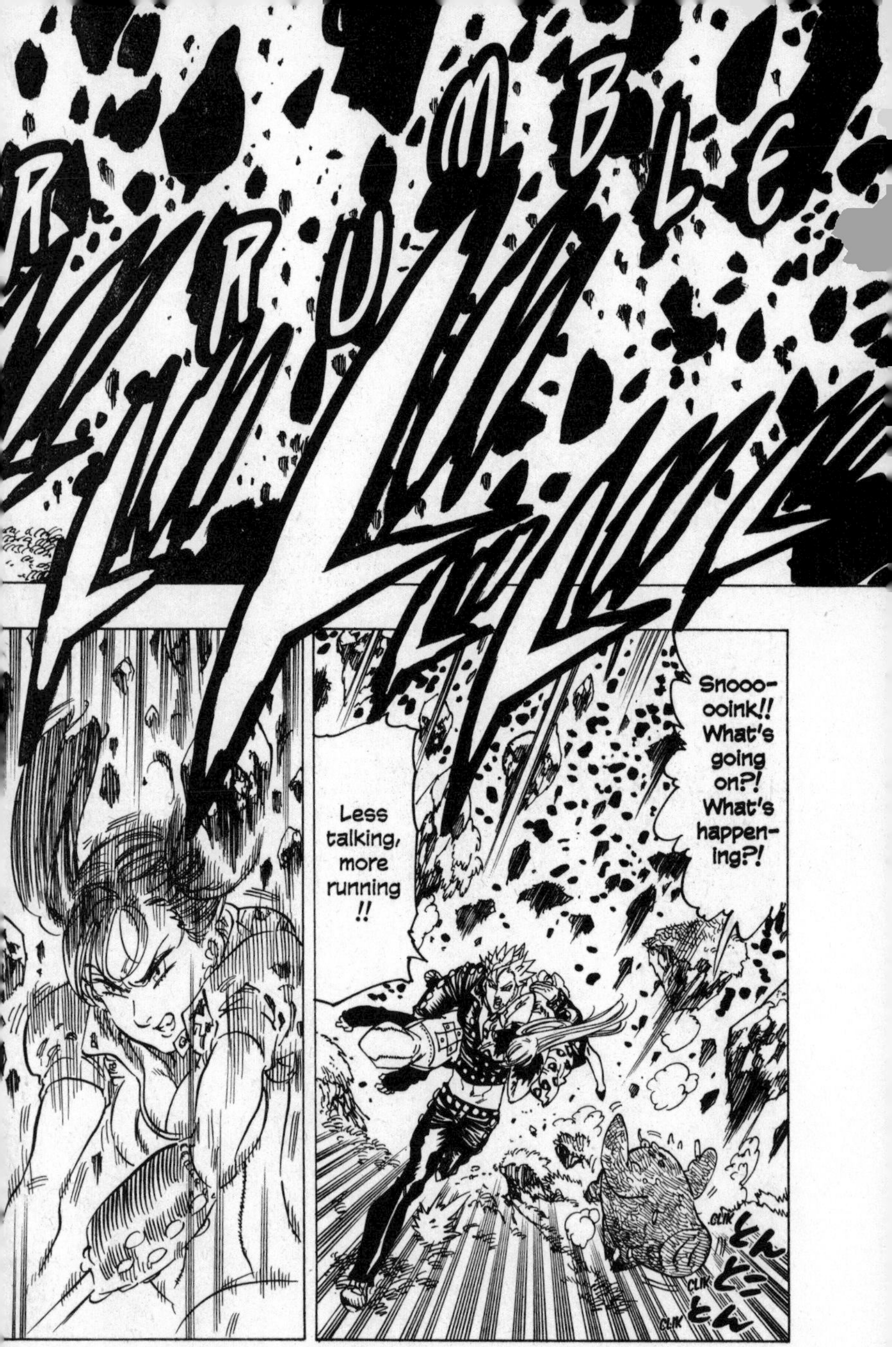
RRUMBLE
Snooo-
ooink!!
What's
going
on?!
What's
happen-
ing?!
Less
talking,
more
running
!!
CLIK
CLIK
CLIK

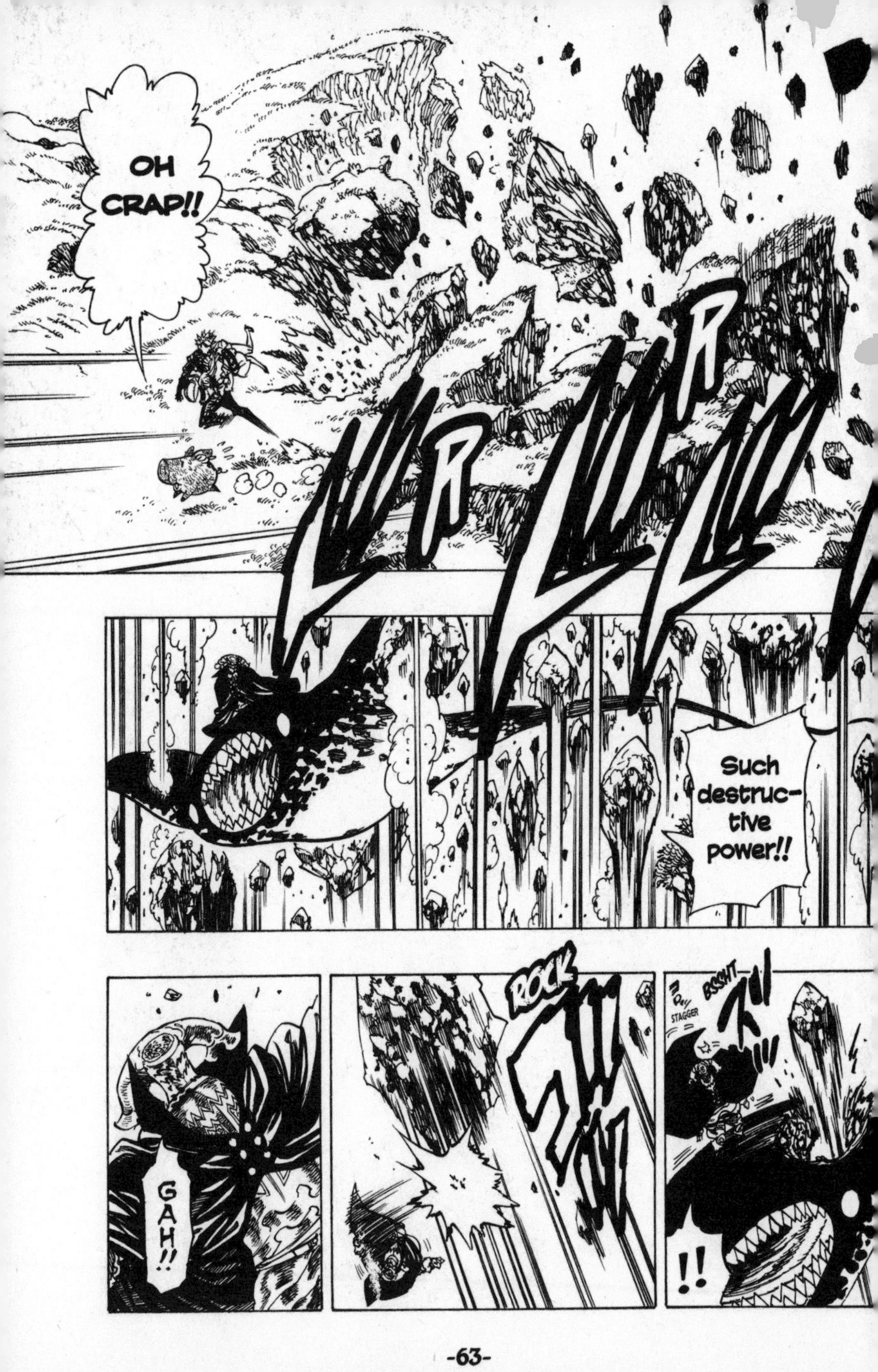
OH CRAP!!
Such destructive power!!
BSSHT
STAGGER
!!
ROCK
GAH!!

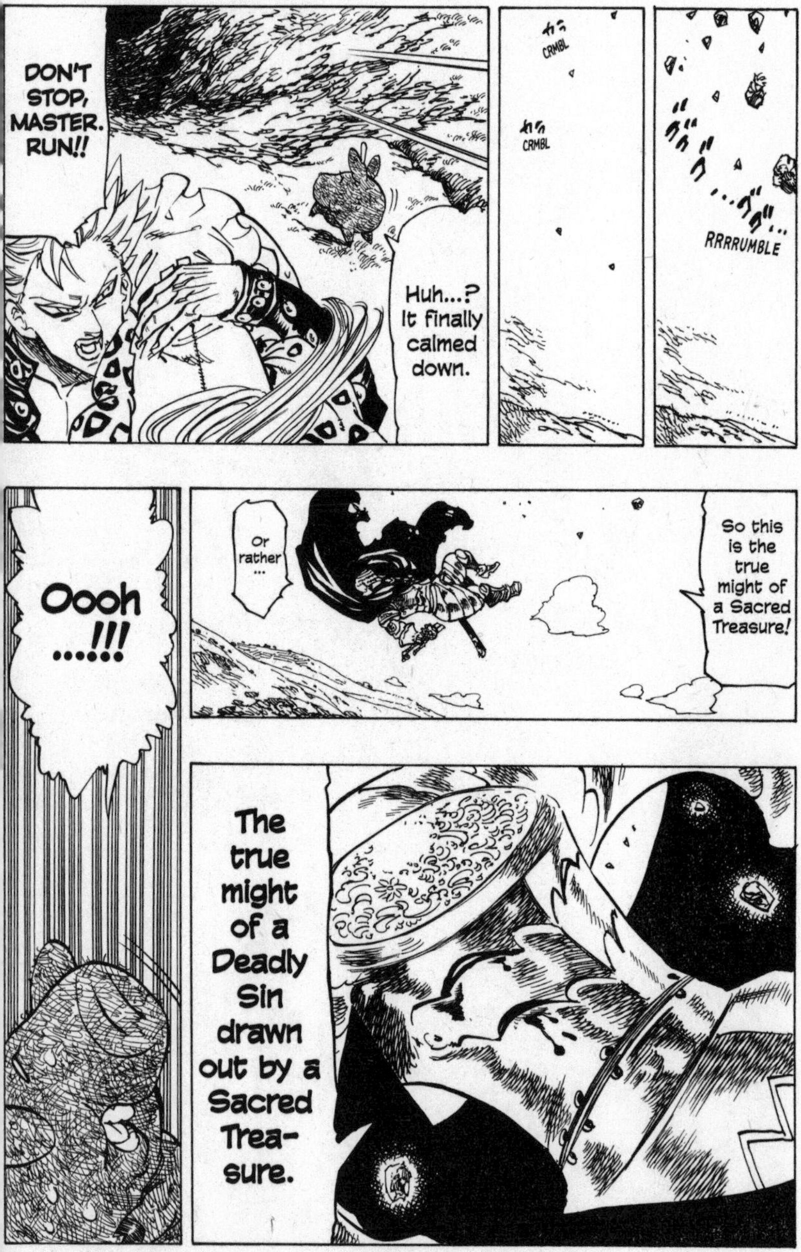
RRRRUMBLE
CRMBL
CRMBL
DON'T STOP, MASTER. RUN!!
Huh...? It finally calmed down.
So this is the true might of a Sacred Treasure!
Or rather ...
The true might of a Deadly Sin drawn out by a Sacred Trea-sure.
Oooh ...!!!

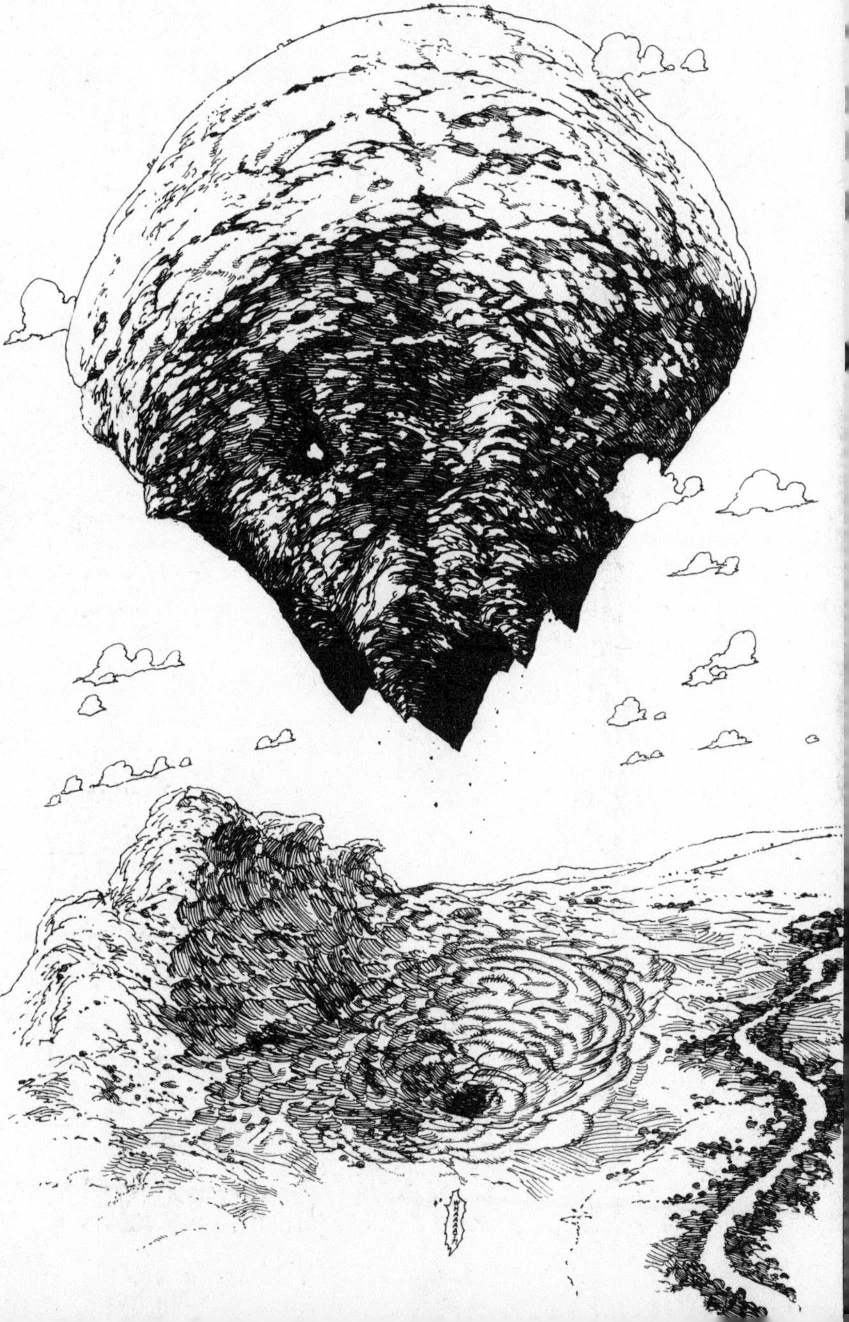
WHAAAAT!!

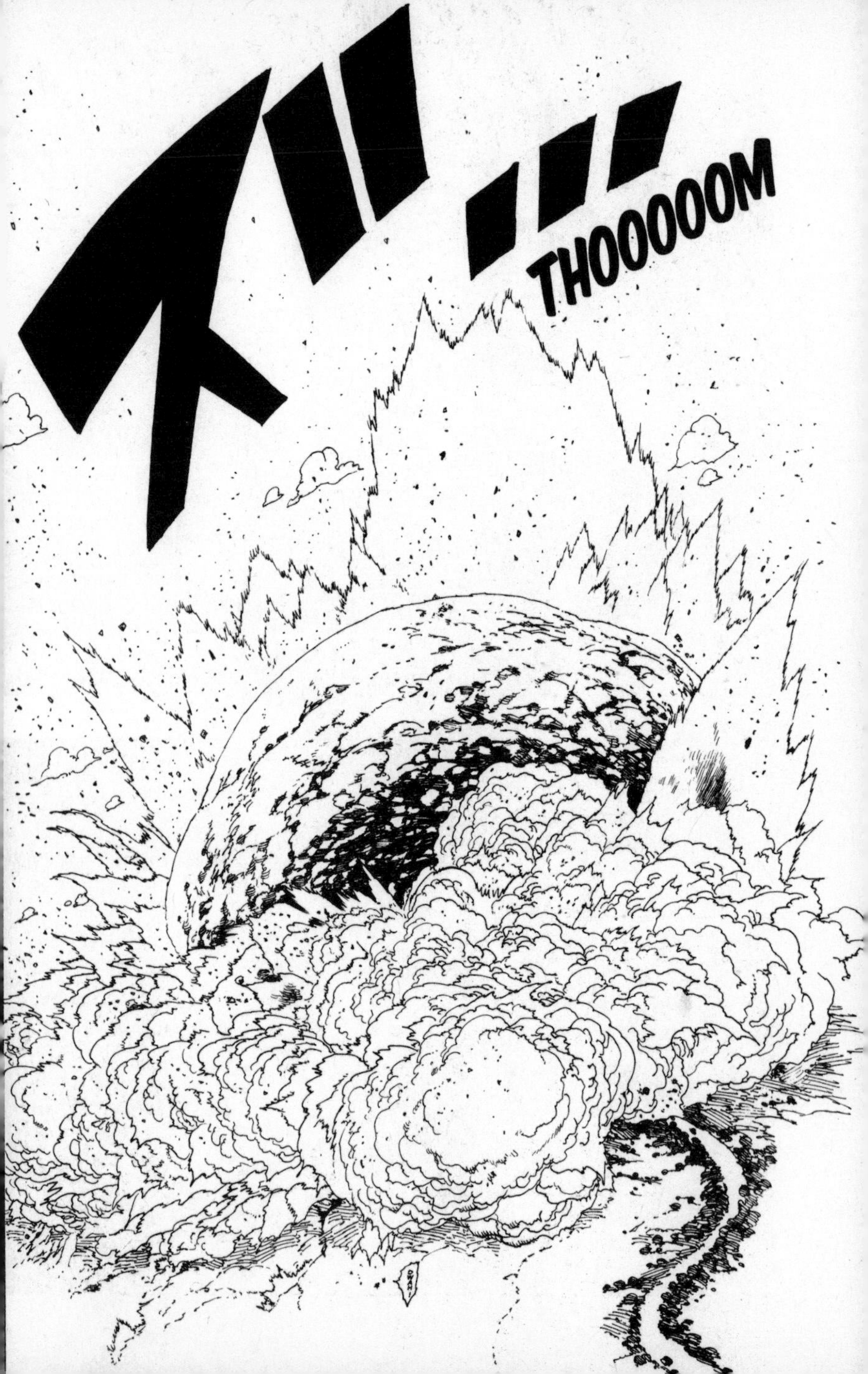
THOOOOOM

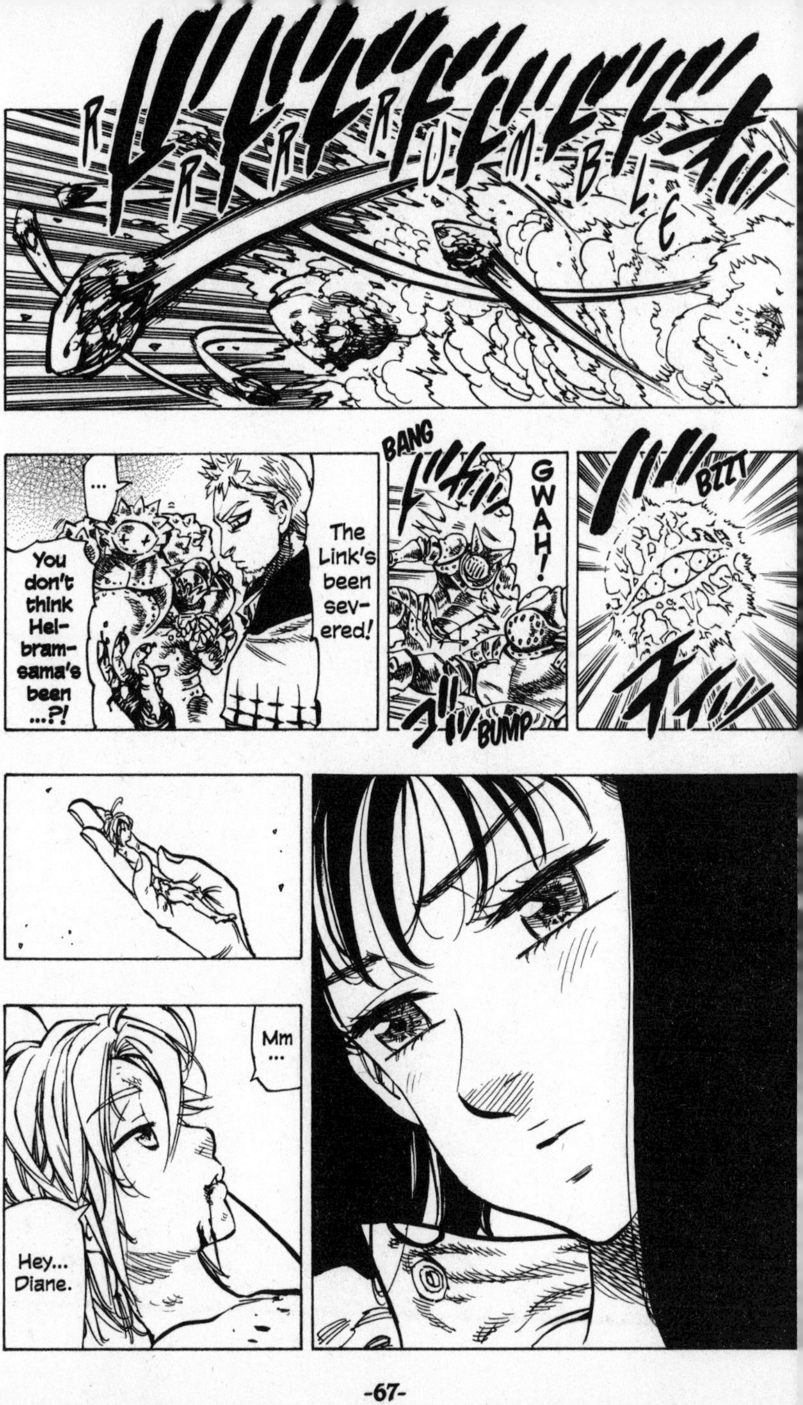
RRRRRUMBLE
BZZT
BANG
GWAH!
BUMP
The Link's been severed!
...
You don't think Helbram-sama's been ...?!
Mm ...
Hey... Diane.

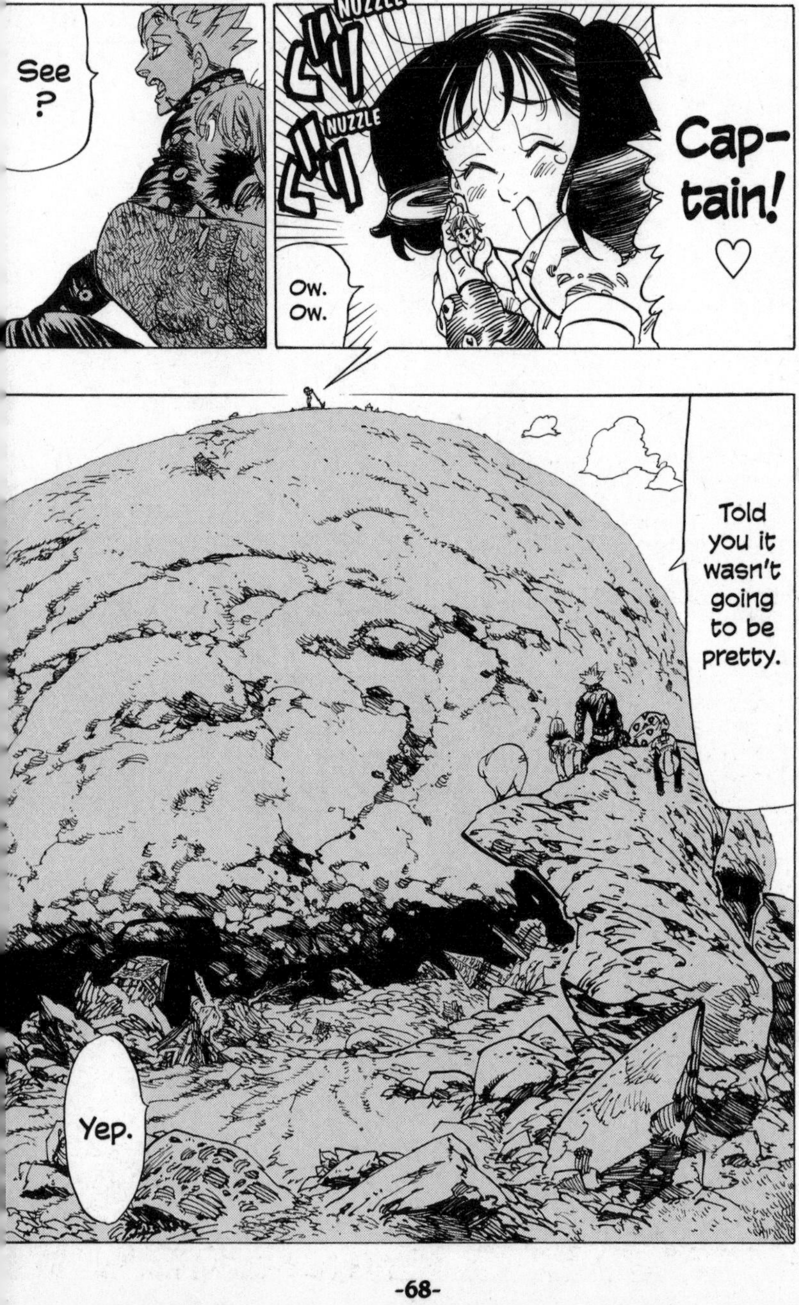
NUZZLE
NUZZLE
Cap-tain! ♡
Ow. Ow.
See ?
Told you it wasn't going to be pretty.
Yep.

Chapter 50 - After the Festival

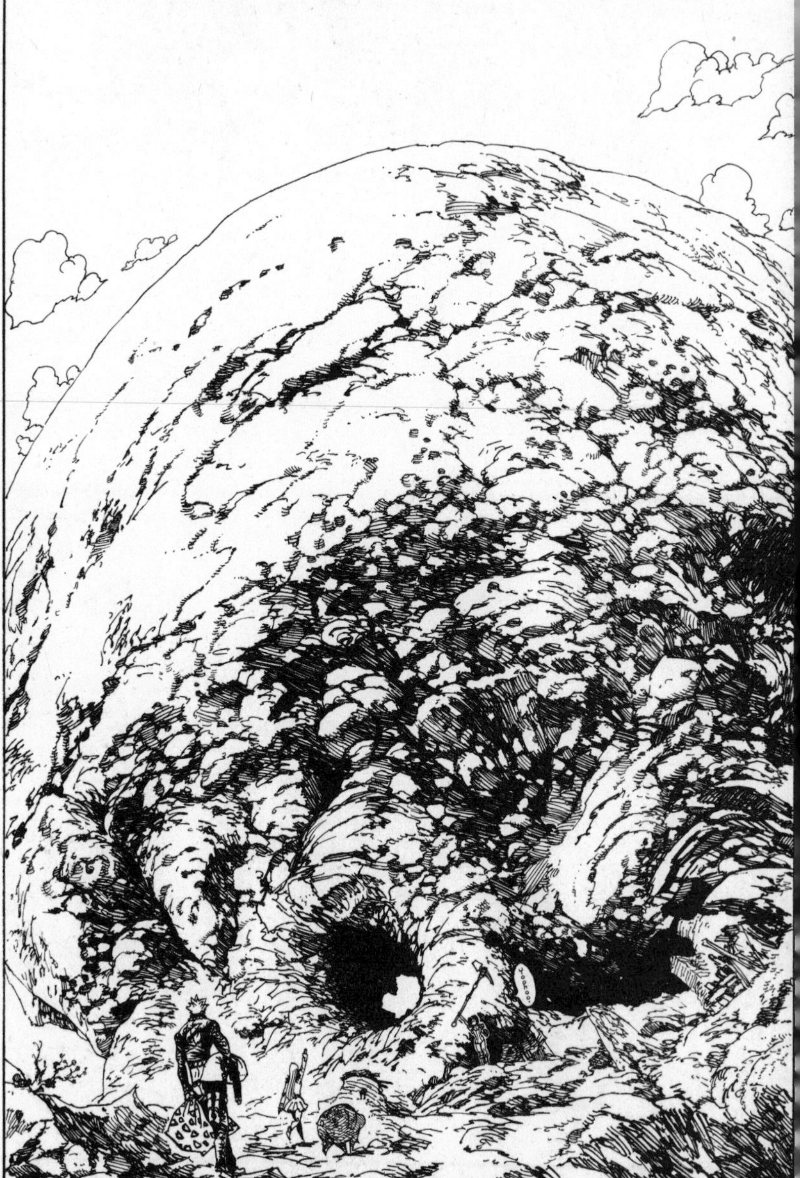
Yoohoo.

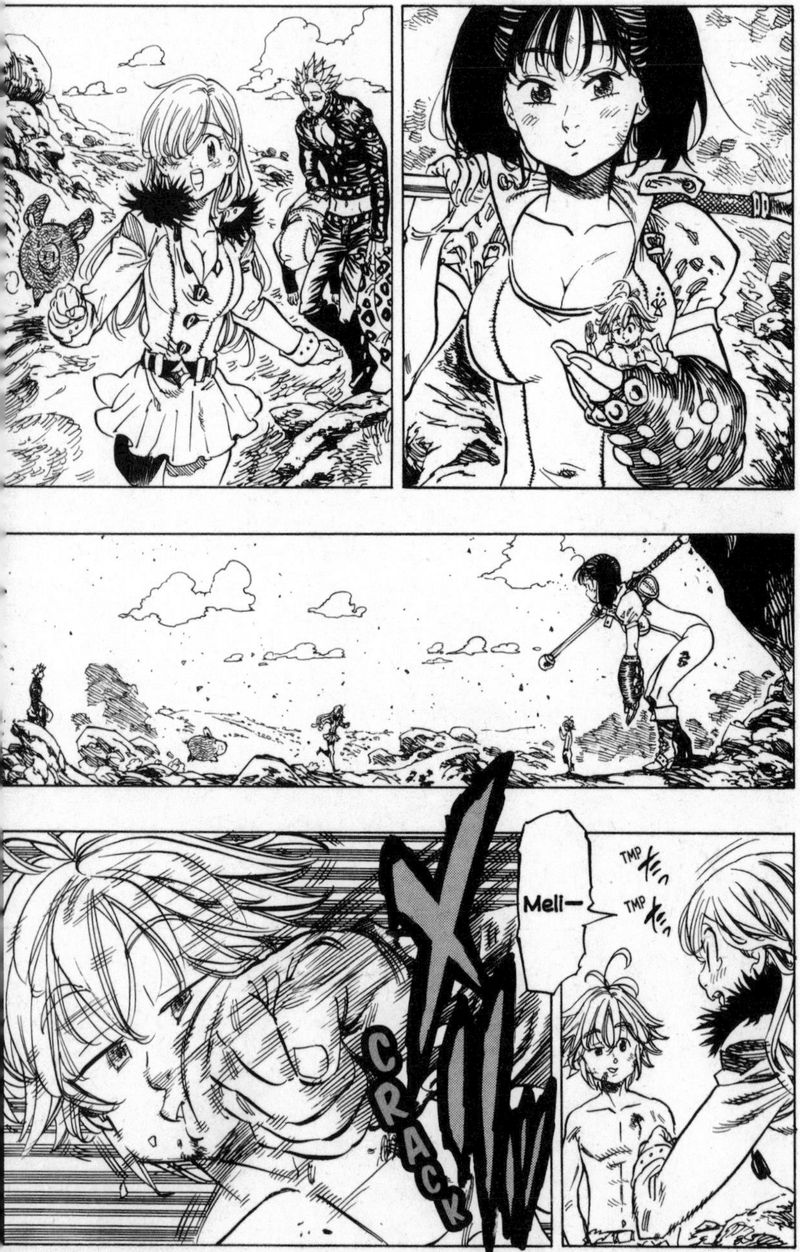
TMP
TMP
Meli—
CRACK

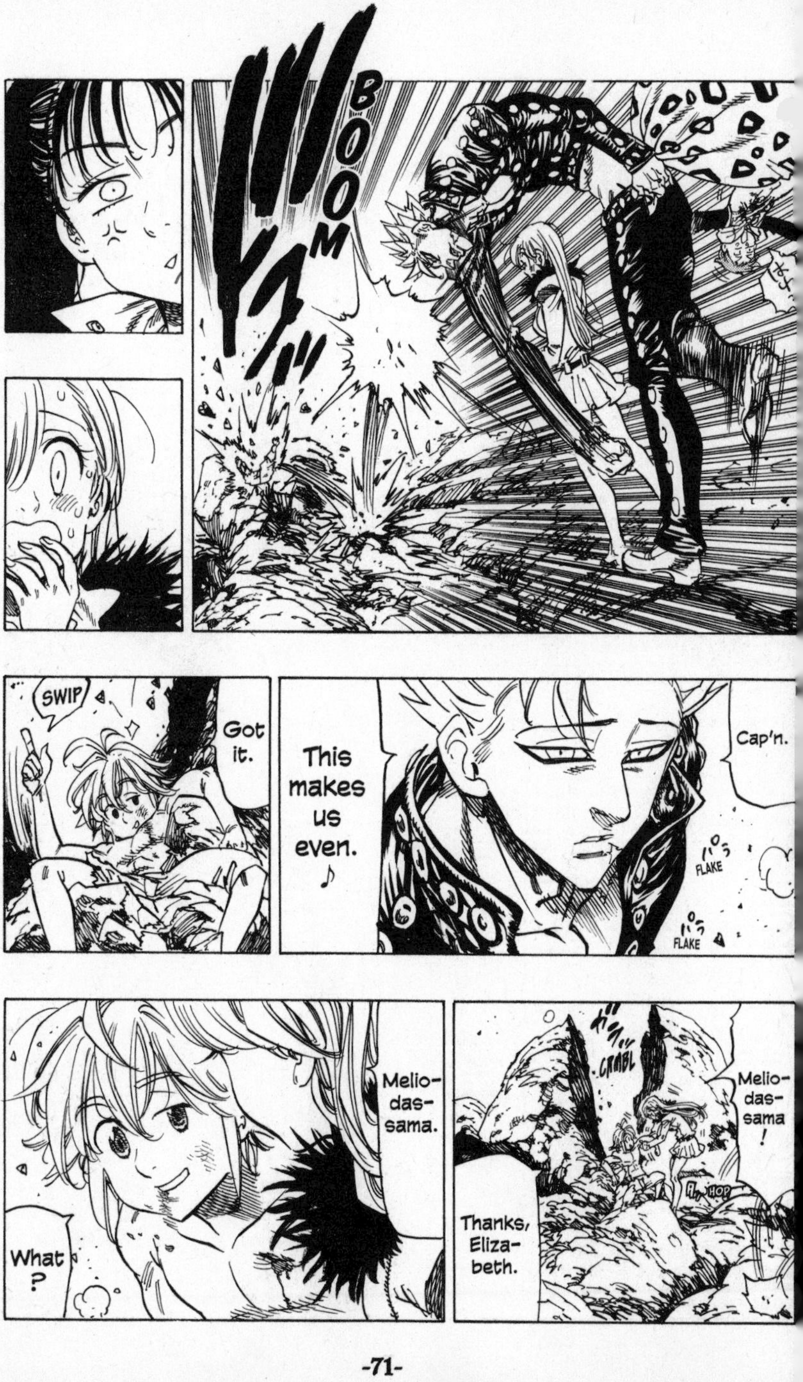
BOOM
Cap'n.
This makes us even. ♪
FLAKE
FLAKE
Got it.
SWIP
Melio-das-sama!
CRABL
HOP
Thanks, Eliza-beth.
Melio-das-sama.
What?

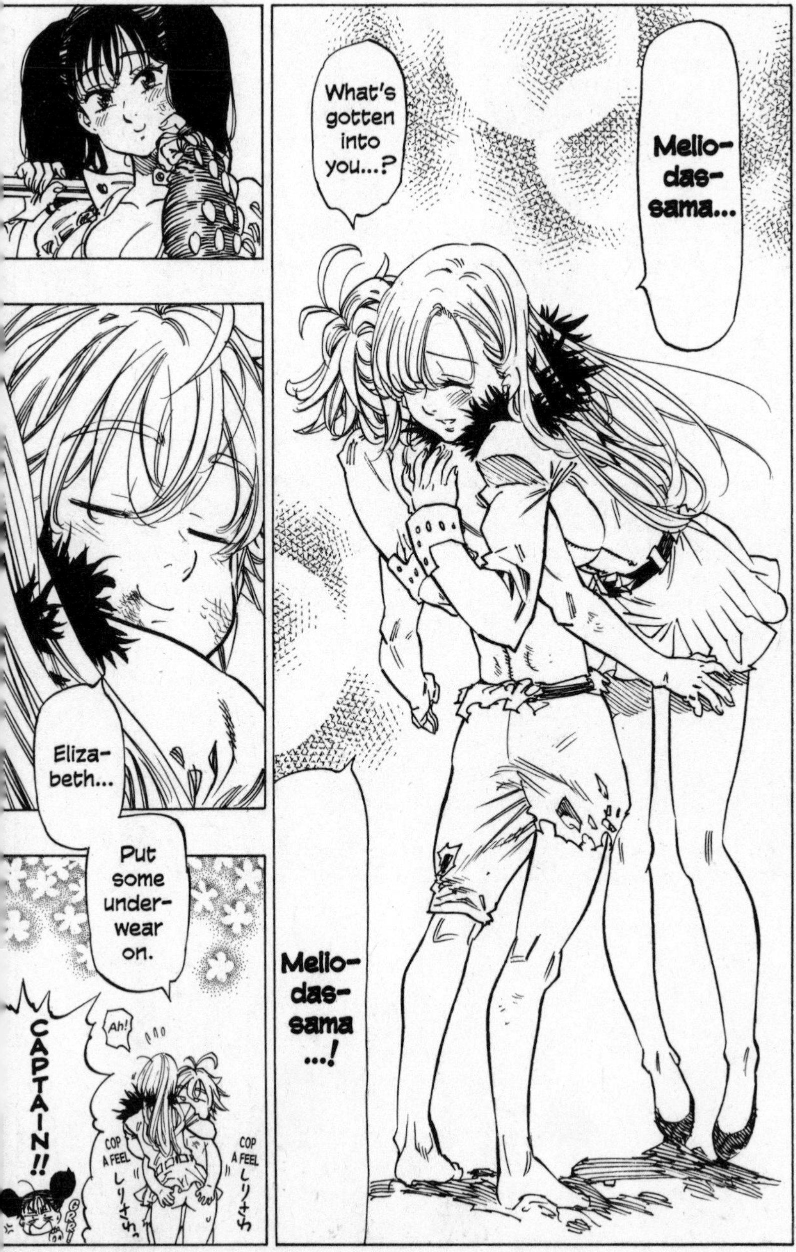
Melio-das-sama...
What's gotten into you...?
Melio-das-sama...!
Eliza-beth...
Put some under-wear on.
Ah!
CAPTAIN!!
COP A FEEL
COP A FEEL

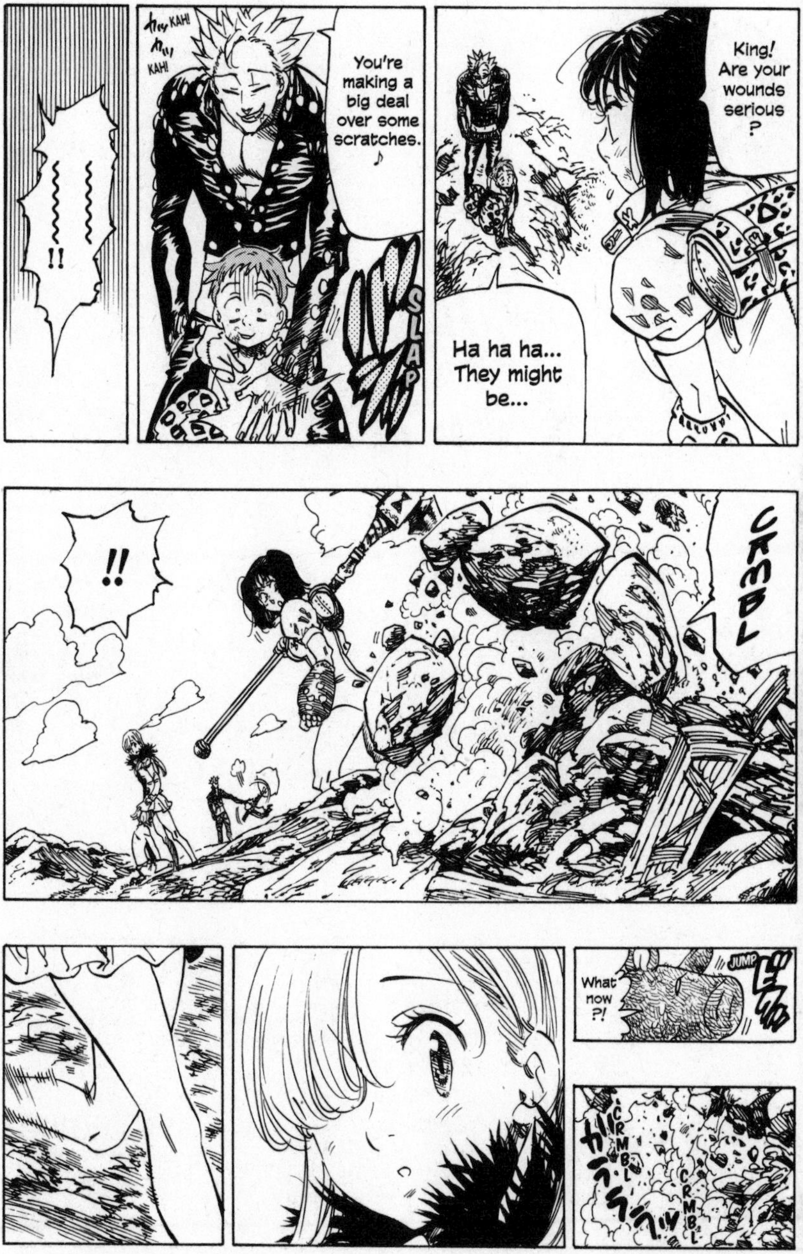
King! Are your wounds serious?
Ha ha ha... They might be...
KAH! KAH!
You're making a big deal over some scratches. ♪
SLAP
~~~~ ~~~~ !!
CRMBL
!!
JUMP
What now?!
CRMBL
CRMBL
~~~~

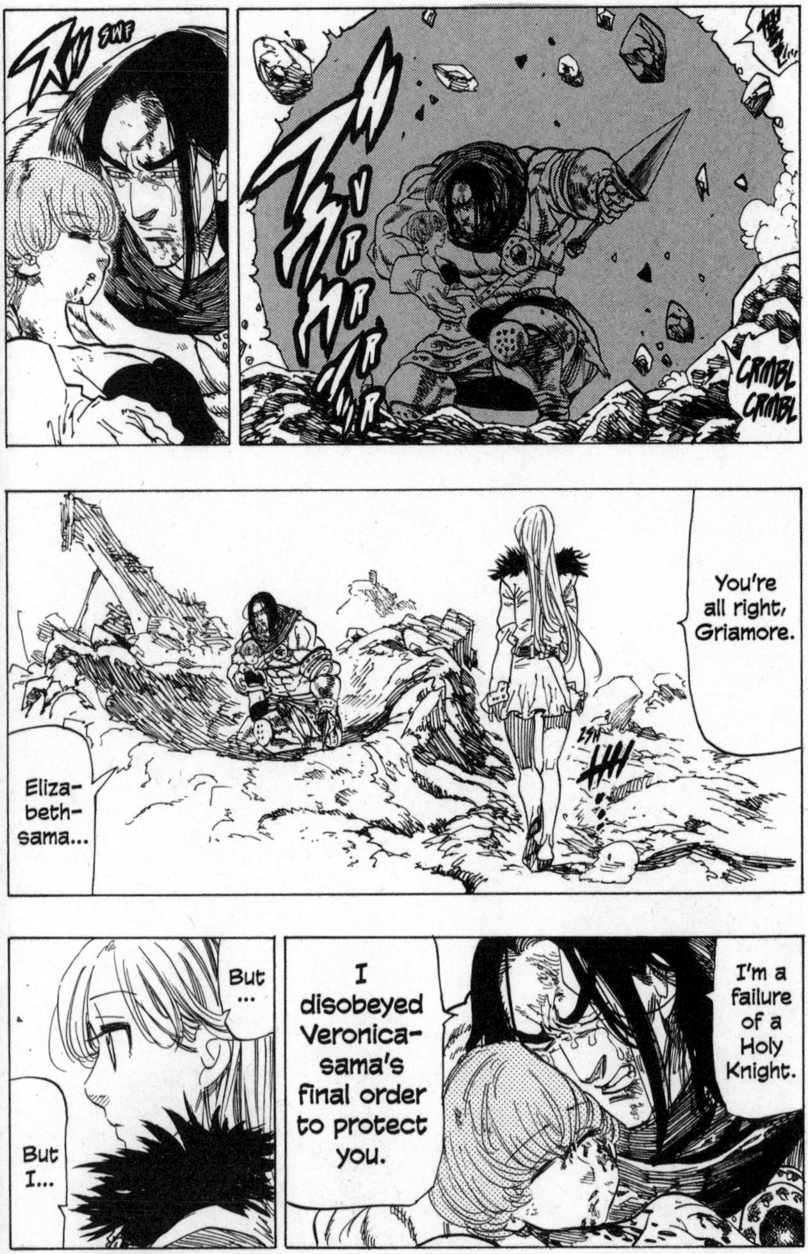
VRRRRR
CRMBL CRMBL
SWF
You're all right, Griamore.
Eliza-beth-sama...
I'm a failure of a Holy Knight.
I disobeyed Veronica-sama's final order to protect you.
But ...
But I...

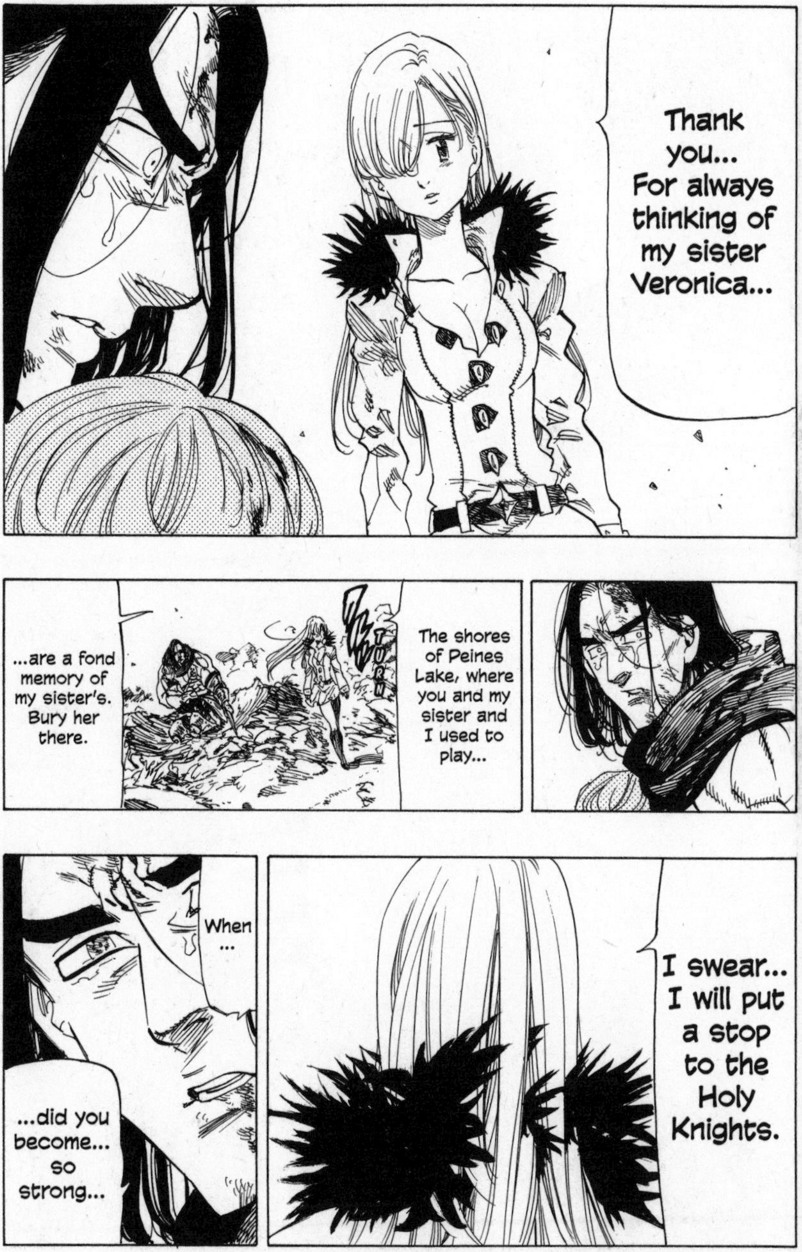
Thank you... For always thinking of my sister Veronica...
The shores of Peines Lake, where you and my sister and I used to play...
TURN
...are a fond memory of my sister's. Bury her there.
I swear... I will put a stop to the Holy Knights.
When...
...did you become... so strong...

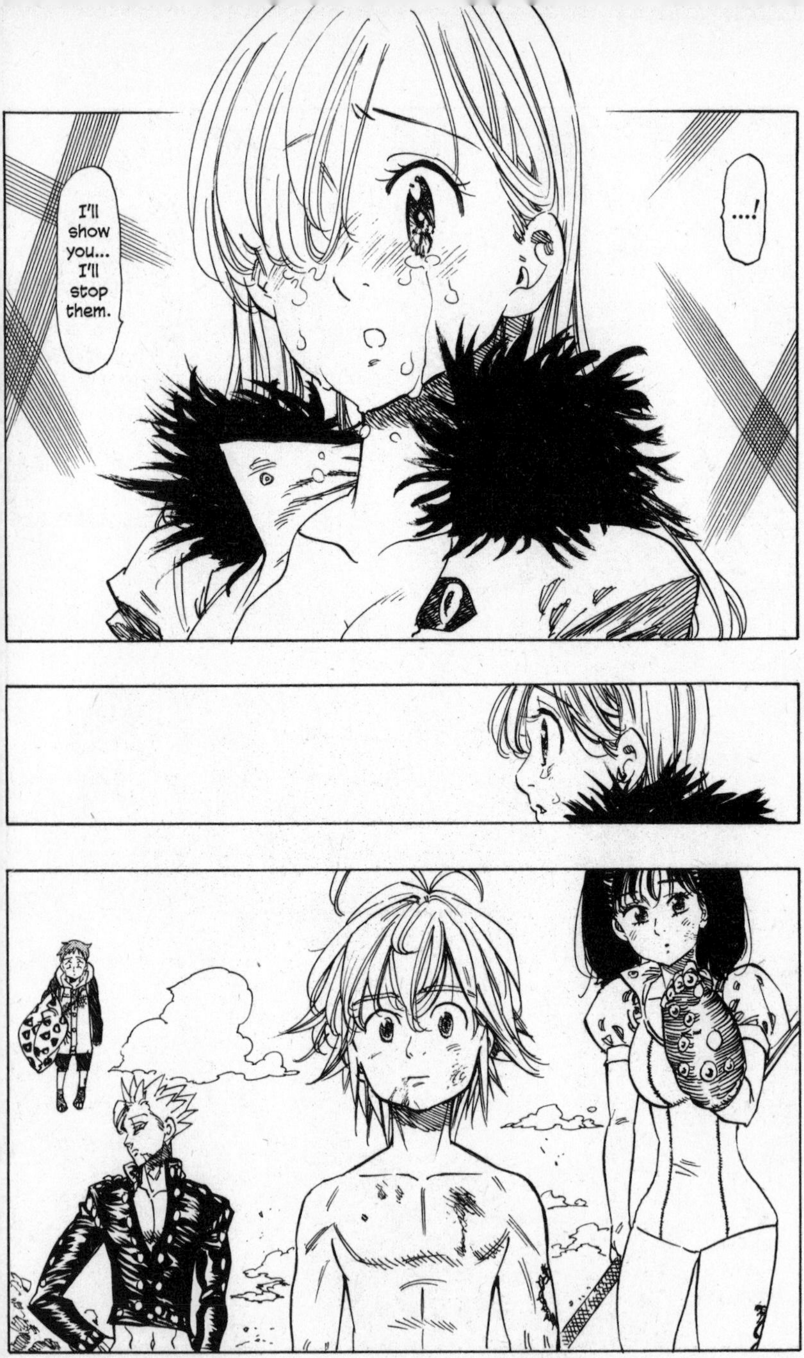
....!
I'll show you... I'll stop them.

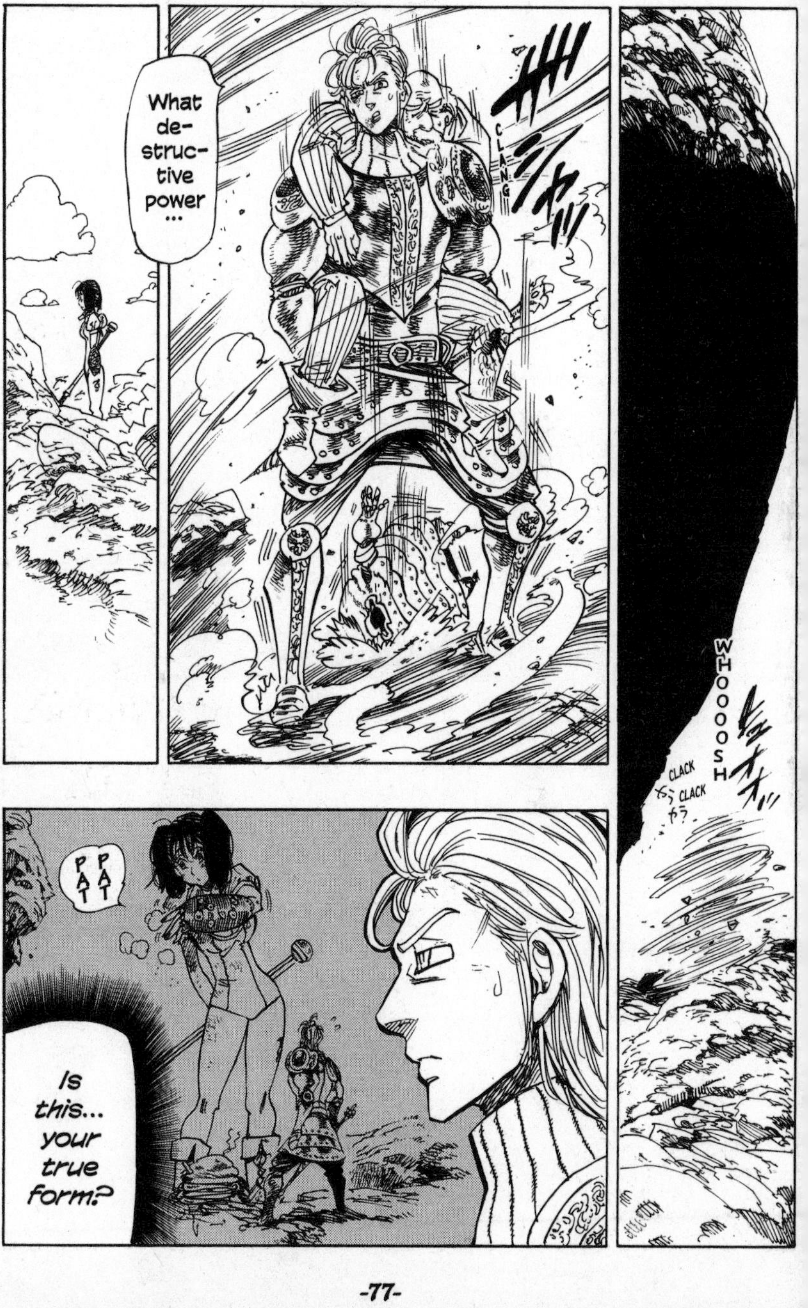
WHOOOOSH
CLACK CLACK
CLANG
What de-struc-tive power...
PAT PAT
Is this... your true form?

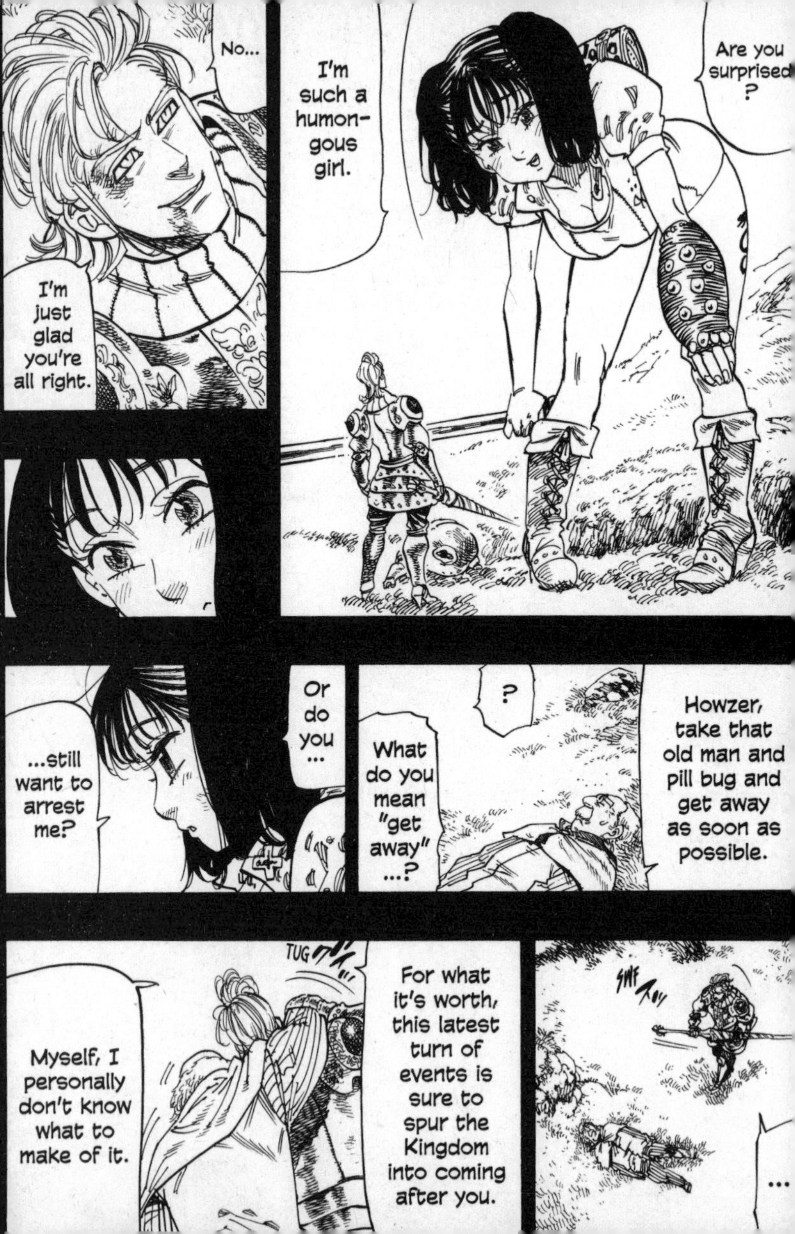

Are you surprised?
I'm such a humongous girl.
No...
I'm just glad you're all right.
Howzer, take that old man and pill bug and get away as soon as possible.
?
What do you mean "get away"...?
Or do you...
...still want to arrest me?
SWF
...
For what it's worth, this latest turn of events is sure to spur the Kingdom into coming after you.
TUG
Myself, I personally don't know what to make of it.

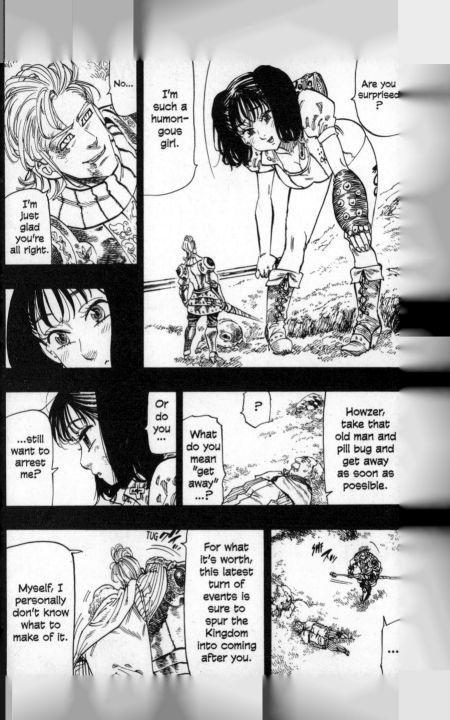

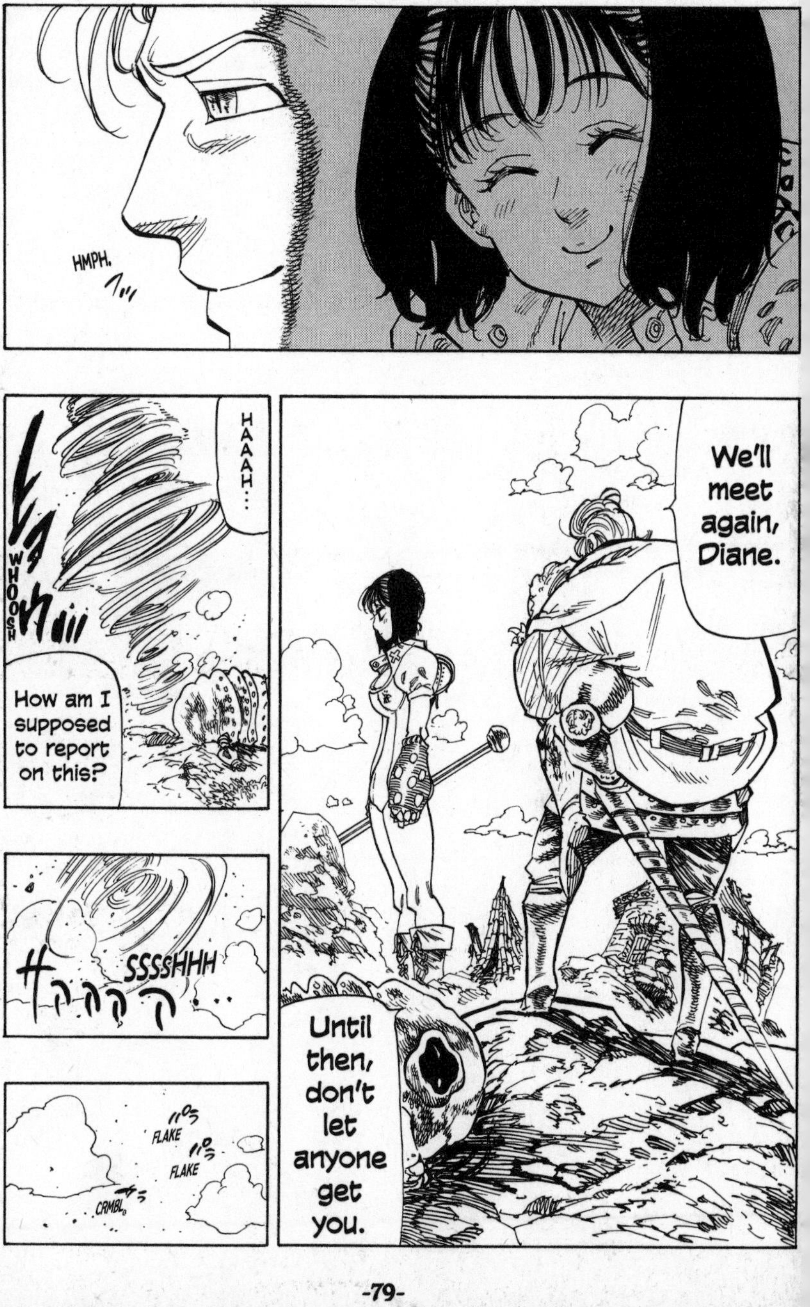
HMPH.
We'll meet again, Diane.
Until then, don't let anyone get you.
HAAAH...
WHOOSH
How am I supposed to report on this?
SSSSHHH
FLAKE
FLAKE
CRMBL

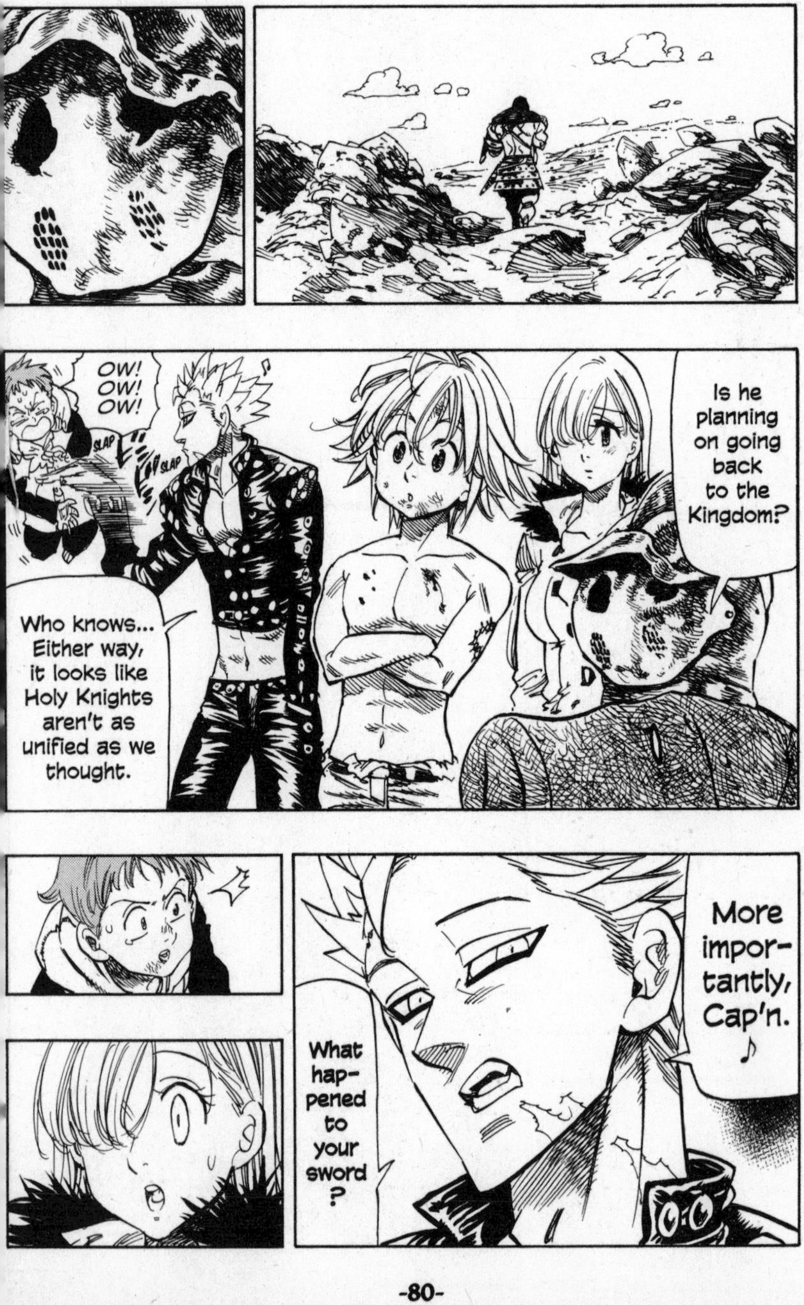
Is he planning on going back to the Kingdom?
OW! OW! OW!
SLAP
SLAP
Who knows... Either way, it looks like Holy Knights aren't as unified as we thought.
More impor-tantly, Cap'n. ♪
What hap-pened to your sword?

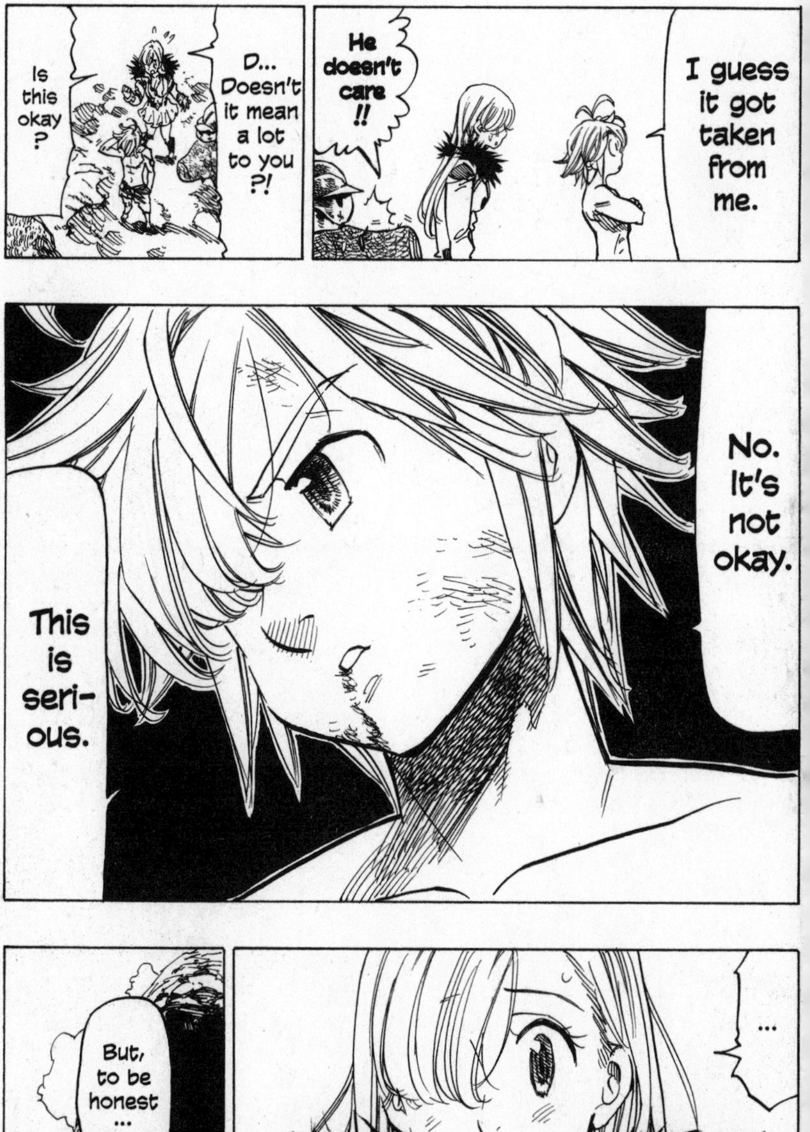
I guess it got taken from me.
He doesn't care!!
D... Doesn't it mean a lot to you?!
Is this okay?
No. It's not okay.
This is seri-ous.
...
But, to be honest...

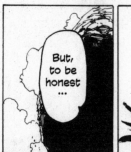

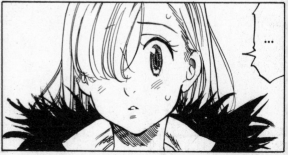

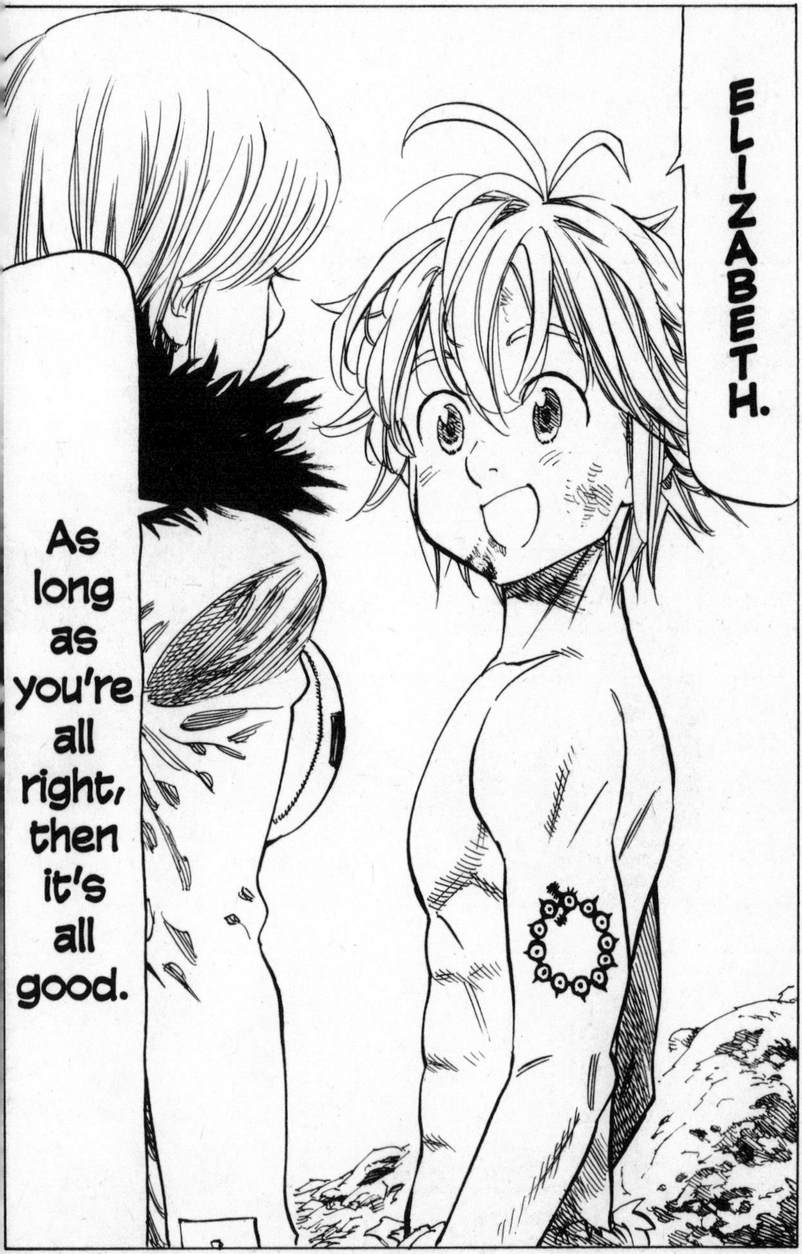
ELIZABETH.
As long as you're all right, then it's all good.

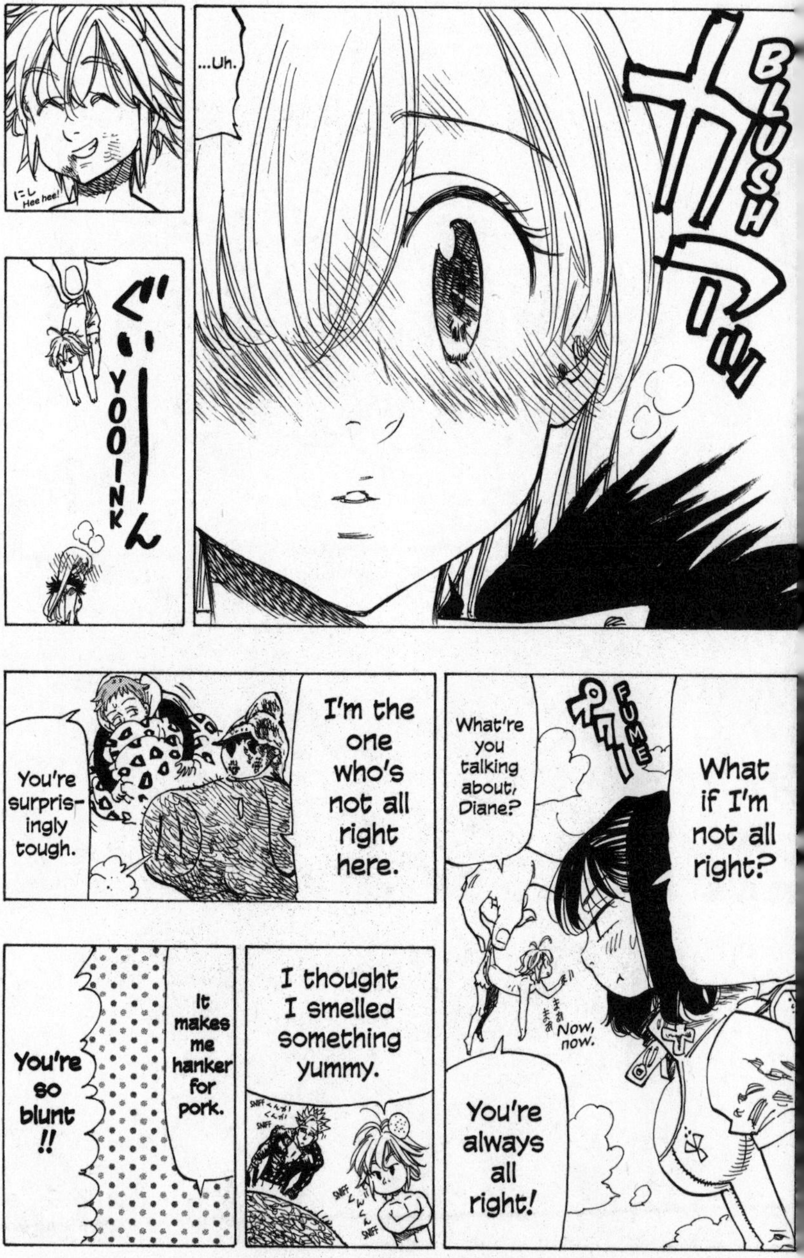
BLUSH
...Uh.
にし Hee hee!
ぐいーん
YOOINK
FUME
What if I'm not all right?
What're you talking about, Diane?
Now, now.
You're always all right!
I'm the one who's not all right here.
You're surprisingly tough.
I thought I smelled something yummy.
SNIFF
SNIFF
SNIFF
SNIFF
It makes me hanker for pork.
You're so blunt!!

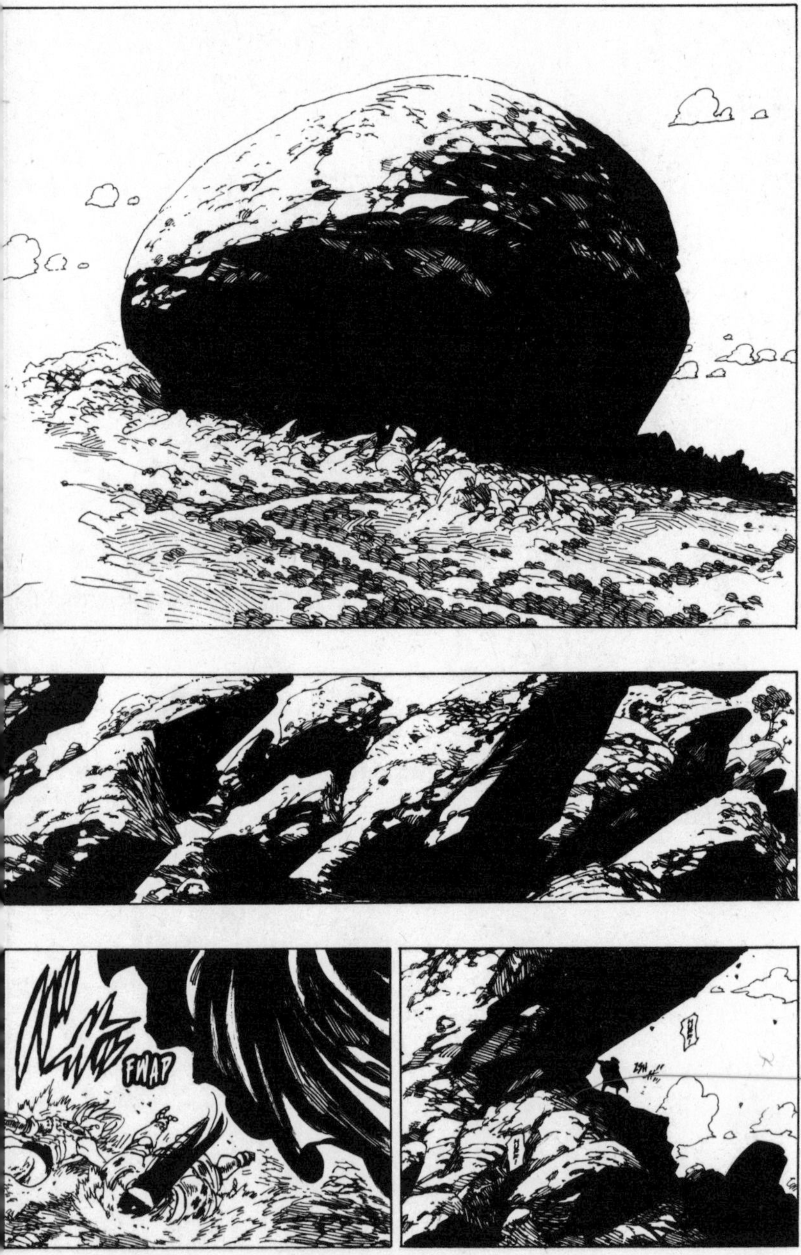
FWAP

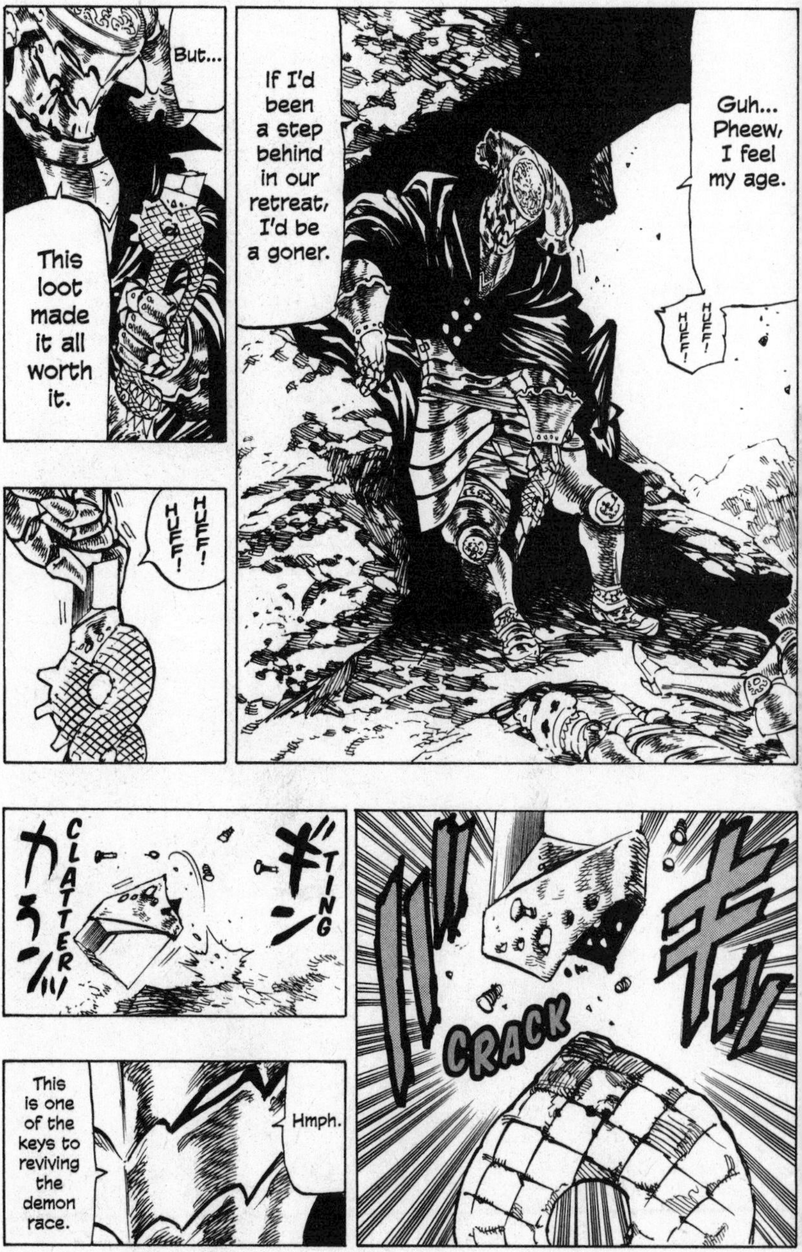
Guh... Pheew, I feel my age.
HUFF! HUFF!
If I'd been a step behind in our retreat, I'd be a goner.
But...
This loot made it all worth it.
HUFF! HUFF!
CRACK
TING
CLATTER
Hmph.
This is one of the keys to reviving the demon race.

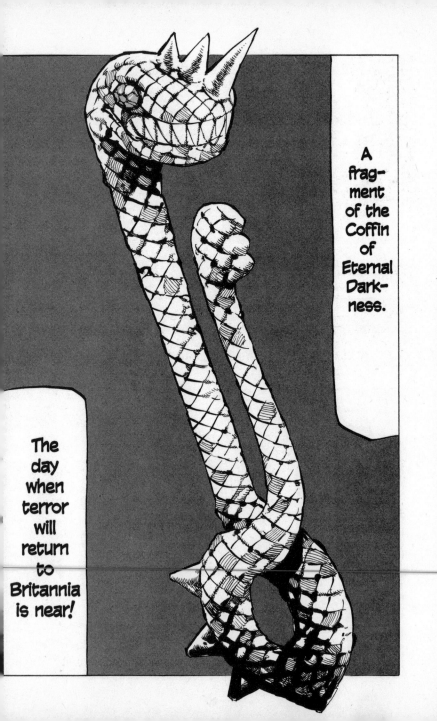

A fragment of the Coffin of Eternal Darkness.

The day when terror will return to Britannia is near!

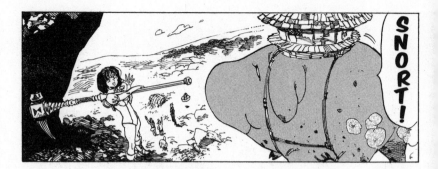

SNORT!
Let's get ready to set off! Starting tomorrow, we'll pick up our regular business...
...and resume our journey to find the remaining Deadly Sins and Sacred Treasures!!

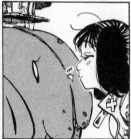

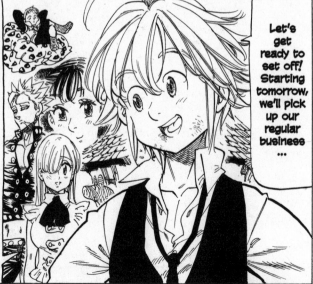

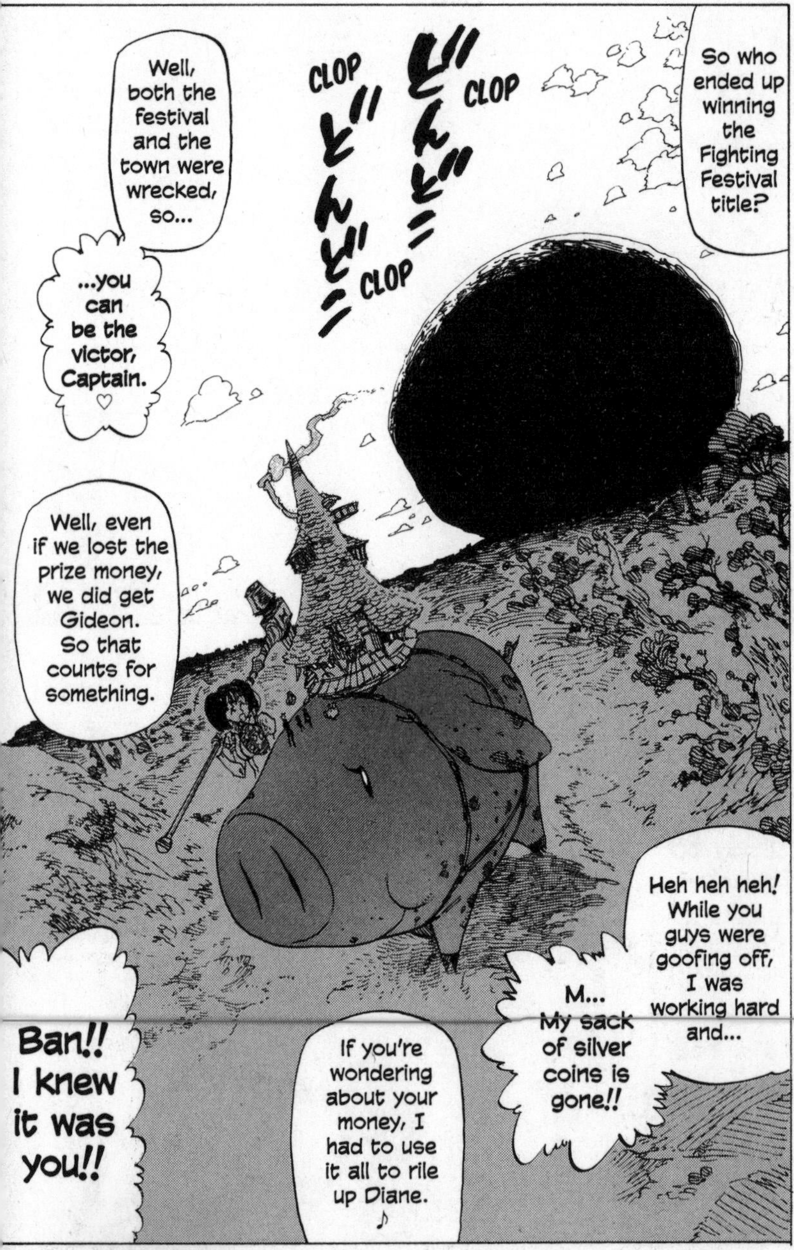

So who ended up winning the Fighting Festival title?
どん どん CLOP
どん どん CLOP
CLOP
CLOP
Well, both the festival and the town were wrecked, so...
...you can be the victor, Captain. ♡
Well, even if we lost the prize money, we did get Gideon. So that counts for something.
Heh heh heh! While you guys were goofing off, I was working hard and...
M... My sack of silver coins is gone!!
If you're wondering about your money, I had to use it all to rile up Diane. ♪
Ban!! I knew it was you!!

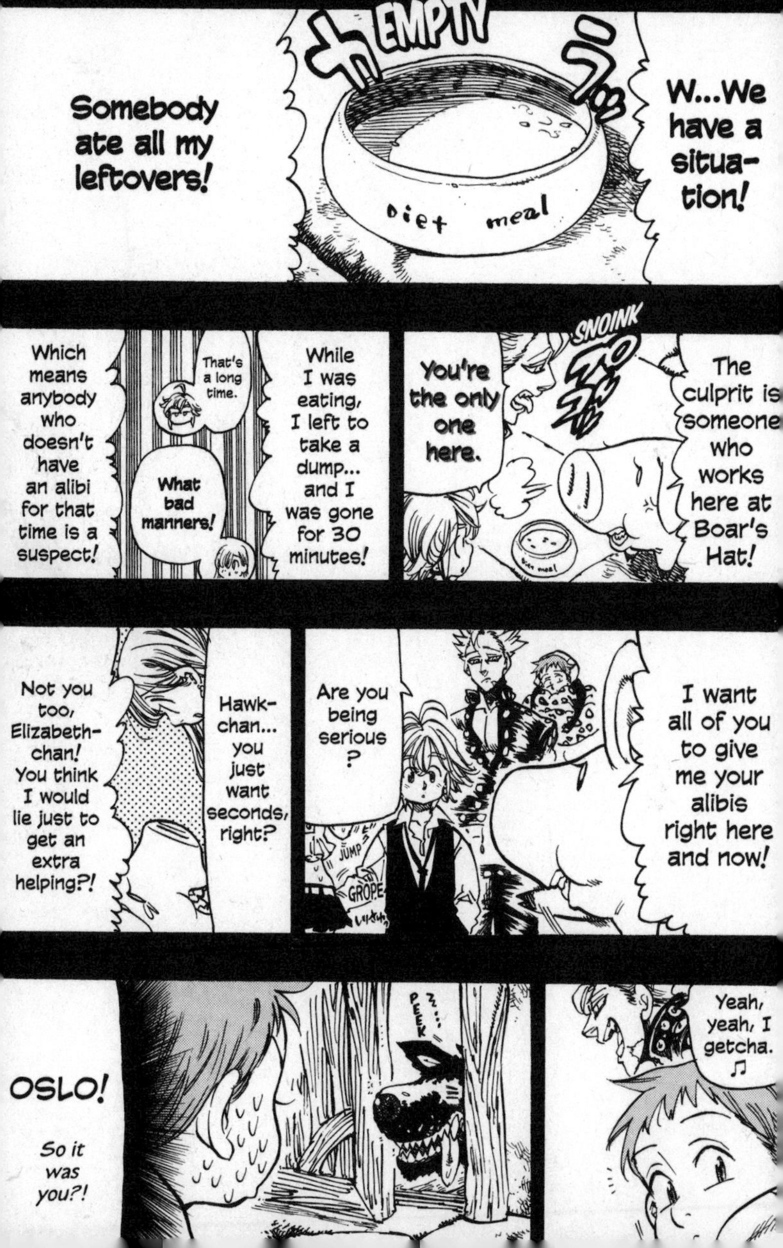
W...We have a situation!
EMPTY
Diet meal
Somebody ate all my leftovers!
SNOINK
The culprit is someone who works here at Boar's Hat!
You're the only one here.
While I was eating, I left to take a dump... and I was gone for 30 minutes!
That's a long time.
What bad manners!
Which means anybody who doesn't have an alibi for that time is a suspect!
I want all of you to give me your alibis right here and now!
Are you being serious?
JUMP
GROPE
Hawk-chan... you just want seconds, right?
Not you too, Elizabeth-chan! You think I would lie just to get an extra helping?!
Yeah, yeah, I getcha. ♫
PEEK
OSLO!
So it was you?!

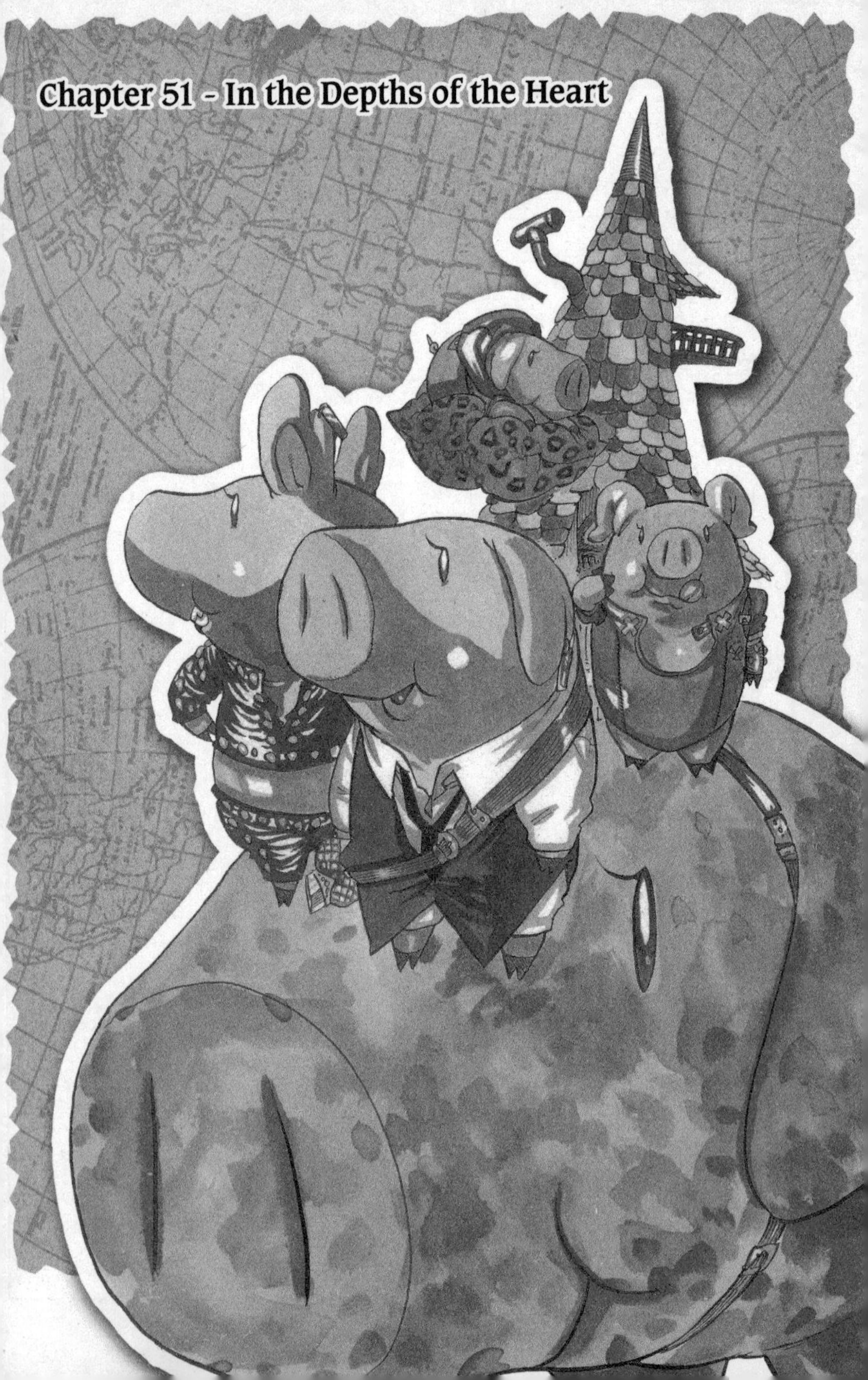
Chapter 51 - In the Depths of the Heart

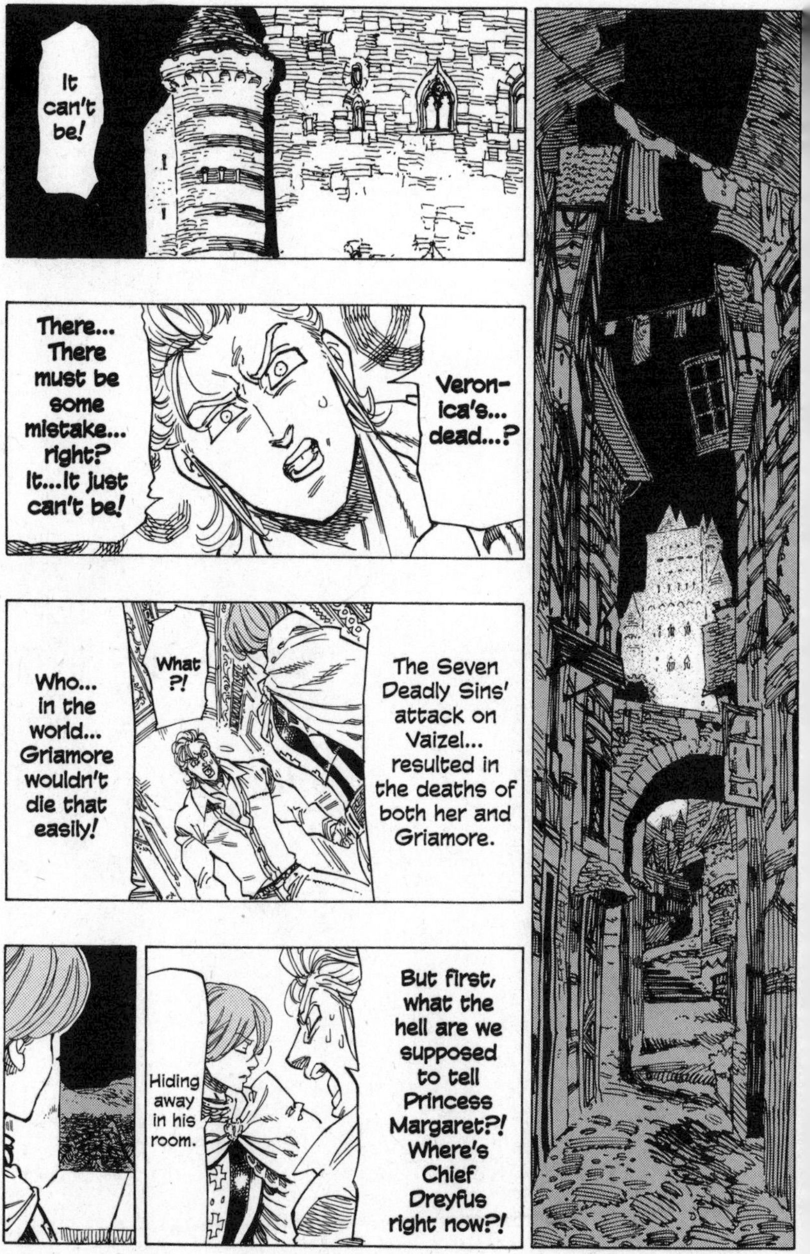
It can't be!
Veronica's... dead...?
There... There must be some mistake... right? It...it just can't be!
The Seven Deadly Sins' attack on Vaizel... resulted in the deaths of both her and Griamore.
What?!
Who... in the world... Griamore wouldn't die that easily!
But first, what the hell are we supposed to tell Princess Margaret?! Where's Chief Dreyfus right now?!
Hiding away in his room.

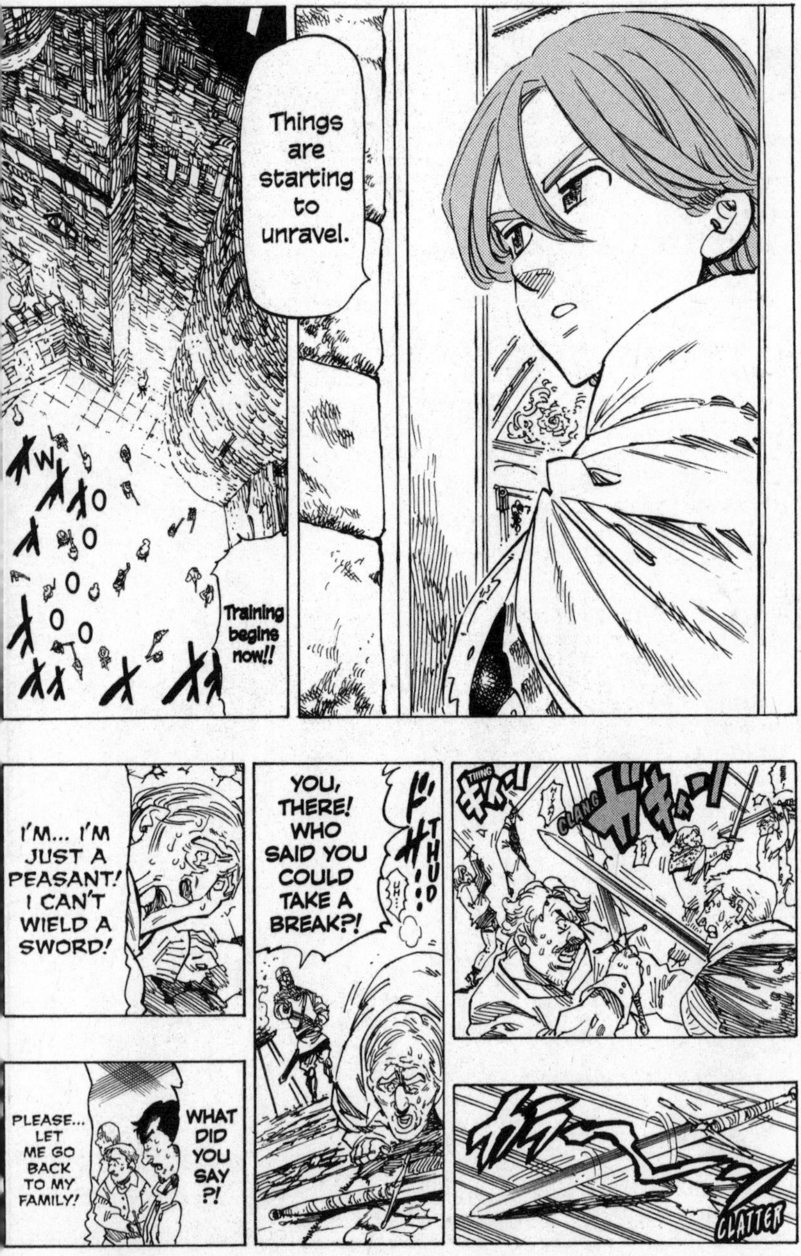
Things are starting to unravel.
Training begins now!!
WOOOOO
THIING
CLANG
CLATTER
YOU, THERE! WHO SAID YOU COULD TAKE A BREAK?!
THUD
I'M... I'M JUST A PEASANT! I CAN'T WIELD A SWORD!
WHAT DID YOU SAY?!
PLEASE... LET ME GO BACK TO MY FAMILY!

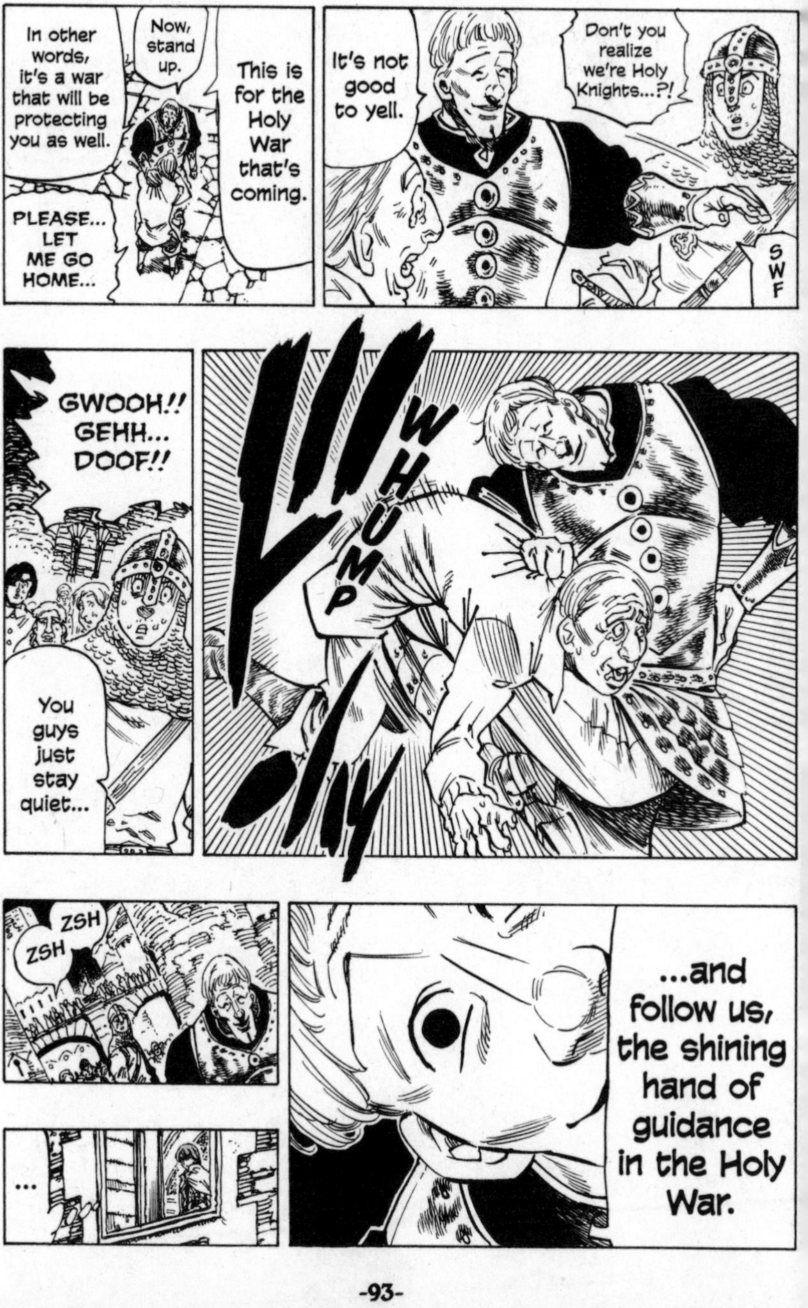

Don't you realize we're Holy Knights...?!
It's not good to yell.
SWF
This is for the Holy War that's coming.
Now, stand up.
In other words, it's a war that will be protecting you as well.
PLEASE... LET ME GO HOME...
WHUMP
GWOOH!! GEHH... DOOF!!
You guys just stay quiet...
...and follow us, the shining hand of guidance in the Holy War.
ZSH
ZSH
...

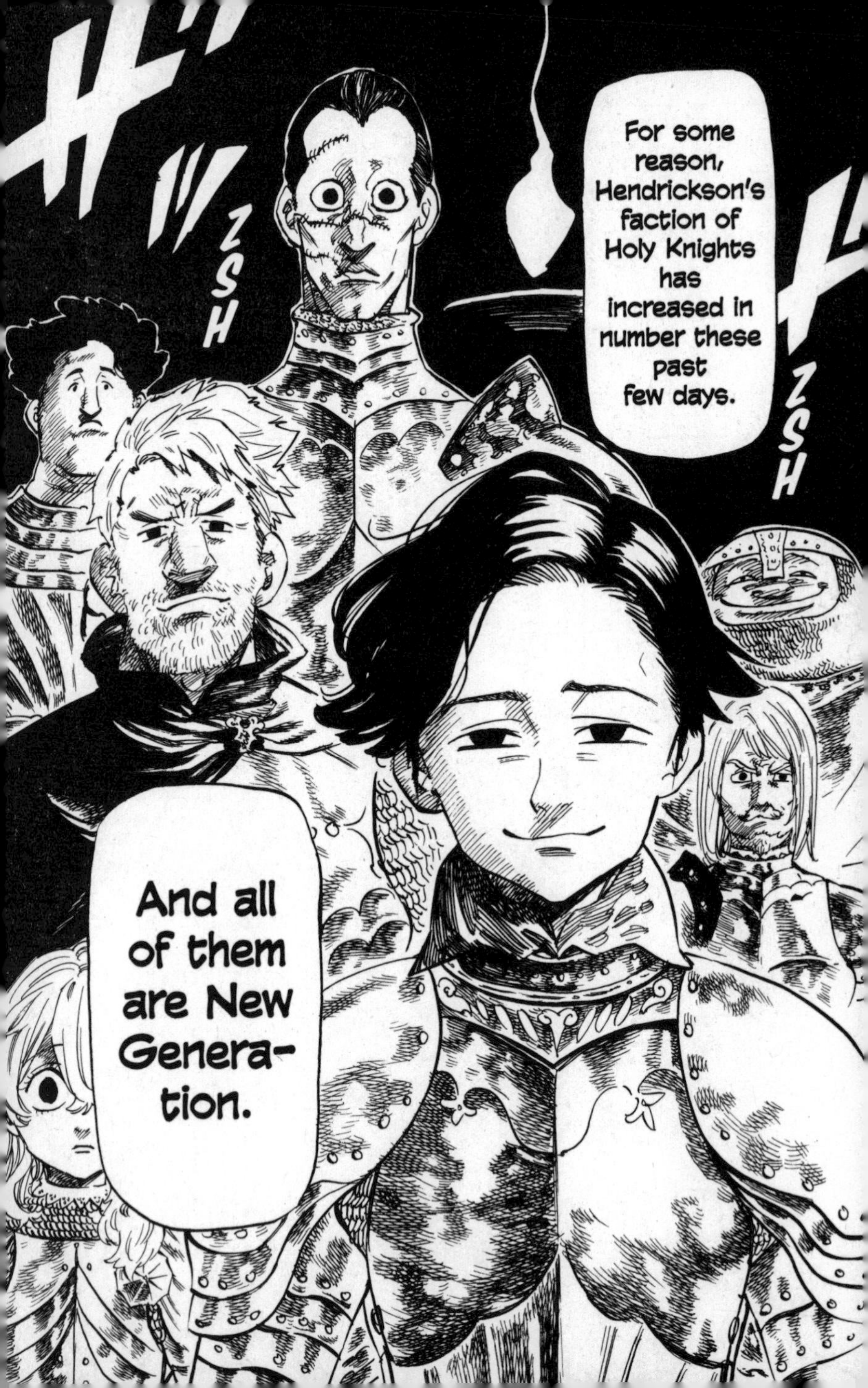

For some reason, Hendrickson's faction of Holy Knights has increased in number these past few days.
ZSH
ZSH
And all of them are New Genera-tion.

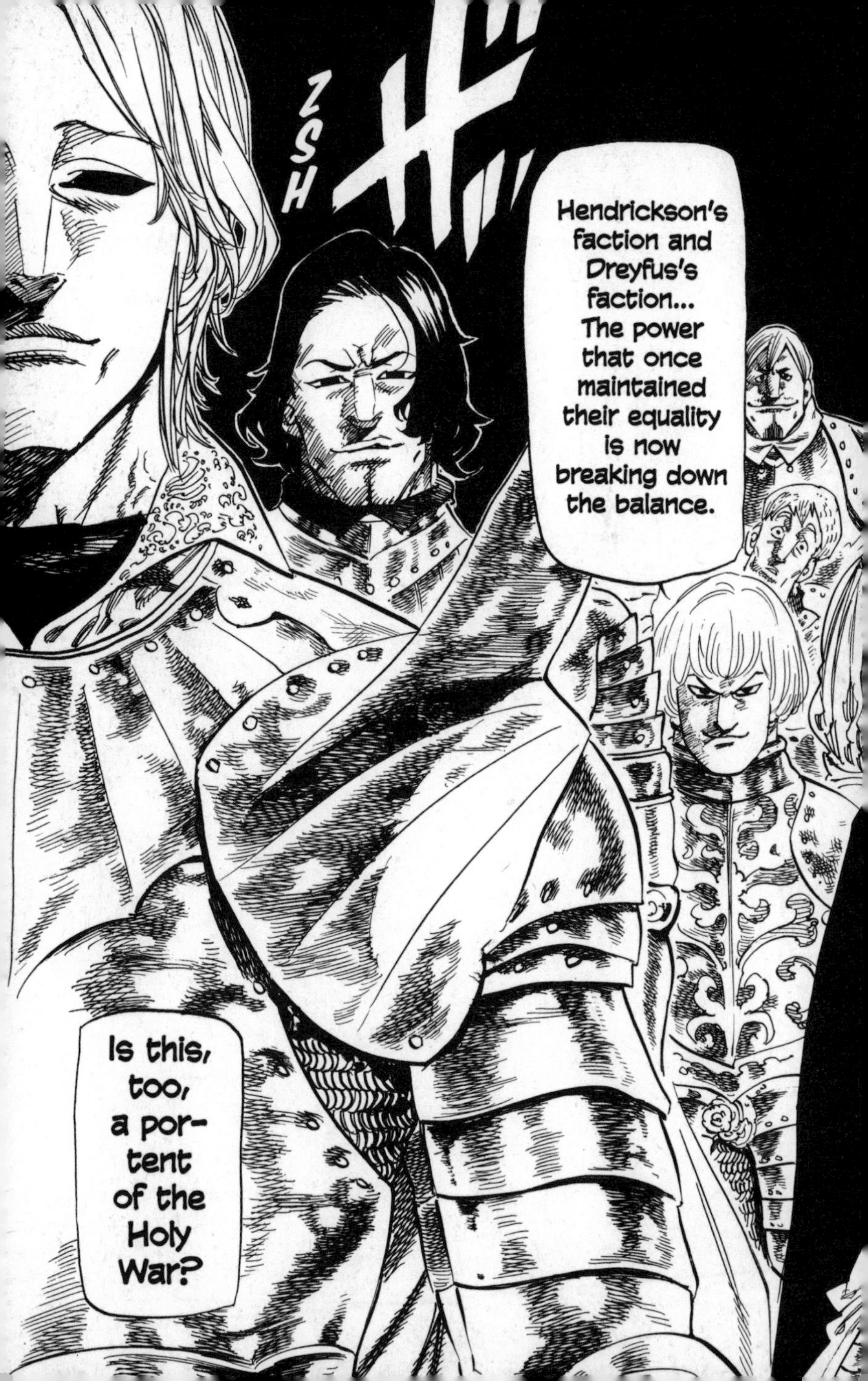
ZSH
Hendrickson's faction and Dreyfus's faction... The power that once maintained their equality is now breaking down the balance.
Is this, too, a portent of the Holy War?

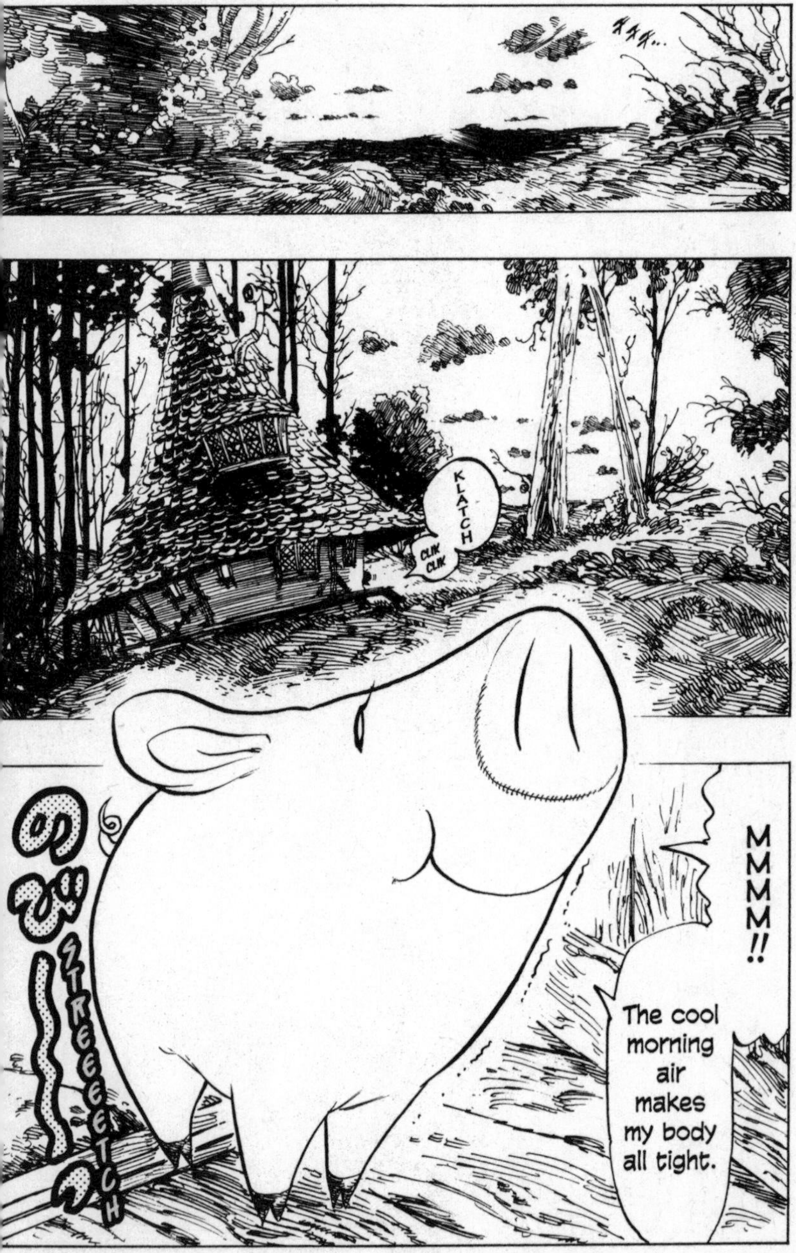
KLATCH
CLIK CLIK
MMMM!!
The cool morning air makes my body all tight.
STREEEETCH

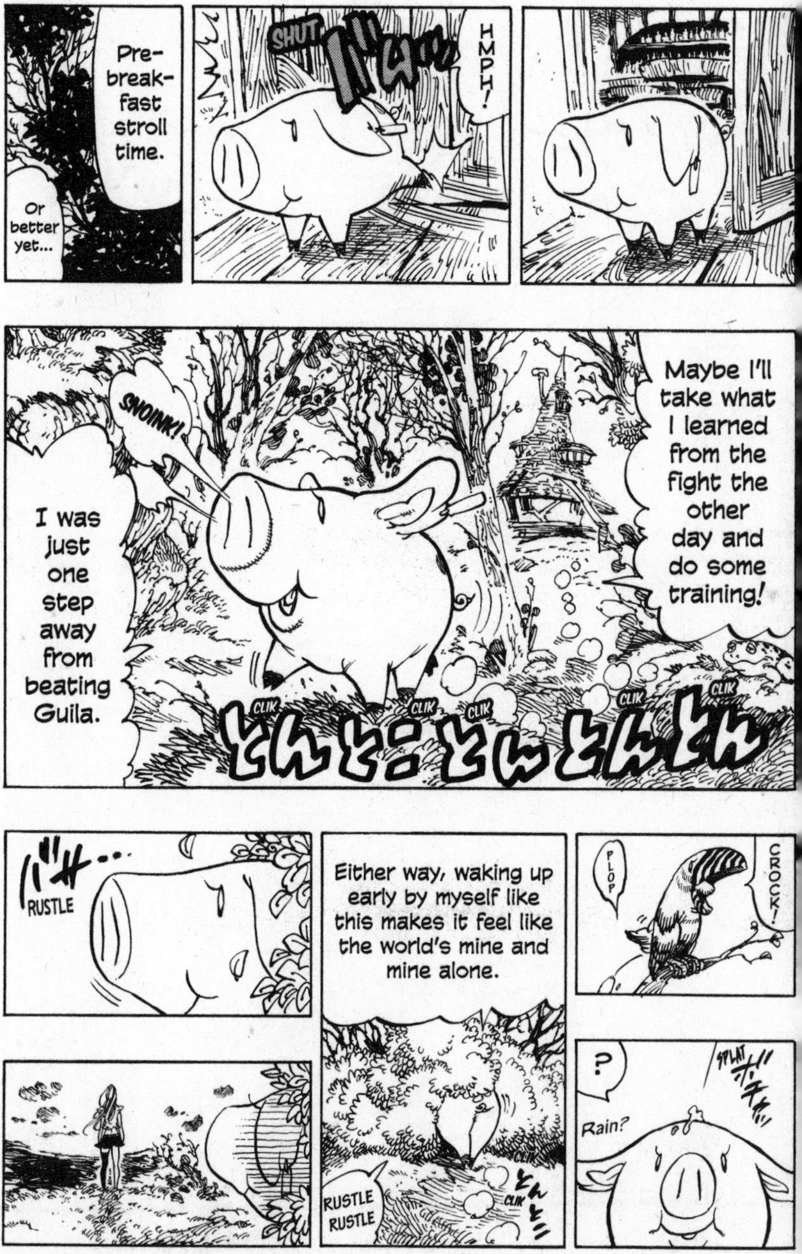
SHUT
HMPH!
Pre-breakfast stroll time.
Or better yet...
Maybe I'll take what I learned from the fight the other day and do some training!
SNOINK!
I was just one step away from beating Guila.
CLIK
CLIK
CLIK
CLIK
CLIK
CROCK!
PLOP
SPLAT
?
Rain?
Either way, waking up early by myself like this makes it feel like the world's mine and mine alone.
RUSTLE RUSTLE
CLIK
RUSTLE

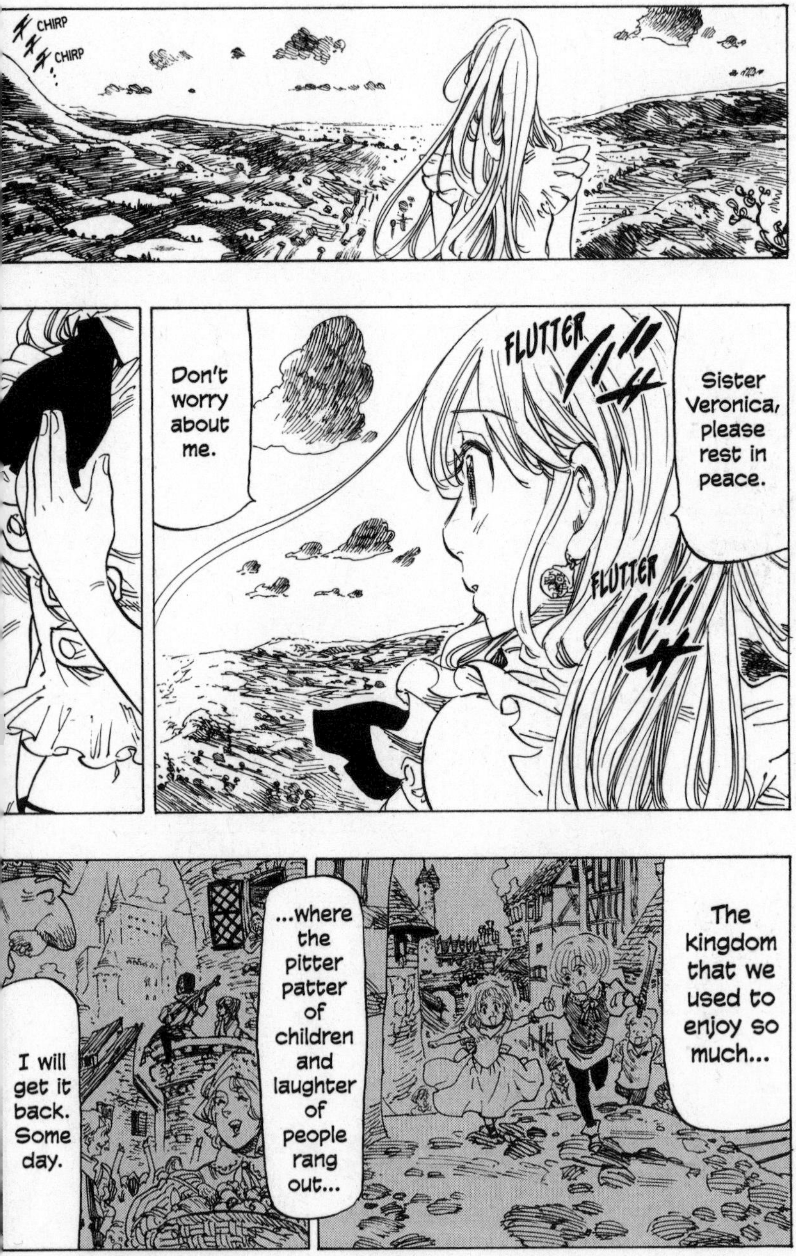
CHIRP
CHIRP
FLUTTER
Sister Veronica, please rest in peace.
FLUTTER
Don't worry about me.
The kingdom that we used to enjoy so much...
...where the pitter patter of children and laughter of people rang out...
I will get it back. Some day.

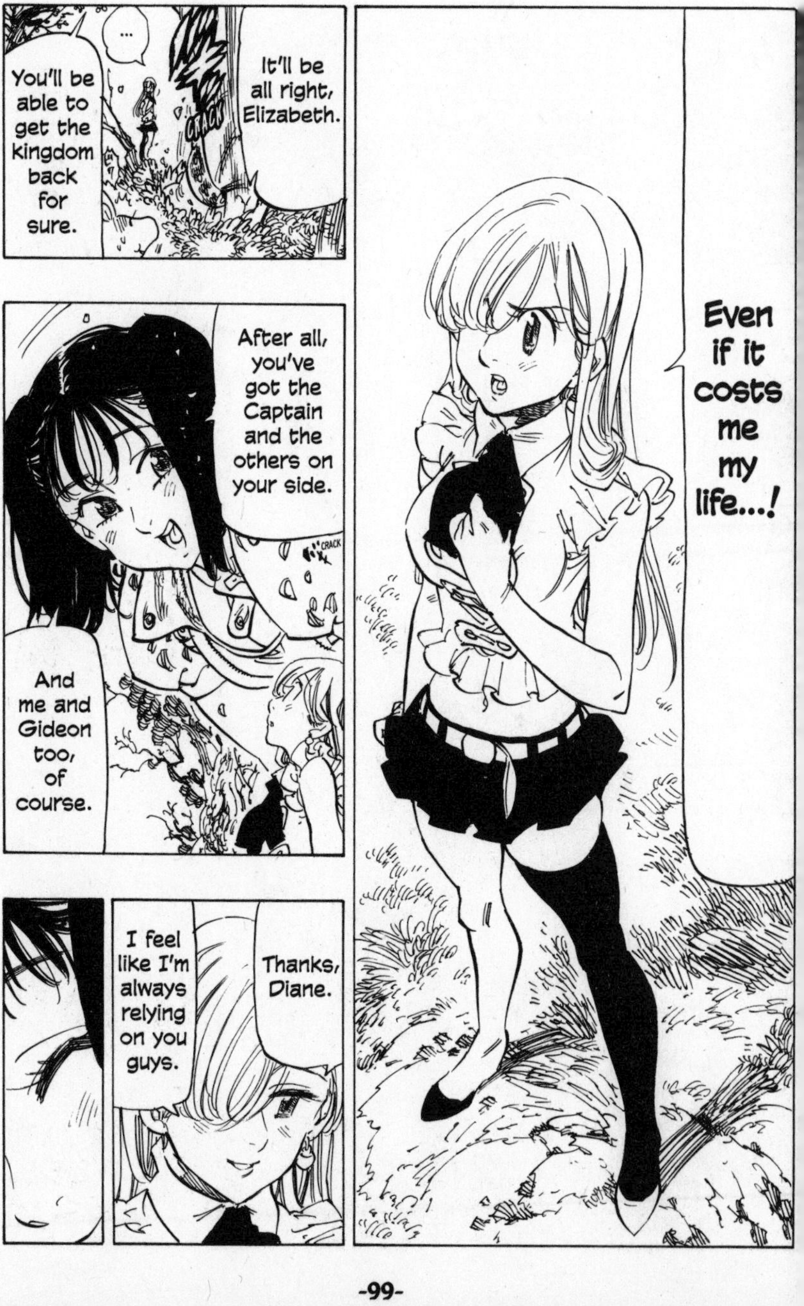
Even if it costs me my life...!
...
It'll be all right, Elizabeth.
CRACK
You'll be able to get the kingdom back for sure.
After all, you've got the Captain and the others on your side.
CRACK
And me and Gideon too, of course.
Thanks, Diane.
I feel like I'm always relying on you guys.

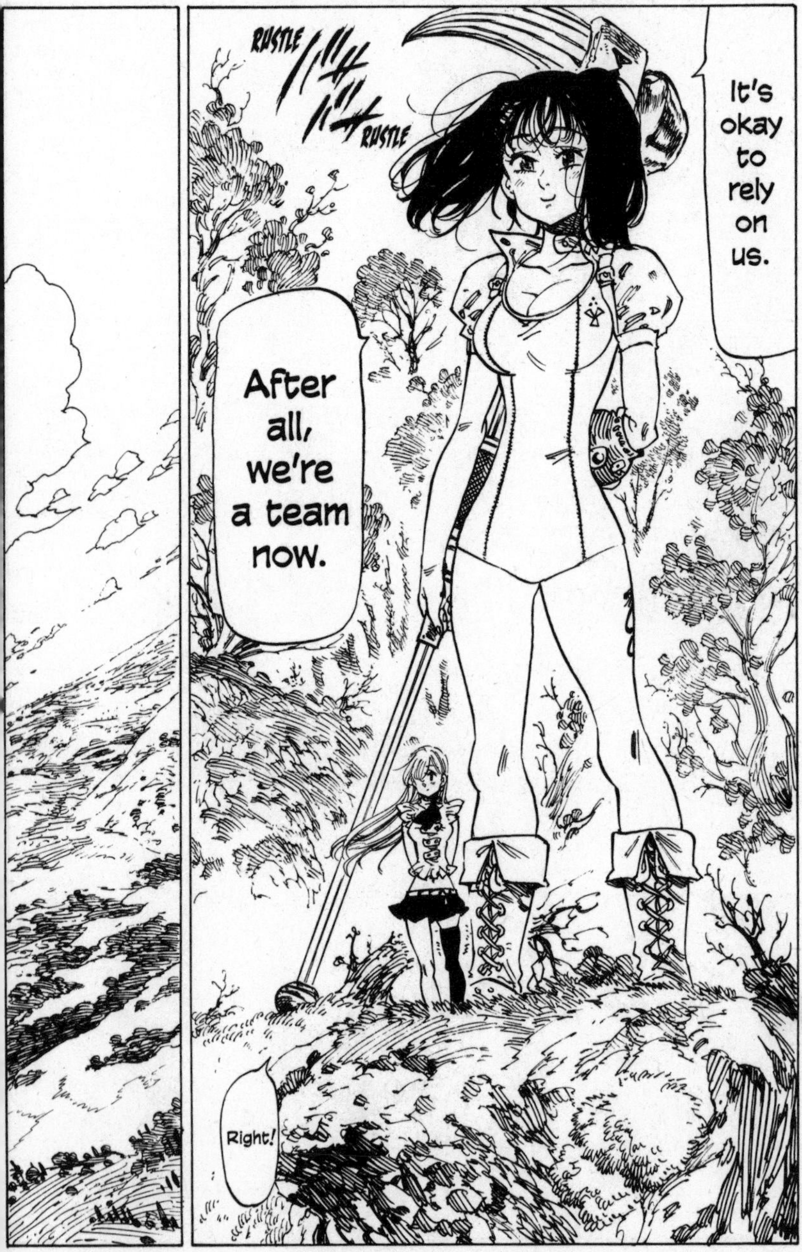
It's okay to rely on us.
RUSTLE
RUSTLE
After all, we're a team now.
Right!

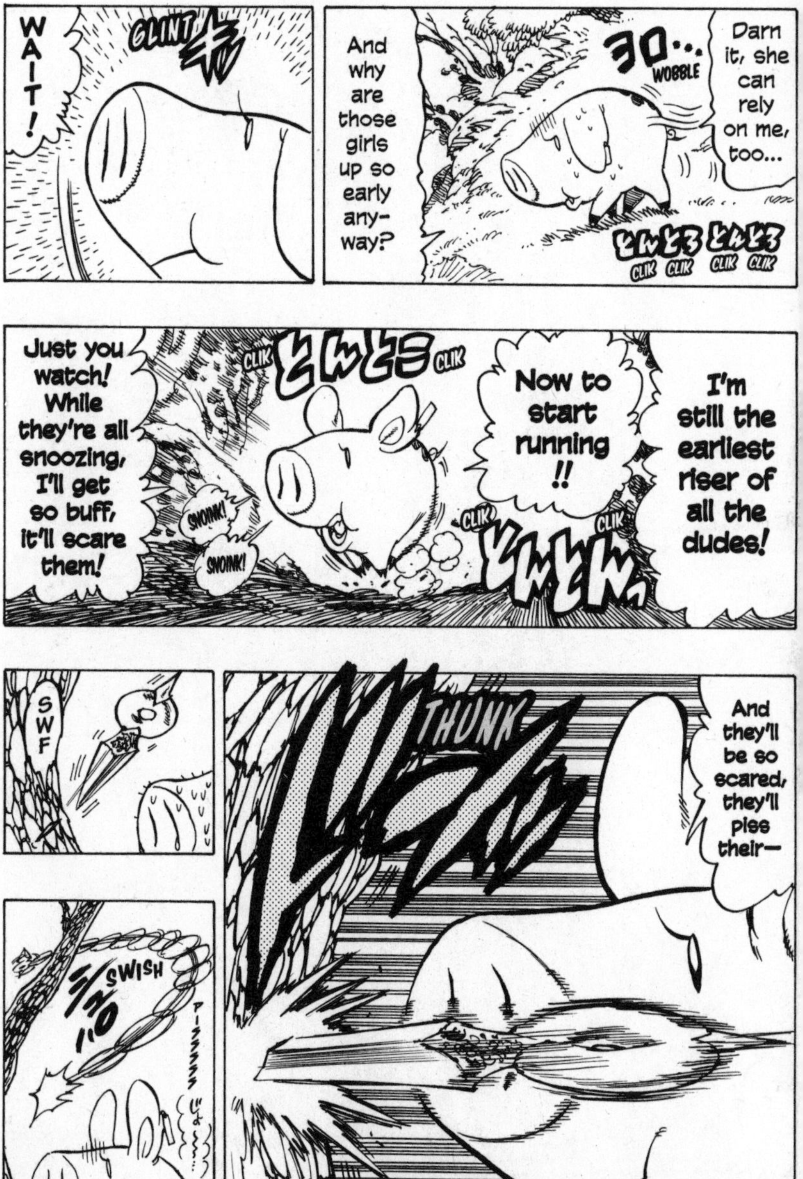
Darn it, she can rely on me, too...
ヨロ...
WOBBLE
And why are those girls up so early anyway?
とんとろ とんとろ
CLIK CLIK CLIK CLIK
GLINT
WAIT!
I'm still the earliest riser of all the dudes!
CLIK
CLIK
Now to start running!!
CLIK
CLIK
SNOINK!
SNOINK!
Just you watch! While they're all snoozing, I'll get so buff, it'll scare them!
And they'll be so scared, they'll piss their—
THUNK
SWF
SWISH

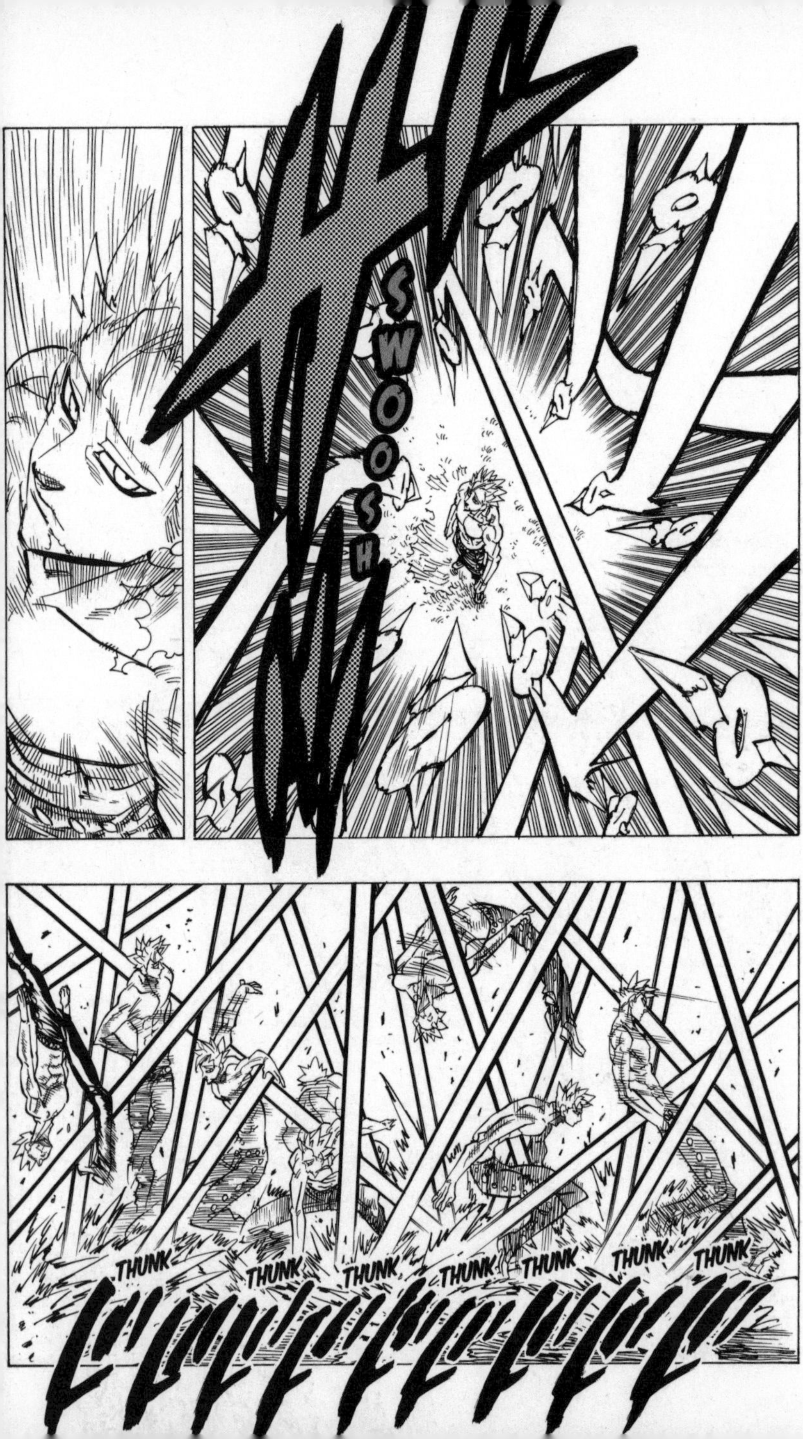
SWOOSH
THUNK
THUNK
THUNK
THUNK
THUNK
THUNK
THUNK

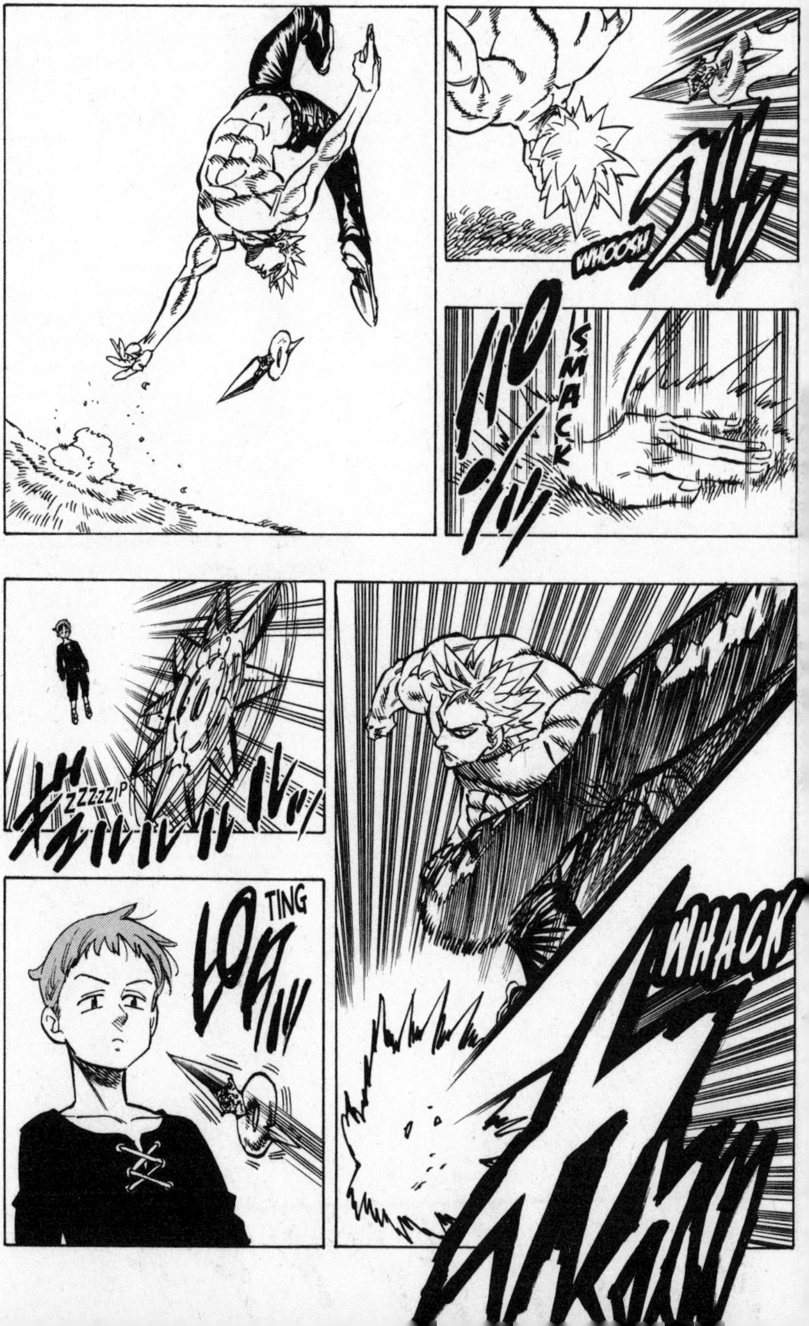
WHOOSH
SMACK
WHACK
ZZZZZIP
TING

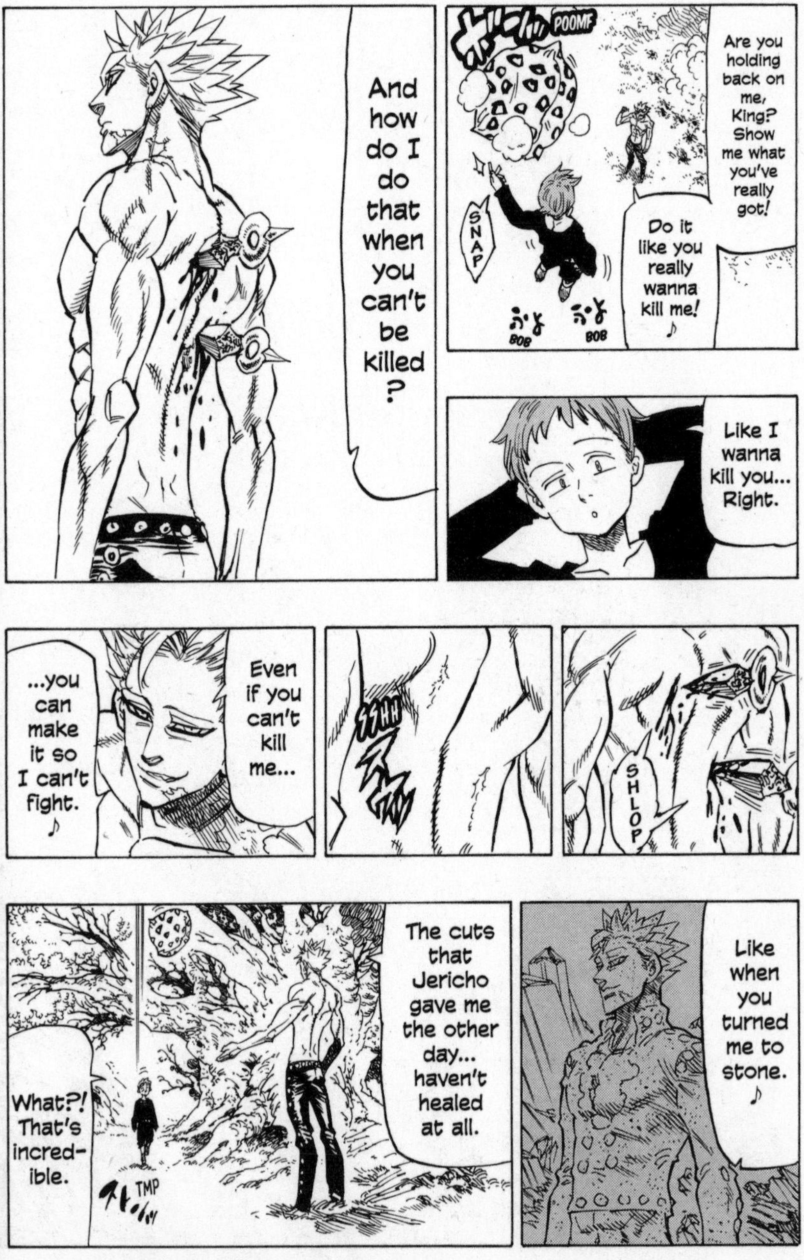
POOMF
Are you holding back on me, King? Show me what you've really got!
Do it like you really wanna kill me! ♪
SNAP
BOB
BOB
Like I wanna kill you... Right.
And how do I do that when you can't be killed?
SHLOP
SSHH
Even if you can't kill me...
...you can make it so I can't fight. ♪
Like when you turned me to stone. ♪
The cuts that Jericho gave me the other day... haven't healed at all.
What?! That's incredible.
TMP

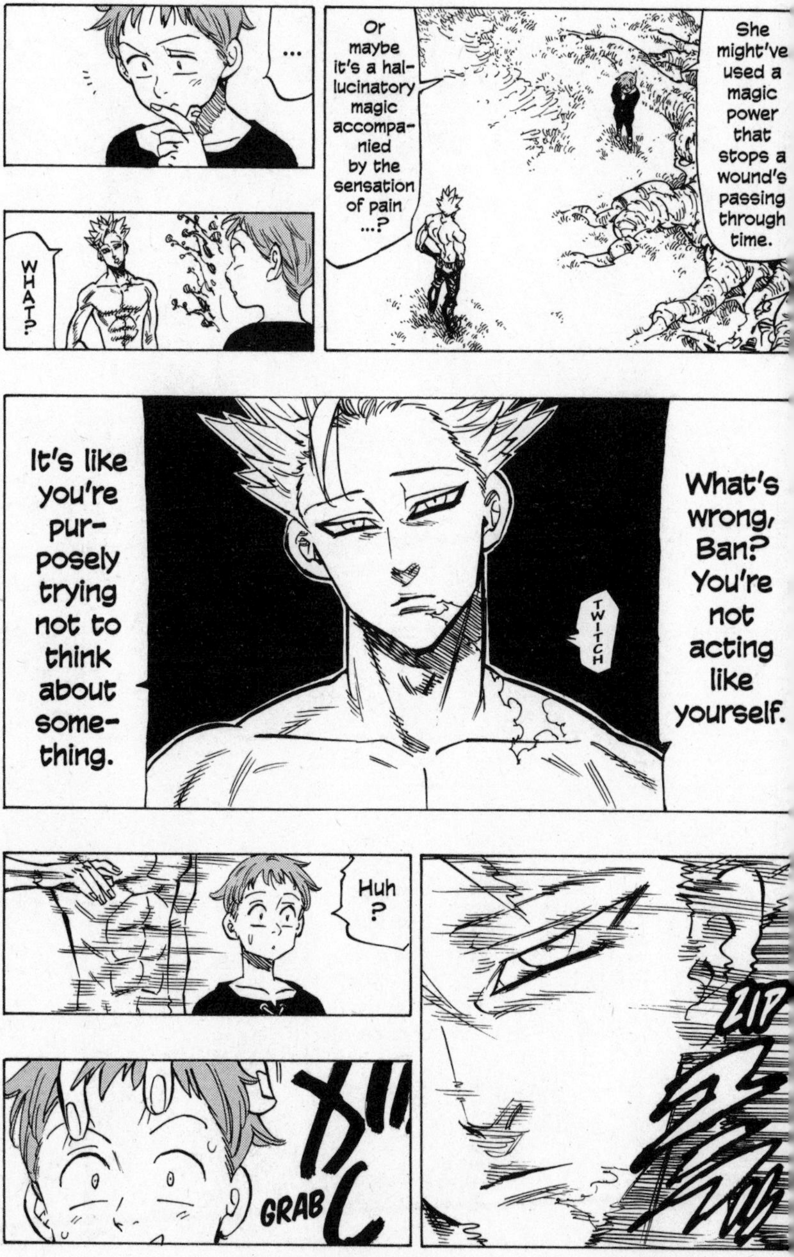
She might've used a magic power that stops a wound's passing through time.
Or maybe it's a hallucinatory magic accompanied by the sensation of pain...?
...
WHAT?
What's wrong, Ban? You're not acting like yourself.
TWITCH
It's like you're purposely trying not to think about something.
ZIP
Huh?
GRAB

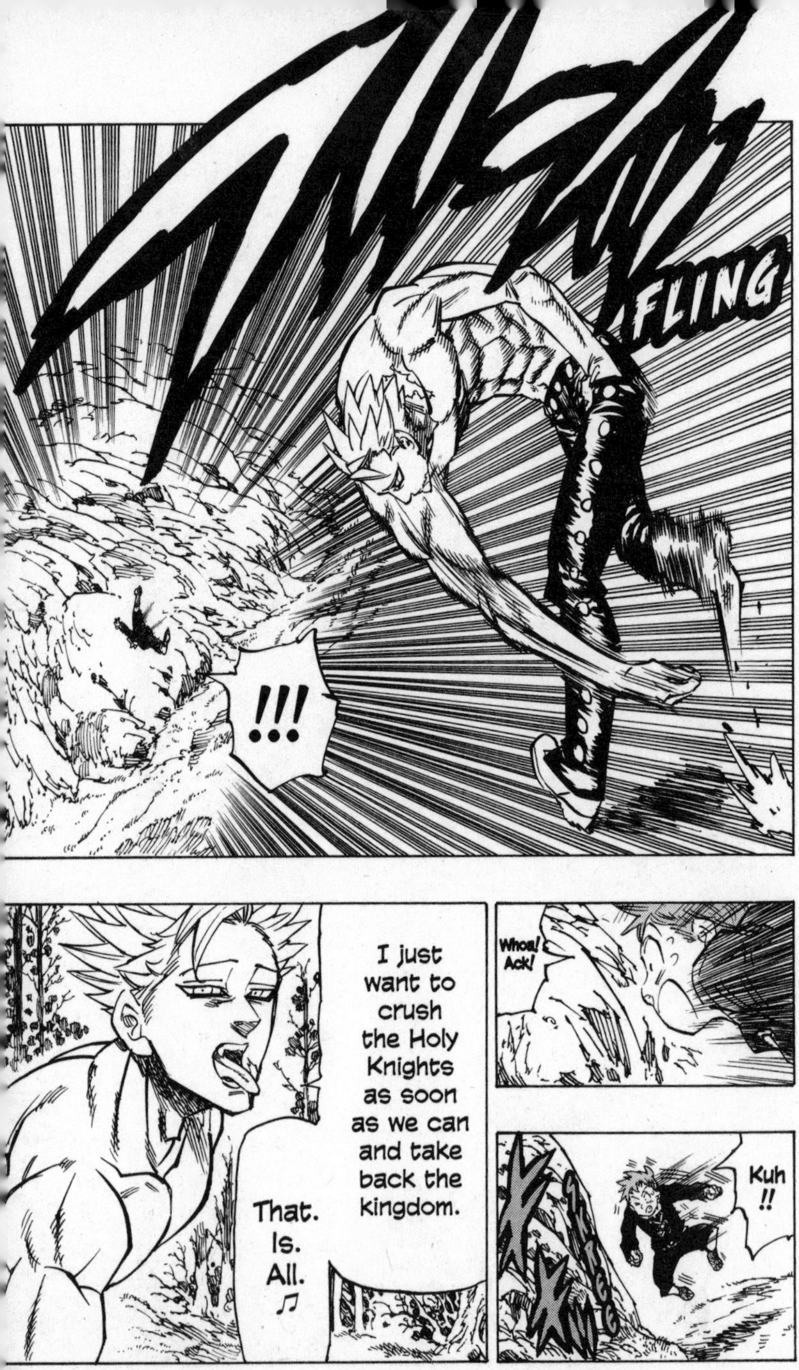
FLING
!!!
Whoa! Ack!
Kuh!!
I just want to crush the Holy Knights as soon as we can and take back the kingdom.
That. Is. All. ♫

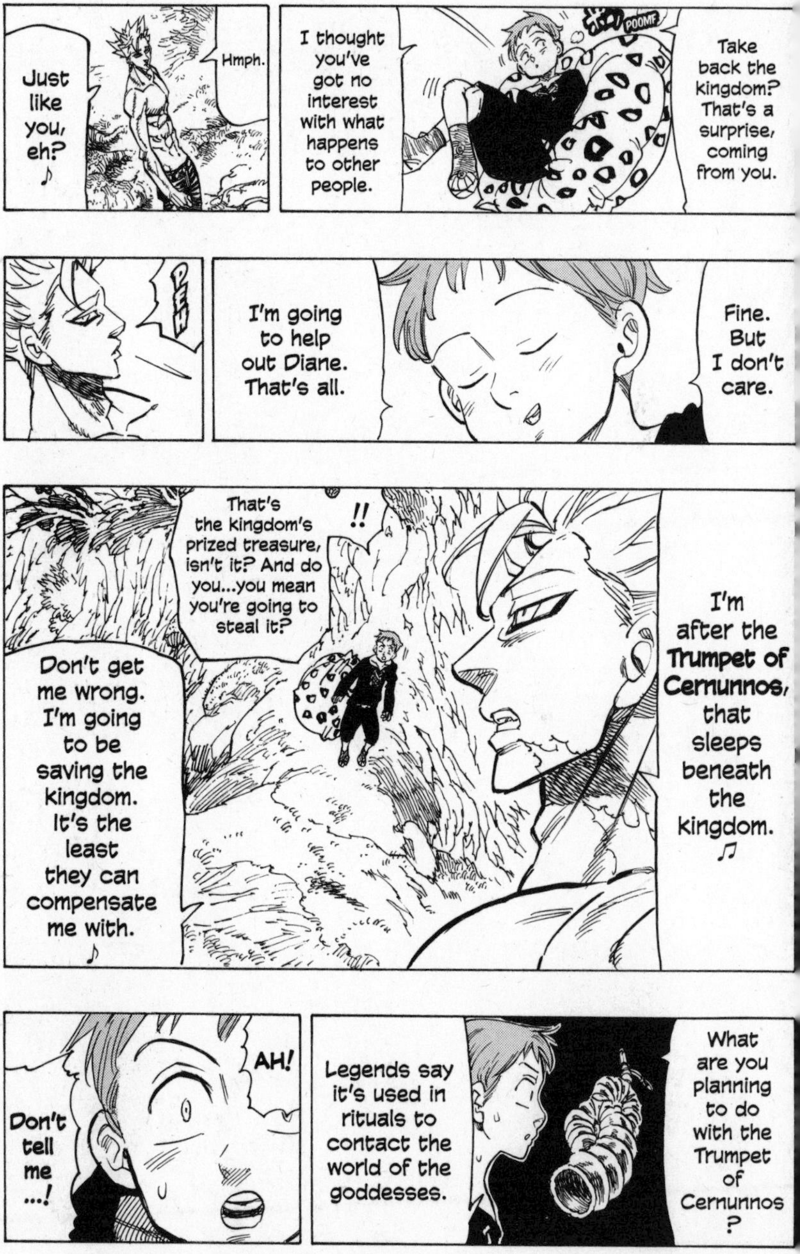
Take back the kingdom? That's a surprise, coming from you.
POOMF
I thought you've got no interest with what happens to other people.
Hmph.
Just like you, eh? ♪
Fine. But I don't care.
I'm going to help out Diane. That's all.
PEW
I'm after the **Trumpet of Cernunnos,** that sleeps beneath the kingdom. ♫
That's the kingdom's prized treasure, isn't it? And do you...you mean you're going to steal it?
!!
Don't get me wrong. I'm going to be saving the kingdom. It's the least they can compensate me with. ♪
What are you planning to do with the Trumpet of Cernunnos?
Legends say it's used in rituals to contact the world of the goddesses.
AH!
Don't tell me ...!

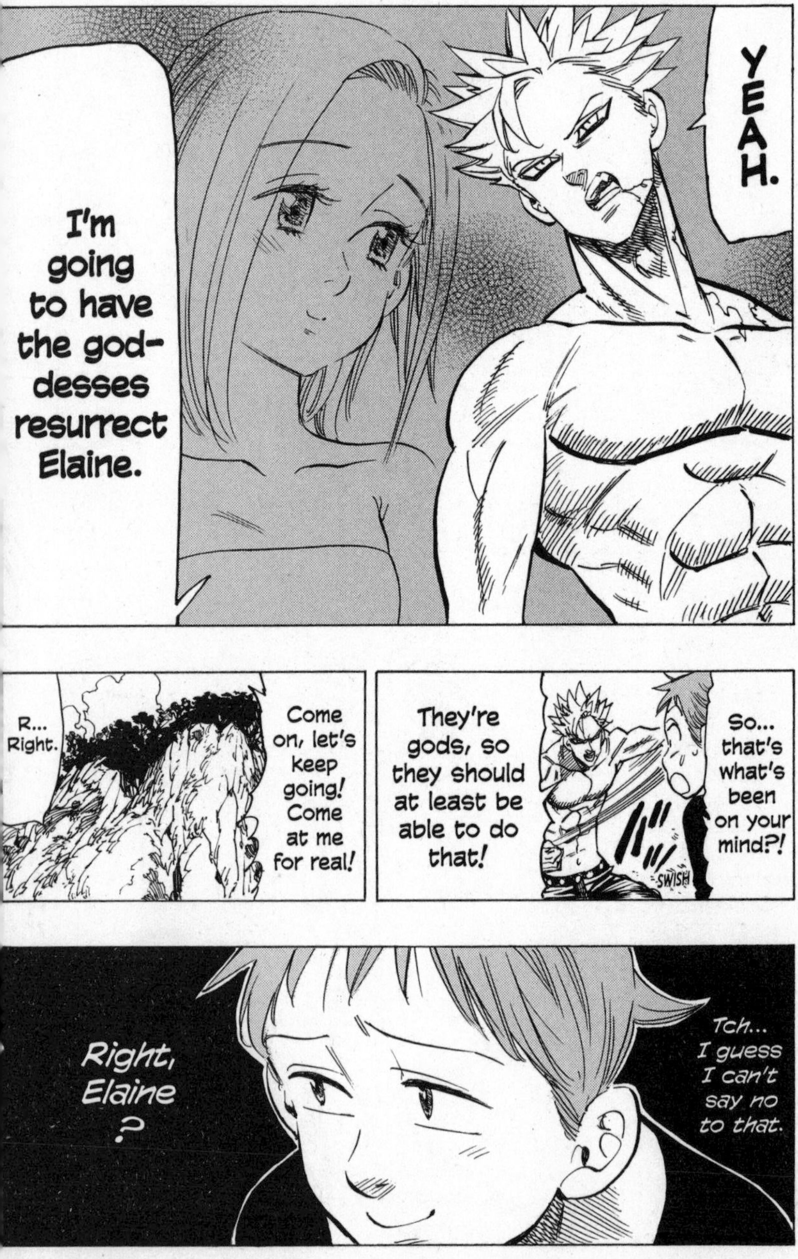
YEAH.
I'm going to have the god-desses resurrect Elaine.
So... that's what's been on your mind?!
SWISH
They're gods, so they should at least be able to do that!
Come on, let's keep going! Come at me for real!
R... Right.
Tch... I guess I can't say no to that.
Right, Elaine?

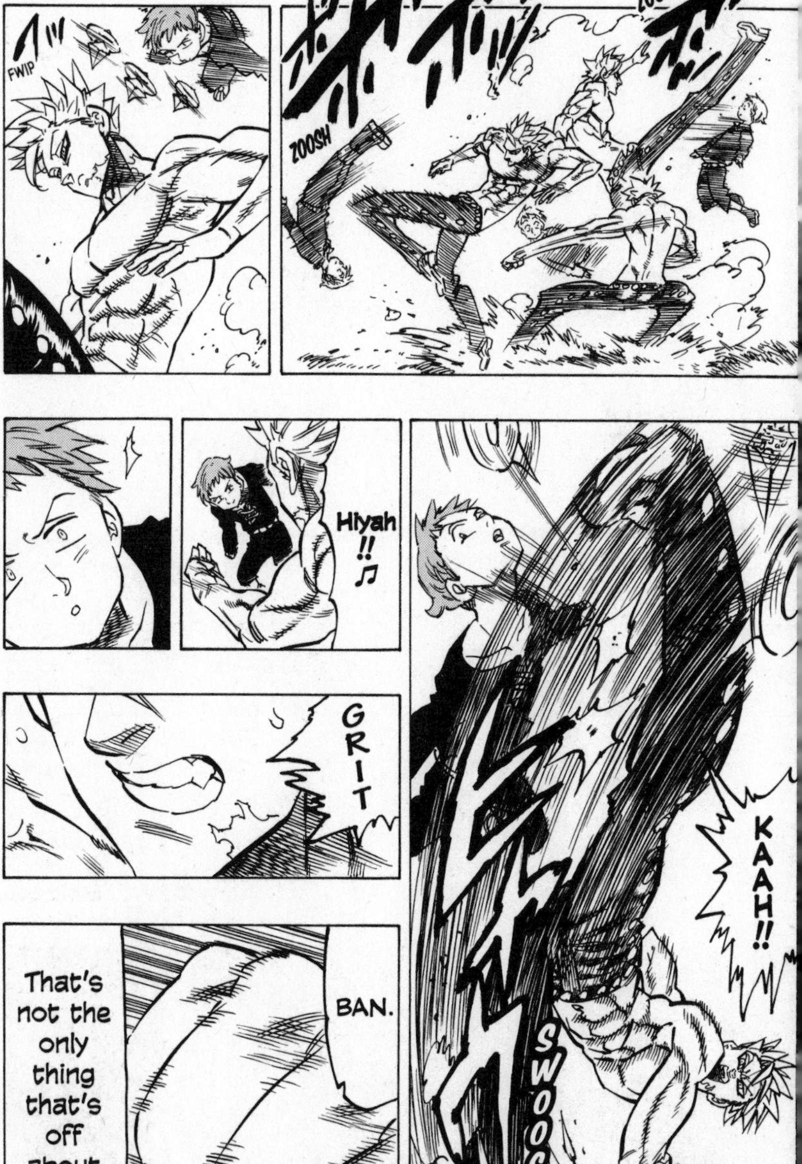
ZOOSH
ZOOSH
ZOOSH
FWIP
KAAH!!
SWOOSH
Hiyah!! ♫
GRIT
BAN.
That's not the only thing that's off about you.

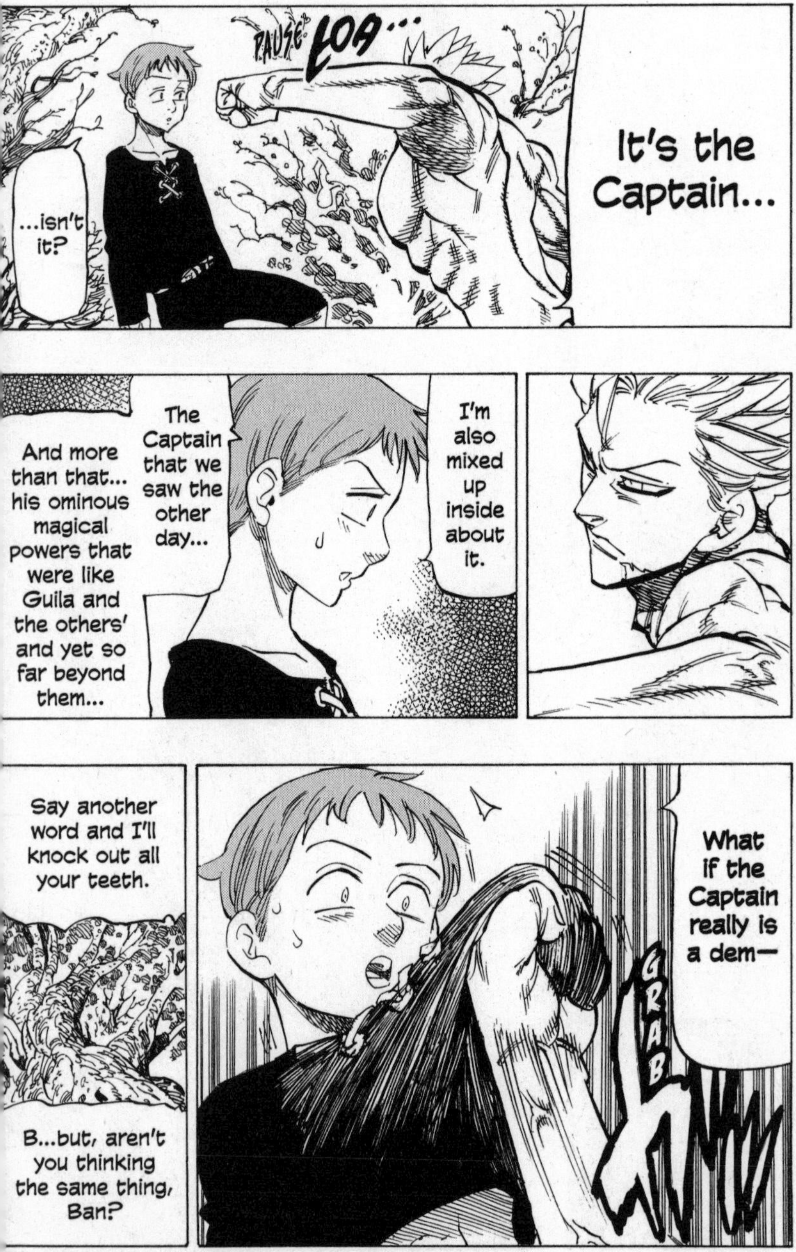
It's the Captain...
PAUSE
...isn't it?
I'm also mixed up inside about it.
The Captain that we saw the other day...
And more than that... his ominous magical powers that were like Guila and the others' and yet so far beyond them...
What if the Captain really is a dem—
GRAB
Say another word and I'll knock out all your teeth.
B...but, aren't you thinking the same thing, Ban?

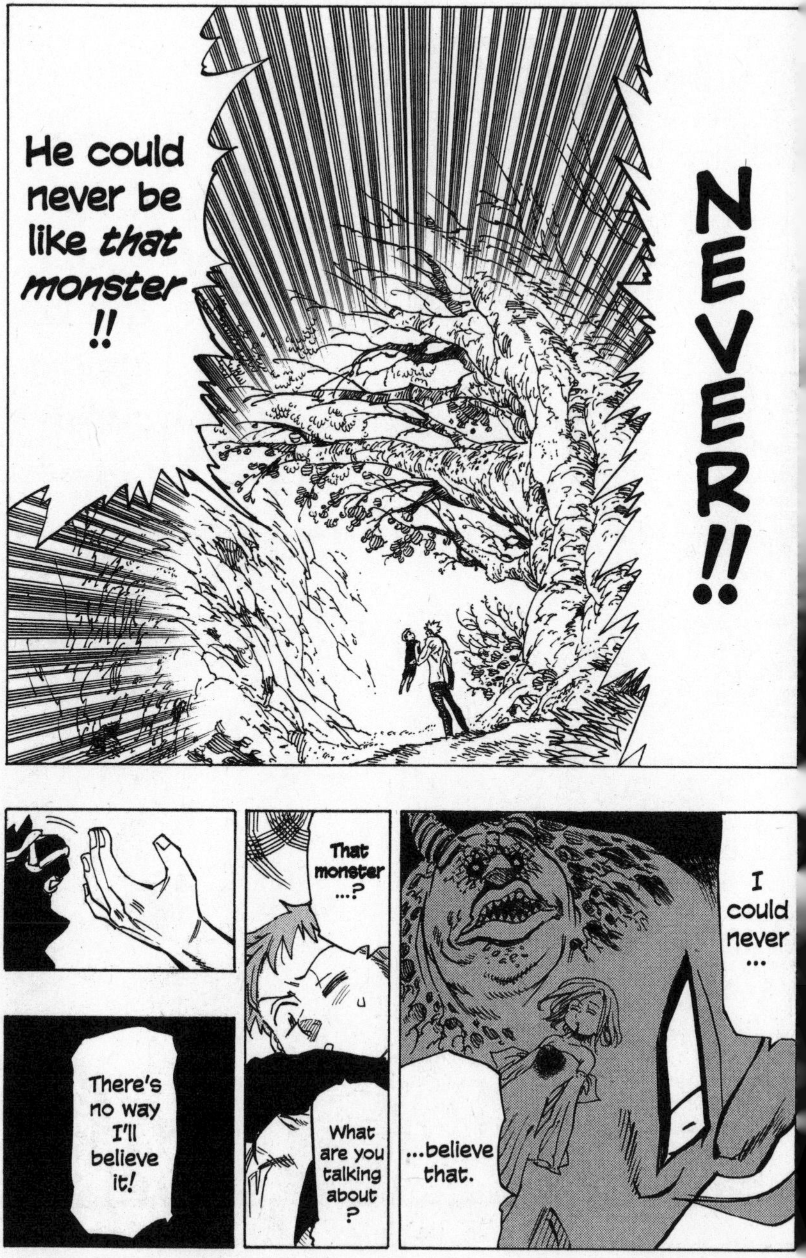
He could never be like *that monster*!!
NEVER!!
I could never...
...believe that.
That monster...?
What are you talking about?
There's no way I'll believe it!

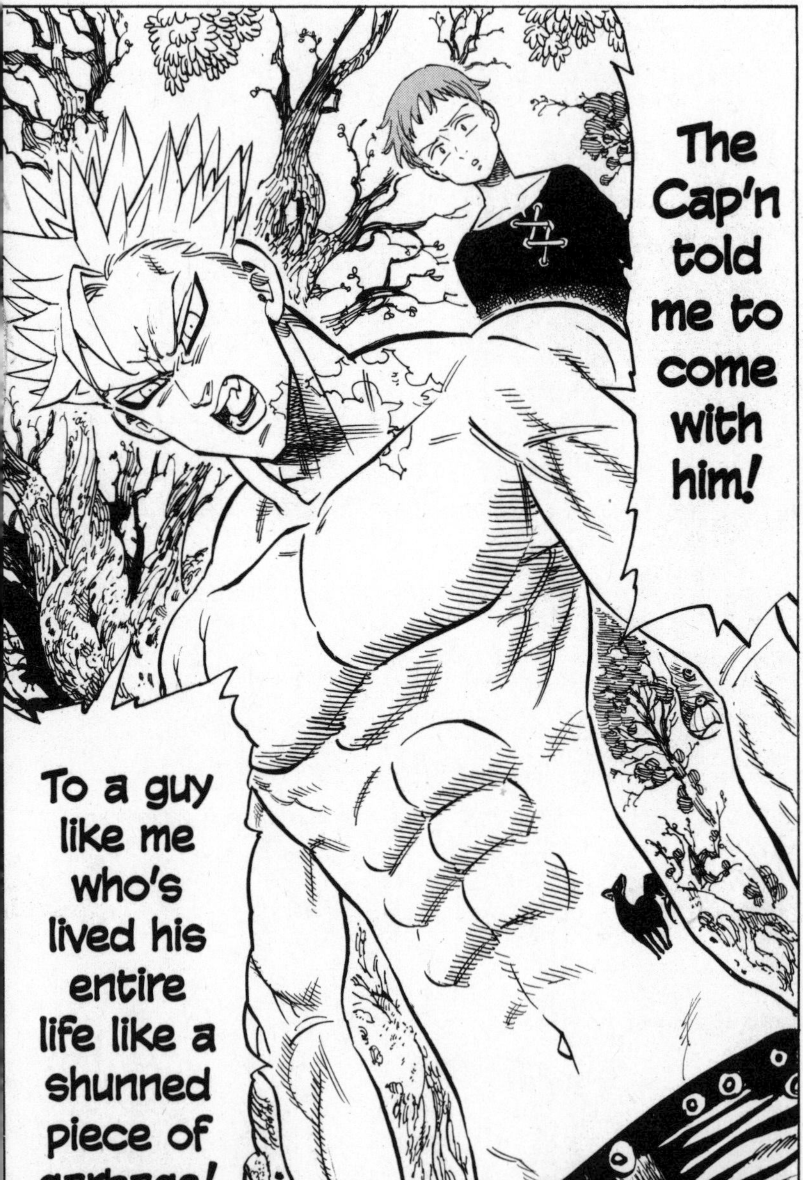
The Cap'n told me to come with him!
To a guy like me who's lived his entire life like a shunned piece of garbage!

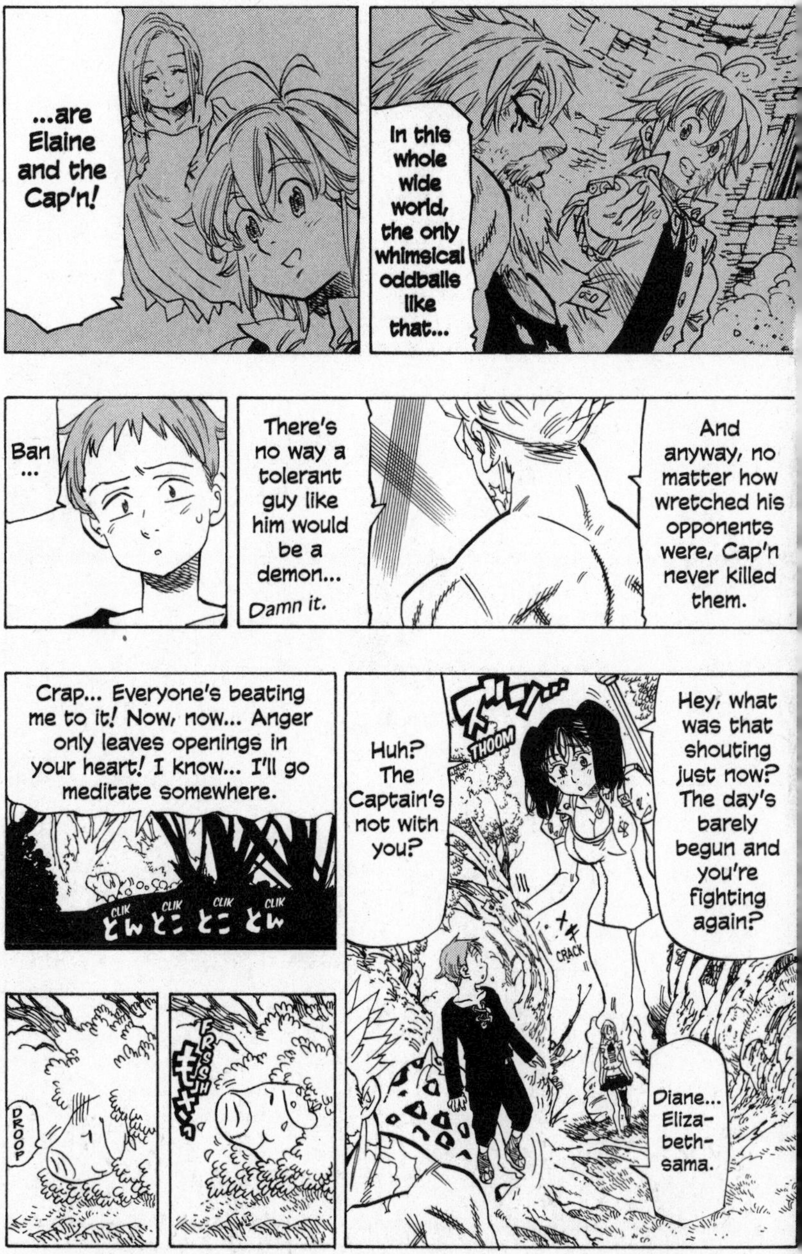
In this whole wide world, the only whimsical oddballs like that...
...are Elaine and the Cap'n!
And anyway, no matter how wretched his opponents were, Cap'n never killed them.
There's no way a tolerant guy like him would be a demon...
Damn it.
Ban ...
Hey, what was that shouting just now? The day's barely begun and you're fighting again?
THOOM
Huh? The Captain's not with you?
CRACK
Diane... Elizabeth-sama.
Crap... Everyone's beating me to it! Now, now... Anger only leaves openings in your heart! I know... I'll go meditate somewhere.
CLIK CLIK CLIK CLIK
FRSSH
DROOP

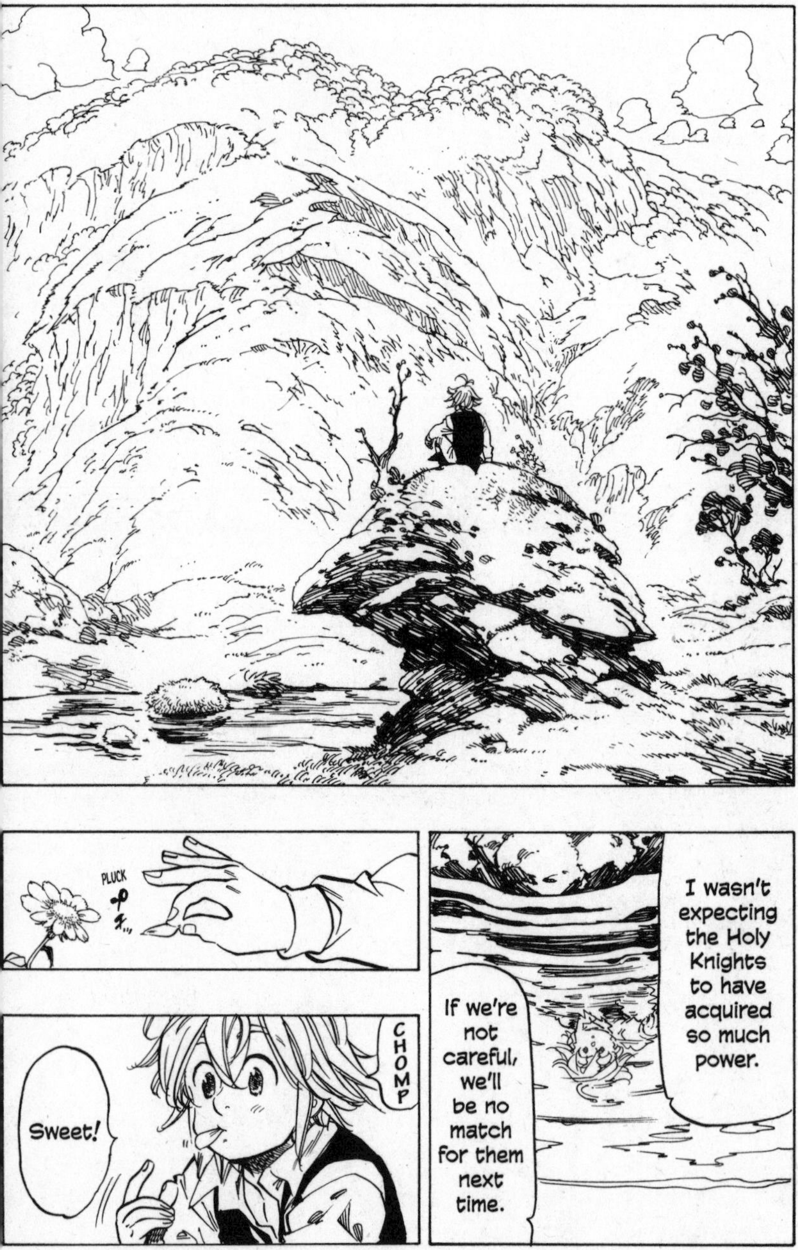

I wasn't expecting the Holy Knights to have acquired so much power.
If we're not careful, we'll be no match for them next time.
PLUCK
CHOMP
Sweet!

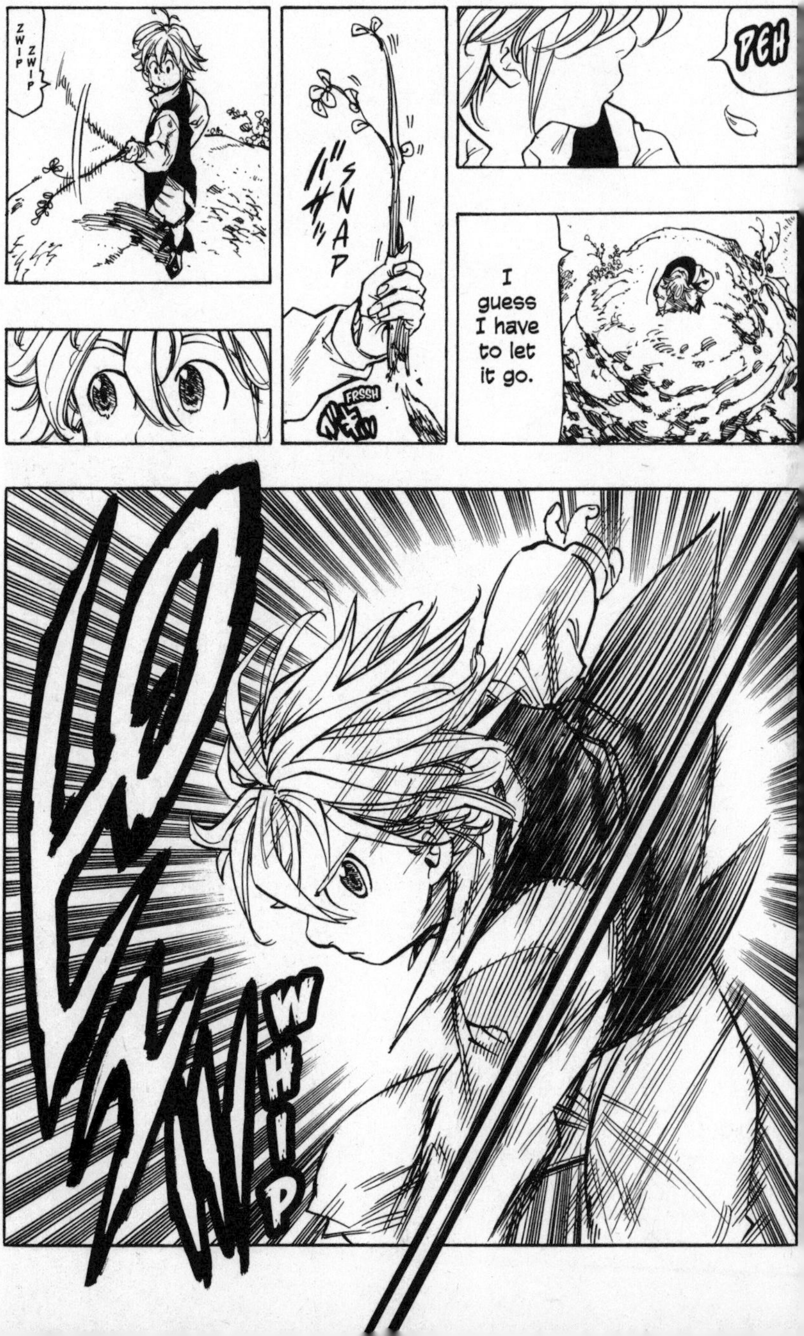
PEH
I guess I have to let it go.
SNAP
FRSSH
ZWIP ZWIP
WHIP

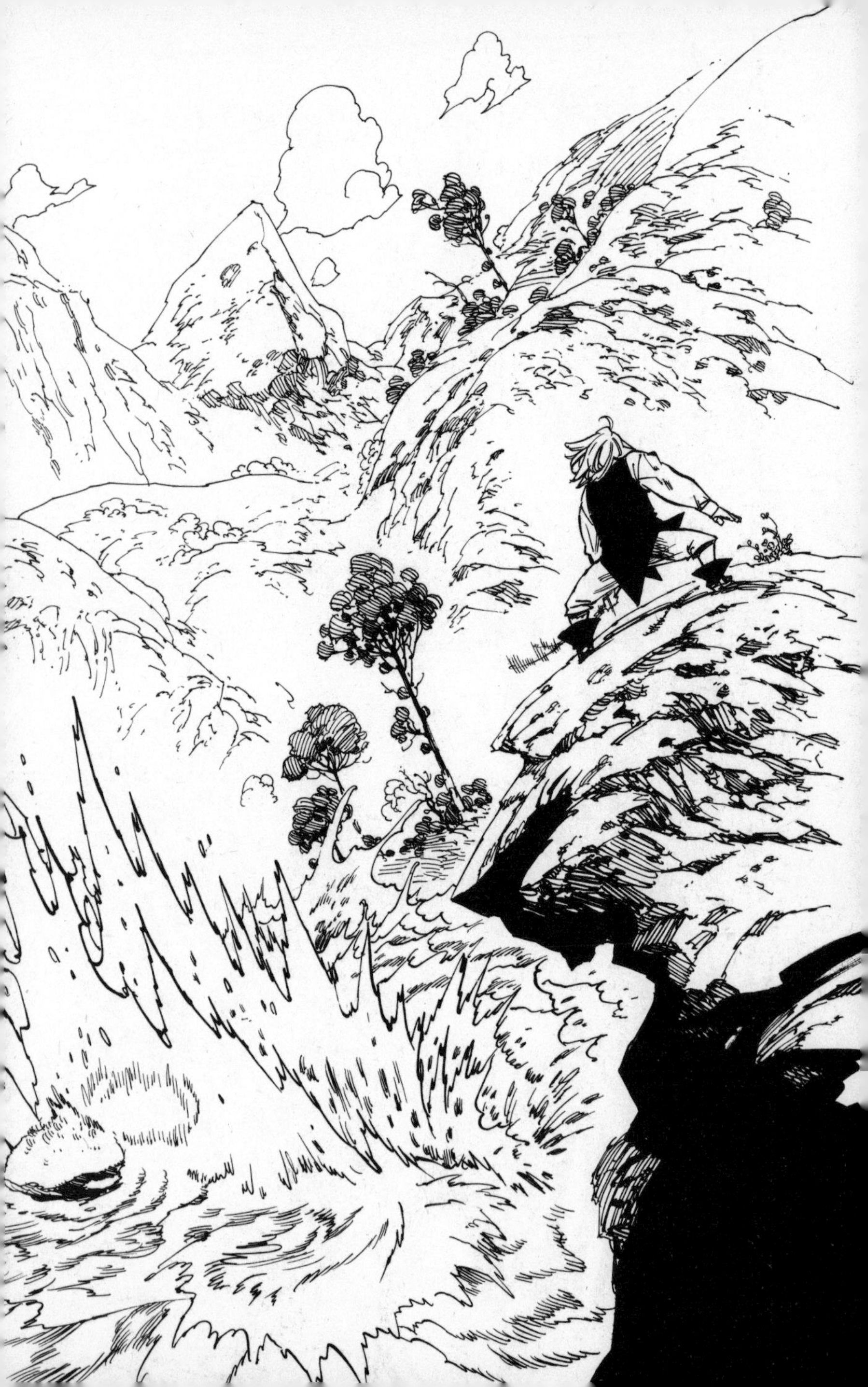

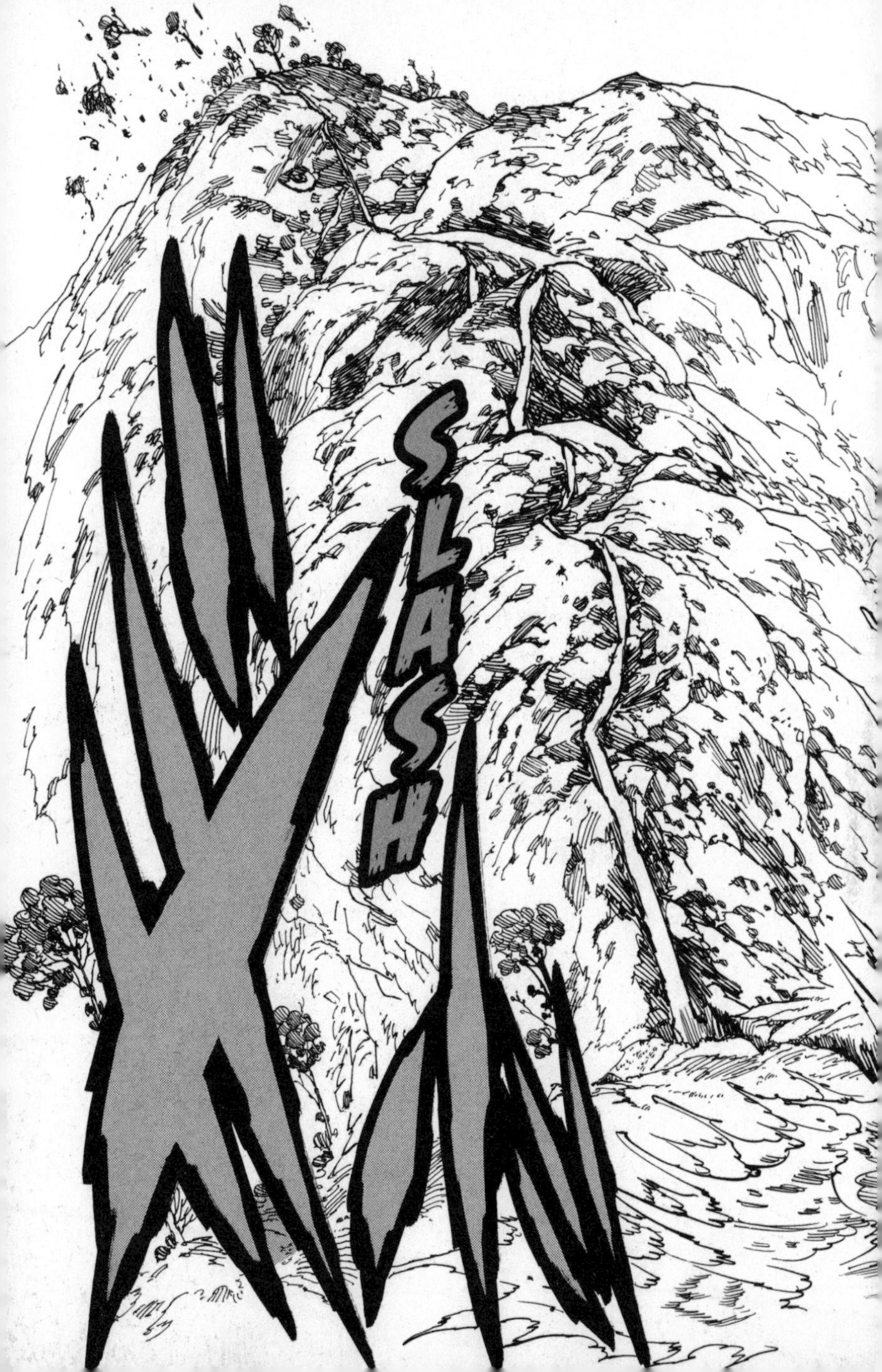
SLASH

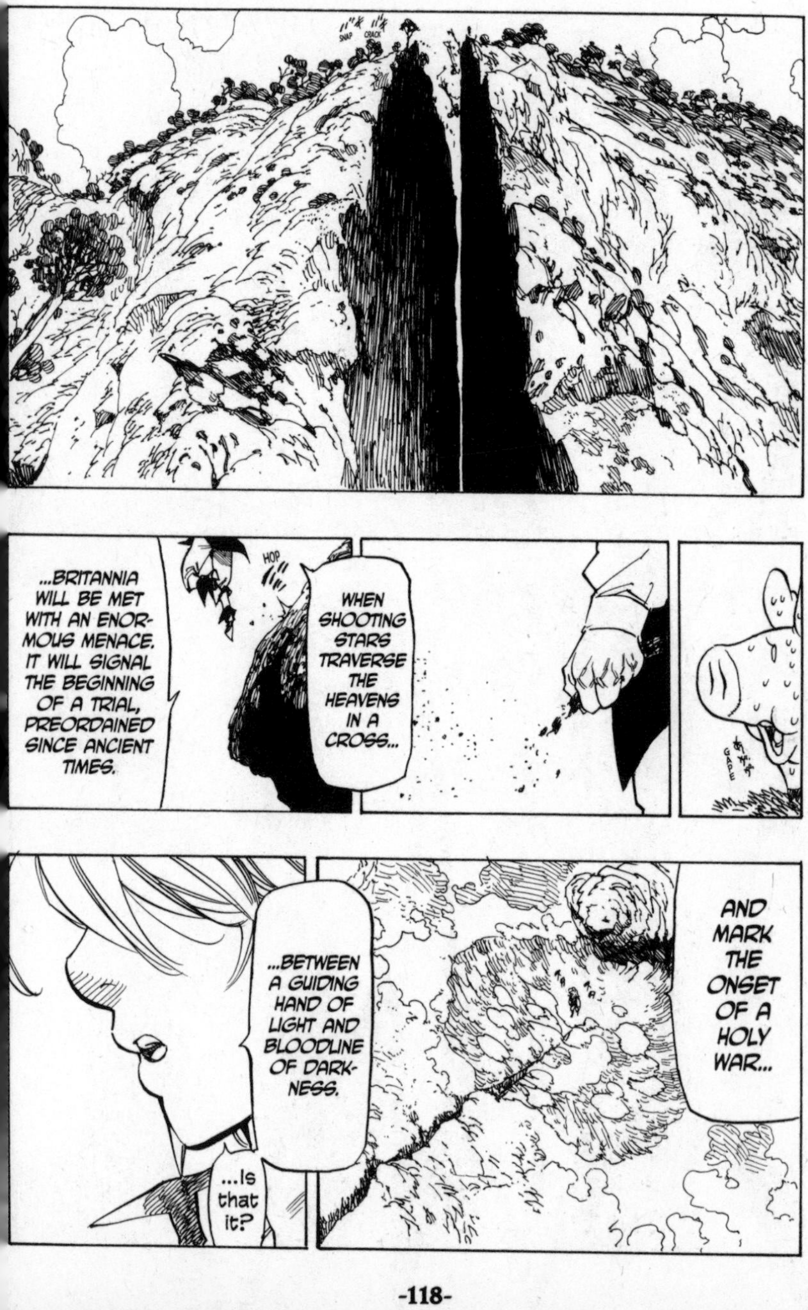
SNAP
CRACK
GAPE
WHEN SHOOTING STARS TRAVERSE THE HEAVENS IN A CROSS...
HOP
...BRITANNIA WILL BE MET WITH AN ENORMOUS MENACE. IT WILL SIGNAL THE BEGINNING OF A TRIAL, PREORDAINED SINCE ANCIENT TIMES.
AND MARK THE ONSET OF A HOLY WAR...
...BETWEEN A GUIDING HAND OF LIGHT AND BLOODLINE OF DARKNESS.
...Is that it?

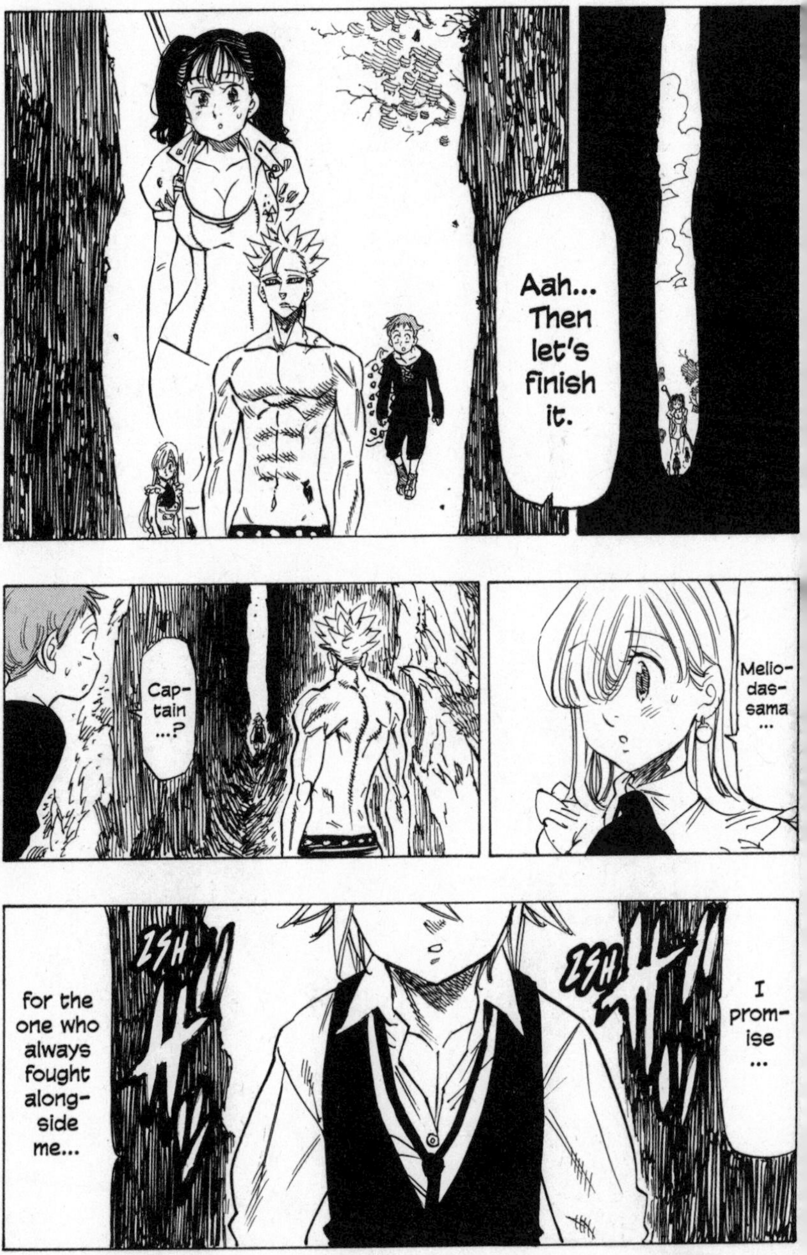
Aah... Then let's finish it.
Melio-das-sama ...
Cap-tain ...?
I prom-ise ...
ZSH
ZSH
for the one who always fought along-side me...

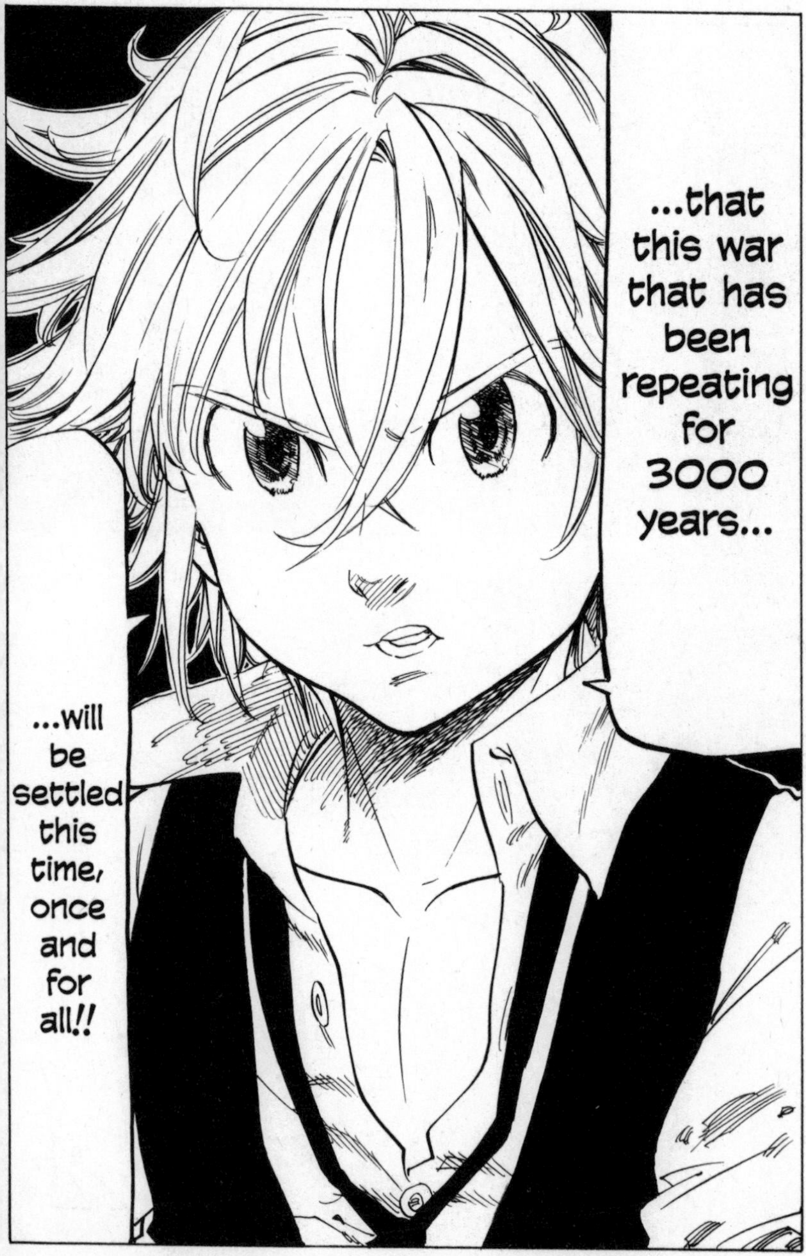
...that this war that has been repeating for 3000 years...
...will be settled this time, once and for all!!

Chapter 52 - The Truth Behind the Rumors

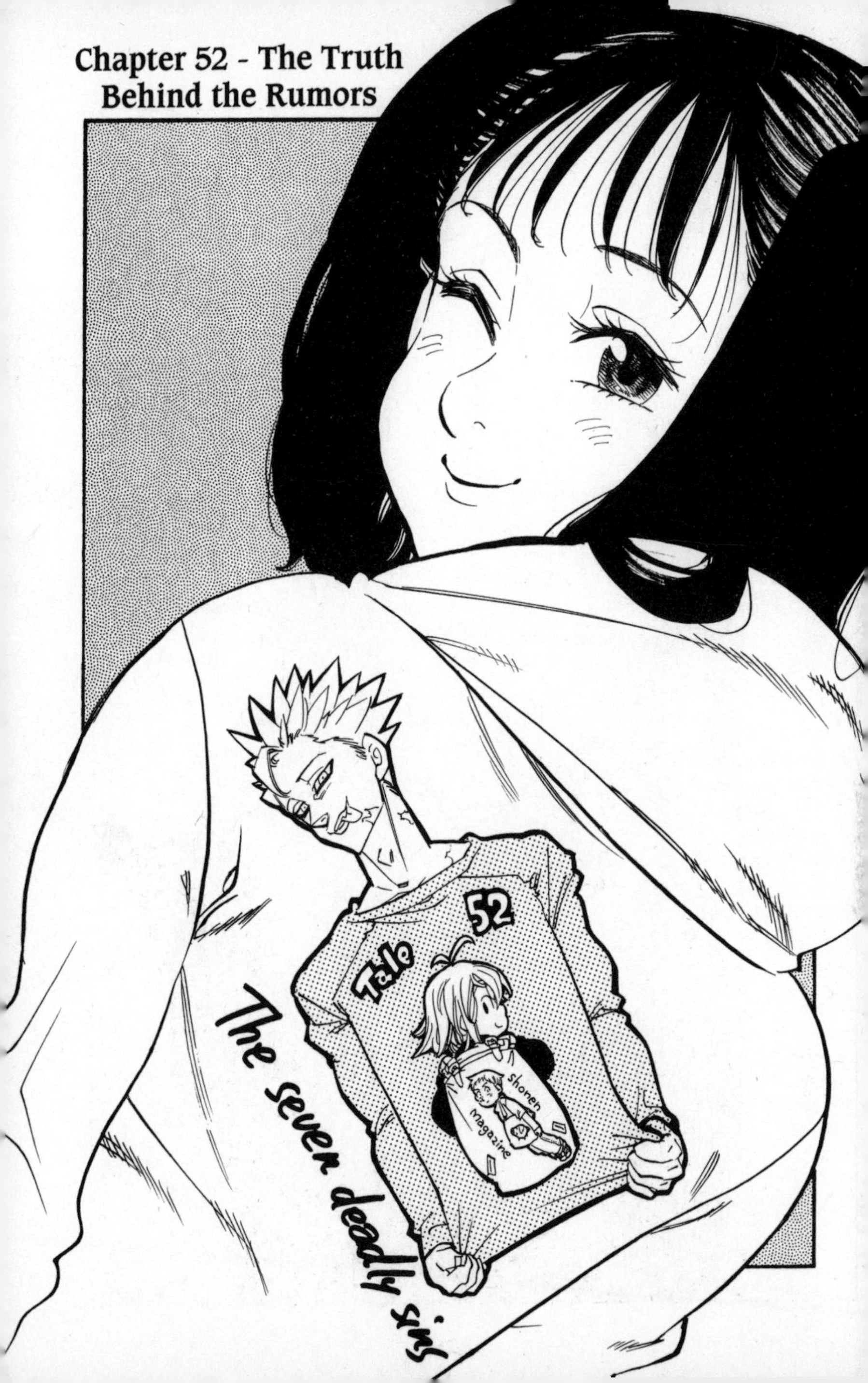

52
Tale
shonen
magazine
The seven deadly sins

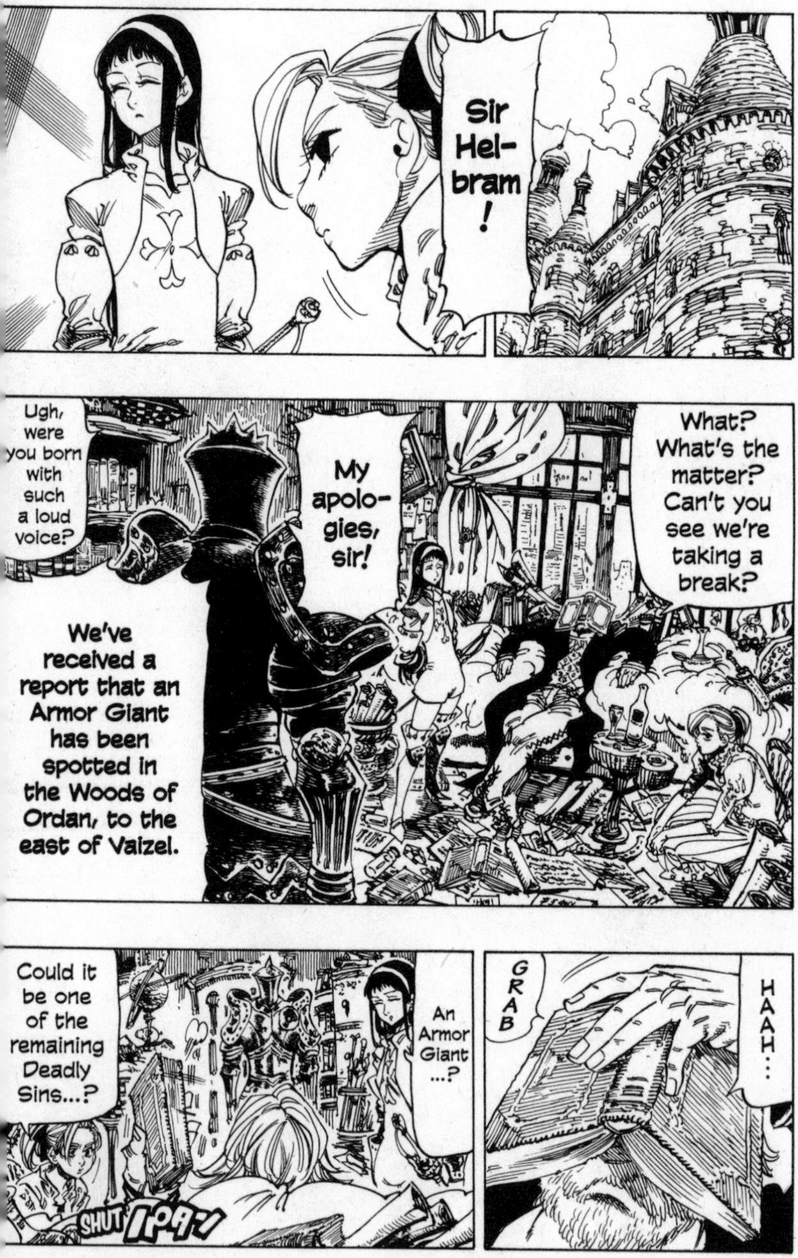
Sir Hel-bram!
What? What's the matter? Can't you see we're taking a break?
Ugh, were you born with such a loud voice?
My apologies, sir!
We've received a report that an Armor Giant has been spotted in the Woods of Ordan, to the east of Vaizel.
HAAH...
GRAB
An Armor Giant...?
Could it be one of the remaining Deadly Sins...?
SHUT

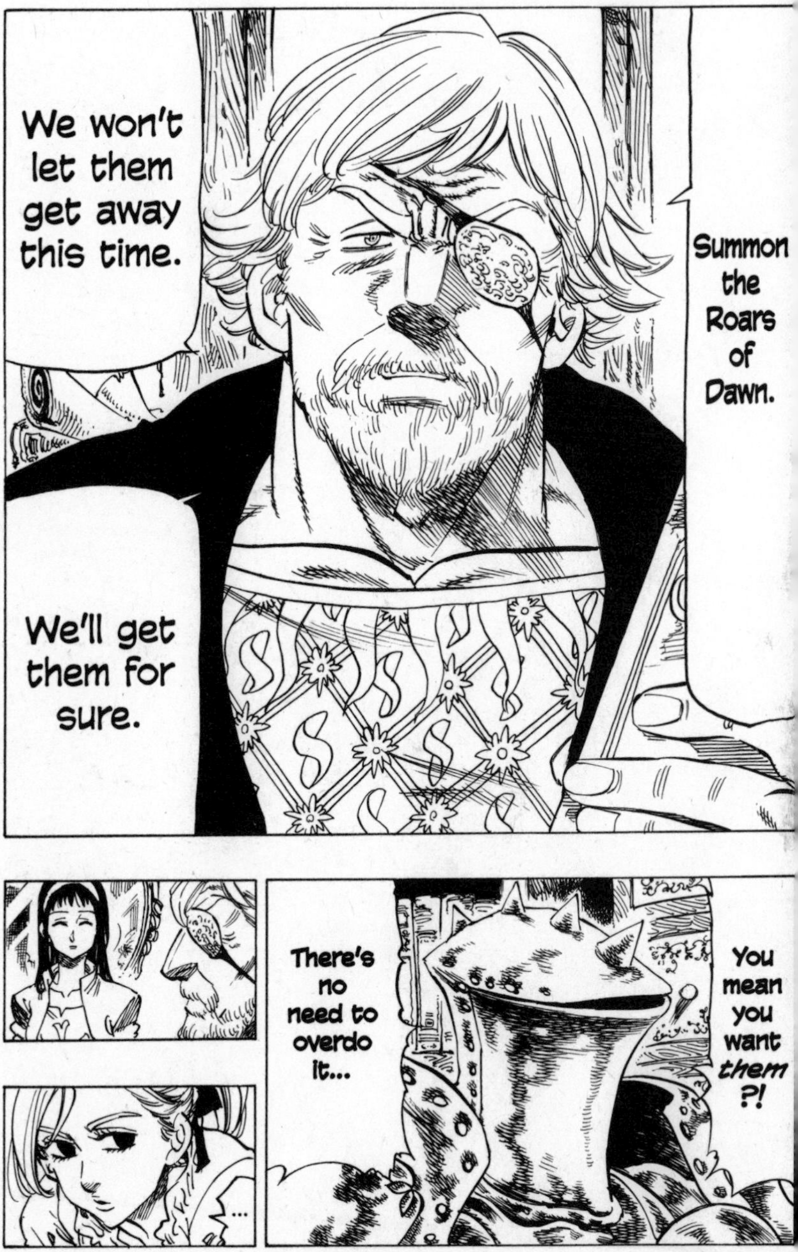
Summon the Roars of Dawn.
We won't let them get away this time.
We'll get them for sure.
You mean you want *them* ?!
There's no need to overdo it...
...

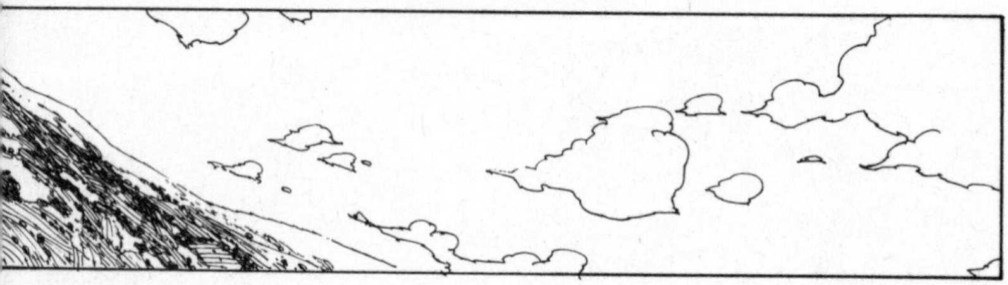

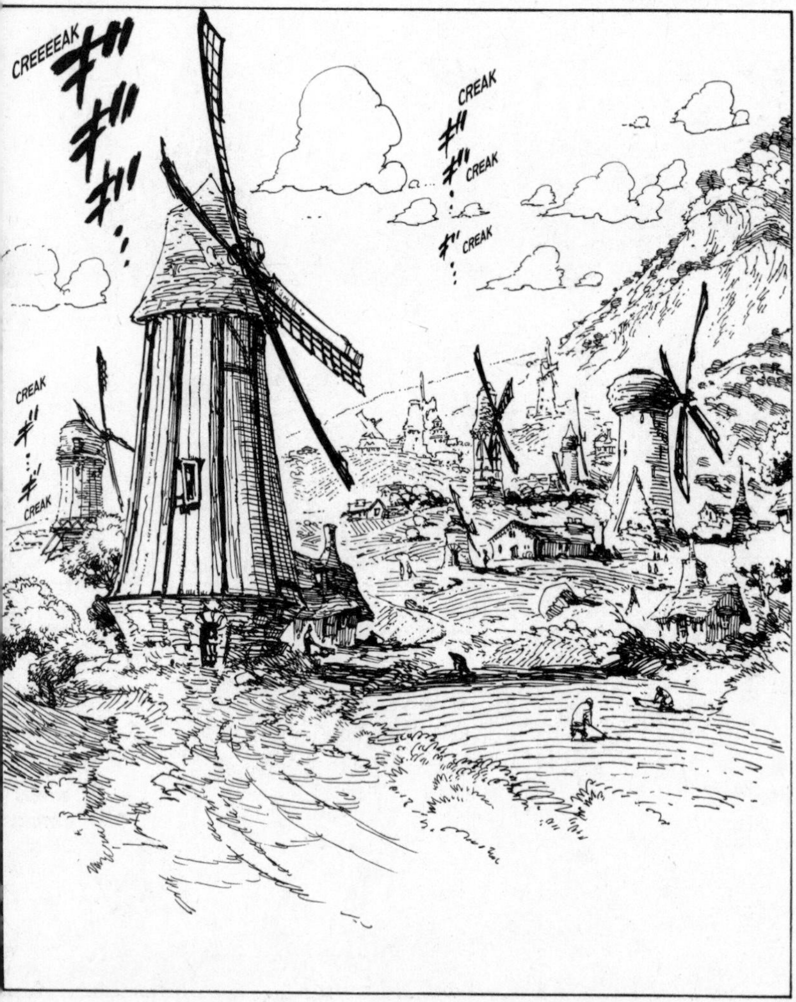
CREAK
CREAK
CREAK
CREEEEAK
CREAK
CREAK

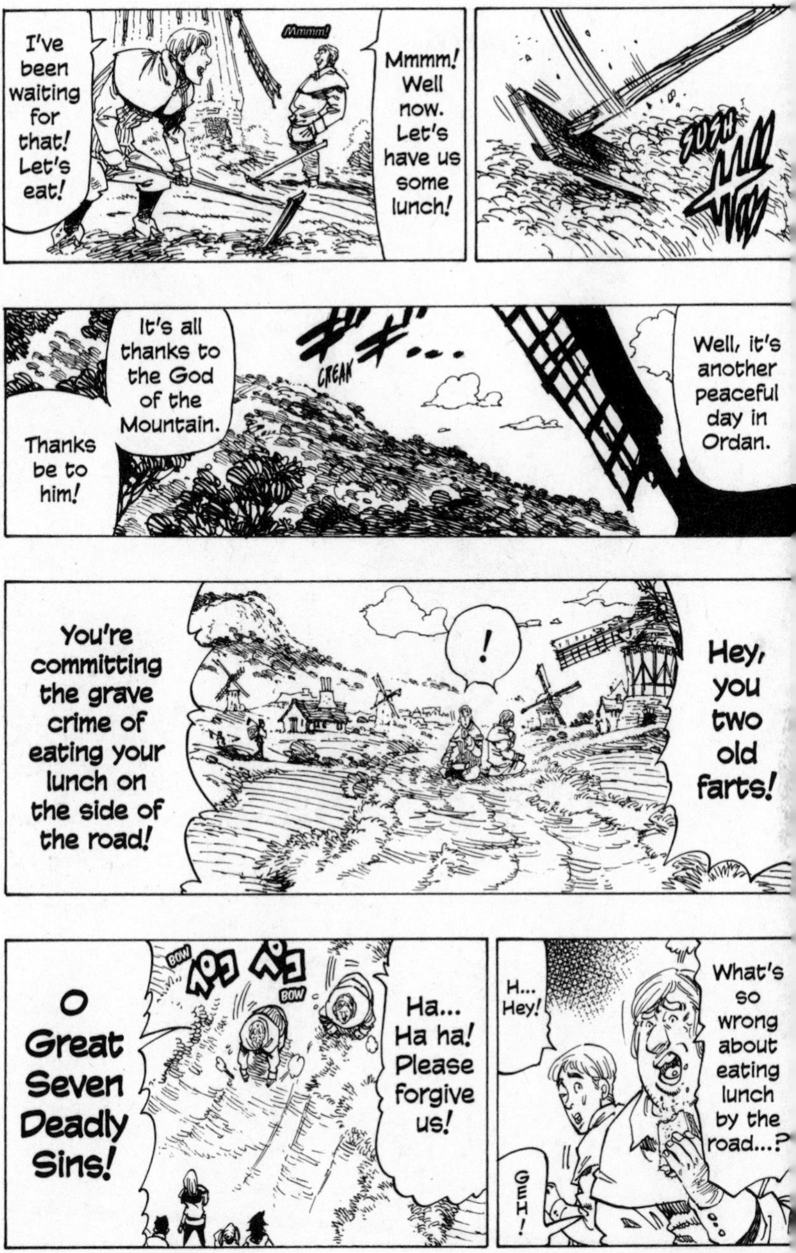
SUSH
Mmmm! Well now. Let's have us some lunch!
Mmmm!
I've been waiting for that! Let's eat!
Well, it's another peaceful day in Ordan.
CREAK
It's all thanks to the God of the Mountain.
Thanks be to him!
Hey, you two old farts!
!
You're committing the grave crime of eating your lunch on the side of the road!
What's so wrong about eating lunch by the road...?
H... Hey!
GEH!
Ha... Ha ha! Please forgive us!
BOW
BOW
O Great Seven Deadly Sins!

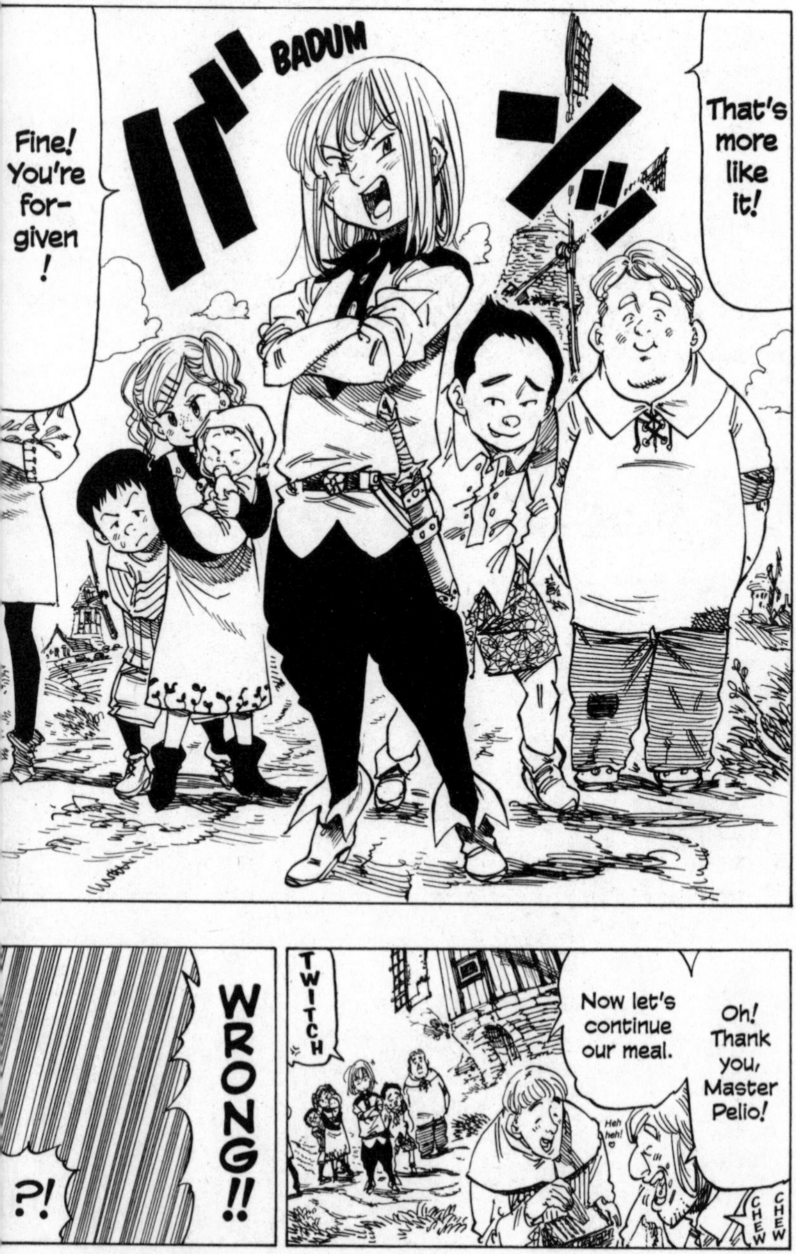

That's more like it!
BADUM
Fine! You're for-given!
Oh! Thank you, Master Pelio!
Now let's continue our meal.
Heh heh ♥
TWITCH
CHEW CHEW
WRONG!!
?!

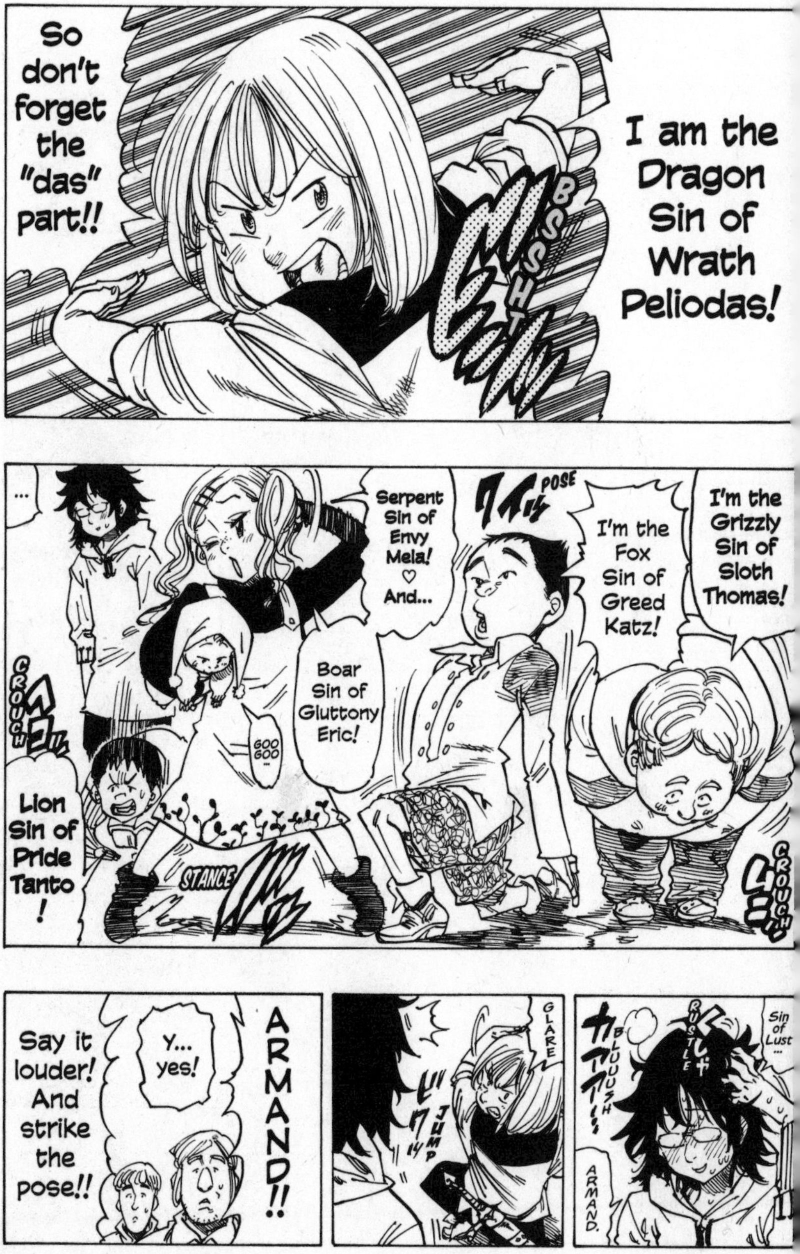

I am the Dragon Sin of Wrath Peliodas!
BSSHT
So don't forget the "das" part!!
I'm the Grizzly Sin of Sloth Thomas!
CROUCH
I'm the Fox Sin of Greed Katz!
POSE
Serpent Sin of Envy Mela! ♡ And...
Boar Sin of Gluttony Eric!
GOO GOO ...
STANCE
...
CROUCH
Lion Sin of Pride Tanto!
Sin of Lust ...
RUSTLE
BLUUUSH
ARMAND.
GLARE
JUMP
ARMAND!!
Y... yes!
Say it louder! And strike the pose!!

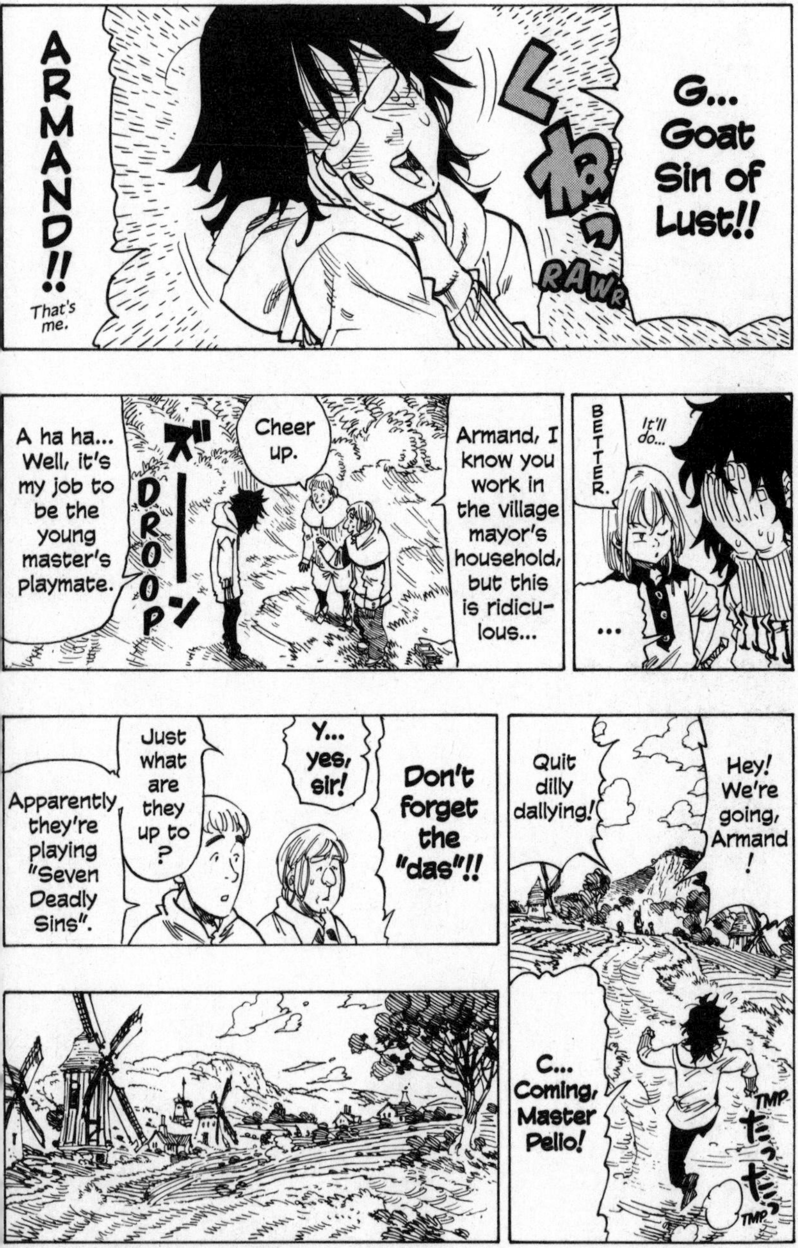
G... Goat Sin of Lust!!
RAWR
ARMAND!!
That's me.
It'll do...
BETTER.
...
Armand, I know you work in the village mayor's household, but this is ridiculous...
Cheer up.
DROOP
A ha ha... Well, it's my job to be the young master's playmate.
Hey! We're going, Armand!
Quit dilly dallying!
C... Coming, Master Pelio!
TMP
TMP
Don't forget the "das"!!
Y... yes, sir!
Just what are they up to?
Apparently they're playing "Seven Deadly Sins".

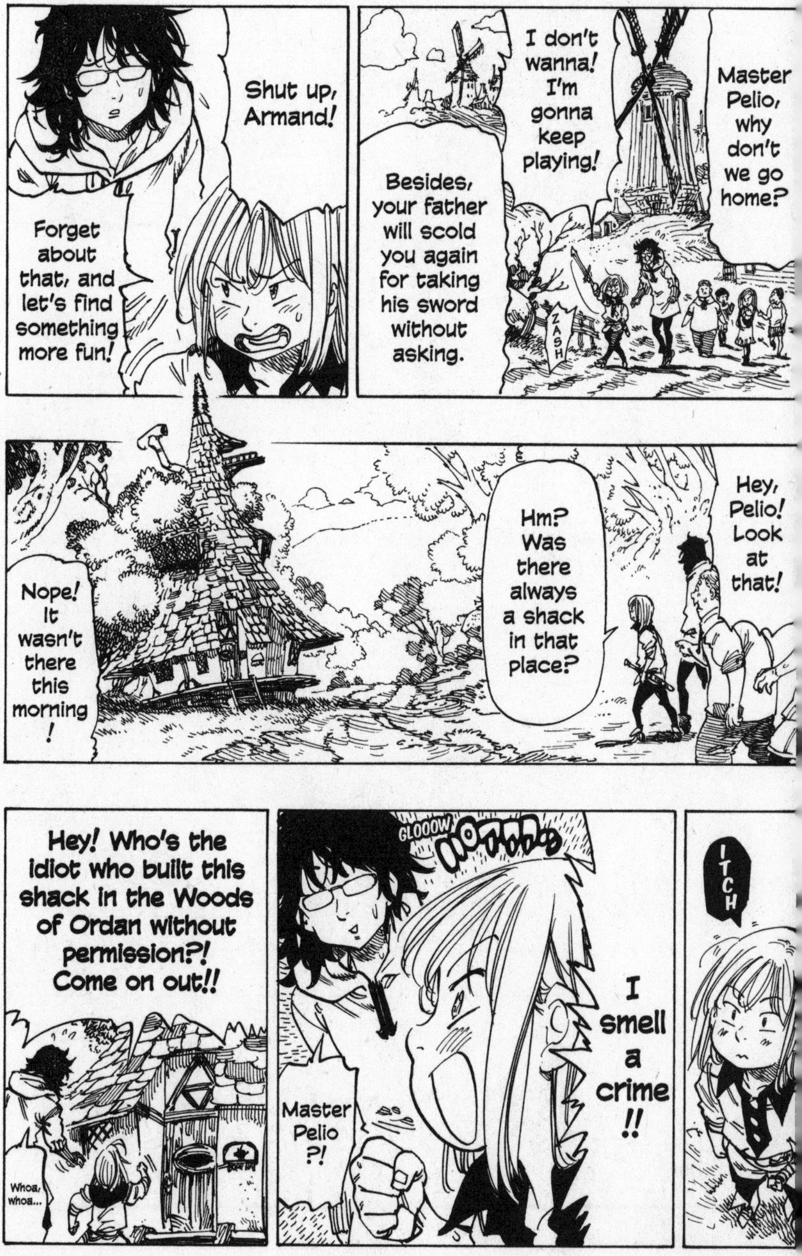
Master Pelio, why don't we go home?
I don't wanna! I'm gonna keep playing!
Besides, your father will scold you again for taking his sword without asking.
ZASH
Shut up, Armand!
Forget about that, and let's find something more fun!
Hey, Pelio! Look at that!
Hm? Was there always a shack in that place?
Nope! It wasn't there this morning!
ITCH
GLOOOW
I smell a crime!!
Master Pelio?!
Hey! Who's the idiot who built this shack in the Woods of Ordan without permission?! Come on out!!
Whoa, whoa...

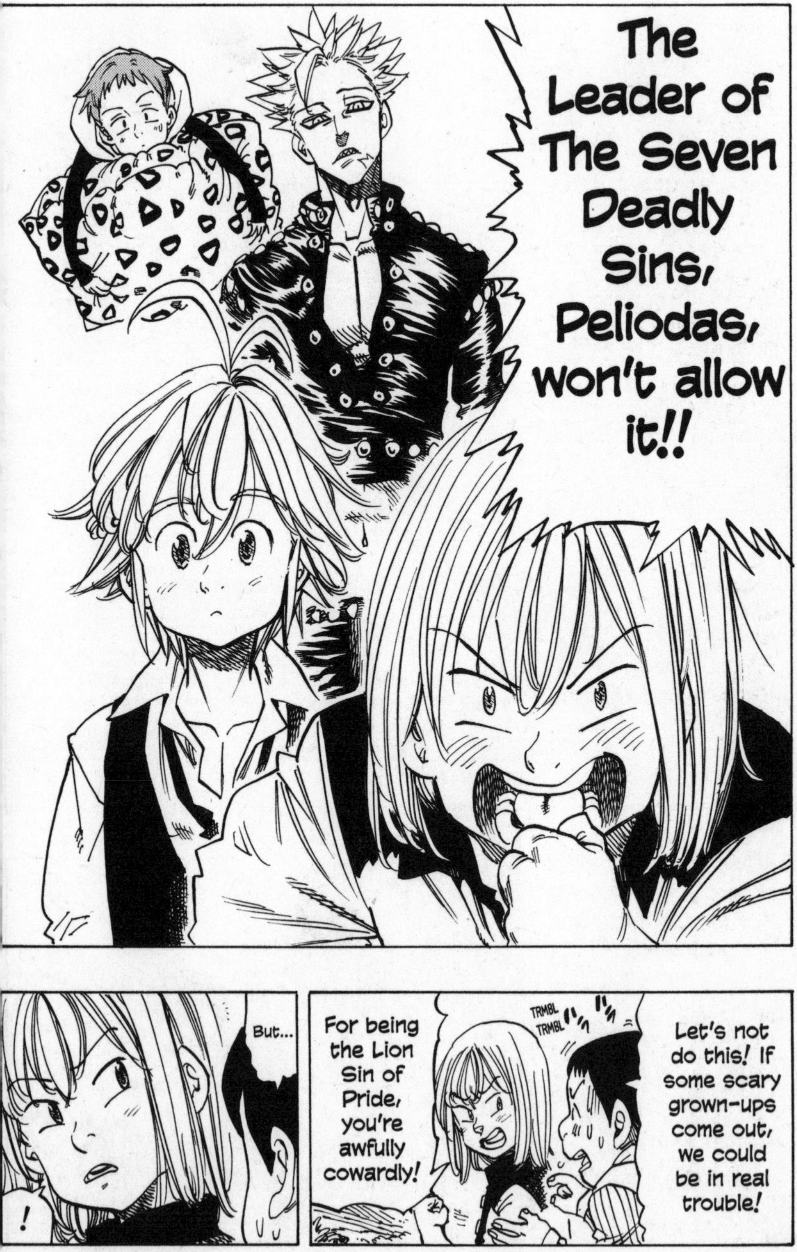
The Leader of The Seven Deadly Sins, Peliodas, won't allow it!!
Let's not do this! If some scary grown-ups come out, we could be in real trouble!
TRMBL TRMBL
For being the Lion Sin of Pride, you're awfully cowardly!
But...
!

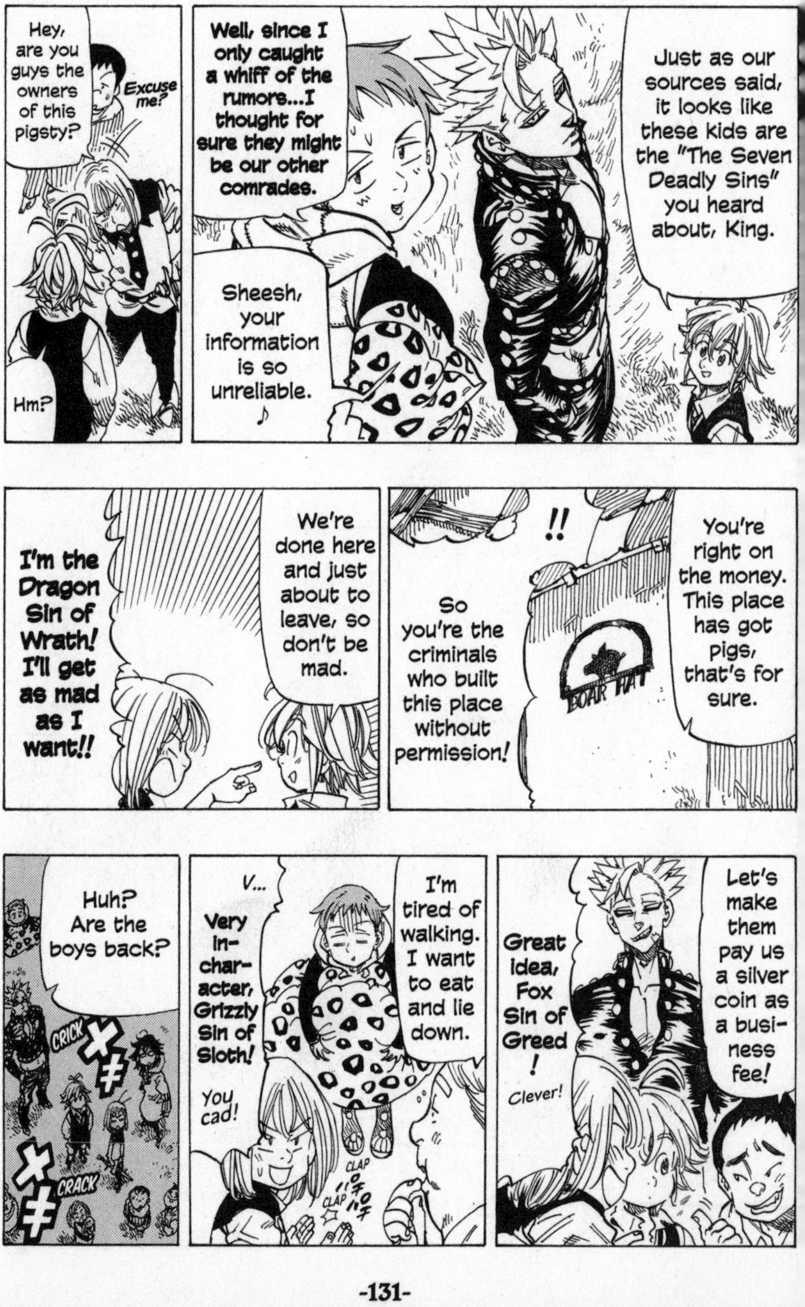

Just as our sources said, it looks like these kids are the "The Seven Deadly Sins" you heard about, King.
Well, since I only caught a whiff of the rumors...I thought for sure they might be our other comrades.
Sheesh, your information is so unreliable. ♪
Hey, are you guys the owners of this pigsty?
Excuse me?
Hm?
You're right on the money. This place has got pigs, that's for sure.
!!
BOAR HAT
So you're the criminals who built this place without permission!
We're done here and just about to leave, so don't be mad.
I'm the Dragon Sin of Wrath! I'll get as mad as I want!!
Let's make them pay us a silver coin as a business fee!
Great idea, Fox Sin of Greed!
Clever!
I'm tired of walking. I want to eat and lie down.
V...
Very in-character, Grizzly Sin of Sloth!
You cad!
CLAP
CLAP
Huh? Are the boys back?
CRICK
CRACK

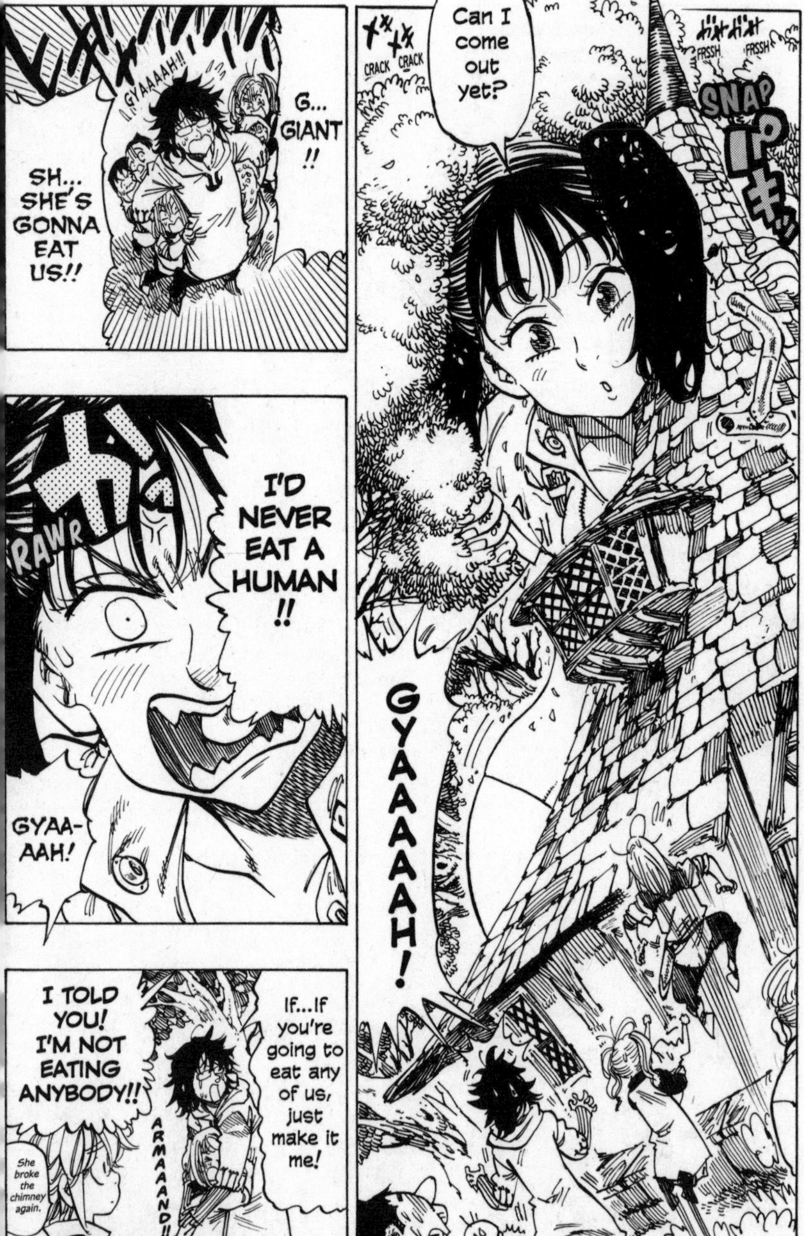
CRACK CRACK
Can I come out yet?
FRSSH FRSSH
SNAP
GYAAAAAAH!
GYAAAAH!!
G... GIANT!!
SH... SHE'S GONNA EAT US!!
RAWR
I'D NEVER EAT A HUMAN!!
GYAA-AAH!
If...If you're going to eat any of us, just make it me!
I TOLD YOU! I'M NOT EATING ANYBODY!!
ARMAAAAND!!
She broke the chimney again.

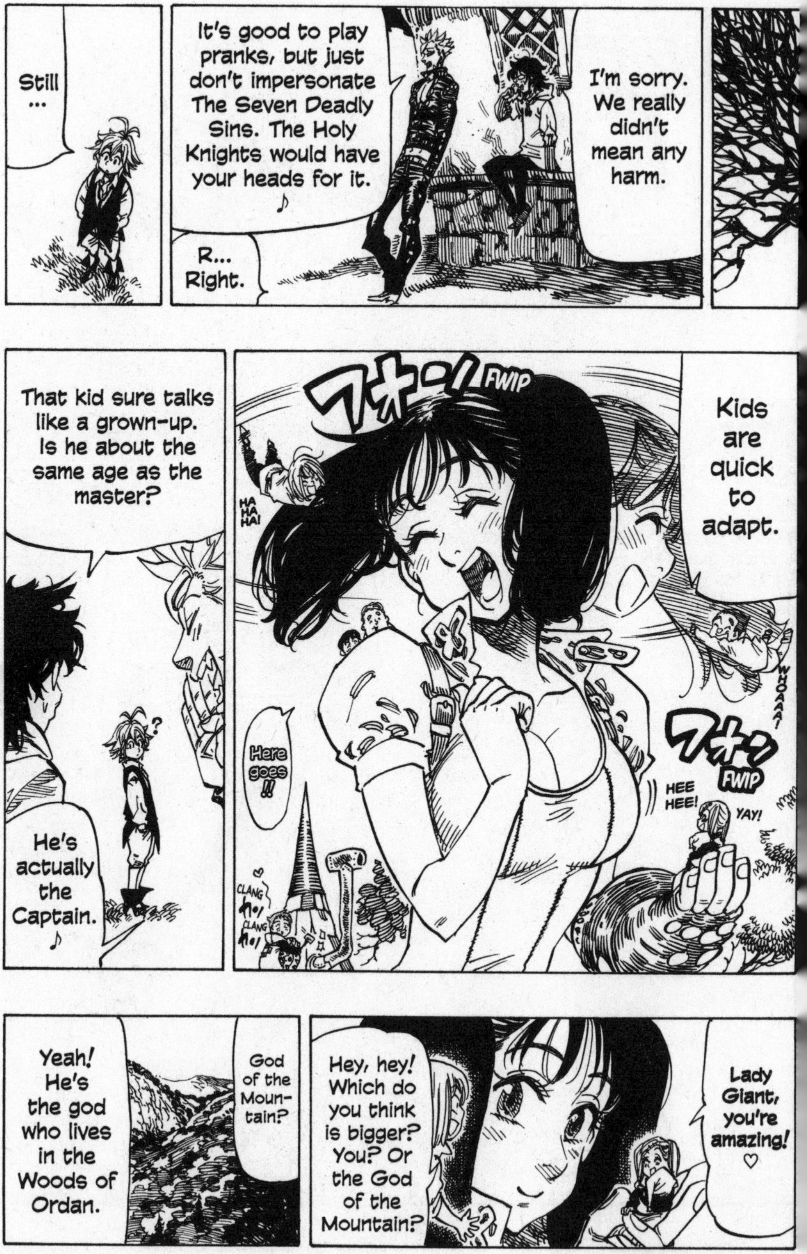
I'm sorry. We really didn't mean any harm.
It's good to play pranks, but just don't impersonate The Seven Deadly Sins. The Holy Knights would have your heads for it. ♪
R... Right.
Still ...
Kids are quick to adapt.
FWIP
HA HA HA!
WHOAAA!
FWIP
HEE HEE!
YAY!
Here goes!!
CLANG
CLANG
That kid sure talks like a grown-up. Is he about the same age as the master?
He's actually the Captain. ♪
Lady Giant, you're amazing! ♡
Hey, hey! Which do you think is bigger? You? Or the God of the Mountain?
God of the Moun-tain?
Yeah! He's the god who lives in the Woods of Ordan.

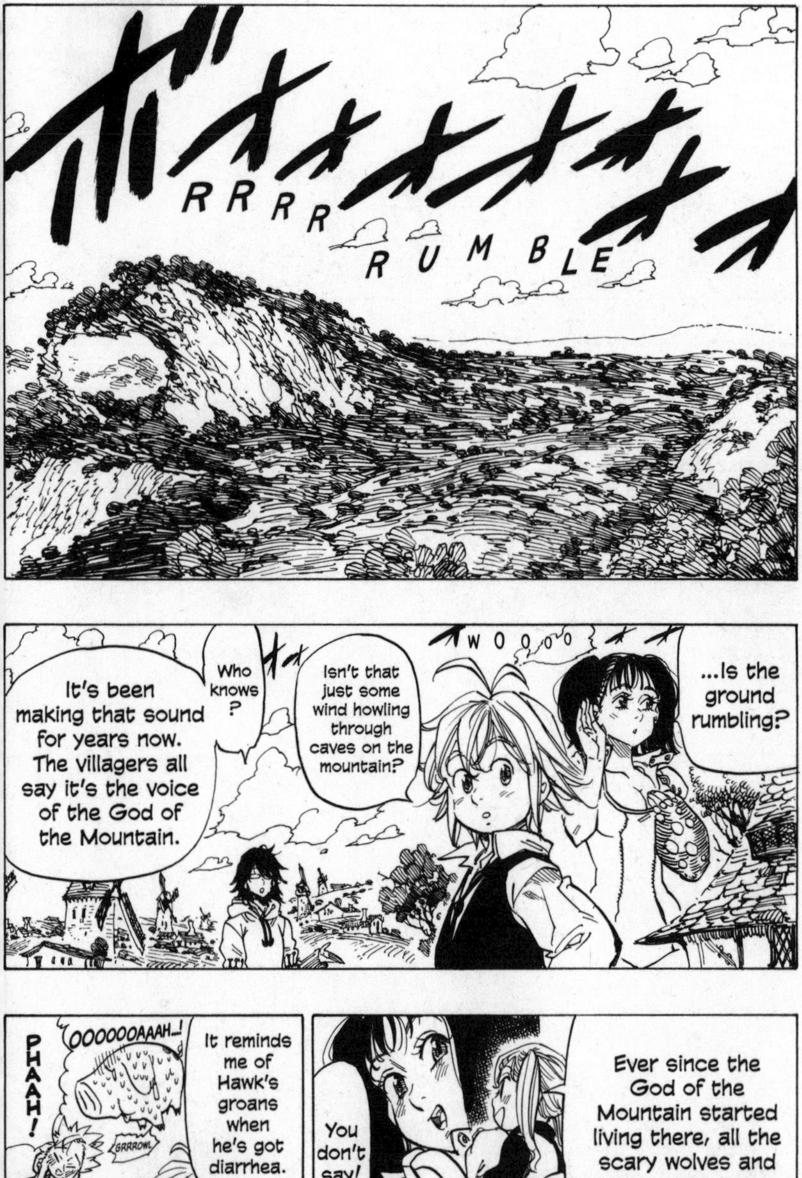
RRRR
RUMBLE
...Is the ground rumbling?
WOOOO
Isn't that just some wind howling through caves on the mountain?
Who knows?
It's been making that sound for years now. The villagers all say it's the voice of the God of the Mountain.
Ever since the God of the Mountain started living there, all the scary wolves and bears went away.
You don't say!
It reminds me of Hawk's groans when he's got diarrhea.
OOOOOOAAAH...!
GRRROWL
PHAAH!

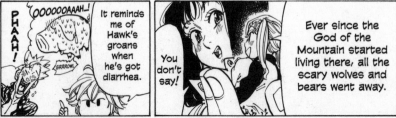

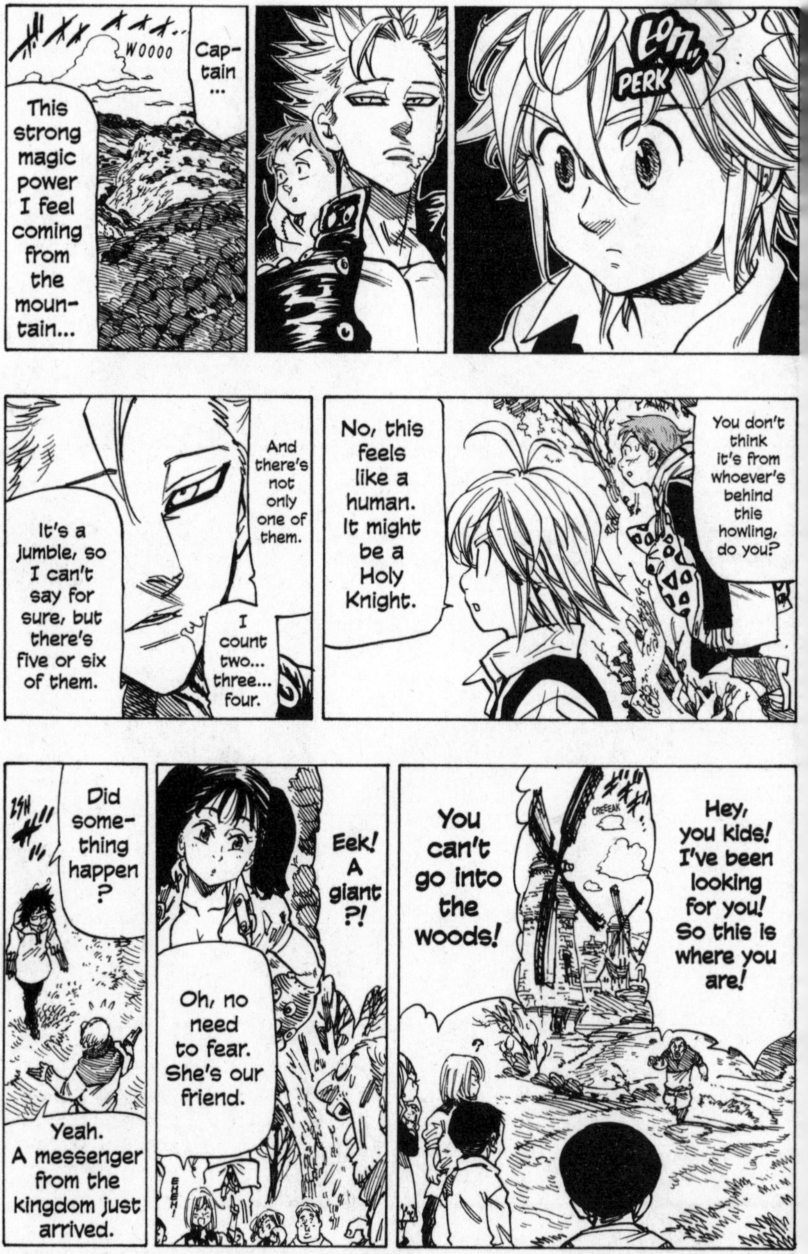
PERK
Cap-tain...
WOOOO
This strong magic power I feel coming from the moun-tain...
You don't think it's from whoever's behind this howling, do you?
No, this feels like a human. It might be a Holy Knight.
And there's not only one of them.
It's a jumble, so I can't say for sure, but there's five or six of them.
I count two... three... four.
Hey, you kids! I've been looking for you! So this is where you are!
CREEEAK
You can't go into the woods!
Eek! A giant?!
Oh, no need to fear. She's our friend.
Did some-thing happen?
Yeah. A messenger from the kingdom just arrived.

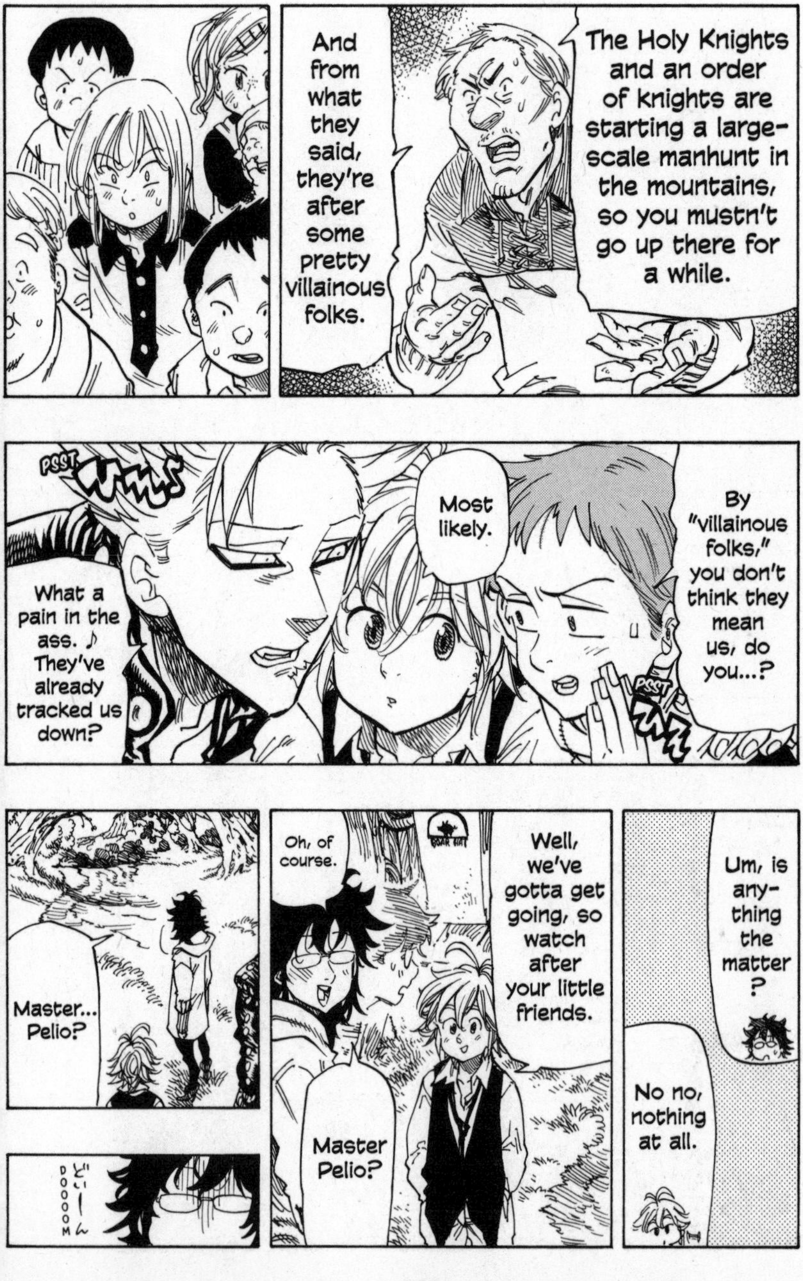
The Holy Knights and an order of knights are starting a large-scale manhunt in the mountains, so you mustn't go up there for a while.
And from what they said, they're after some pretty villainous folks.
By "villainous folks," you don't think they mean us, do you...?
PSST
Most likely.
PSST
What a pain in the ass. ♪ They've already tracked us down?
Um, is anything the matter?
No no, nothing at all.
Well, we've gotta get going, so watch after your little friends.
Oh, of course.
Master Pelio?
Master... Pelio?
DOOOOM

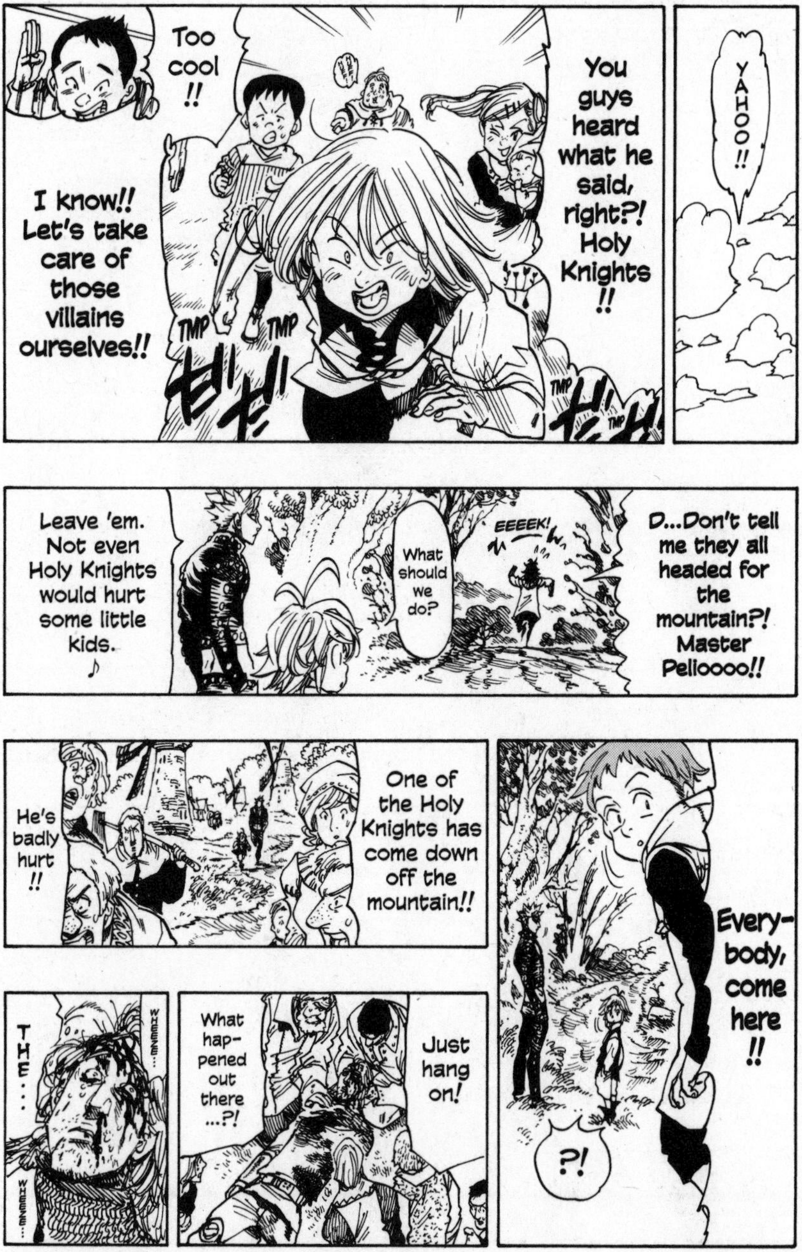
YAHOO!!
You guys heard what he said, right?! Holy Knights!!
Too cool!!
I know!! Let's take care of those villains ourselves!!
TMP
TMP
TMP
TMP
D...Don't tell me they all headed for the mountain?! Master Peliooo!!
EEEEK!
What should we do?
Leave 'em. Not even Holy Knights would hurt some little kids. ♪
Every-body, come here!!
?!
One of the Holy Knights has come down off the mountain!!
He's badly hurt!!
Just hang on!
What hap-pened out there ...?!
WHEEZE...
THE...
WHEEZE...

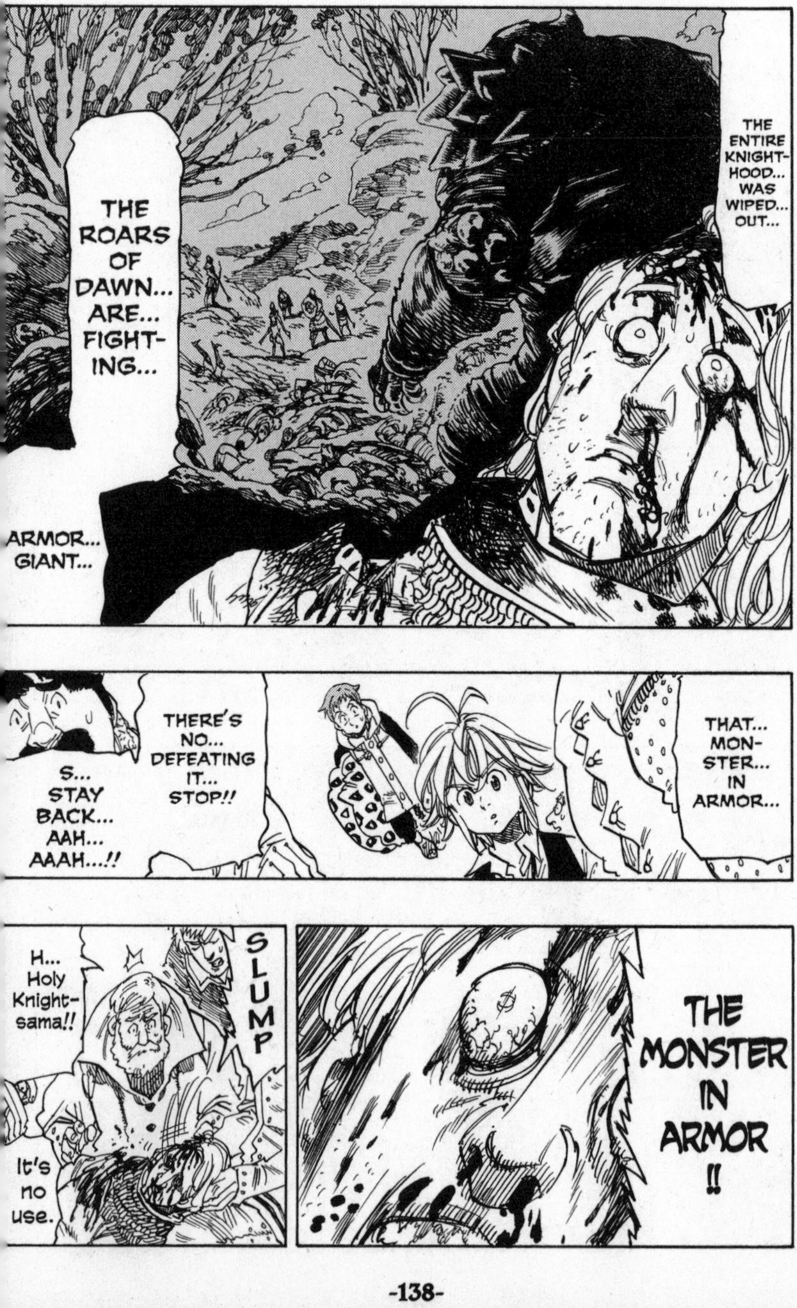
THE ENTIRE KNIGHTHOOD... WAS WIPED... OUT...
THE ROARS OF DAWN... ARE... FIGHTING...
ARMOR... GIANT...
THAT... MONSTER... IN ARMOR...
THERE'S NO... DEFEATING IT... STOP!!
S... STAY BACK... AAH... AAAH...!!
THE MONSTER IN ARMOR !!
SLUMP
H... Holy Knight-sama!!
It's no use.

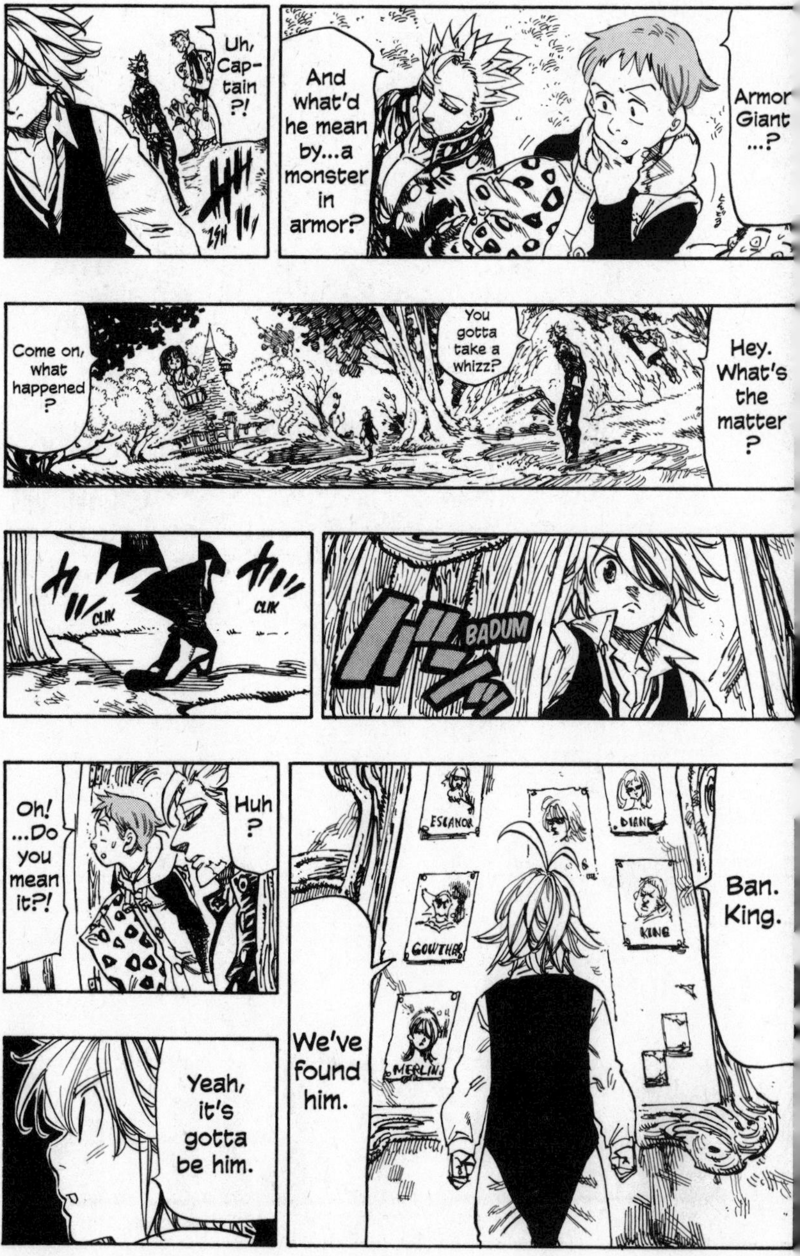
Armor Giant ...?
And what'd he mean by...a monster in armor?
Uh, Captain?!
ZSH
Hey. What's the matter?
You gotta take a whizz?
Come on, what happened?
BADUM
CLIK
CLIK
Ban. King.
We've found him.
Huh?
Oh! ...Do you mean it?!
Yeah, it's gotta be him.

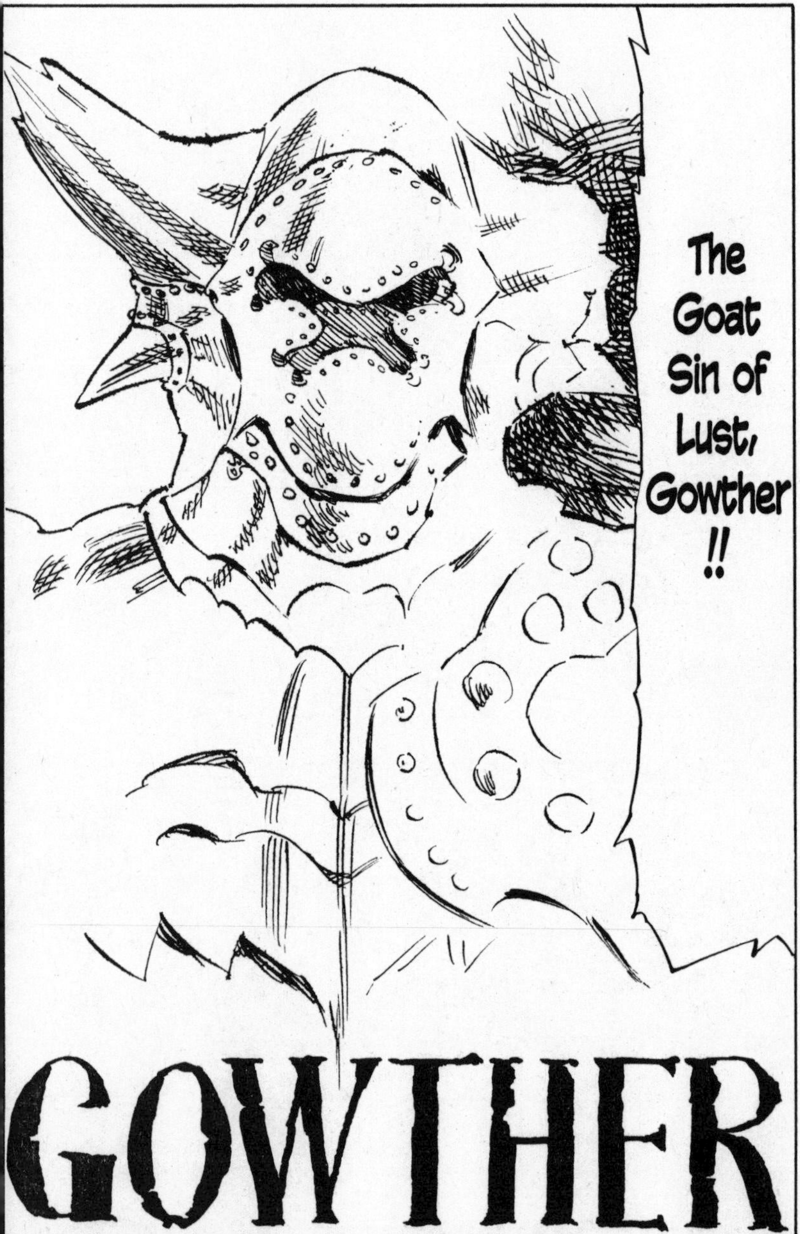
The Goat Sin of Lust, Gowther !!
GOWTHER

Chapter 53 - The Armor Giant vs. The Roars of Dawn

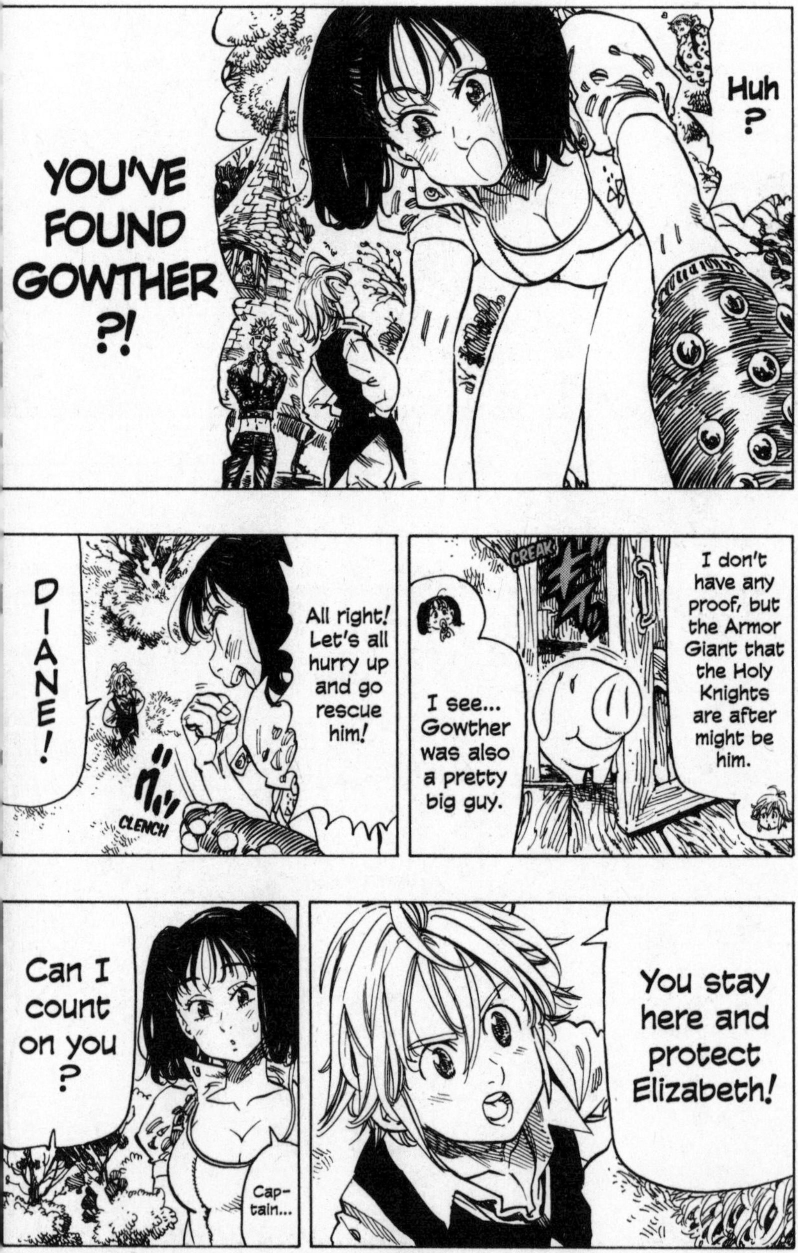
Huh?
YOU'VE FOUND GOWTHER?!
CREAK
I don't have any proof, but the Armor Giant that the Holy Knights are after might be him.
I see... Gowther was also a pretty big guy.
All right! Let's all hurry up and go rescue him!
DIANE!
CLENCH
You stay here and protect Elizabeth!
Can I count on you?
Captain...

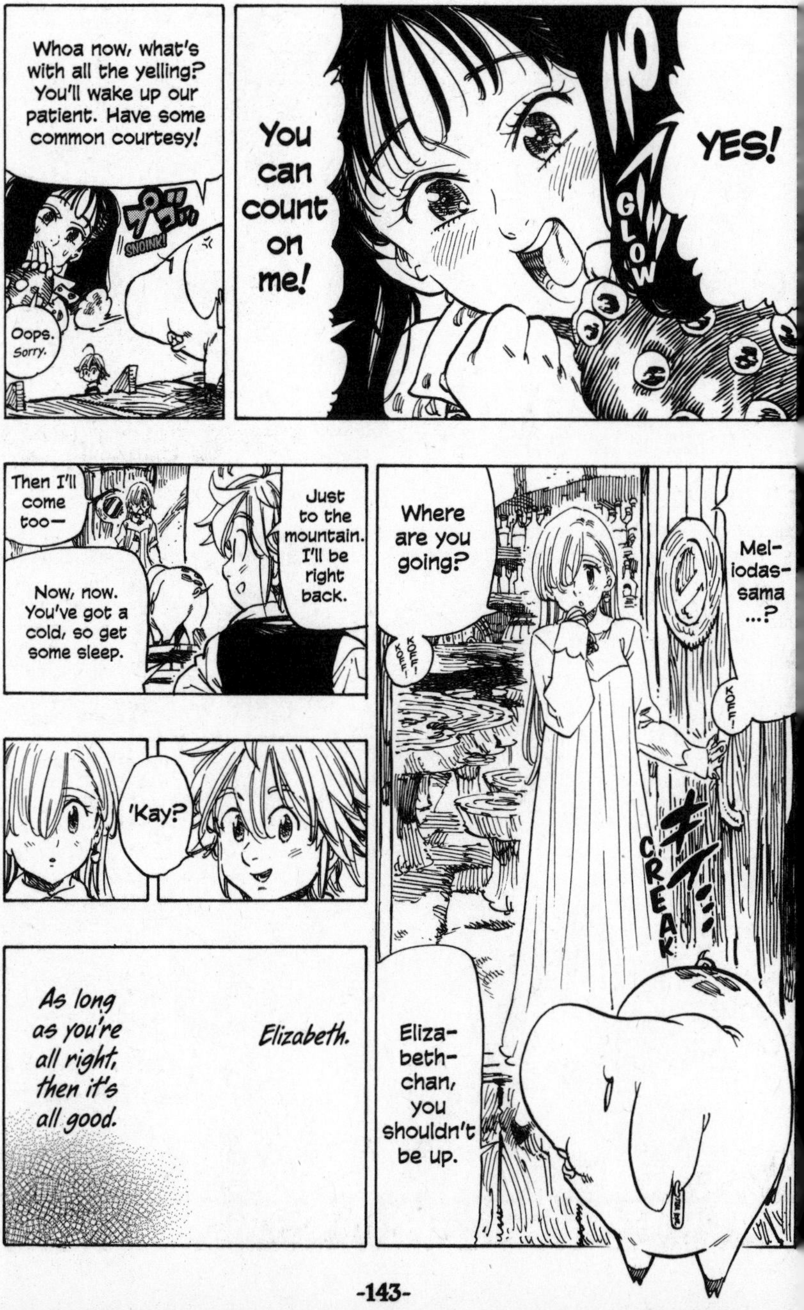
YES!
GLOW
You can count on me!
Whoa now, what's with all the yelling? You'll wake up our patient. Have some common courtesy!
SNOINK!
Oops. Sorry.
Mel-iodas-sama ...?
KOFF!
Where are you going?
KOFF! KOFF!
CREAK
Eliza-beth-chan, you shouldn't be up.
Just to the mountain. I'll be right back.
Then I'll come too—
Now, now. You've got a cold, so get some sleep.
'Kay?
Elizabeth.
As long as you're all right, then it's all good.

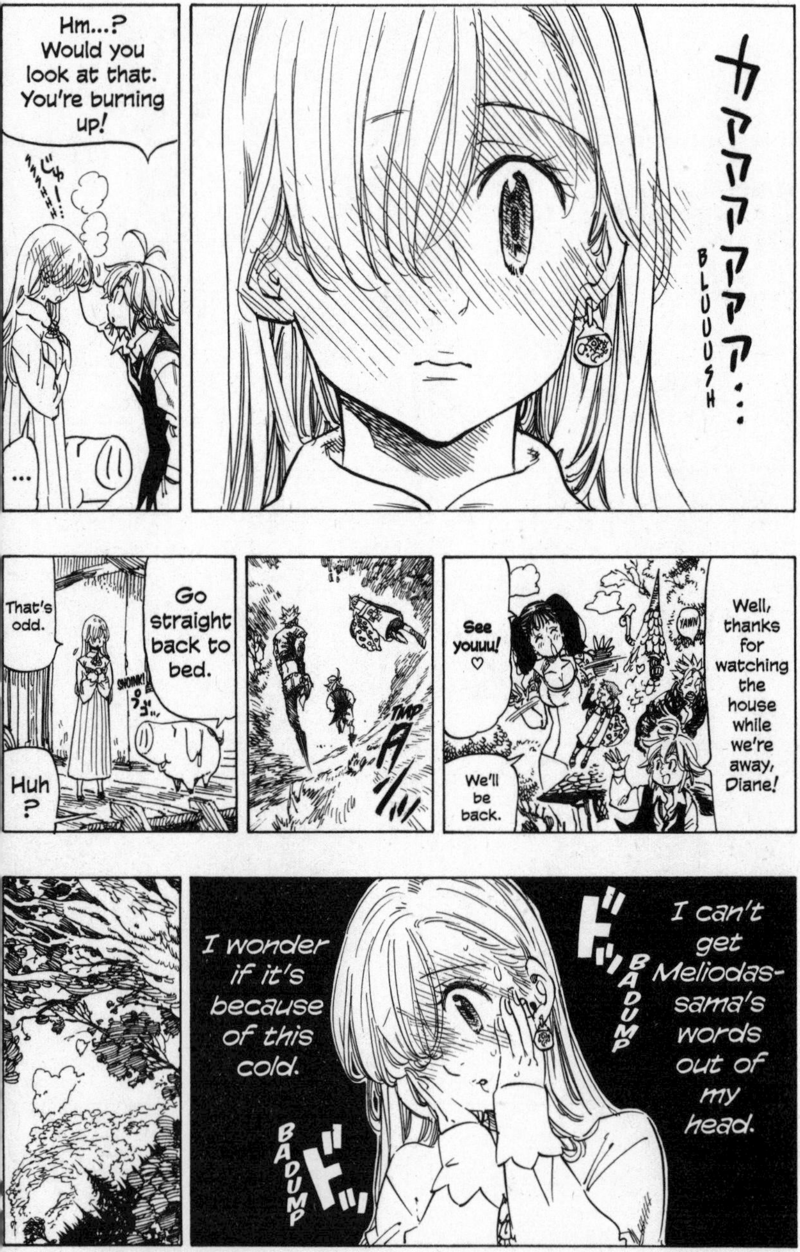
カアアアア…
BLUUUSH
Hm...? Would you look at that. You're burning up!
...
Well, thanks for watching the house while we're away, Diane!
YAWN
See youuu! ♡
We'll be back.
TMP
Go straight back to bed.
SNOINK!
That's odd.
Huh?
I can't get Meliodas-sama's words out of my head.
ドッ
BADUMP
I wonder if it's because of this cold.
ドッ
BADUMP

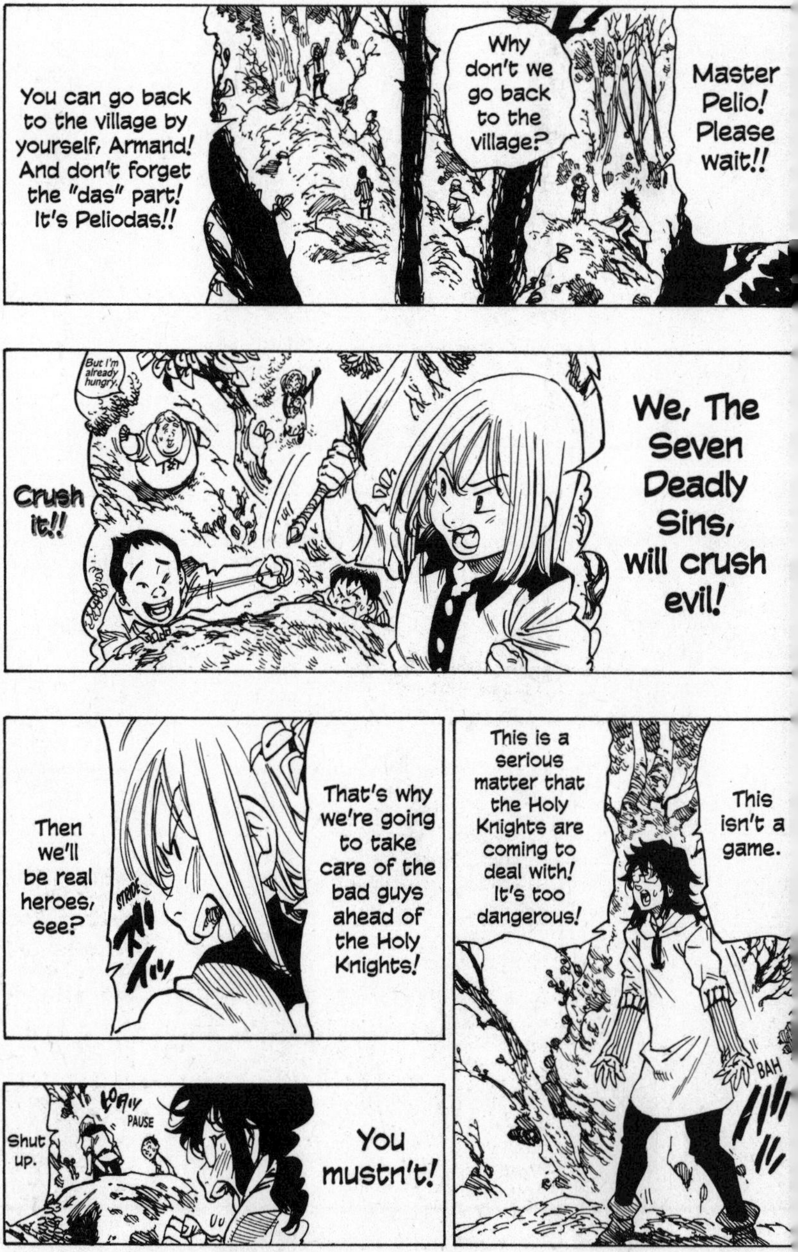
Master Pelio! Please wait!!
Why don't we go back to the village?
You can go back to the village by yourself, Armand! And don't forget the "das" part! It's Peliodas!!
We, The Seven Deadly Sins, will crush evil!
But I'm already hungry.
Crush it!!
This isn't a game.
This is a serious matter that the Holy Knights are coming to deal with! It's too dangerous!
BAH
That's why we're going to take care of the bad guys ahead of the Holy Knights!
STRIDE
Then we'll be real heroes, see?
You mustn't!
PAUSE
Shut up.

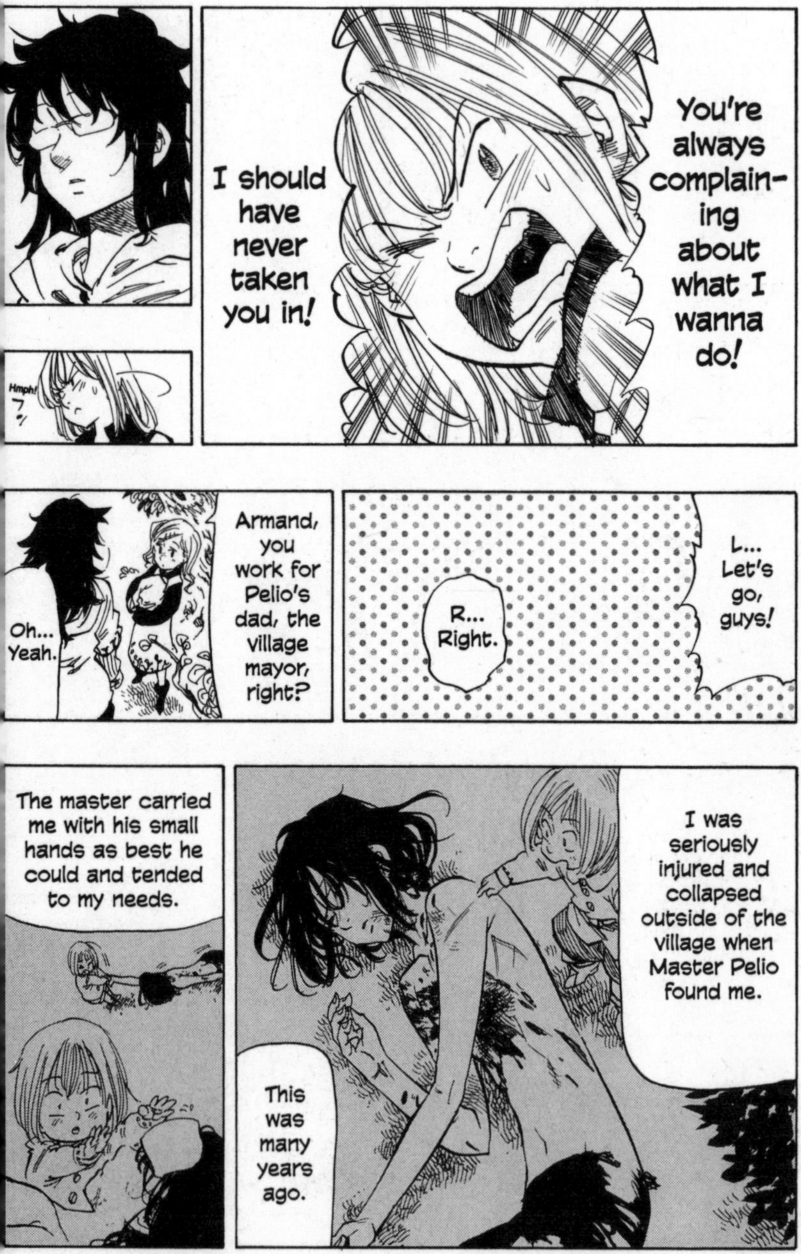
You're always complaining about what I wanna do!
I should have never taken you in!
Hmph!
L... Let's go, guys!
R... Right.
Armand, you work for Pelio's dad, the village mayor, right?
Oh... Yeah.
I was seriously injured and collapsed outside of the village when Master Pelio found me.
This was many years ago.
The master carried me with his small hands as best he could and tended to my needs.

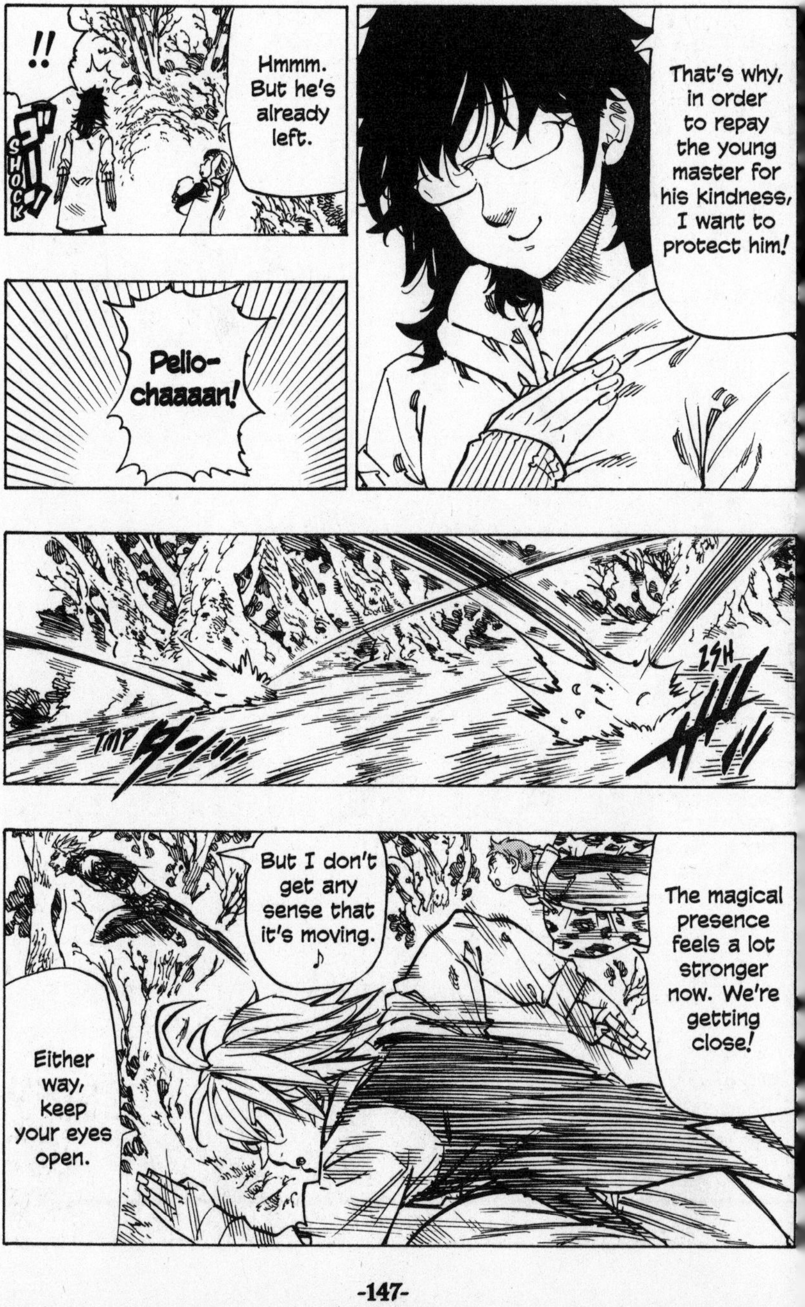
That's why, in order to repay the young master for his kindness, I want to protect him!
!!
SHOCK
Hmmm. But he's already left.
Pelio-chaaaan!
ISH
TMP
The magical presence feels a lot stronger now. We're getting close!
But I don't get any sense that it's moving. ♪
Either way, keep your eyes open.

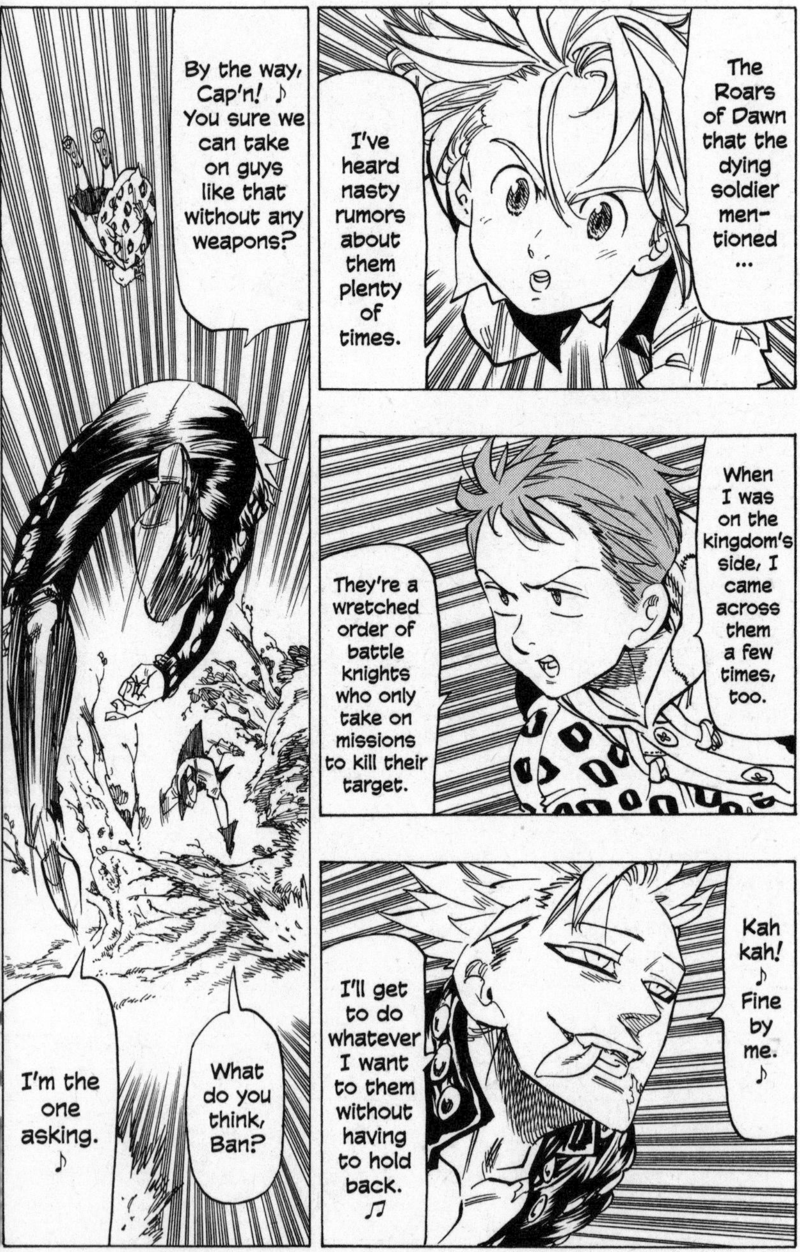
The Roars of Dawn that the dying soldier mentioned ...
I've heard nasty rumors about them plenty of times.
When I was on the kingdom's side, I came across them a few times, too.
They're a wretched order of battle knights who only take on missions to kill their target.
Kah kah! ♪ Fine by me. ♪
I'll get to do whatever I want to them without having to hold back. ♫
By the way, Cap'n! ♪ You sure we can take on guys like that without any weapons?
What do you think, Ban?
I'm the one asking. ♪

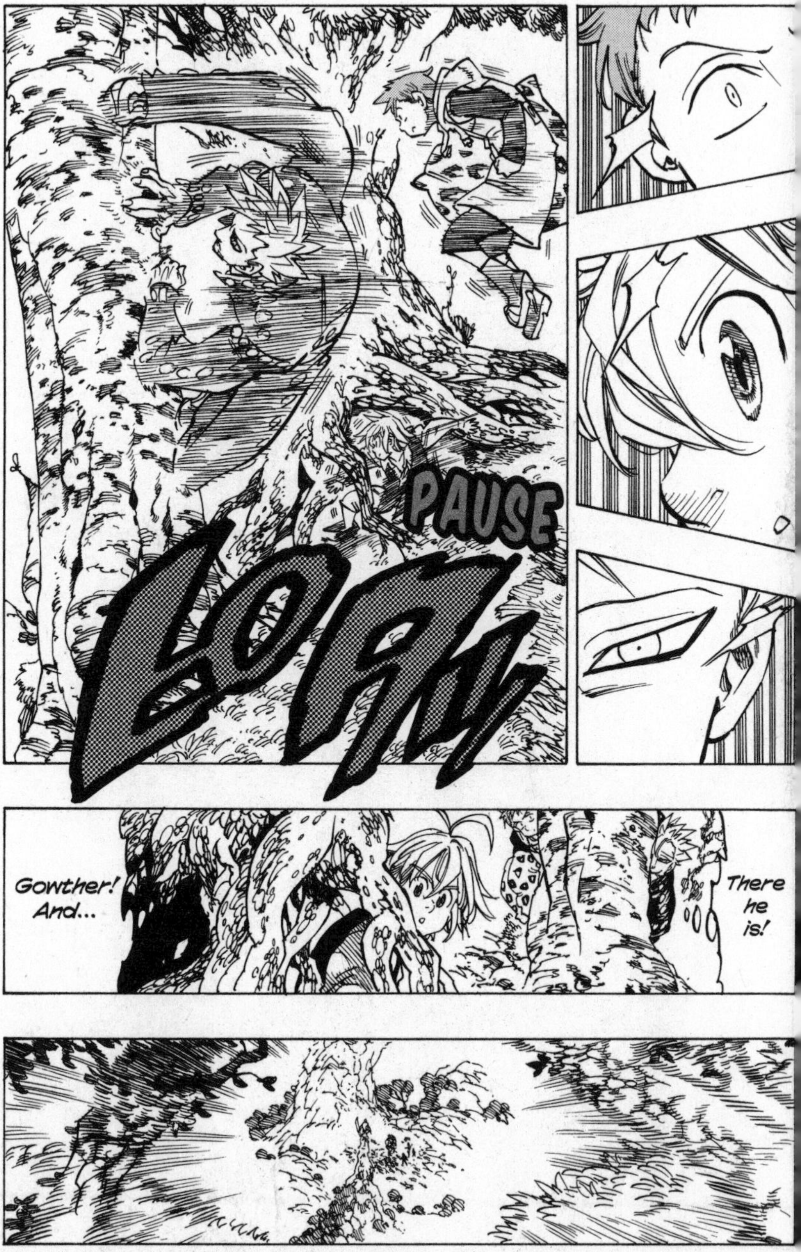
PAUSE
There he is!
Gowther! And...

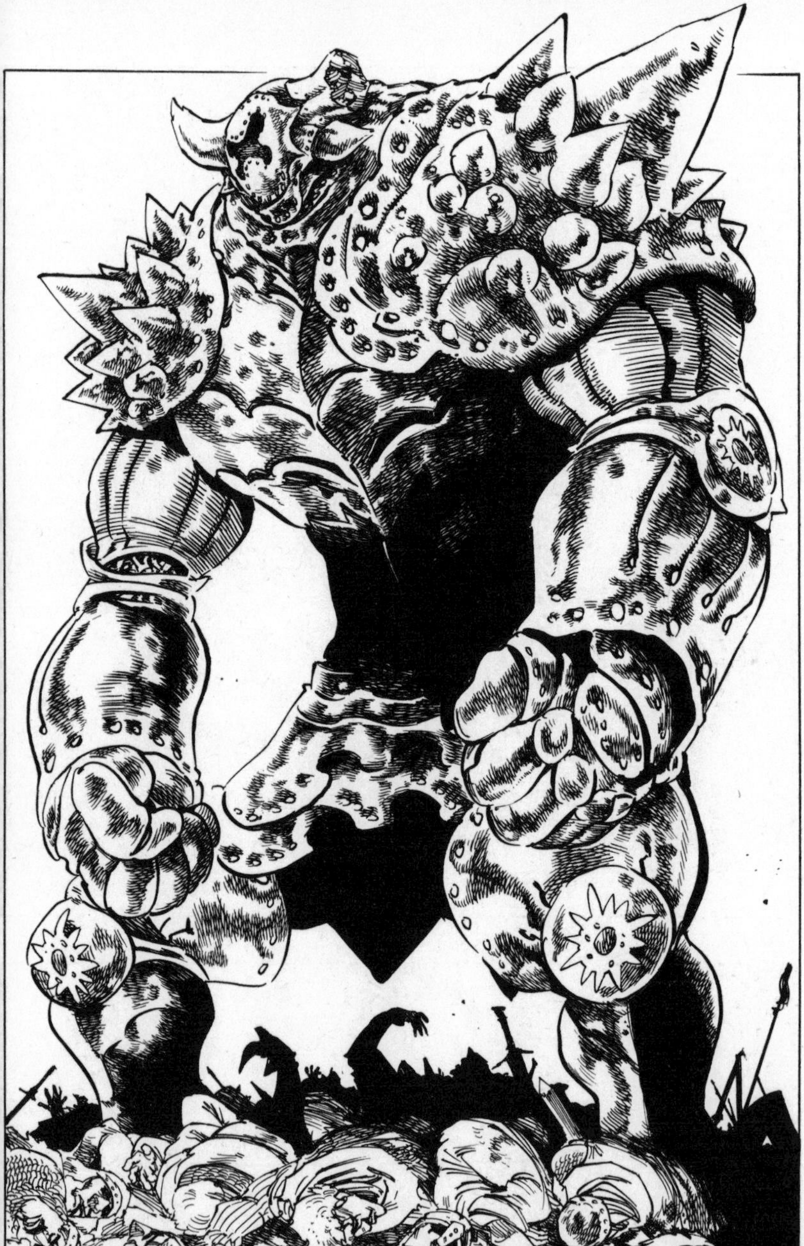

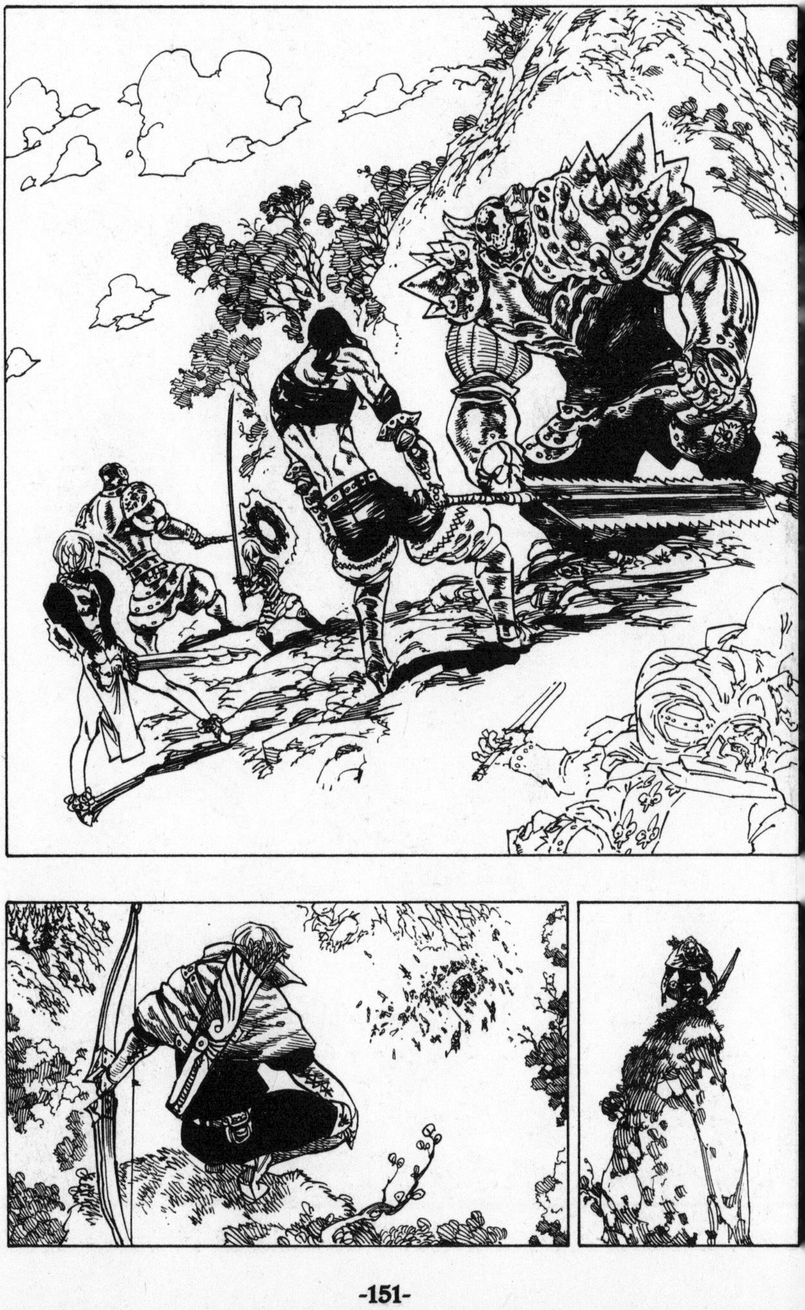

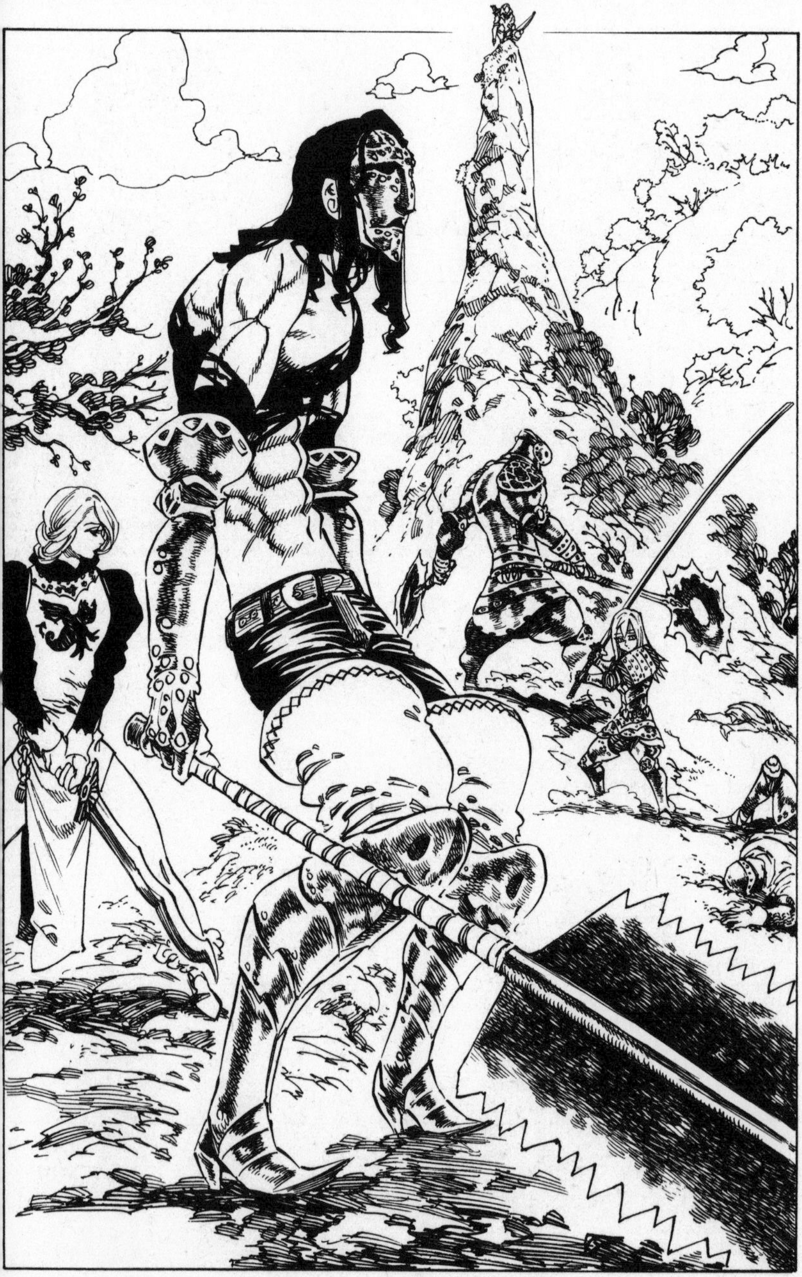

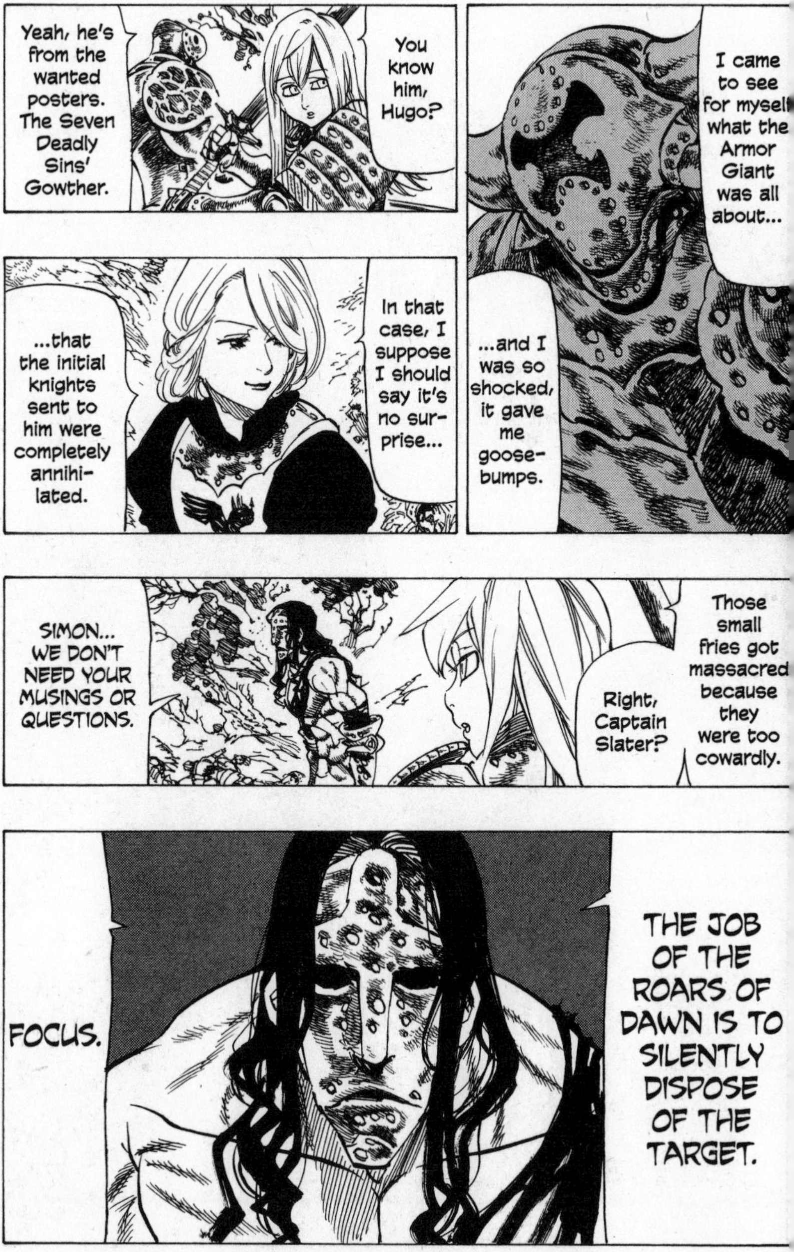
I came to see for mysel what the Armor Giant was all about...
...and I was so shocked, it gave me goose-bumps.
You know him, Hugo?
Yeah, he's from the wanted posters. The Seven Deadly Sins' Gowther.
In that case, I suppose I should say it's no surprise...
...that the initial knights sent to him were completely annihilated.
Those small fries got massacred because they were too cowardly.
Right, Captain Slater?
SIMON... WE DON'T NEED YOUR MUSINGS OR QUESTIONS.
THE JOB OF THE ROARS OF DAWN IS TO SILENTLY DISPOSE OF THE TARGET.
FOCUS.

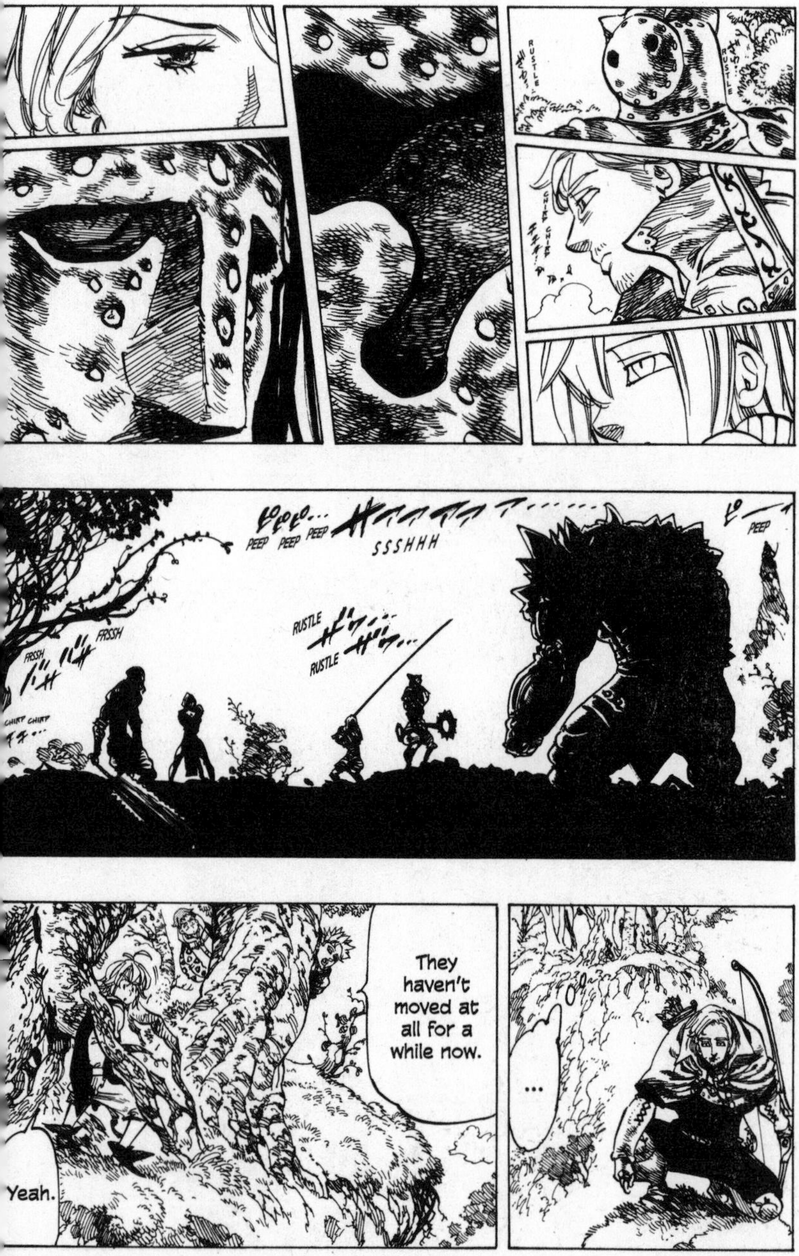
RUSTLE
RUSTLE
CHIRP CHIRP
PEEP
SSSHHH
PEEP PEEP PEEP
RUSTLE
RUSTLE
FRSSH
FRSSH
CHIRP CHIRP
...
They haven't moved at all for a while now.
Yeah.

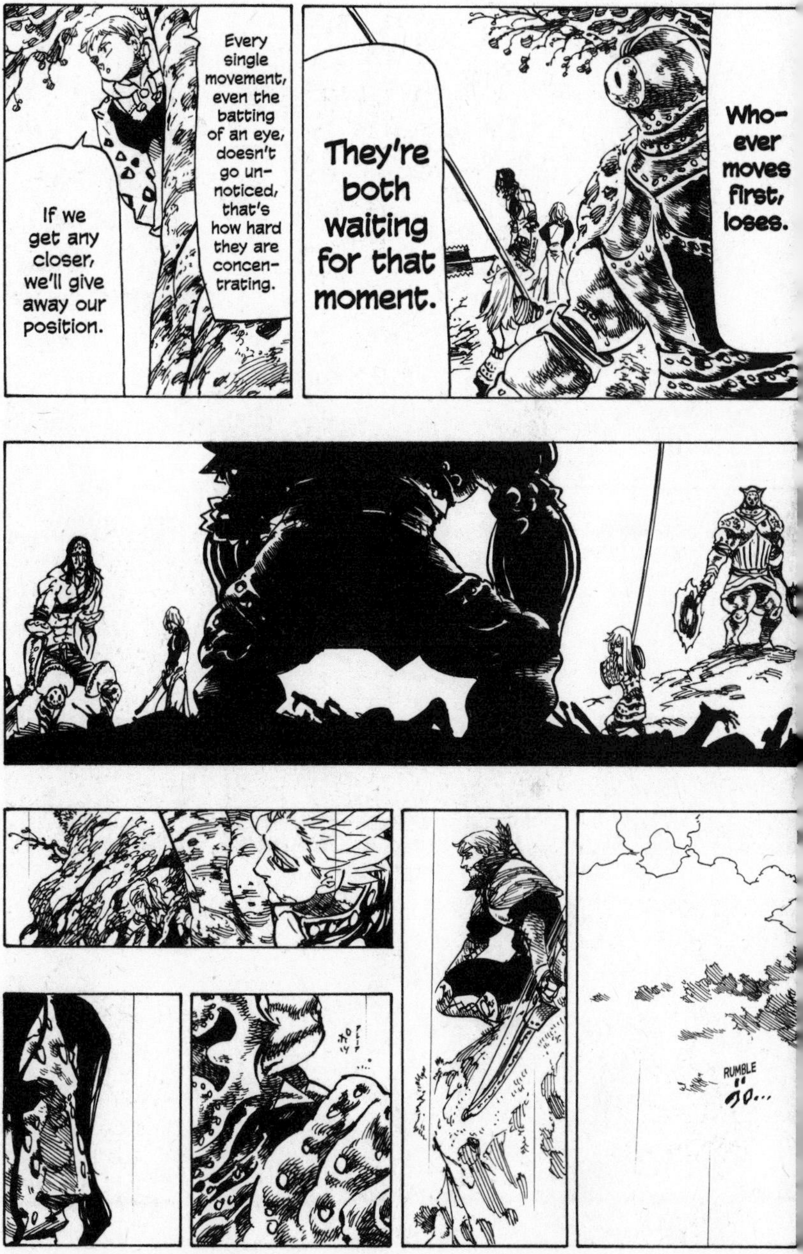
Who-ever moves first, loses.
They're both waiting for that moment.
Every single movement, even the batting of an eye, doesn't go un-noticed, that's how hard they are concen-trating.
If we get any closer, we'll give away our position.
RUMBLE

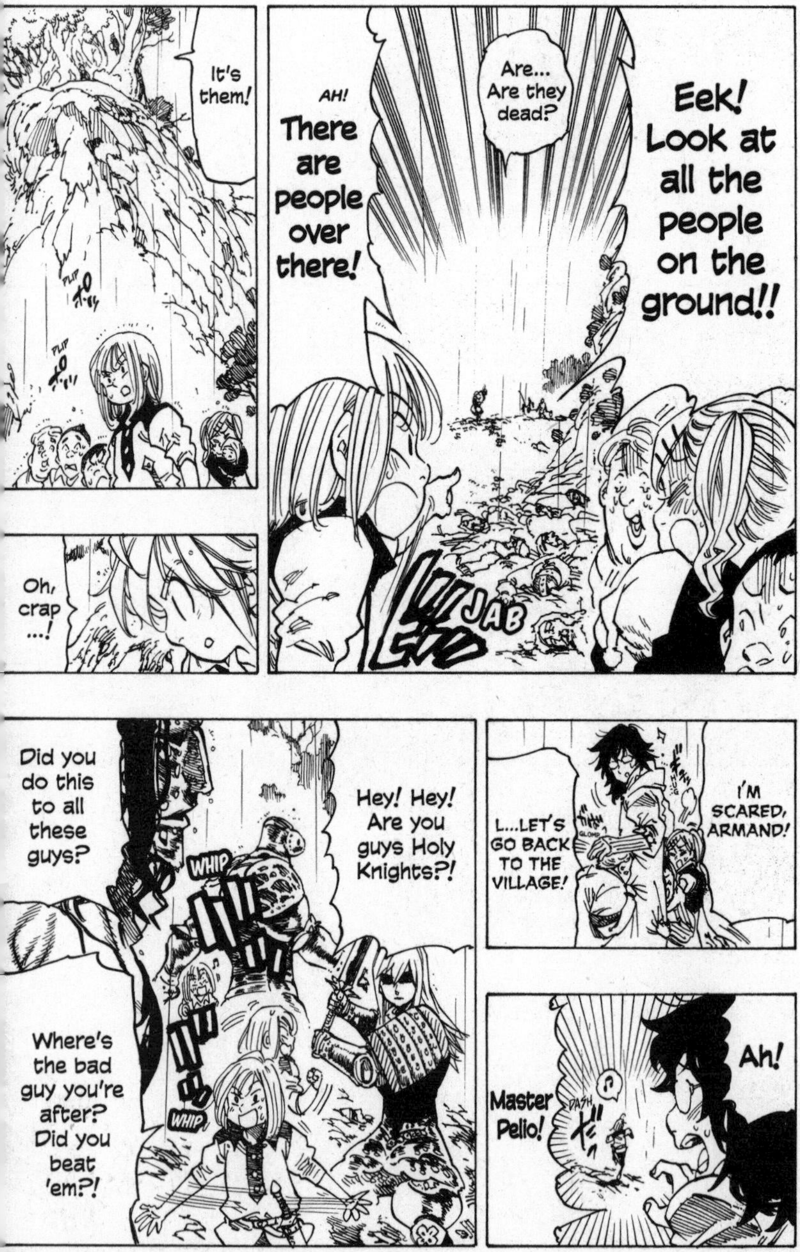
Are... Are they dead?
Eek! Look at all the people on the ground!!
AH! There are people over there!
JAB
It's them!
FLIP
FLIP
Oh, crap ...!
I'M SCARED, ARMAND!
HUG
L...LET'S GO BACK TO THE VILLAGE!
GLOMP
Ah!
Master Pelio!
DASH
Hey! Hey! Are you guys Holy Knights?!
Did you do this to all these guys?
WHIP
WHIP
Where's the bad guy you're after? Did you beat 'em?!

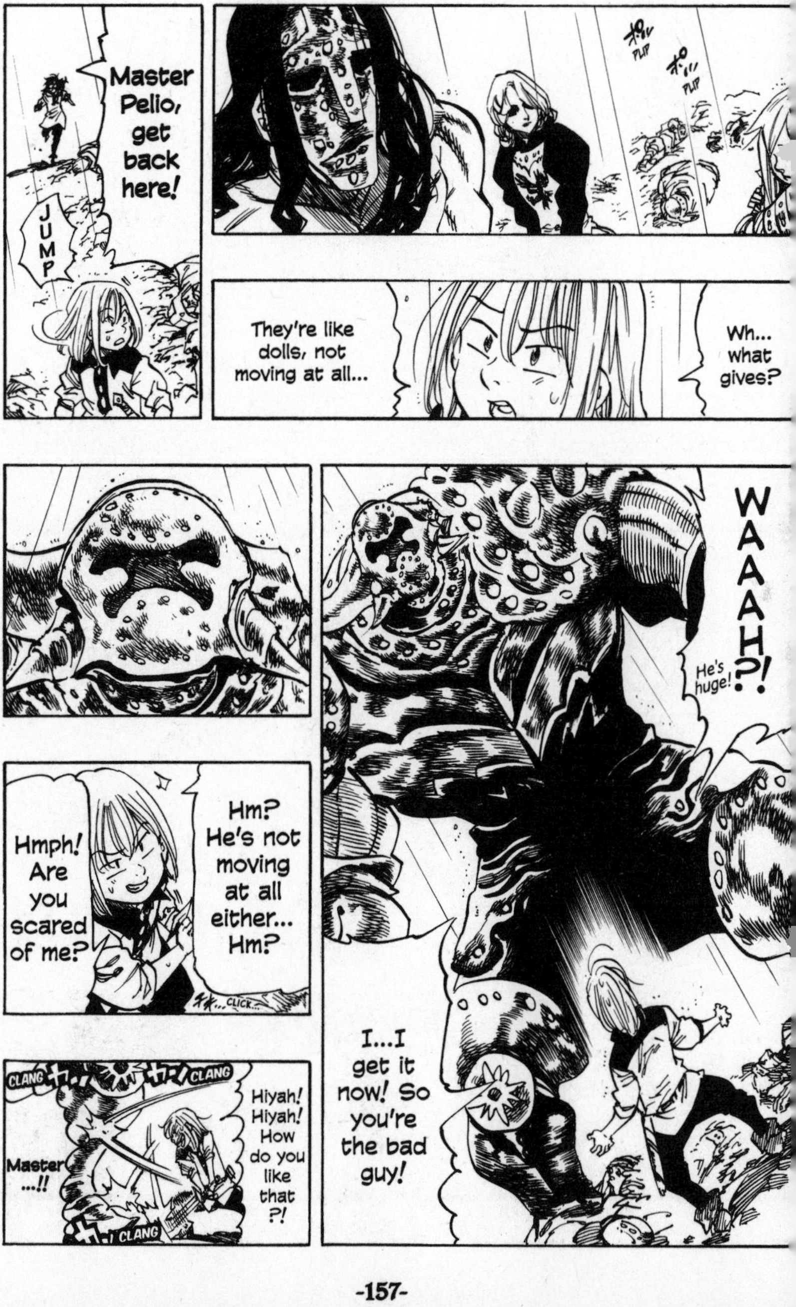
PLIP
PLIP
Wh... what gives?
They're like dolls, not moving at all...
Master Pelio, get back here!
JUMP
WAAAH?!
He's huge!
I...I get it now! So you're the bad guy!
Hm? He's not moving at all either... Hm?
Hmph! Are you scared of me?
CLICK...
CLANG
CLANG
Hiyah! Hiyah! How do you like that?!
Master...!!
CLANG

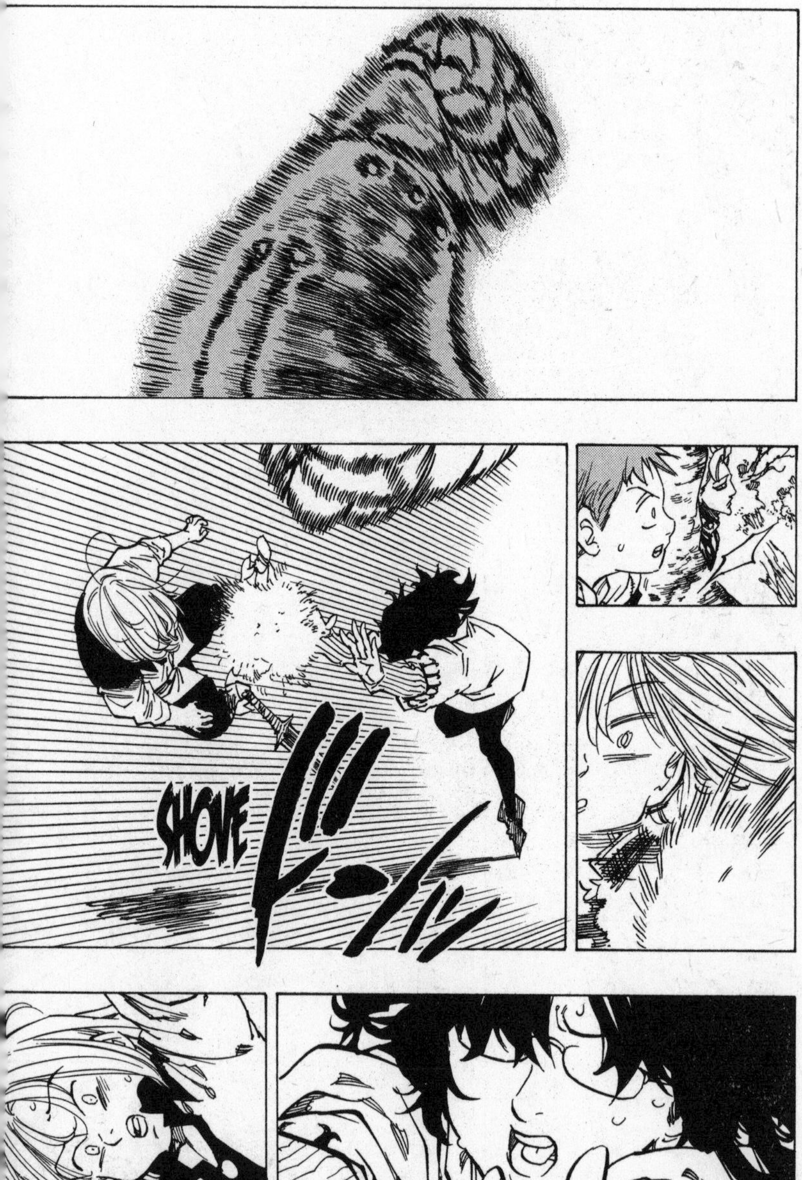
SHOVE

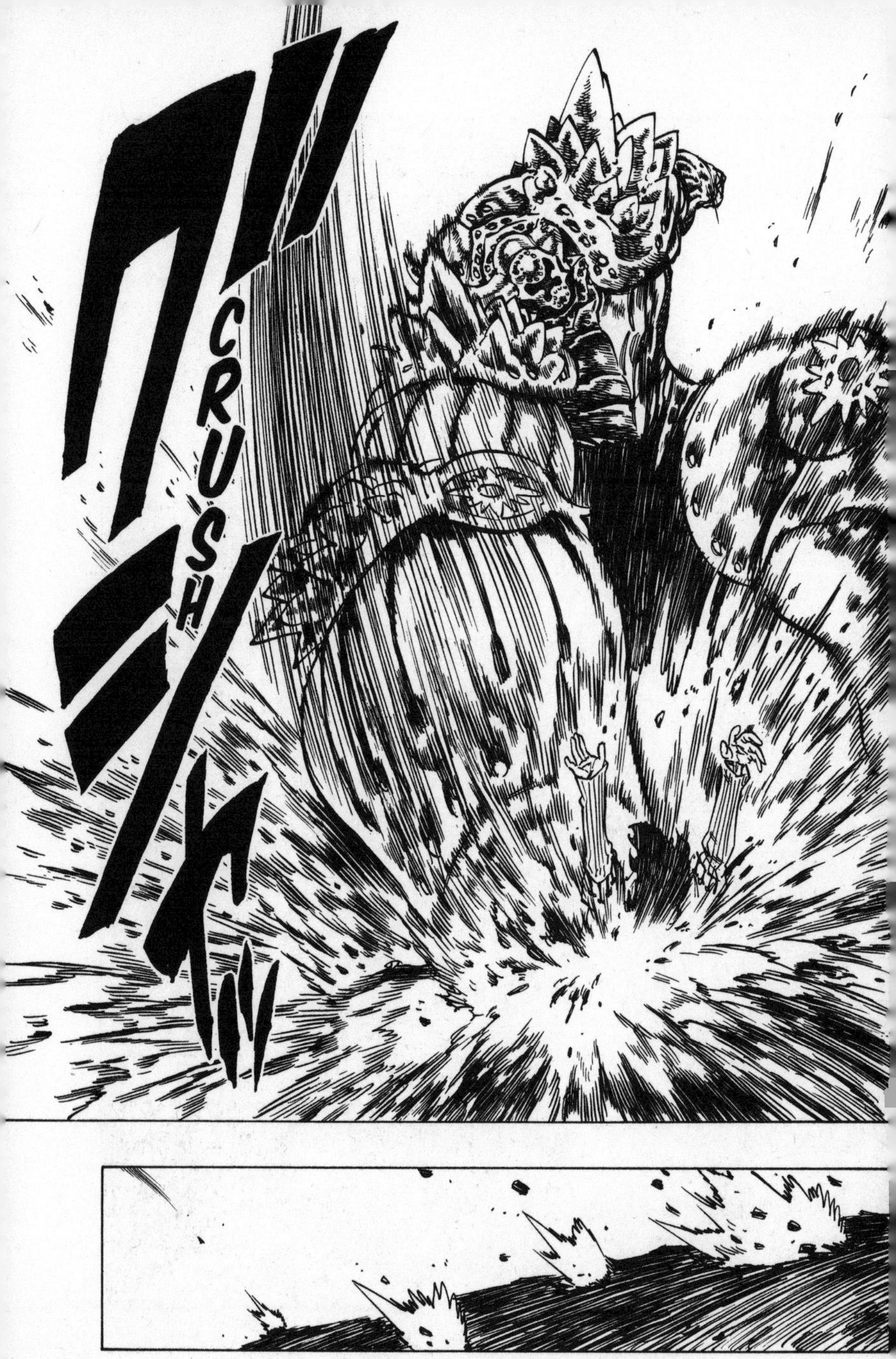
CRUSH

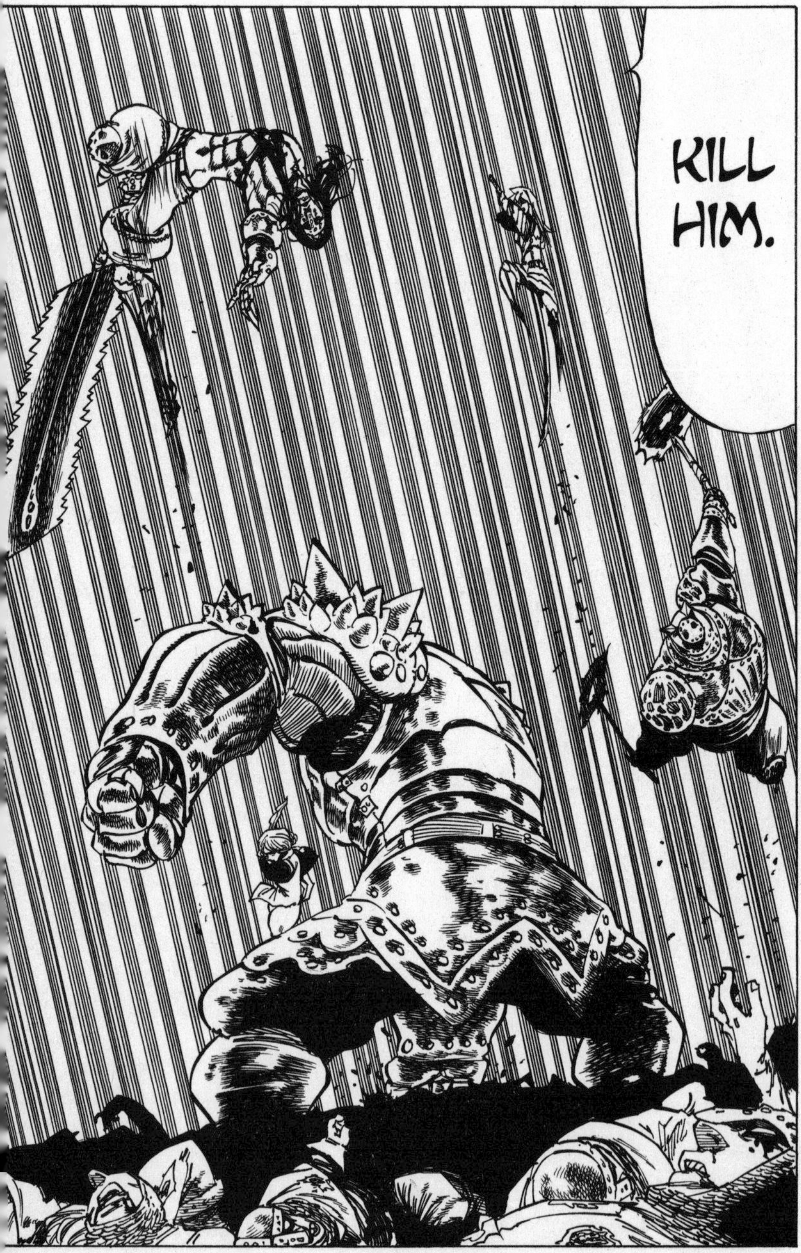
KILL HIM.

the Seven deadly sins

Chapter 54 - The Man Who Didn't Move

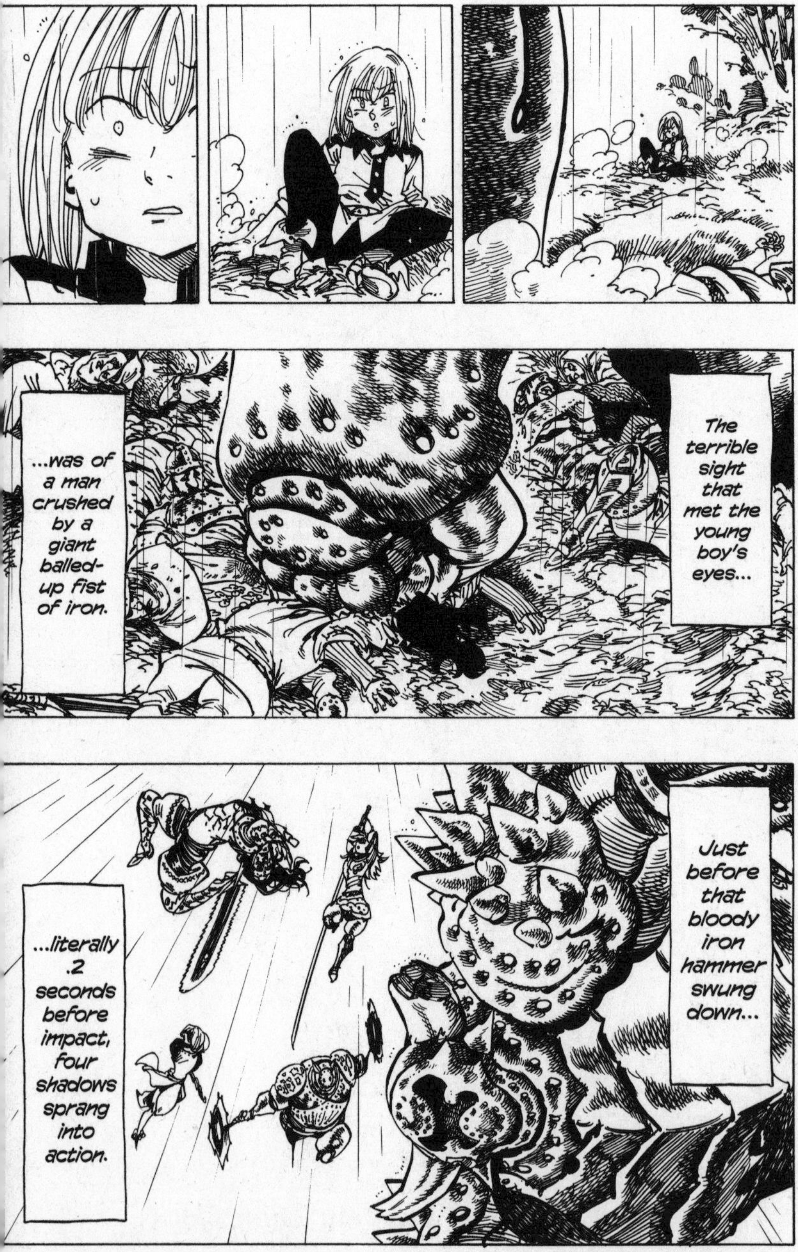
The terrible sight that met the young boy's eyes...
...was of a man crushed by a giant balled-up fist of iron.
Just before that bloody iron hammer swung down...
...literally .2 seconds before impact, four shadows sprang into action.

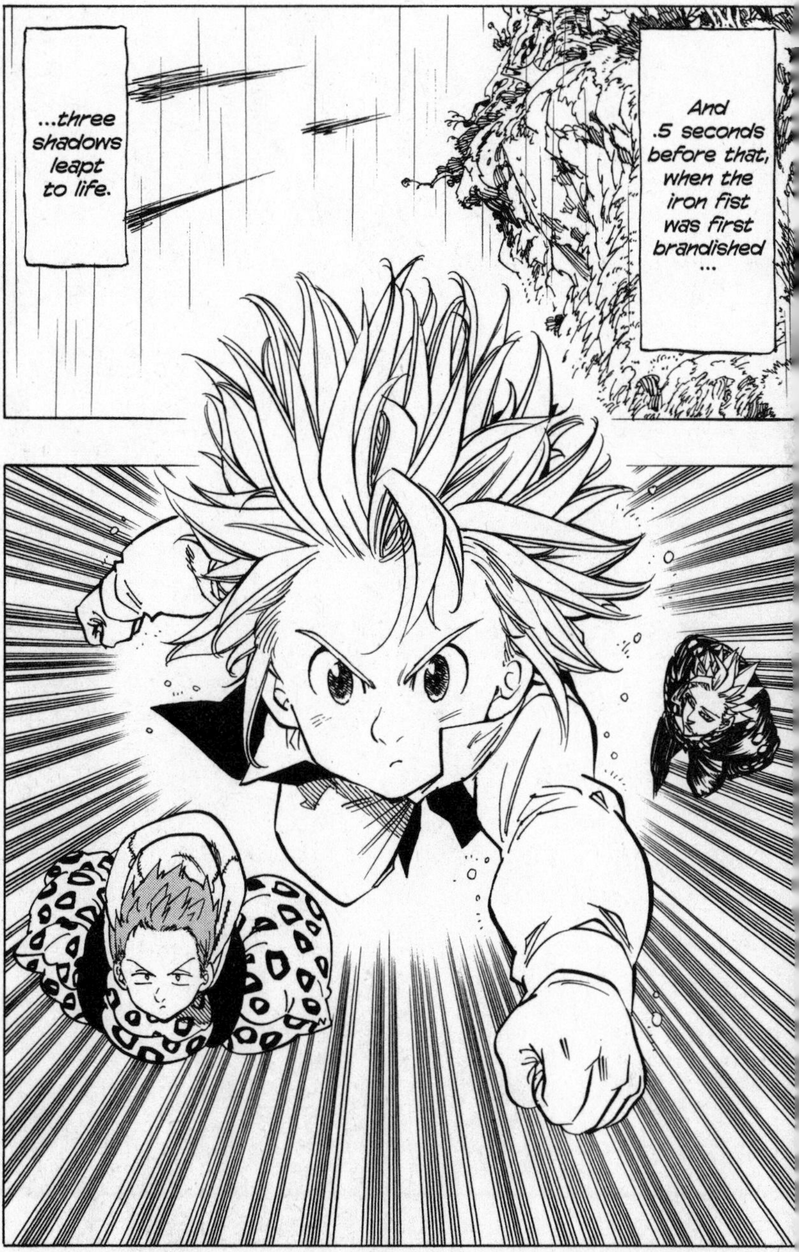
And .5 seconds before that, when the iron fist was first brandished ...
...three shadows leapt to life.

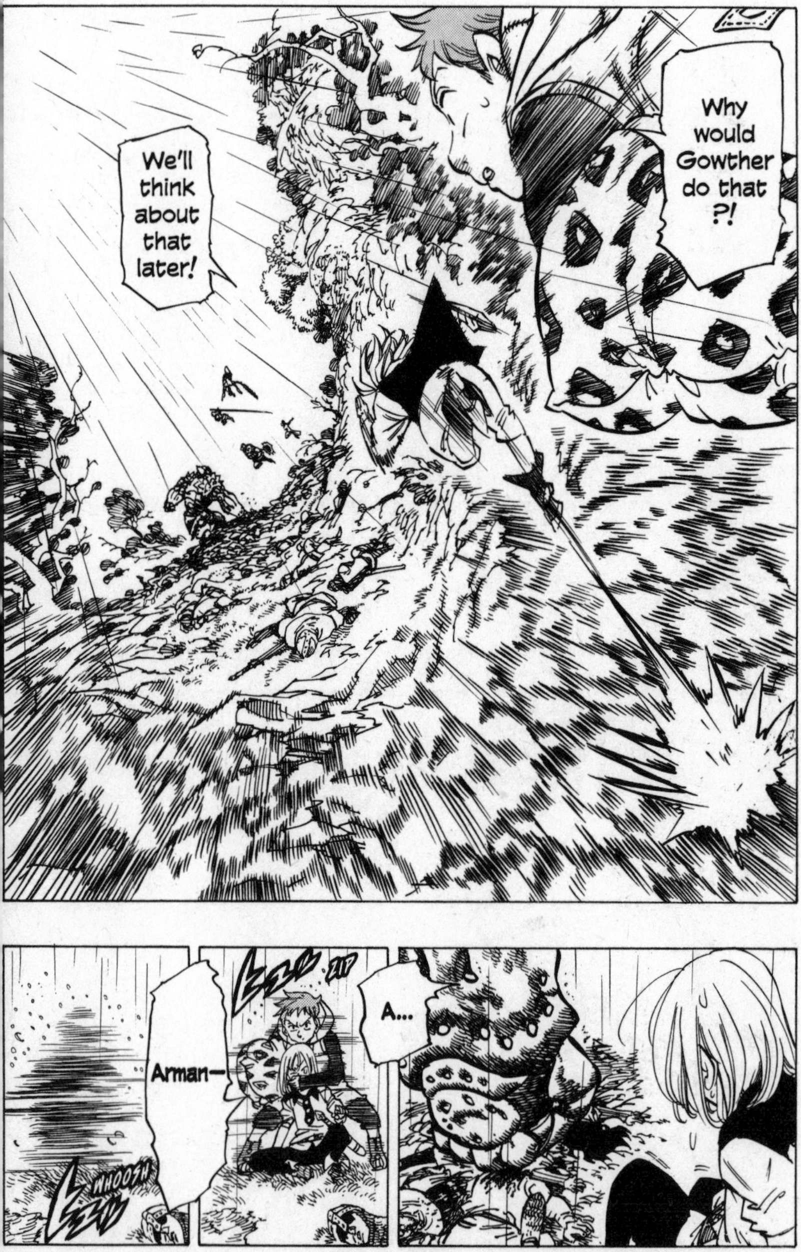
Why would Gowther do that?!
We'll think about that later!
A...
ZIP
Arman—
WHOOSH

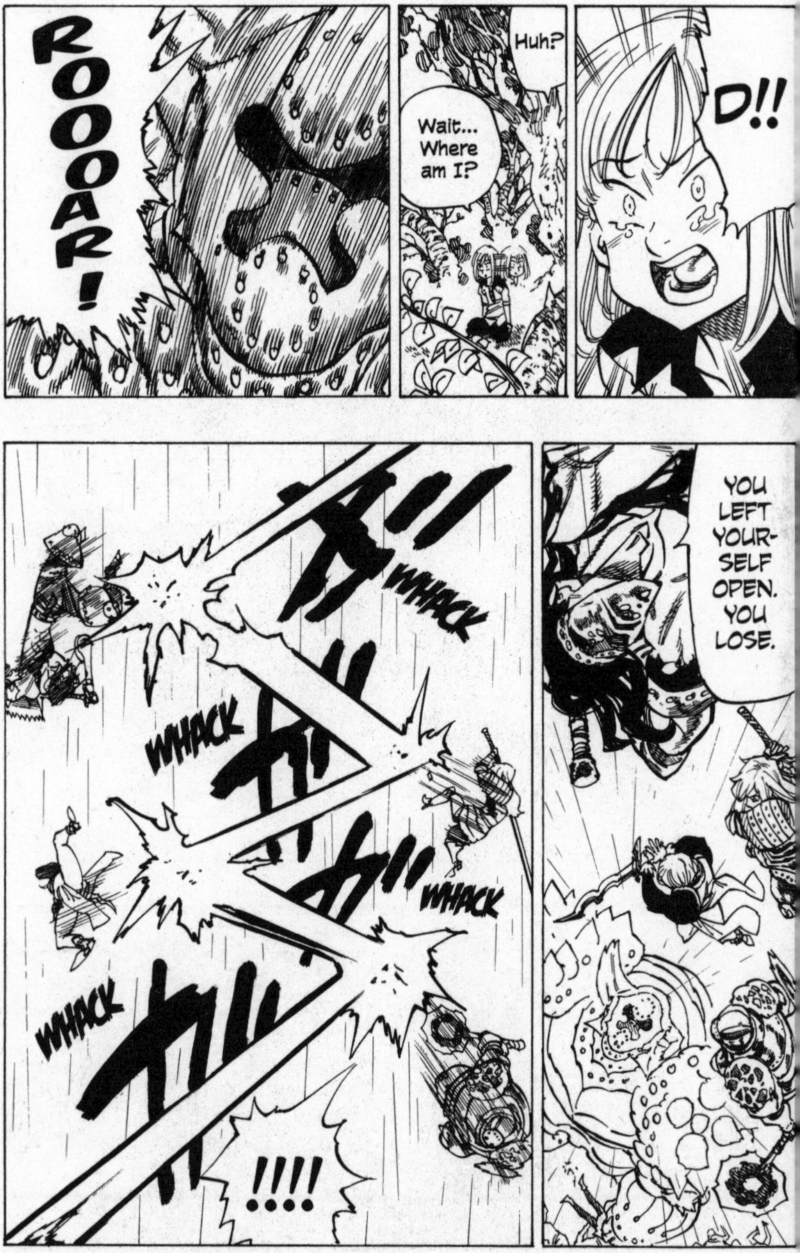
D!!
Huh?
Wait... Where am I?
ROOOAR!
YOU LEFT YOUR-SELF OPEN. YOU LOSE.
WHACK
WHACK
WHACK
WHACK
!!!!

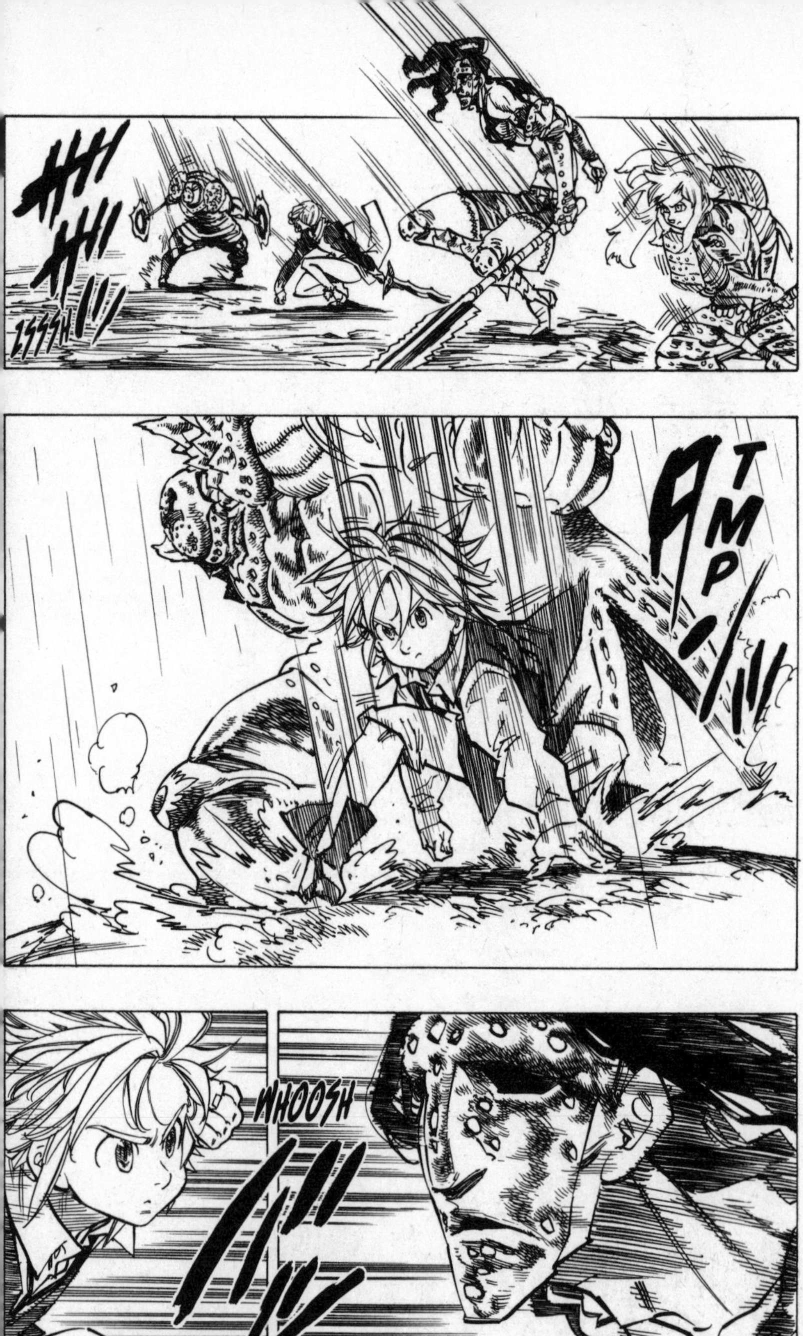
ZSSSH
TMP
WHOOSH

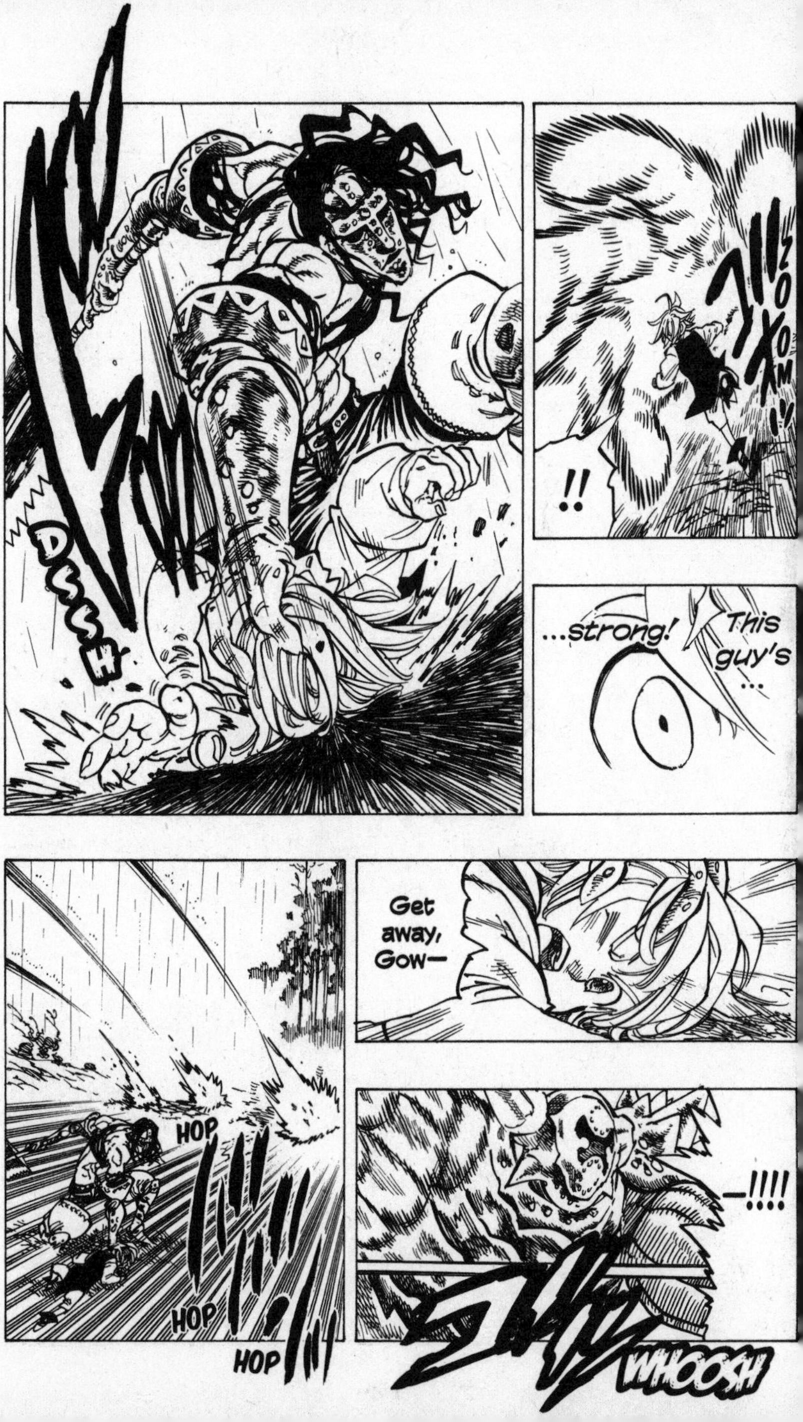
ZOOM!!
!!
This guy's...
...strong!
DSSH
Get away, Gow—
—!!!!
WHOOSH
HOP
HOP
HOP

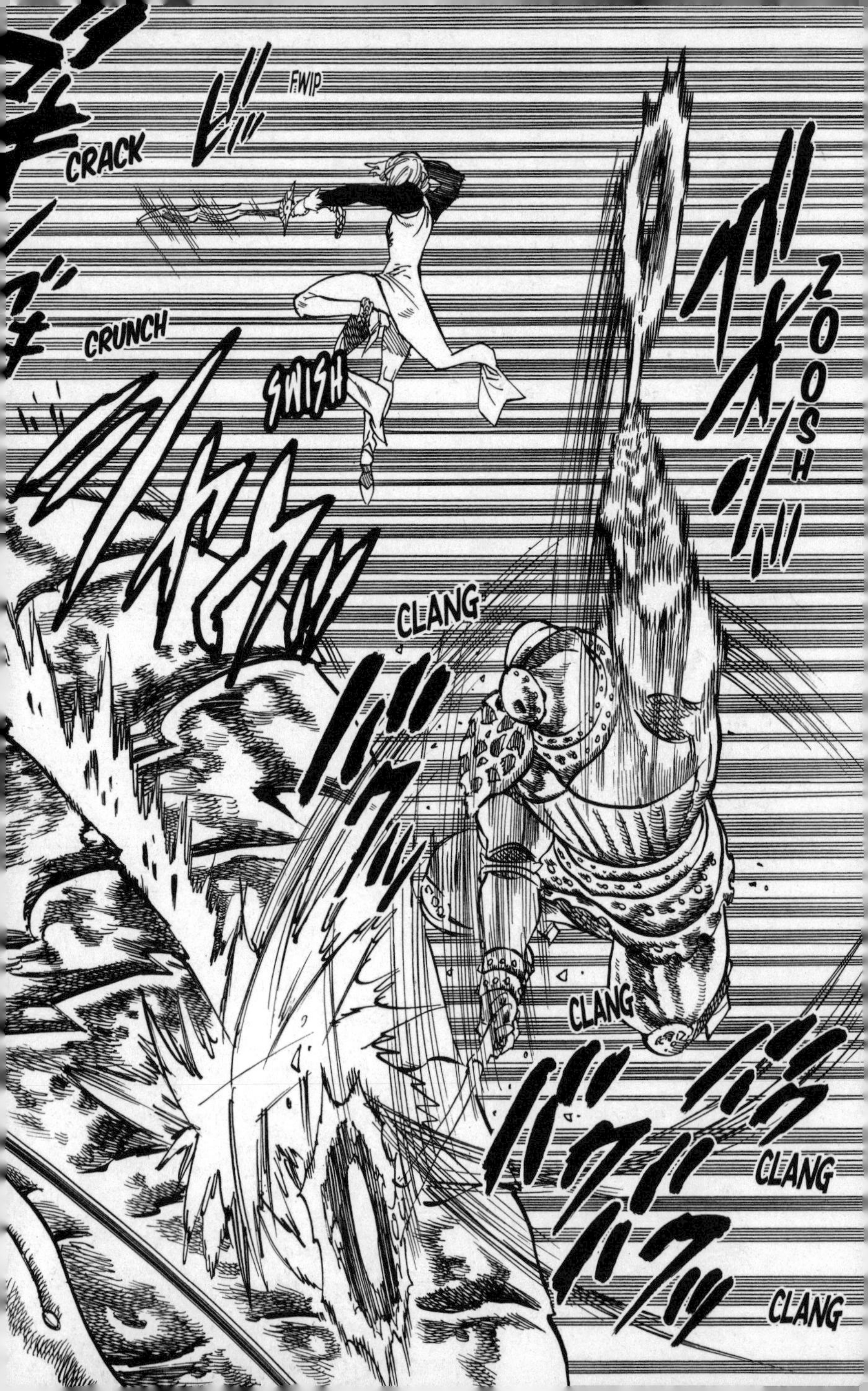
ZOOSH
FWIP
CRACK
SWISH
CRUNCH
CLANG
CLANG
CLANG
CLANG

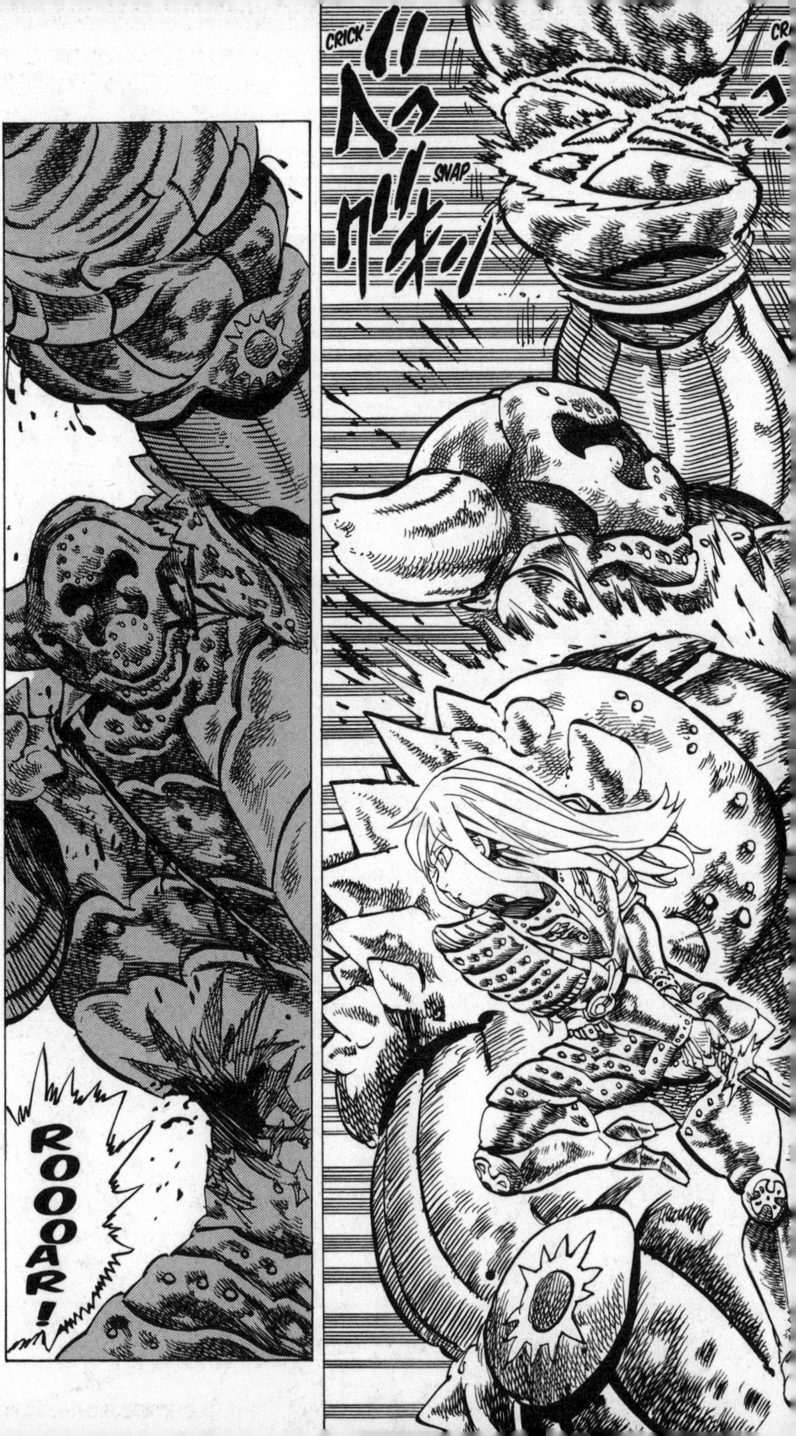
CRICK
SNAP
ROOOOAR!

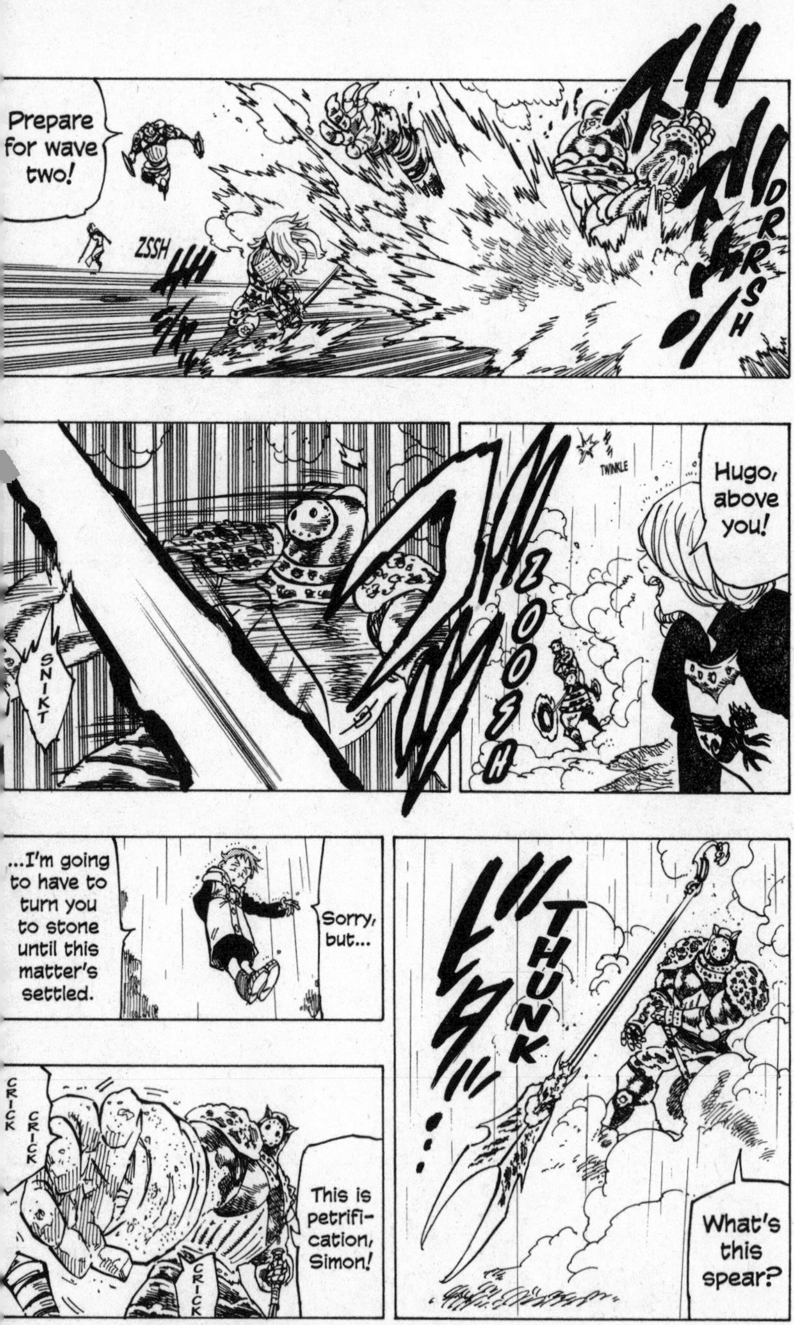
DORRSH
Prepare for wave two!
ZSSH
Hugo, above you!
TWINKLE
ZOOOSH
SNIKT
THUNK
What's this spear?
Sorry, but...
...I'm going to have to turn you to stone until this matter's settled.
This is petrification, Simon!
CRICK
CRICK
CRICK

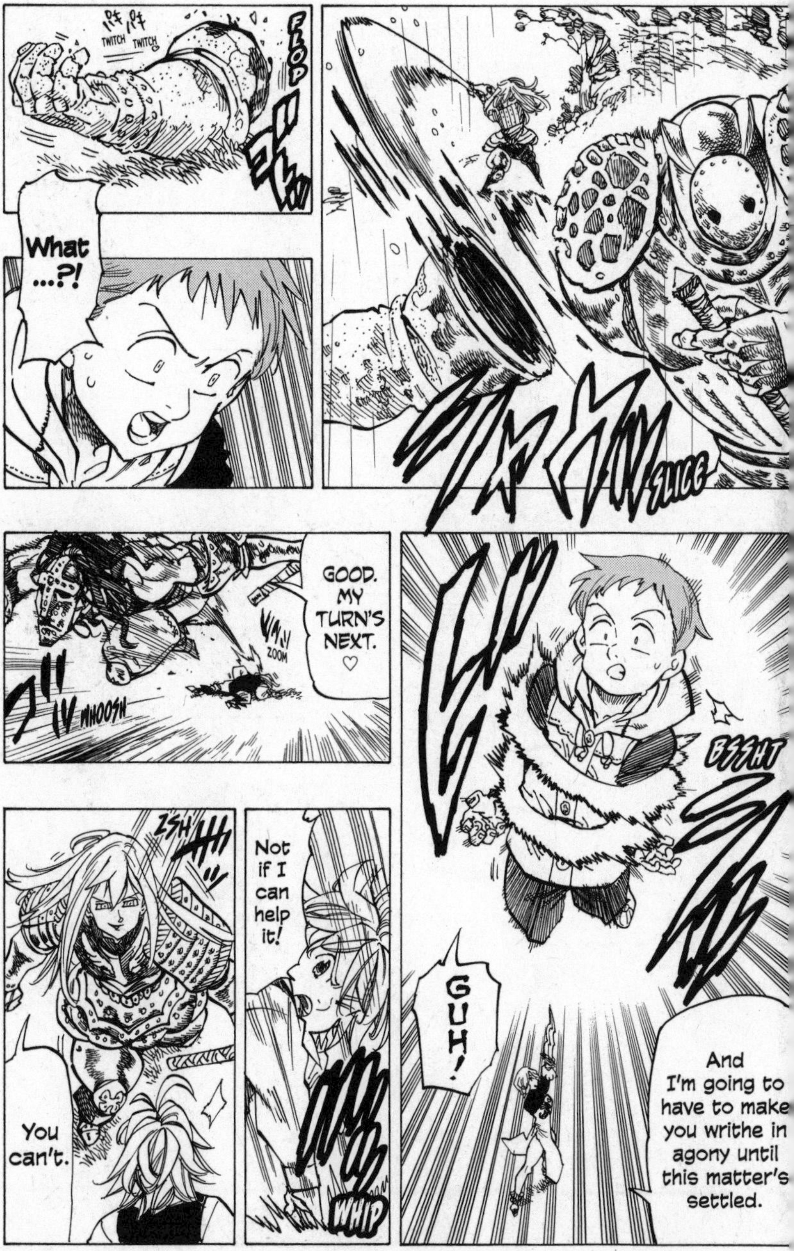
SLICE
TWITCH TWITCH
FLOP
What ...?!
BSSHT
GUH!
And I'm going to have to make you writhe in agony until this matter's settled.
GOOD. MY TURN'S NEXT. ♡
ZOOM
WHOOSH
Not if I can help it!
WHIP
ZSH
You can't.

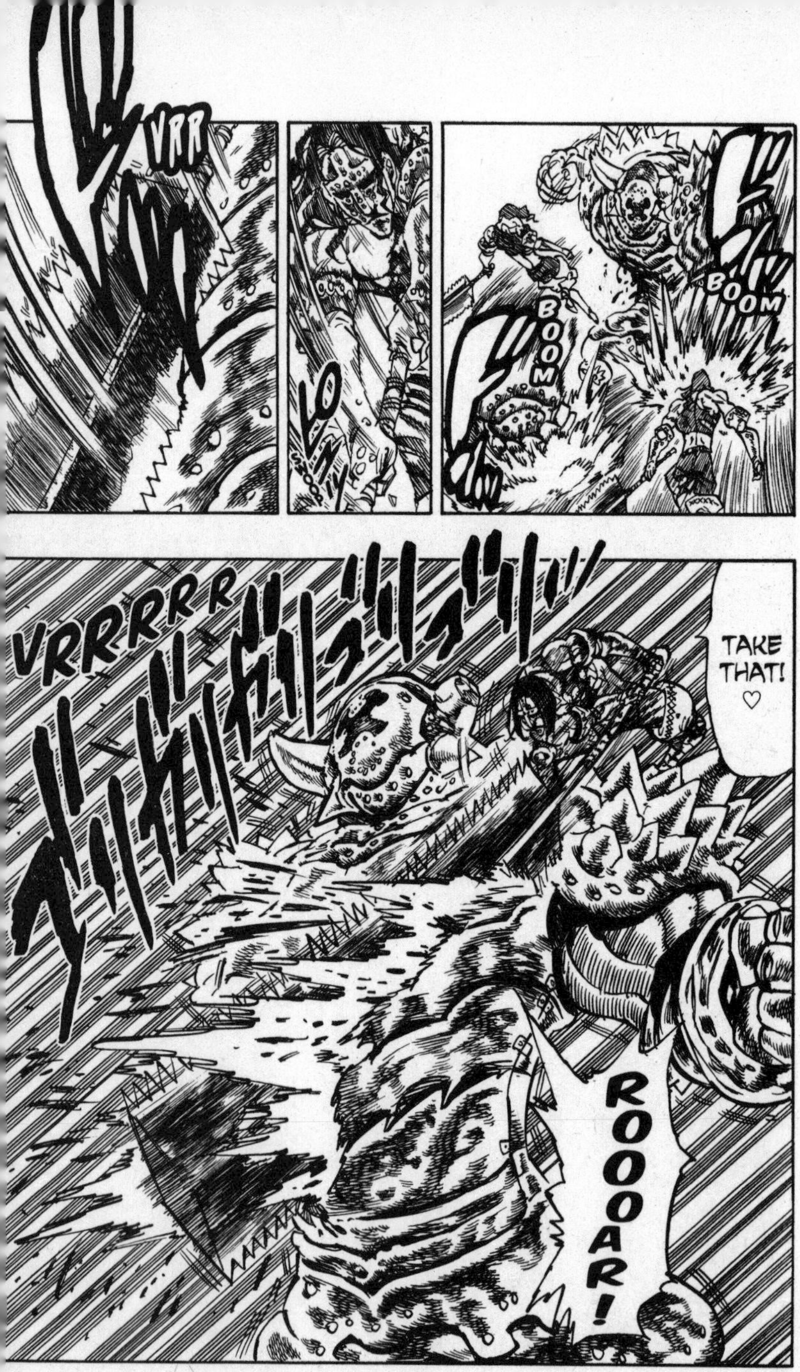
BOOM
BOOM
SWOOP
VRR
TAKE THAT! ♡
VRRRRRR
ROOOAR!

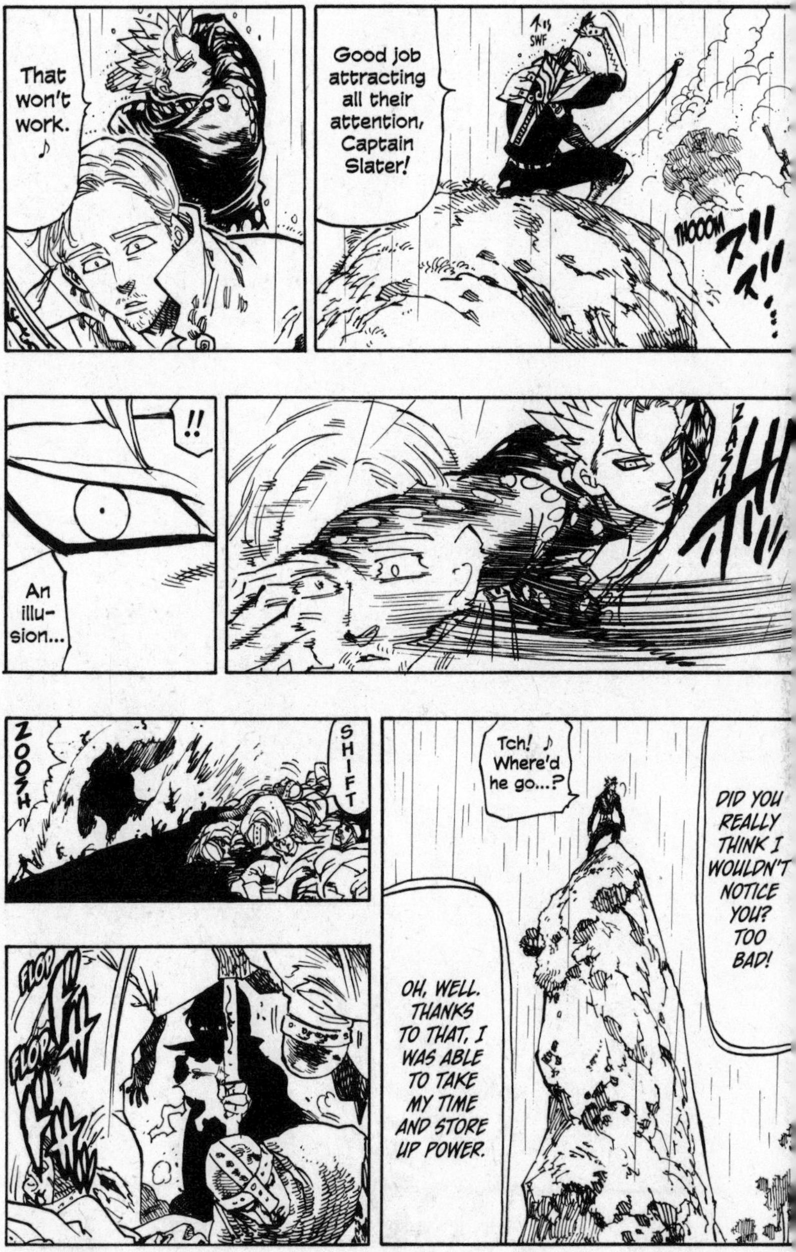
SWF
Good job attracting all their attention, Captain Slater!
THOOOM
That won't work. ♪
ZASH
!!
An illusion...
Tch! ♪ Where'd he go...?
DID YOU REALLY THINK I WOULDN'T NOTICE YOU? TOO BAD!
OH, WELL. THANKS TO THAT, I WAS ABLE TO TAKE MY TIME AND STORE UP POWER.
SHIFT
ZOOSH
FLOP
FLOP

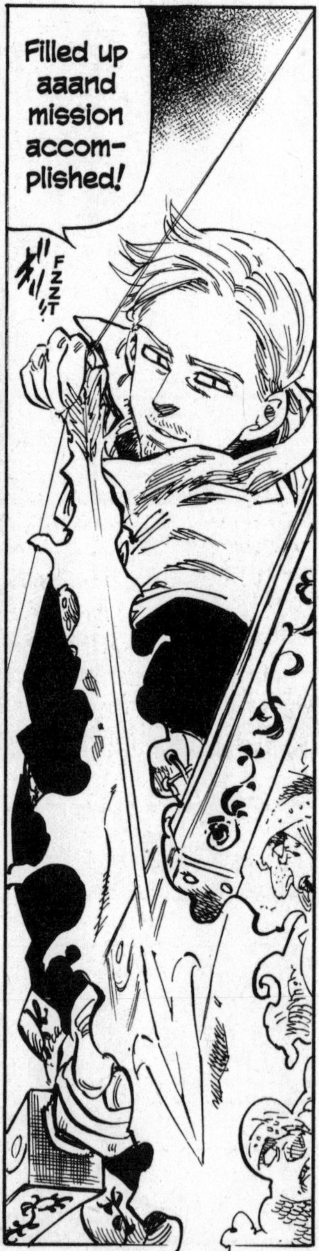
Filled up aaand mission accom-plished!
FZZT

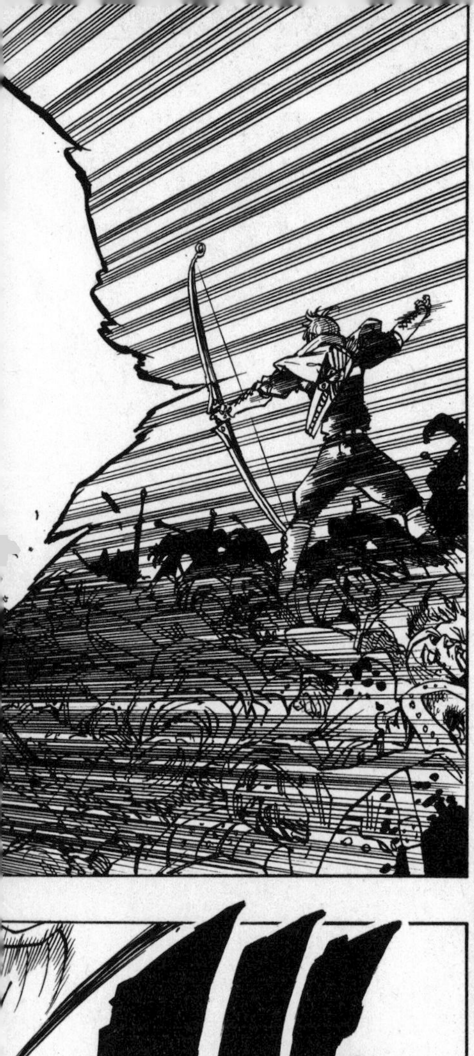

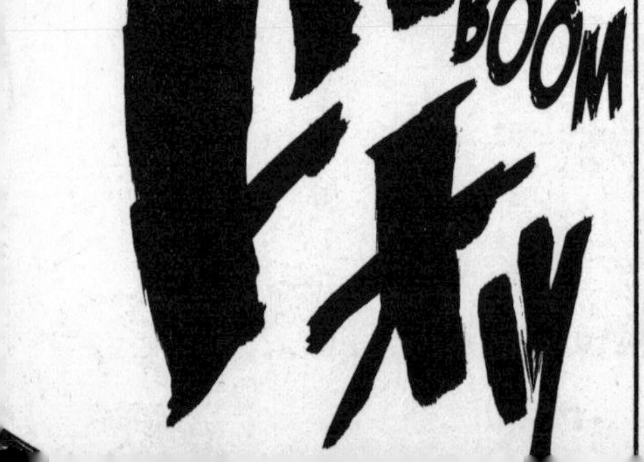
BOOM

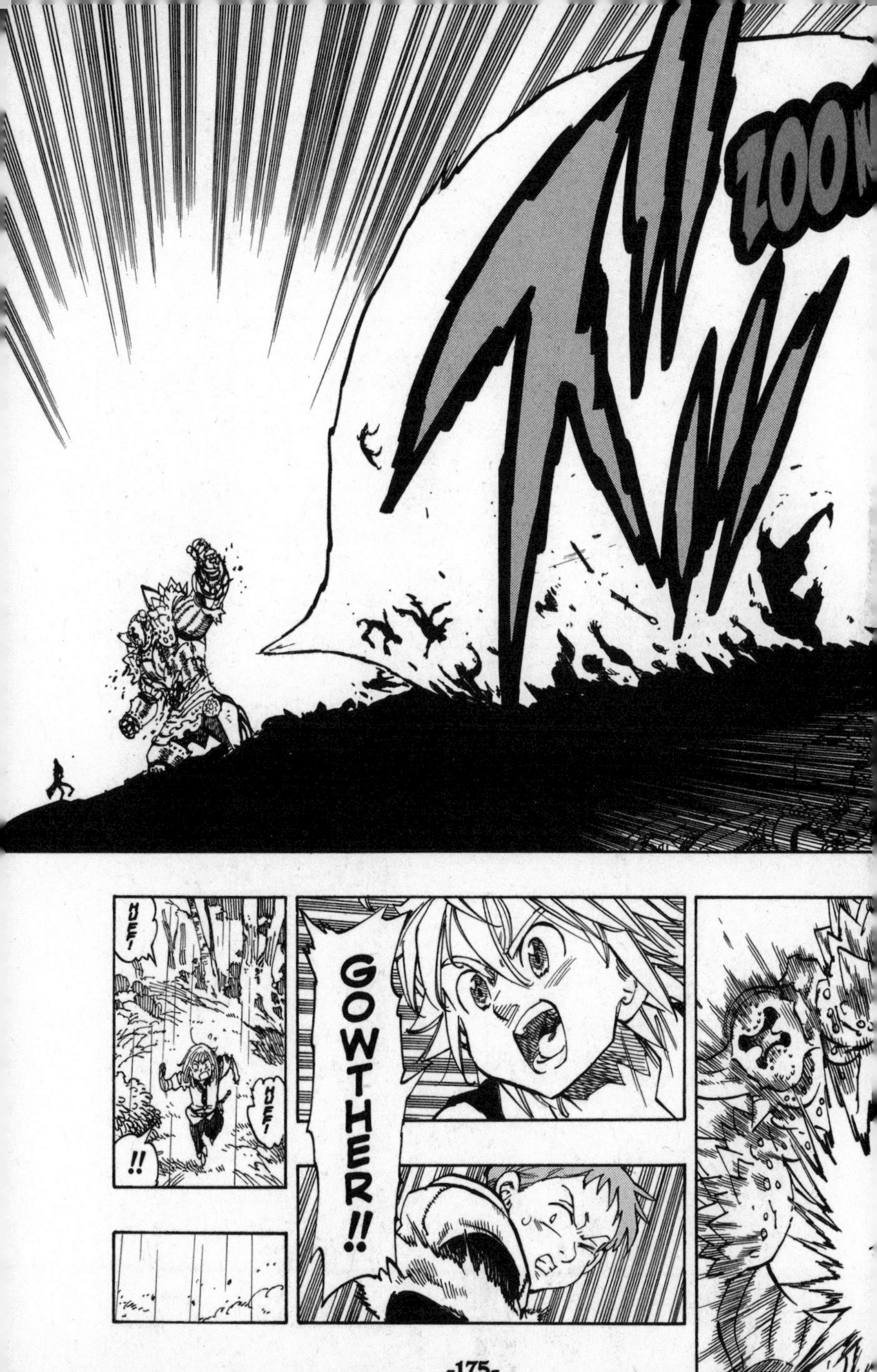
ZOO
GOWTHER!!
HUF!
HUF!
!!

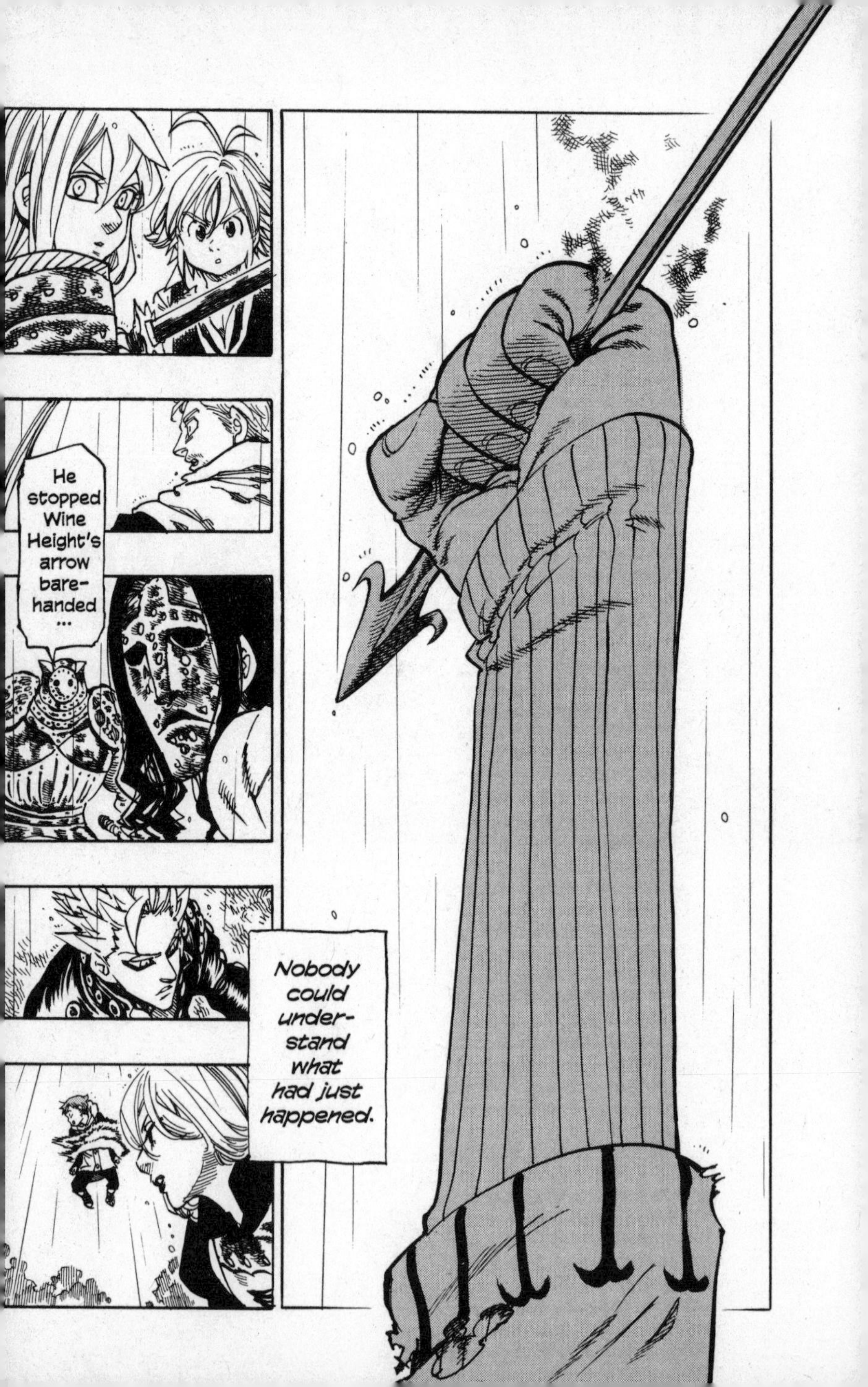

He stopped Wine Height's arrow bare-handed ...
Nobody could under-stand what had just happened.

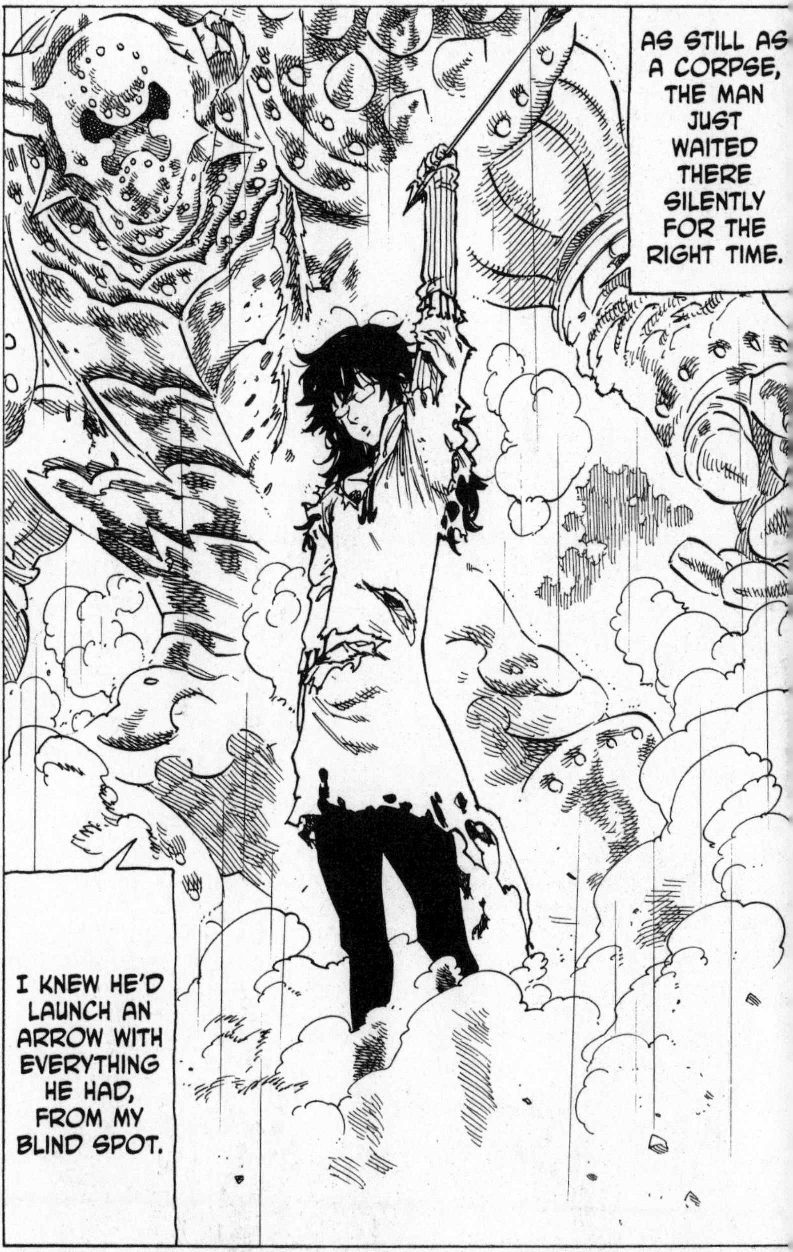
AS STILL AS A CORPSE, THE MAN JUST WAITED THERE SILENTLY FOR THE RIGHT TIME.
I KNEW HE'D LAUNCH AN ARROW WITH EVERYTHING HE HAD, FROM MY BLIND SPOT.

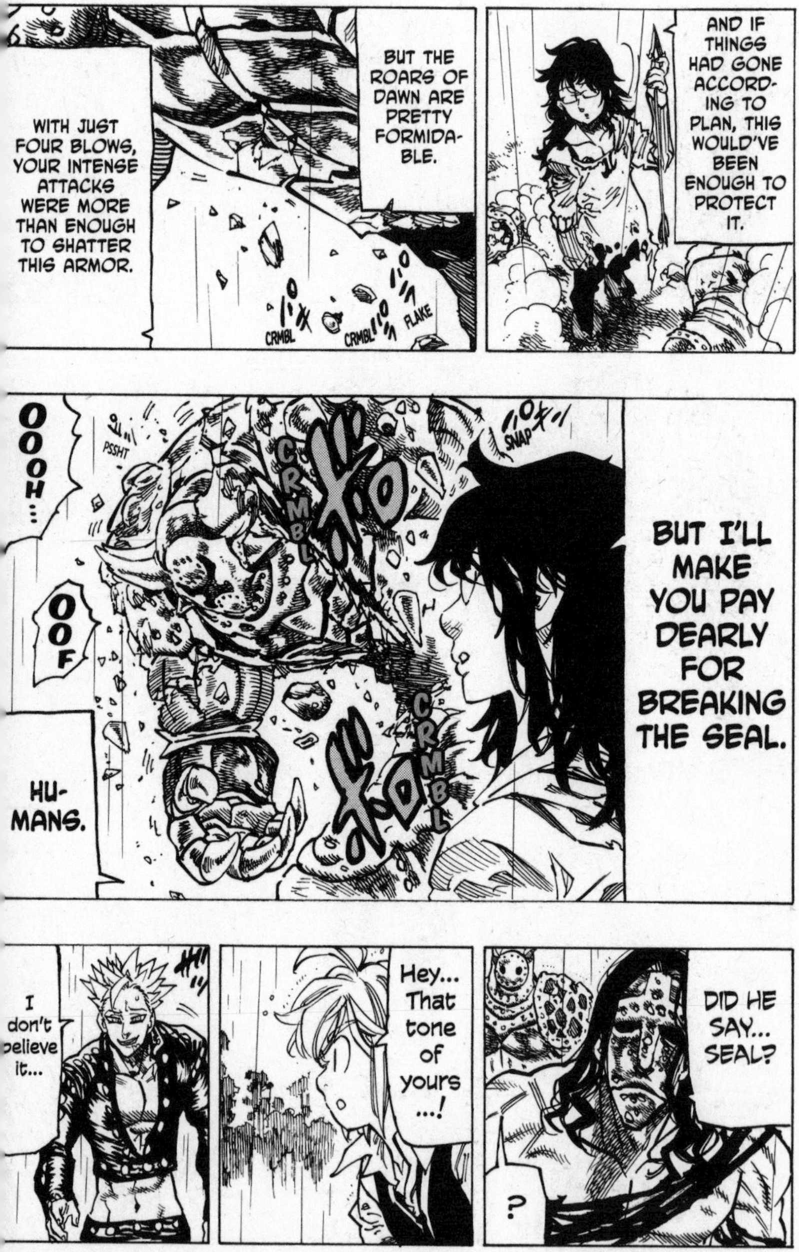
AND IF THINGS HAD GONE ACCORD-ING TO PLAN, THIS WOULD'VE BEEN ENOUGH TO PROTECT IT.
BUT THE ROARS OF DAWN ARE PRETTY FORMIDA-BLE.
WITH JUST FOUR BLOWS, YOUR INTENSE ATTACKS WERE MORE THAN ENOUGH TO SHATTER THIS ARMOR.
FLAKE
CRMBL
CRMBL
BUT I'LL MAKE YOU PAY DEARLY FOR BREAKING THE SEAL.
SNAP
CRMBL
CRMBL
PSSHT
OOOOH...
OOF
HU-MANS.
DID HE SAY... SEAL?
?
Hey... That tone of yours ...!
I don't believe it...

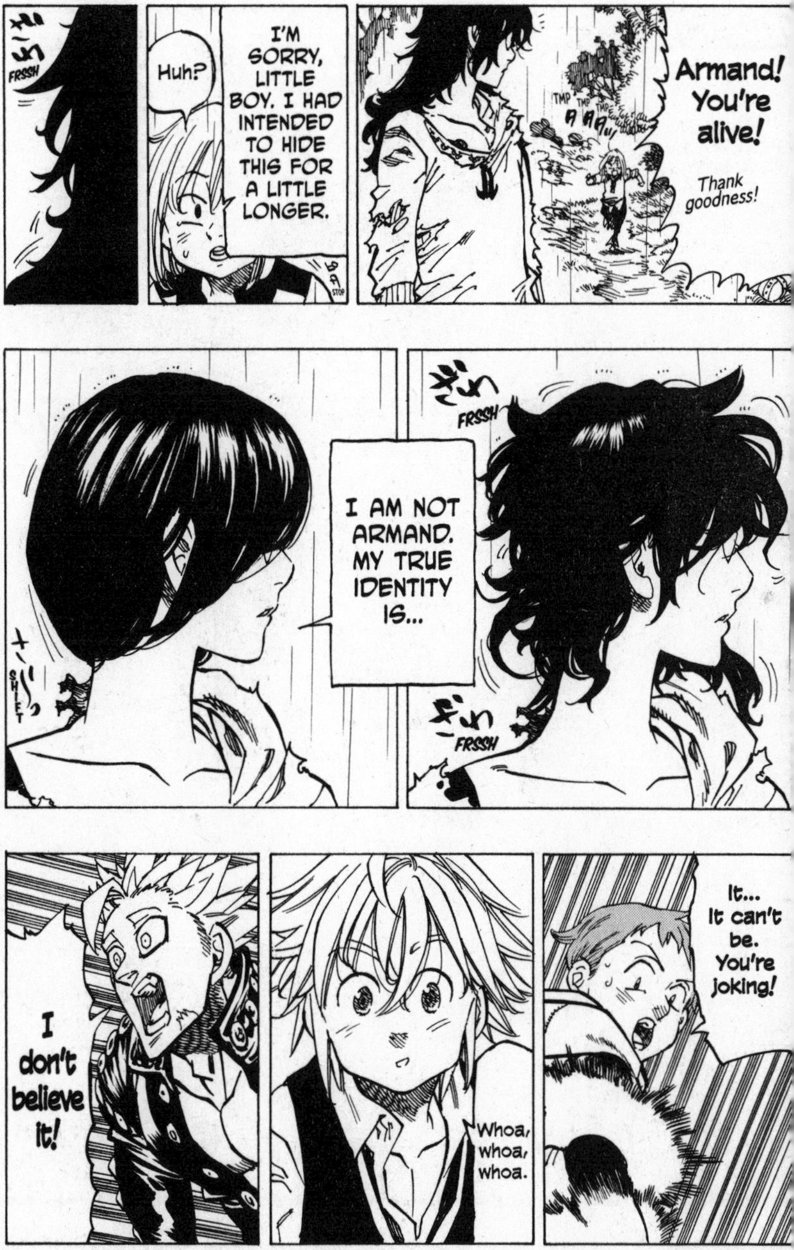
Armand! You're alive!
Thank goodness!
TMP TMP TMP
I'M SORRY, LITTLE BOY. I HAD INTENDED TO HIDE THIS FOR A LITTLE LONGER.
Huh?
STOP
FRSSH
FRSSH
FRSSH
I AM NOT ARMAND. MY TRUE IDENTITY IS...
SHIFT
It... It can't be. You're joking!
Whoa, whoa, whoa.
I don't believe it!

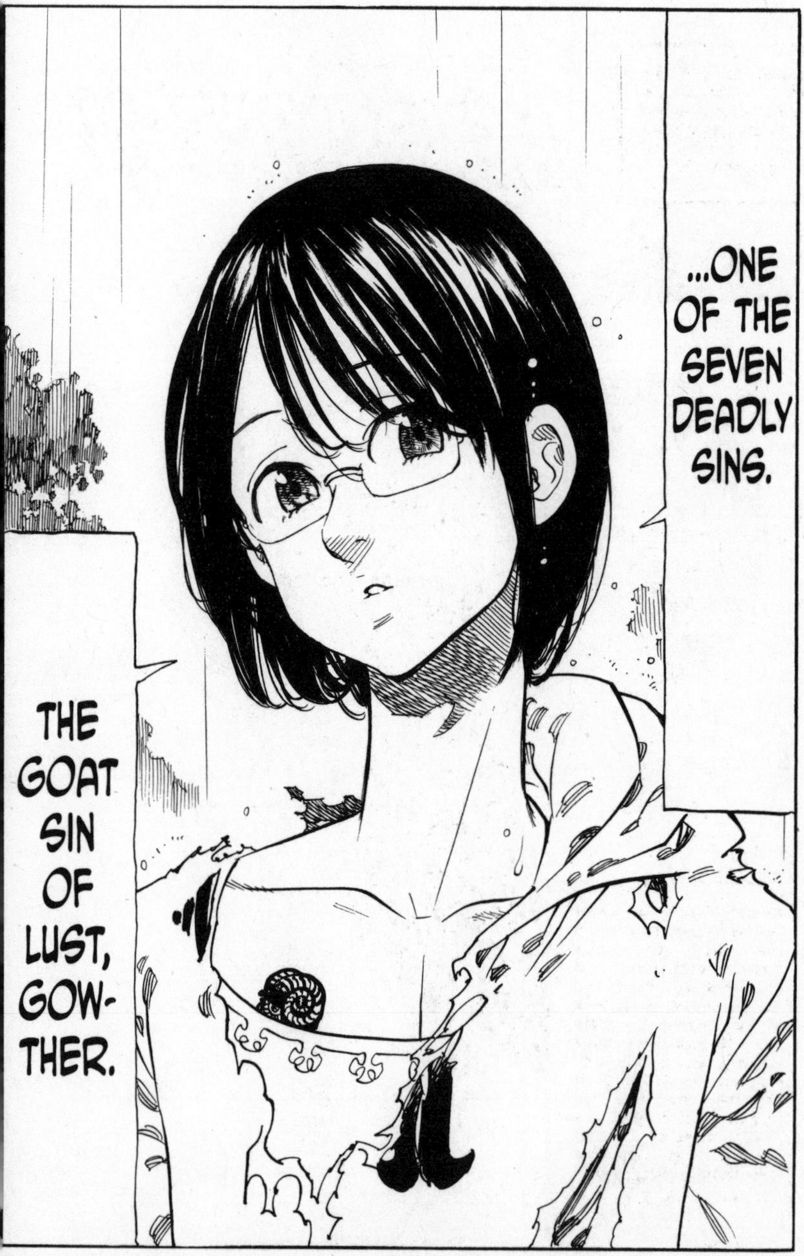
...ONE OF THE SEVEN DEADLY SINS.
THE GOAT SIN OF LUST, GOW-THER.

To be continued in volume 8.

As one of the Chief Holy Knights in the Liones Kingdom, his magic powers are said to surpass even those of the former Chief Holy Knight, Zaratras.

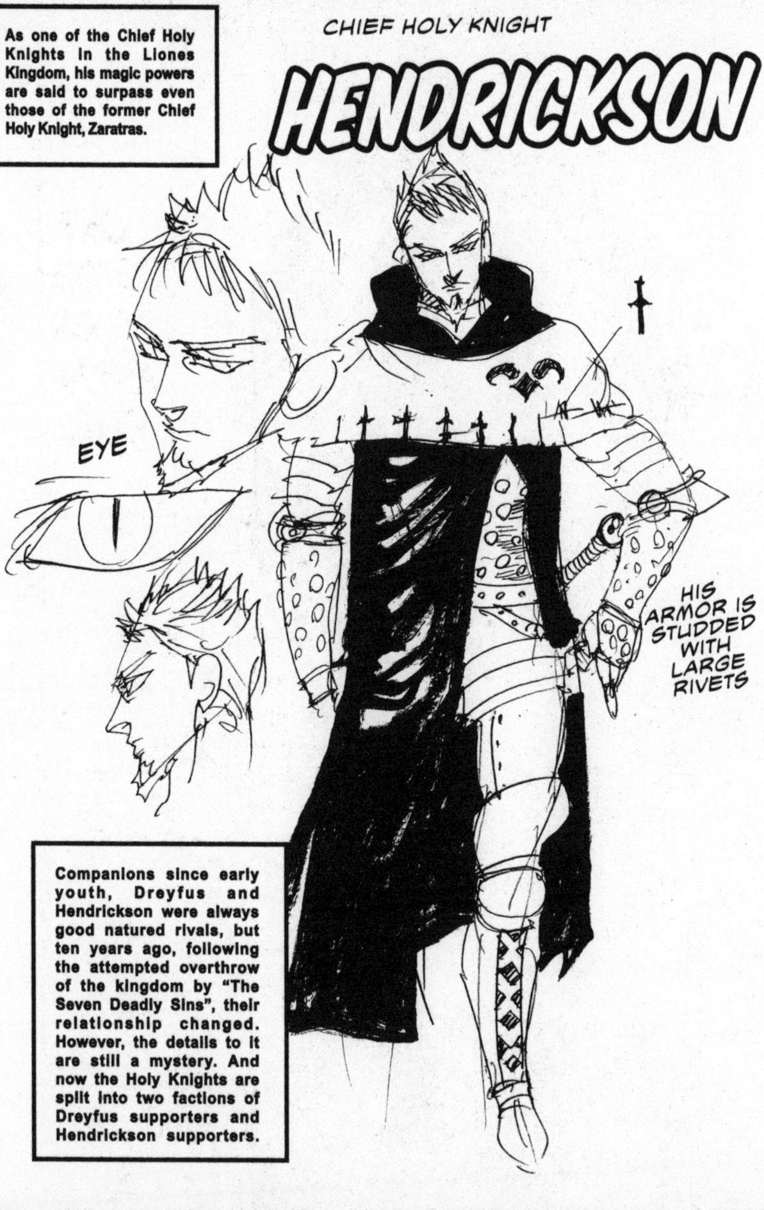
CHIEF HOLY KNIGHT
HENDRICKSON
EYE
HIS ARMOR IS STUDDED WITH LARGE RIVETS

Companions since early youth, Dreyfus and Hendrickson were always good natured rivals, but ten years ago, following the attempted overthrow of the kingdom by "The Seven Deadly Sins", their relationship changed. However, the details to it are still a mystery. And now the Holy Knights are split into two factions of Dreyfus supporters and Hendrickson supporters.

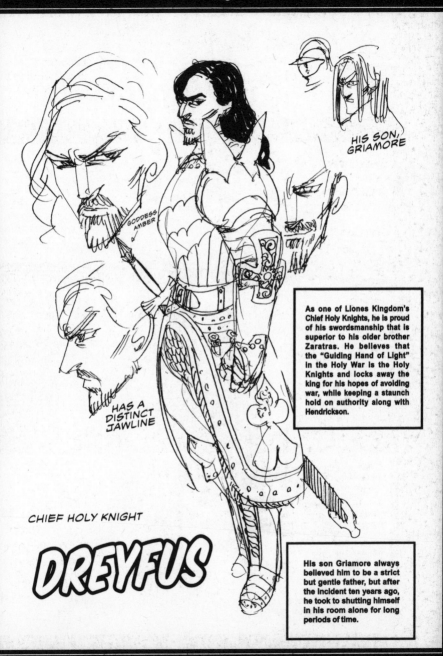

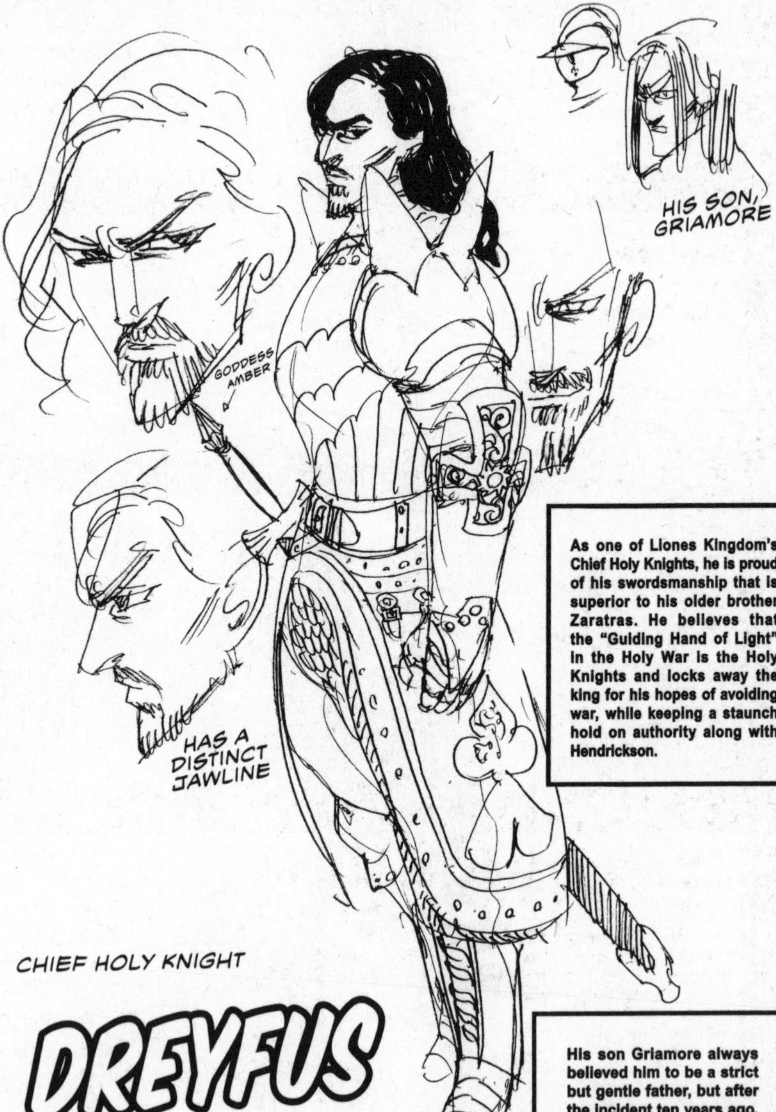
HIS SON, GRIAMORE
GODDESS AMBER
HAS A DISTINCT JAWLINE

As one of Liones Kingdom's Chief Holy Knights, he is proud of his swordsmanship that is superior to his older brother Zaratras. He believes that the "Guiding Hand of Light" in the Holy War is the Holy Knights and locks away the king for his hopes of avoiding war, while keeping a staunch hold on authority along with Hendrickson.

CHIEF HOLY KNIGHT

DREYFUS

His son Griamore always believed him to be a strict but gentle father, but after the incident ten years ago, he took to shutting himself in his room alone for long periods of time.

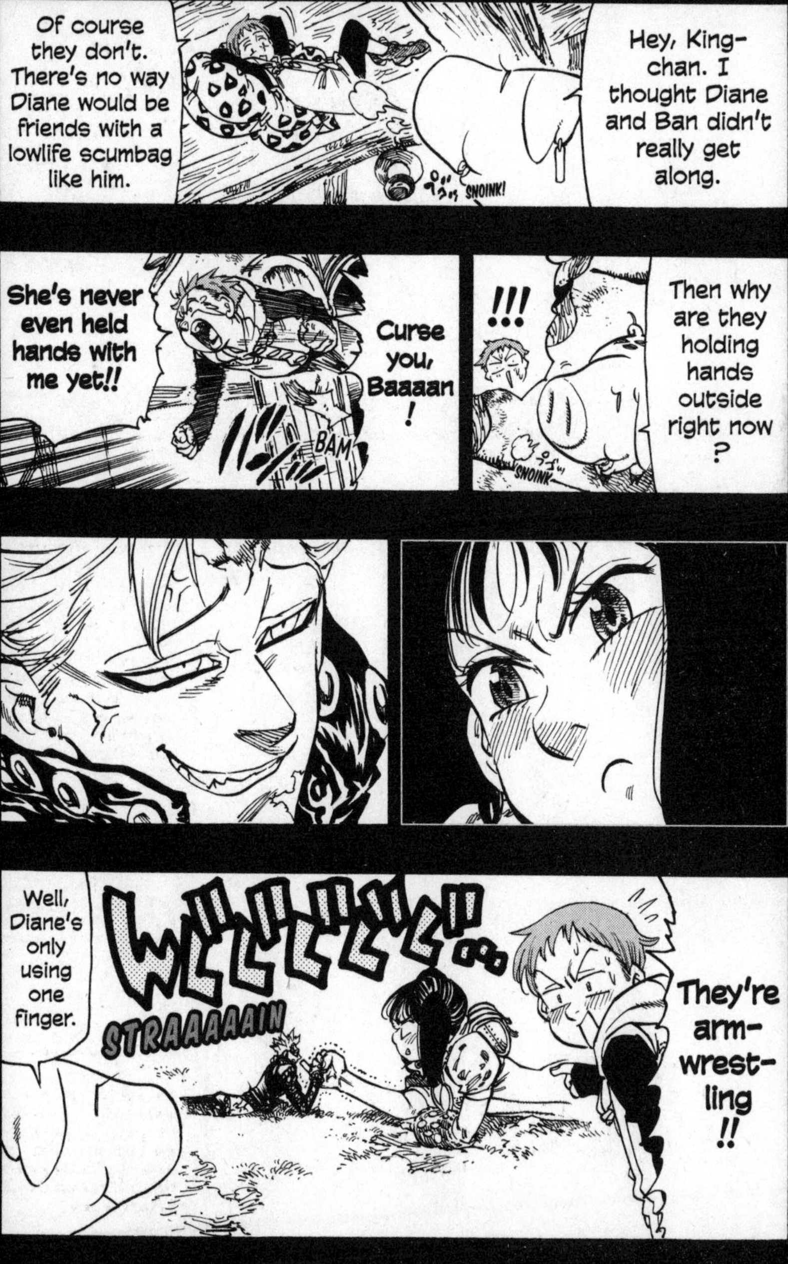
Hey, King-chan. I thought Diane and Ban didn't really get along.
Of course they don't. There's no way Diane would be friends with a lowlife scumbag like him.
SNOINK!
!!!
Then why are they holding hands outside right now?
SNOINK
Curse you, Baaaan!
She's never even held hands with me yet!!
BAM
They're arm-wrestling!!
STRAAAAAAIN
Well, Diane's only using one finger.

CONTINUED ON THE NEXT PAGE

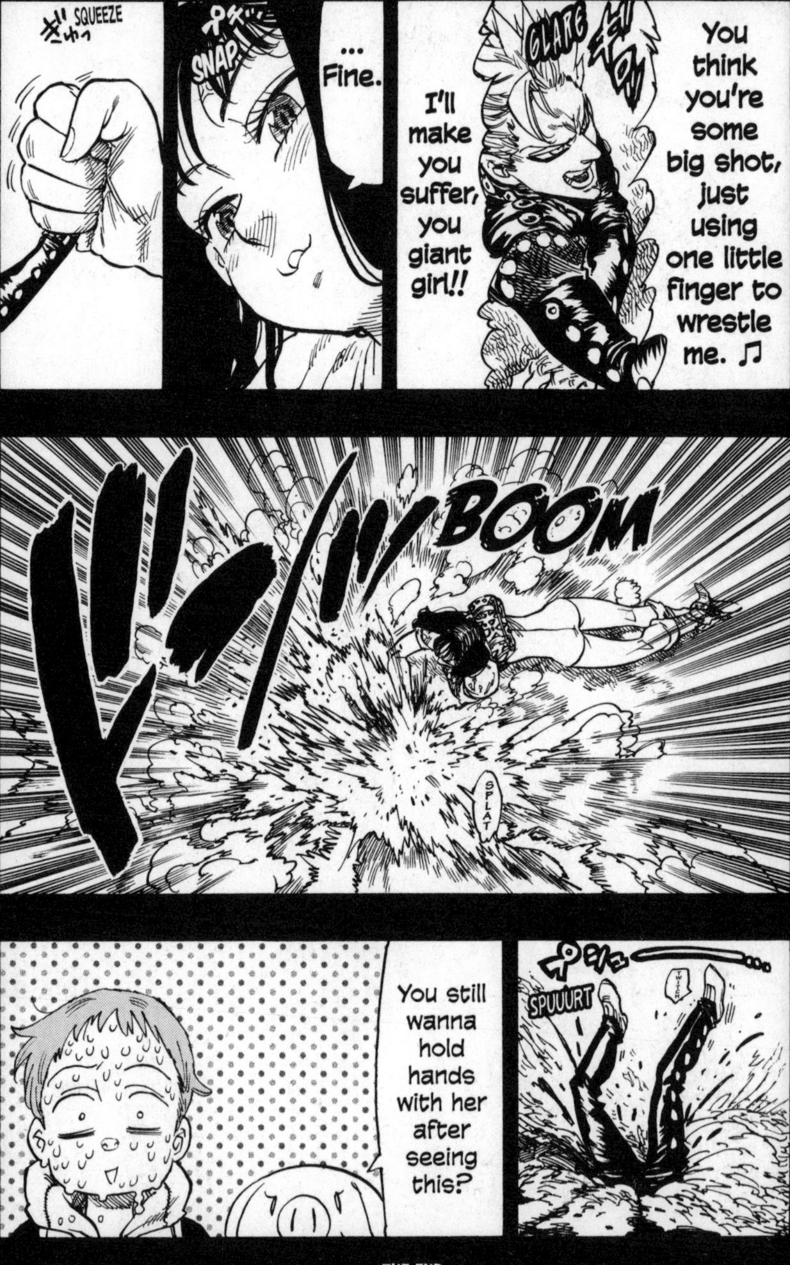
GLARE
You think you're some big shot, just using one little finger to wrestle me. ♫
I'll make you suffer, you giant girl!!
SNAP
... Fine.
SQUEEZE
BOOM
SPLAT
SPUUURT
TWITCH
You still wanna hold hands with her after seeing this?

THE END

"THE SEVEN DEADLY SINS" ILLUSTRATION CORNER

"THE DRAWING KNIGHTHOOD" SPACE

Be sure to include your name and address on your postcard!

SPECIAL PRIZE

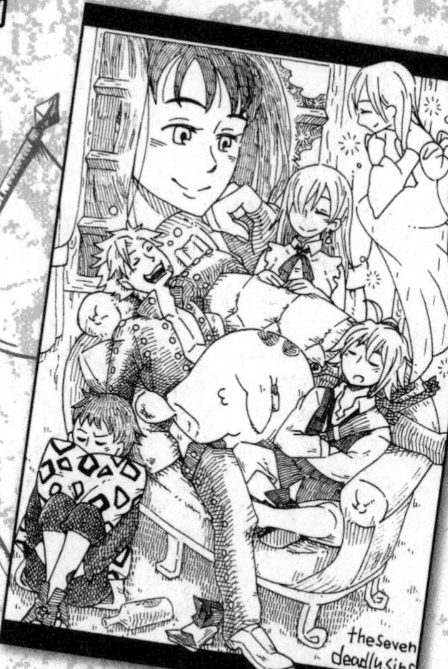

the Seven deadly sins

BORO-SAN FROM SHIZUOKA PREFECTURE

E "Looks like we all fell asleep on the sofa together..."

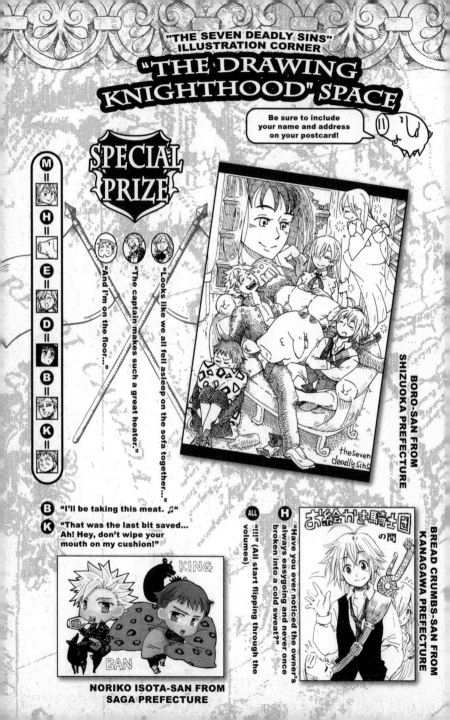

B "The captain makes such a great heater."

K "And I'm on the floor..."

B "I'll be taking this meat. ♫"

K "That was the last bit saved... Ah! Hey, don't wipe your mouth on my cushion!"

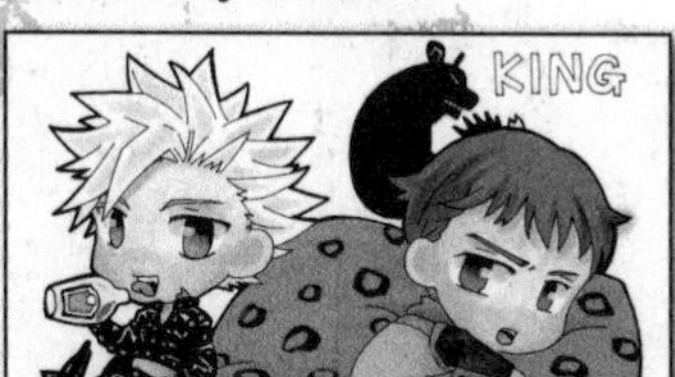

KING
BAN

NORIKO ISOTA-SAN FROM SAGA PREFECTURE

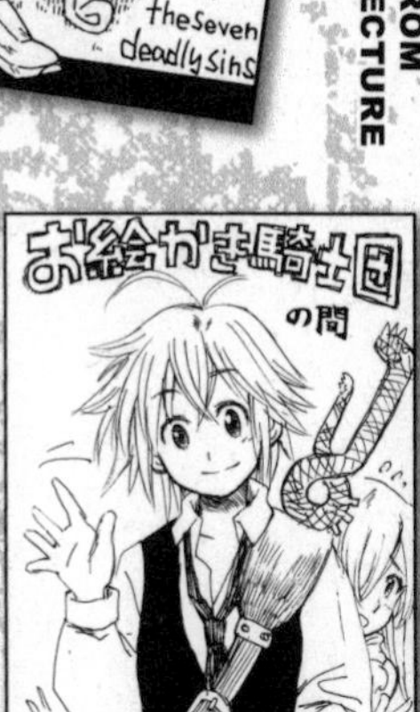

お絵かき騎士団の間

BREAD CRUMBS-SAN FROM KANAGAWA PREFECTURE

H "Have you ever noticed the owner's always easygoing and never once broken into a cold sweat?"

ALL "!!!" (All start flipping through the volumes)

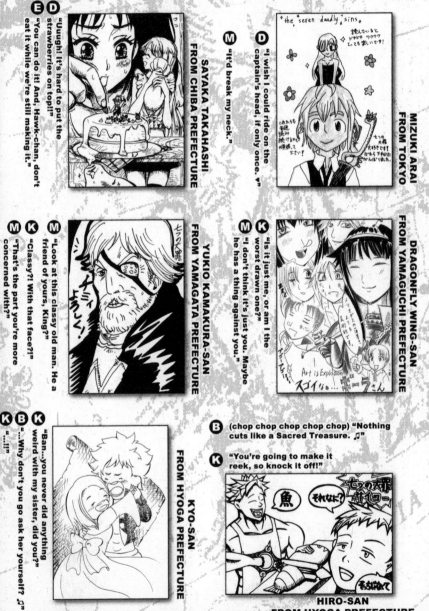

MIZUKI ARAI
FROM TOKYO

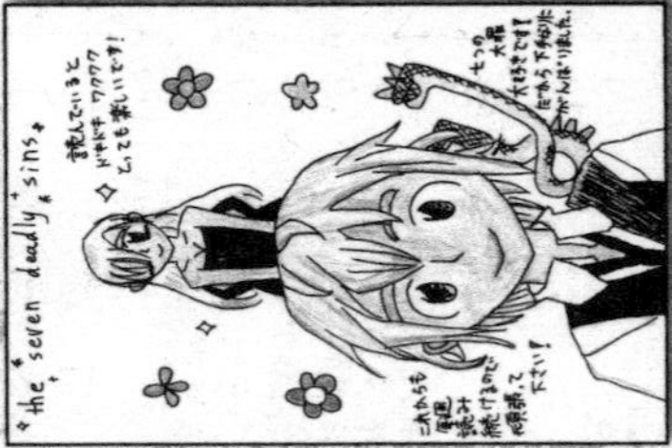
the seven deadly sins

D "I wish I could ride on the captain's head, if only once. ♥"

M "It'd break my neck."

DRAGONFLY WING-SAN
FROM YAMAGUCHI PREFECTURE

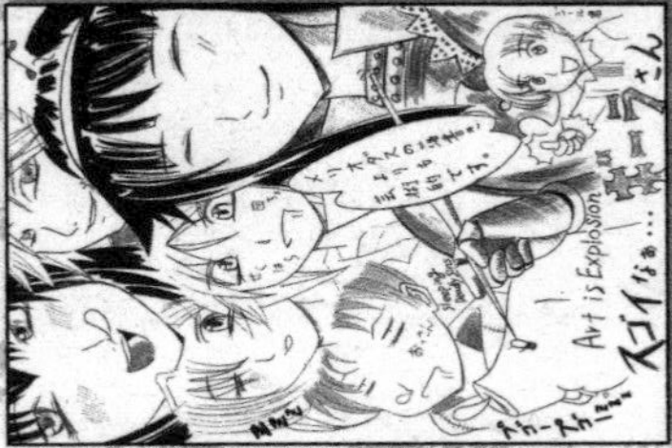
Art is Explosion

K "Is it just me, or am I the worst drawn one?"

M "I don't think it's just you. Maybe he has a thing against you."

B (chop chop chop chop chop) "Nothing cuts like a Sacred Treasure. ♫"

K "You're going to make it reek, so knock it off!"

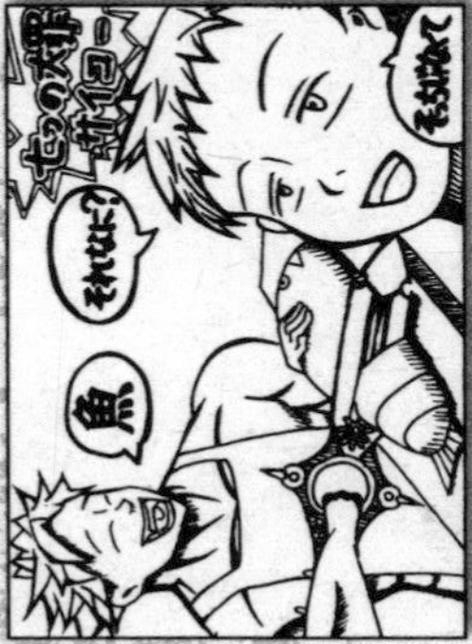
魚
それなに?

HIRO-SAN
FROM HYOGA PREFECTURE

SAYAKA TAKAHASHI
FROM CHIBA PREFECTURE

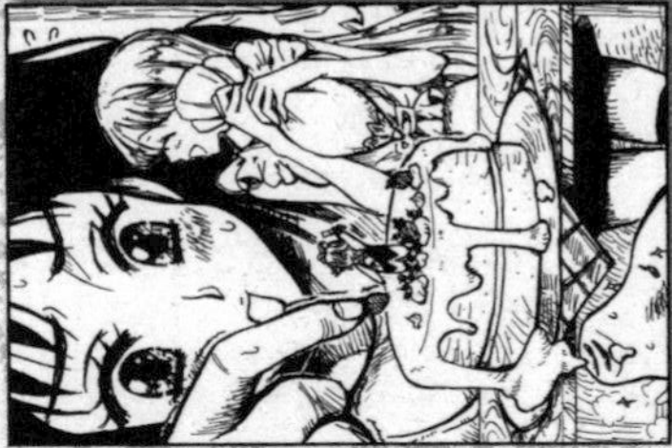

D "Uuugh! It's hard to put the strawberries on top!!"

E "You can do it! And, Hawk-chan, don't eat it while we're still making it."

YUKIO KAMAKURA-SAN
FROM YAMAGATA PREFECTURE

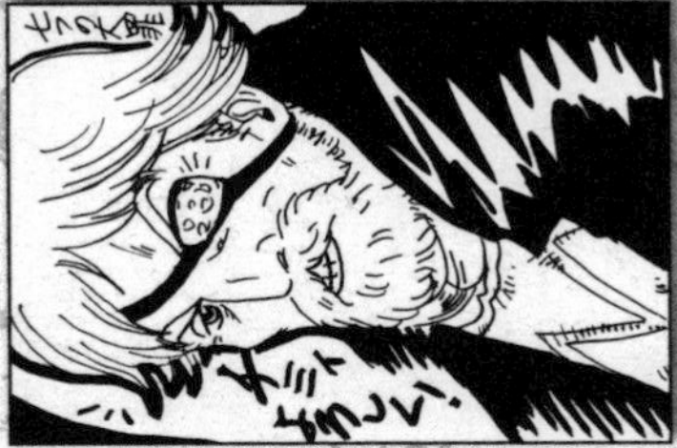

M "Look at this classy old man. He a friend of yours, King?"

K "Classy?! With that face?!"

M "That's the part you're more concerned with?"

KYO-SAN
FROM HYOGA PREFECTURE

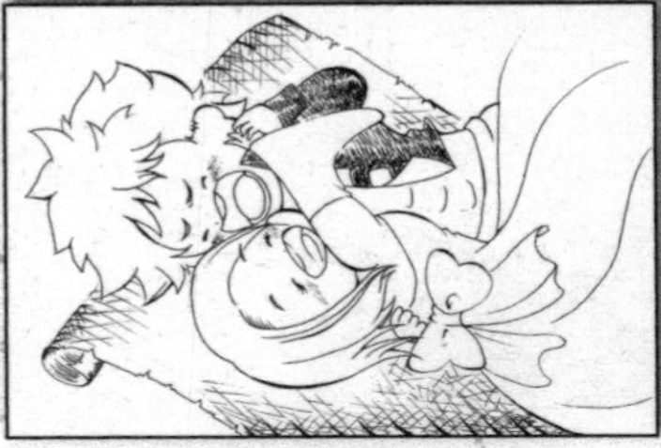

K "Ban...you never did anything weird with my sister, did you?"

B "...Why don't you go ask her yourself? ♫"

K "...!!"

FROM KUMAMOTO PREFECTURE

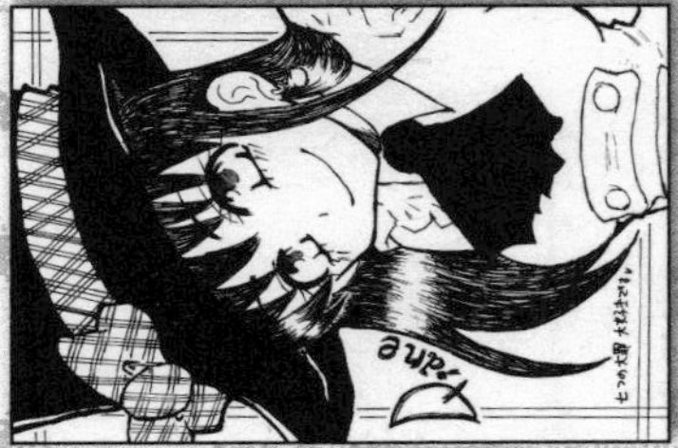
Diane
七つの大罪 大好きです。

D “Aah! I wish I’d saved some of that Chicken Matango in a bottle for future use!”

E “D...Diane.”

FROM TOKYO

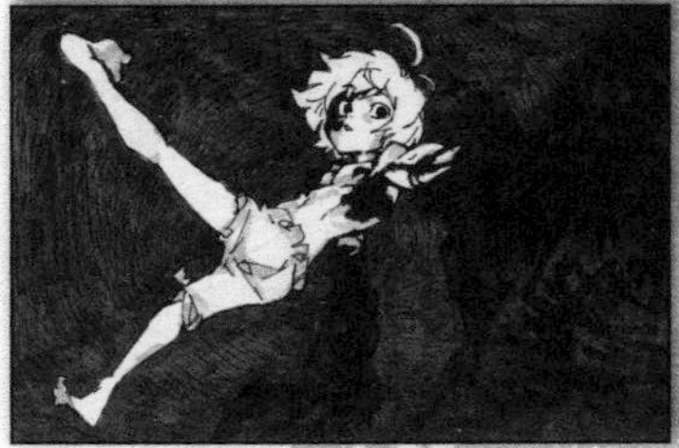

K&D “This is a creepy Captain.”

H “Ditto! I’m about ready to piss myself!”

E “...I don’t find anything scary about it...”

ALL “Whaaat?!”

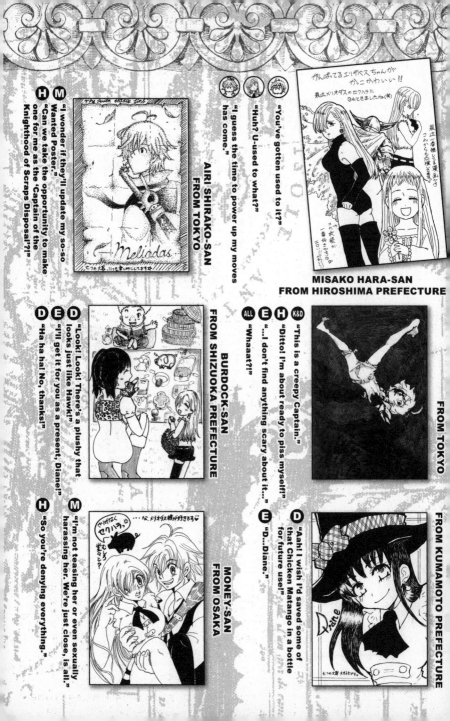

MISAKO HARA-SAN
FROM HIROSHIMA PREFECTURE

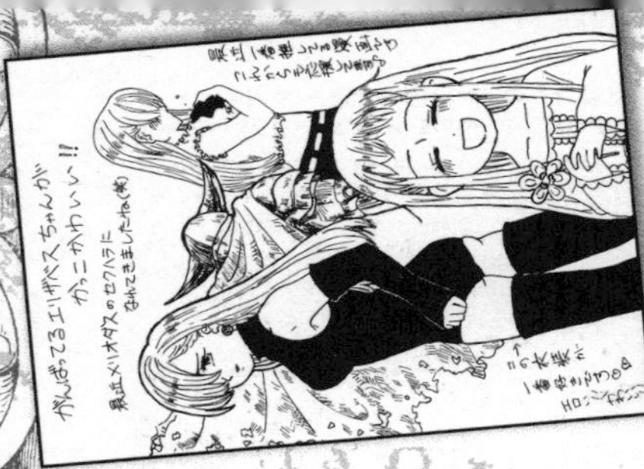
がんばってるエリザベスちゃんがかっこかわいい!!
最近メリオダスのセクハラになれてきましたね(笑)

“You’ve gotten used to it?”

“Huh? U-used to what?”

“I guess the time to power up my moves has come.”

MONEY-SAN
FROM OSAKA

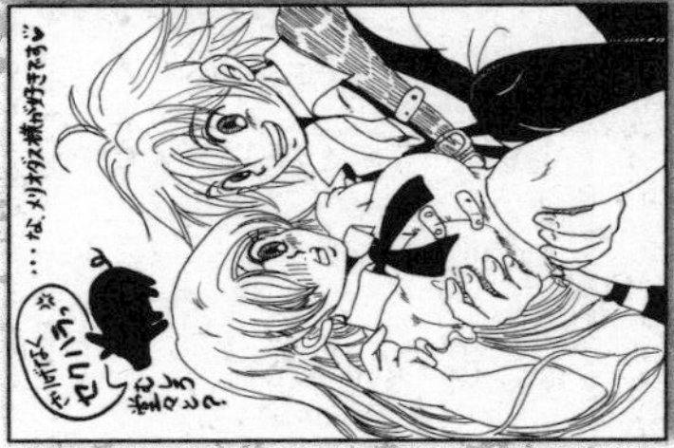
…な、メリオダス様が好きです♡
さりげなくセクハラっ☆
むしろ堂々と?

M “I’m not teasing her or even sexually harassing her. We’re just close, is all.”

H “So you’re denying everything.”

BURDOCK-SAN
FROM SHIZUOKA PREFECTURE

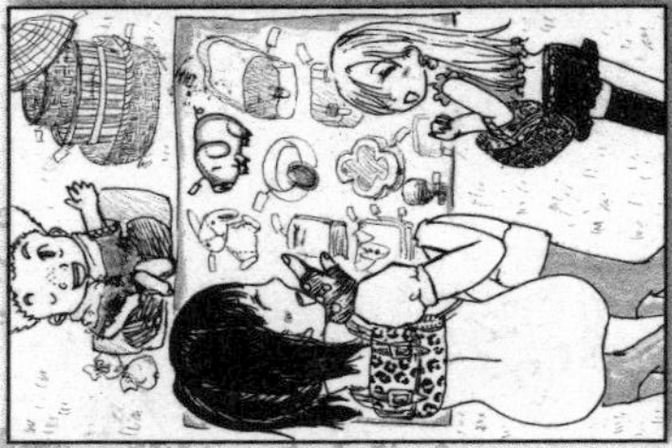

D “Look! Look! There’s a plushy that looks just like Hawk!”

E “I’ll get it for you as a present, Diane!”

D “Ha ha ha! No, thanks!”

AIRI SHIRAKO-SAN
FROM TOKYO

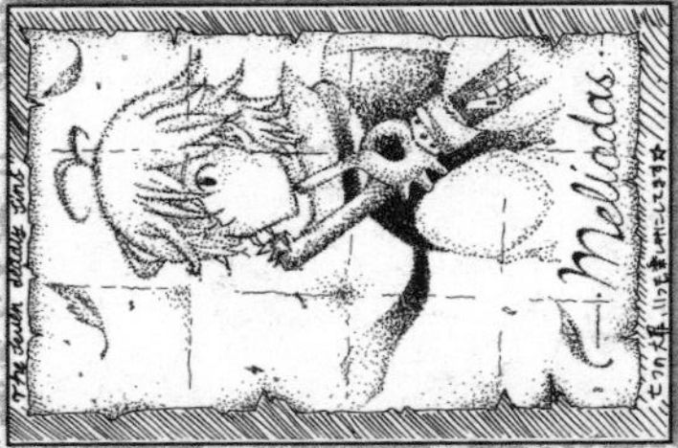
The seven deadly sins
Meliodas
七つの大罪、いつも楽しみにしてます☆

M “I wonder if they’ll update my so-so Wanted Poster.”

H “Can we take the opportunity to make one for me as the ‘Captain of the Knighthood of Scraps Disposal’?!”

"Dreyfus is Zaratras' little brother, right? Darn, he looks cool here."

"We used to drink together all the time." ♫

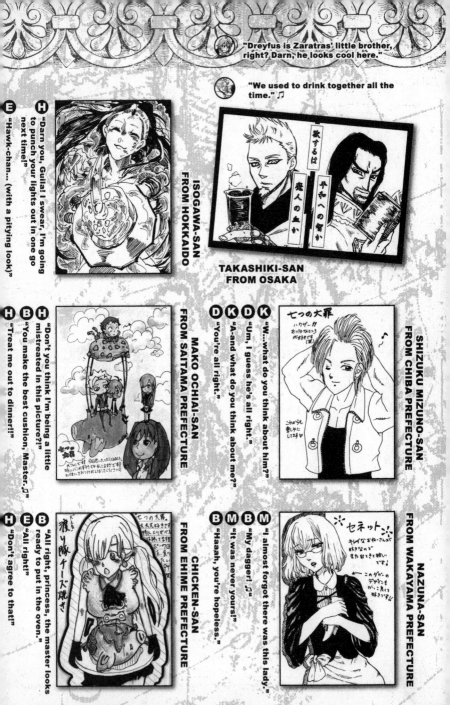

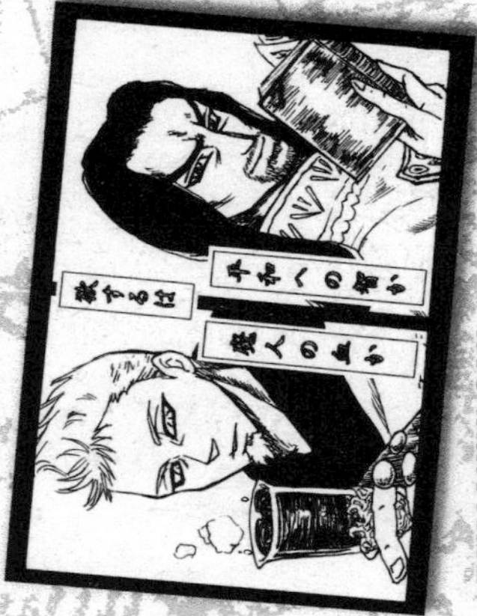
欲するは
平和への智か

TAKASHIKI-SAN
FROM OSAKA

ISOGAWA-SAN
FROM HOKKAIDO

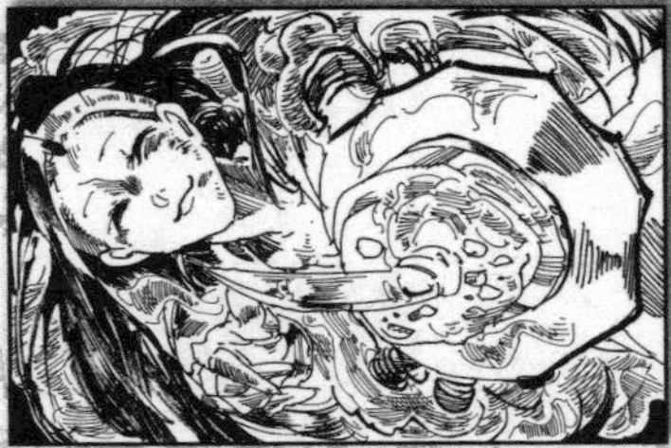

H "Darn you, Guila! I swear, I'm going to punch your lights out in one go next time!"

E "Hawk-chan... (with a pitying look)"

SHIZUKU MIZUNO-SAN
FROM CHIBA PREFECTURE

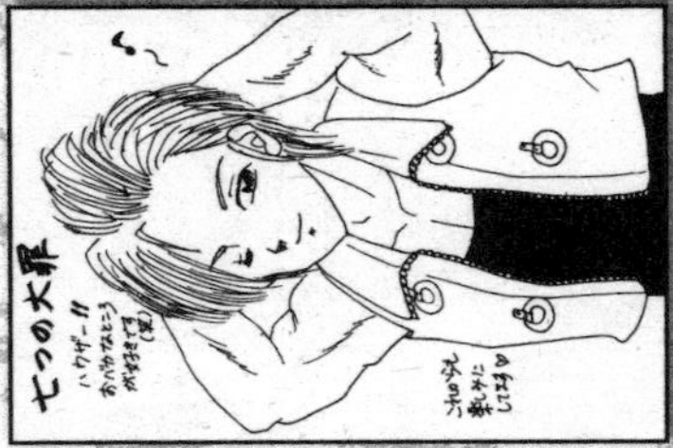
七つの大罪
ハウザー!!
おバカなところが好きです(笑)
これからも楽しみにしてます♡

K "W...what do you think about him?"

D "Um, I guess he's all right."

K "A-and what do you think about me?"

D "You're all right."

MAKO OCHIAI-SAN
FROM SAITAMA PREFECTURE

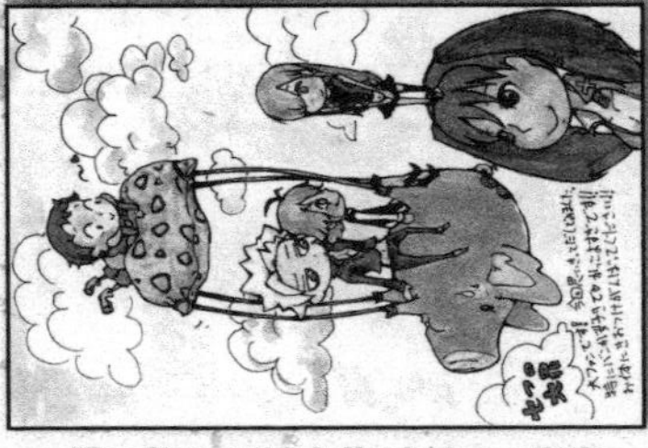
七つの大罪

H "Don't you think I'm being a little mistreated in this picture?!"

B "You make the best cushion, Master. ♫"

H "Treat me out to dinner!!"

NAZUNA-SAN
FROM WAKAYAMA PREFECTURE

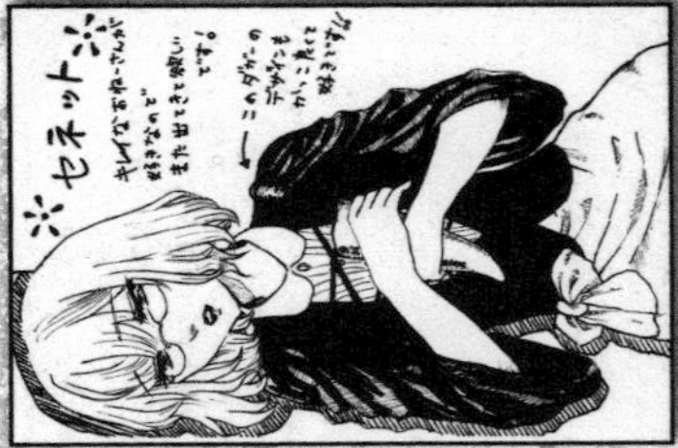
セネット
キレイなおねーさんが好きなので また出てきて嬉しいです!
このダガーのデザインもかっこ良くて好きです!!

M "I almost forgot there was this lady."

B "My dagger! ♫"

M "It was never yours!"

B "Haaah, you're hopeless."

CHICKEN-SAN
FROM EHIME PREFECTURE

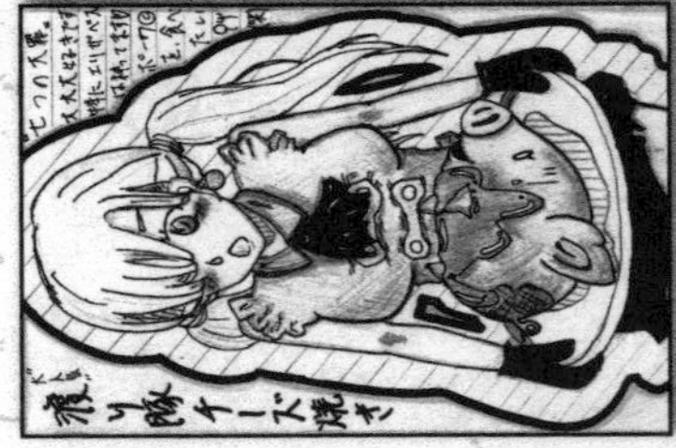
七つの大罪
渡り豚チーズ焼き

B "All right, princess, the master looks ready to put in the oven."

E "All right!"

H "Don't agree to that!"

RINAKO HAMAGAKI FROM KYOTO

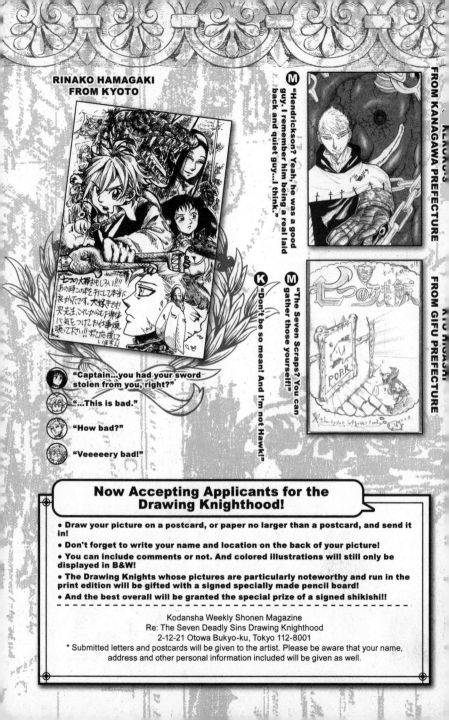

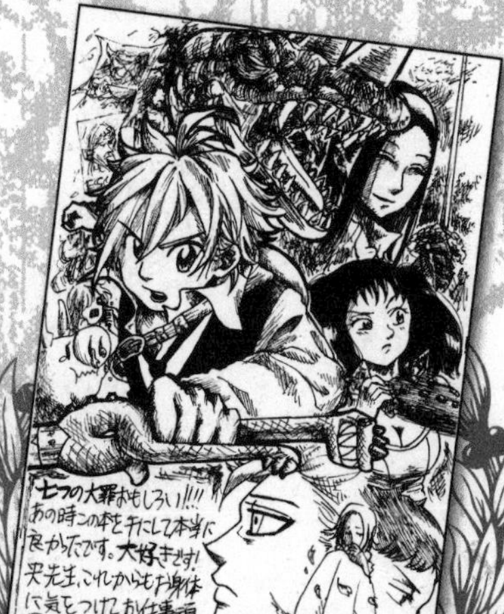
七つの大罪おもしろい!!!!
あの時この本を手にして本当に良かったです。大好きです!
央先生、これからもお身体に気をつけてお仕事頑張って下さい!! ずっと応援しています!!

"Captain...you had your sword stolen from you, right?"

"...This is bad."

"How bad?"

"Veeeeery bad!"

KEROKO'S FROM KANAGAWA PREFECTURE

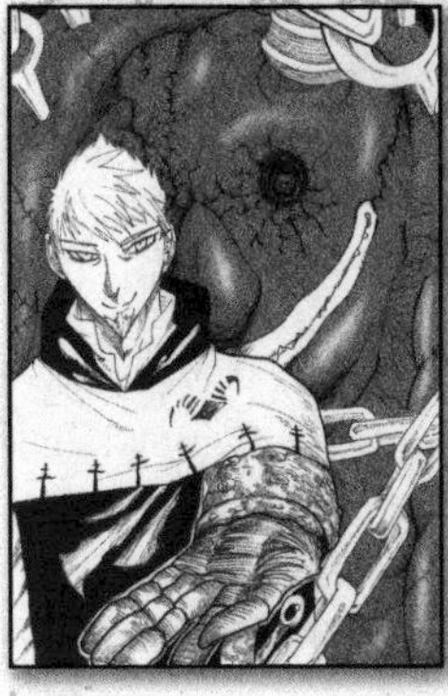

M "Hendrickson? Yeah, he was a good guy. I remember him being a real laid back and quiet guy...I think."

RYO HIGASHI FROM GIFU PREFECTURE

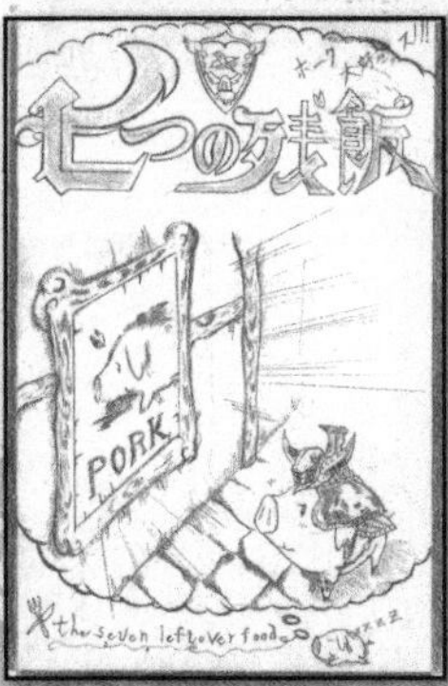
七つの残飯
PORK
the seven leftover food

M "The Seven Scraps? You can gather those yourself!"

K "Don't be so mean! And I'm not Hawk!"

Now Accepting Applicants for the Drawing Knighthood!

- Draw your picture on a postcard, or paper no larger than a postcard, and send it in!
- Don't forget to write your name and location on the back of your picture!
- You can include comments or not. And colored illustrations will still only be displayed in B&W!
- The Drawing Knights whose pictures are particularly noteworthy and run in the print edition will be gifted with a signed specially made pencil board!
- And the best overall will be granted the special prize of a signed shikishi!!

Kodansha Weekly Shonen Magazine
Re: The Seven Deadly Sins Drawing Knighthood
2-12-21 Otowa Bukyo-ku, Tokyo 112-8001

* Submitted letters and postcards will be given to the artist. Please be aware that your name, address and other personal information included will be given as well.

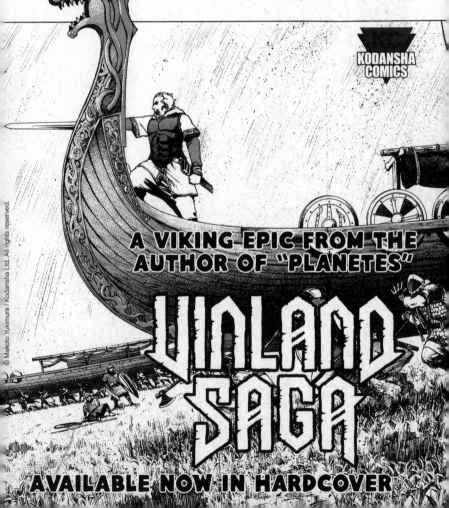

NO.6

A PERFECT LIFE IN A PERFECT CITY

For Shion, an elite student in the technologically sophisticated city No. 6, life is carefully choreographed. One fateful day, he takes a misstep, sheltering a fugitive his age from a typhoon. Helping this boy throws Shion's life down a path to discovering the appalling secrets behind the "perfection" of No. 6.

KODANS COMIC

The Seven Deadly Sins volume 7 is a work of fiction. Names, characters, places, and incidents are the products of the author's imagination or are used fictitiously. Any resemblance to actual events, locales, or persons, living or dead, is entirely coincidental.

A Kodansha Comics Trade Paperback Original.

Published in the United States by Kodansha Comics, an imprint of Kodansha USA Publishing, LLC, New York.

Publication rights for this English edition arranged through Kodansha Ltd., Tokyo.

First published in Japan in 2014 by Kodansha Ltd., Tokyo.

ISBN 978-1-61262-583-6

Printed in the United States of America.

www.kodanshacomics.com

9 8 7 6 5 4 3 2 1

Translator: Christine Dashiell
Lettering: James Dashiell